# RENAL DIET
## COOKBOOK

*Discover and Enjoy 600 Delicious, Healthy, and Quick Recipes
Low in Sodium, Phosphorus, and Potassium
to Fully Manage Your Kidney Disease, Avoid Dialysis and Eat Flavorful.*

*Includes a 4-Weeks Meal Plan*

April Ellis - Rachel Wiley

© **Copyright 2021 by April Ellis and Rachel Wiley - All rights reserved.**
This document is geared towards providing exact and reliable information in regards to the topic and issue covered. The publication is sold with the idea that the publisher is not required to render accounting, officially permitted, or otherwise, qualified services. If advice is necessary, legal or professional, a practiced individual in the profession should be ordered.
- From a Declaration of Principles which was accepted and approved equally by a Committee of the American Bar Association and a Committee of Publishers and Associations.
 It is illegal to reproduce, duplicate, or transmit any part of this document in either electronic means or in printed format. Recording of this publication is strictly prohibited, and any storage of this document is not allowed unless with written permission from the publisher. All rights reserved.
The information provided herein is stated to be truthful and consistent, in that any liability, in terms of inattention or otherwise, by any usage or abuse of any policies, processes, or directions contained within is the solitary and utter responsibility of the recipient reader. Under no circumstances will any legal responsibility or blame be held against the publisher for any reparation, damages, or monetary loss due to the information herein, either directly or indirectly.
Respective authors own all copyrights not held by the publisher.
The information herein is offered for informational purposes solely and is universal as so. The presentation of the information is without contract or any type of guarantee assurance.
The trademarks used are without any consent, and the publication of the trademark is without permission or backing by the trademark owner. All trademarks and brands within this book are for clarifying purposes only and are owned by the owners themselves, not affiliated with this document.

# TABLE OF CONTENTS

**INTRODUCTION** ..................................... 9

**YOUR FREE GIFT** .................................. 11

**UNDERSTANDING THE BASICS OF KIDNEY DISEASE** ............................... 12
- Various Forms of Kidney Disease ................. 12
- Signs and Symptoms of Kidney Disease ....... 13
- Various Kinds of Kidney Disorders and their Treatments ........................................... 14

**FUNDAMENTALS OF RENAL DIET** ......... 17
- What is Renal Diet? ..................................... 17

**FOODS TO AVOID ON RENAL DIET** ........ 19

**ADVANTAGES OF RENAL DIET** ............... 24
- 5 Benefits of Renal Diet ................................ 24

**BREAKFAST RECIPES** .............................. 25
- Mexican Egg & Tortilla Skillet ...................... 25
- Fresh Fruit Compote .................................... 25
- Burritos with Eggs and Mexican Sausage ..... 25
- Master Mix .................................................. 25
- Fig and Goat Cheese Quesadilla .................. 25
- Puffy Chili Rellenos Casserole ..................... 26
- Sudden Quiche ............................................. 26
- Spiced Applesauce Bread or Muffins ........... 26
- Mexican Brunch Eggs .................................. 27
- Buckwheat Pancakes ................................... 27
- 40-Second Omelet ....................................... 27
- Apple Bran Muffins ..................................... 27
- Biscuits with Master Mix ............................. 28
- Bran Breakfast Bars ..................................... 28
- Burritos Rapido's ......................................... 28
- Stuffed Breakfast Biscuits ............................ 29
- Easy Turkey Breakfast Burritos .................... 29
- Fluffy Homemade Buttermilk Pancakes ...... 29
- Cheesesteak Quiche ..................................... 30
- Spicy Tofu Scrambler ................................... 30
- Southwest Baked Egg Breakfast Cups .......... 30
- Summer Harvest Egg Muffin Cups ............... 30
- Smoky Ham Omelet ..................................... 31
- Toad in a Hole ............................................. 31
- Eggs with Chiles .......................................... 31
- Homemade Muesli ...................................... 32
- Egg and Rice Muffins ................................... 32
- Overnight Oatmeal of Blueberry Peanut Butter .. 32
- Asparagus and Swiss Cheese Frittata .......... 33
- Savory Egg Muffins ..................................... 33
- Egg Sandwich .............................................. 33
- Southern Style Grits .................................... 34
- Quinoa Porridge .......................................... 34
- German Pancake (Dutch Baby) .................... 34
- Veggie Mug Omelet ..................................... 34
- Huevos Rancheros ....................................... 35
- Cheddar Frittata .......................................... 35
- Cherry Overnight Oats ................................. 35
- Cheesy Scrambled Eggs with Fresh Herbs ... 36
- Corn Pudding ............................................... 36
- Curried Egg Pita Pockets ............................. 36
- Chili Wheat Treats ....................................... 37
- Country Biscuits and Gravy (Maple Crisp Bars) ... 37
- Holiday Eggnog ........................................... 37
- Ice Cream Sandwiches ................................ 37
- Onion Bagel Chips ....................................... 38
- Oriental Egg Rolls ....................................... 38
- Snack Mix .................................................... 38
- Parmesan Cheese Spread ............................ 38
- Spiced Pineapple Appetizer ......................... 38
- Popcorn Munch ............................................ 39
- Fruit and Oat Pancakes ................................ 39
- Three Pepper Quiche ................................... 39
- Cream Cheese Salad .................................... 39
- Cranberry Salad ........................................... 40
- Strawberry Stuffing ...................................... 40
- Red Hot Jell-O Salad ................................... 40
- Moroccan Couscous .................................... 40
- Pasta with Pesto ........................................... 40
- Crispy Fried Okra ........................................ 41

**VEGETABLE RECIPES** .............................. 42
- Italian Eggplant Salad .................................. 42
- Carrots & Cabbage in Mustard Sauce .......... 42
- Pineapple Coleslaw ..................................... 42
- Basil Oil ...................................................... 42
- Black-Eyed Peas .......................................... 43
- Blasted Brussels Sprouts ............................. 43
- Kidney friendly Pico de Gallo ..................... 43
- Roasted tomatillo salsa ................................ 43
- Kidney Friendly Beans ................................ 43
- Sweet Korean lentils .................................... 44
- Chickpea sunflower sandwich ..................... 44
- Kidney-friendly balsamic vinaigrette ........... 45
- Easy chia seed pudding ................................ 45
- Herb pesto ................................................... 45
- Smoothie bowl ............................................. 45
- Irish colcannon ............................................ 45
- Vegan shortbread cookies ............................ 46
- Asparagus Medley ....................................... 46
- Crepes with passion fruit ............................. 47
- Vegan bread ................................................. 47
- Vegetable broth ............................................ 47
- Festive Cranberry Stuffing ........................... 48
- Everyday Spanish style beans ...................... 48
- Simple Puerto Rican sofrito ......................... 48
- Glazed Green Beans .................................... 48
- Broccoli blossom ......................................... 49
- Spicy Kenyan Greens .................................. 49
- Pasta with peas and lemon .......................... 49
- Coconut curry cauliflower ........................... 50

| | |
|---|---|
| Red lentil stew | 50 |
| Vegetable curry | 50 |
| Stuffed Poblano pepper | 51 |
| Vegetarian Egg Fried Rice | 51 |
| Tempeh Pita Sandwiches | 51 |
| Vegetable Crumble | 52 |
| Vegetable Frittata | 52 |
| Bulgur Vegetable Salad | 53 |
| White bean veggies burgers | 53 |
| German braised cabbage | 53 |
| Greek couscous salad | 53 |
| Citrus Orzo salad | 54 |
| Vegetable Biriyani | 54 |
| Lettuce falafel wrap | 54 |
| Roasted root vegetables | 55 |
| Broccoli Salad | 55 |
| Parmesan Zucchini & Squash | 55 |
| Zucchini Cake | 55 |
| Ratatouille | 56 |
| Veggie Strata | 56 |
| Carrot Cake | 57 |
| Roasted Red Pepper, Vegan Provolone Cheese Sandwiches | 57 |
| Spicy Chickpeas (Chana Masala) | 57 |
| Four Ingredient Vegetable Broth | 58 |
| Honeyed Carrots & Leeks | 58 |
| Rice O'Brien | 58 |
| Steamed Asparagus | 58 |
| Macaroni Salad | 59 |
| Fried Onion Rings | 59 |
| Baked Yellow Squash | 59 |
| Yellow Squash & Green Onions | 59 |

## POULTRY RECIPES .................................... 61

| | |
|---|---|
| Chicken Veronique | 61 |
| Grilled Chicken Sesame | 61 |
| Lemon Tarragon Chicken | 61 |
| Oven-Fried Chicken | 62 |
| Slow Chicken Meatloaf | 62 |
| Barley-Rice Pilaf | 62 |
| Chicken Cabbage Stir Fry | 62 |
| Chicken Salad | 63 |
| Rice Pilaf | 63 |
| Turkey Nuggets with Honey Mustard | 63 |
| Turkey Salad | 64 |
| Easy Gravy | 64 |
| Curry Chicken | 64 |
| Stuffing of Tacos with Chicken | 64 |
| Chicken and Summer Vegetable Kebabs | 65 |
| Chicken Nuggets with Honey Mustard | 65 |
| Easy Chicken and Pasta Dinner | 65 |
| Herb-Roasted Chicken Breasts | 66 |
| Indian Chicken Curry | 66 |
| Chicken Stir-Fry | 66 |
| Low sodium instant pot turkey chili | 67 |
| Chicken Fried Rice | 67 |
| Chicken Waldorf salad | 67 |
| Chicken Casserole | 68 |
| Turkey Waldorf salad | 68 |
| Chicken Stew | 68 |
| Salisbury Steak | 68 |
| Special Pizza | 69 |
| Homemade Pan Sausage (Chicken) | 69 |
| Basic Chicken Loaf | 69 |
| Stir Fry Meal | 70 |
| New Orleans-Style Rice Dressing | 70 |
| Fajitas | 70 |
| White Bread Dressing | 71 |
| Cornbread Dressing | 71 |
| Giblet Gravy | 71 |
| Herb Rice Casserole | 72 |
| Crunchy Chicken Nuggets | 72 |
| Fiesta Lime Fajitas | 72 |
| Chicken Tikka | 72 |
| Chicken Vegetable Salad | 73 |
| Chicken'N Rice | 73 |
| Lemon Chicken | 73 |
| Stuffed Green Peppers | 73 |
| Chicken Salad Delight | 74 |
| Jalapeno Pepper Chicken | 74 |
| Easy low sodium Lemon chicken | 74 |
| BBQ Chicken Pita Pizza | 75 |
| Curried Turkey and Rice | 75 |
| Polynesian Turkey Kabobs | 75 |
| Turkey Fajitas | 76 |
| Oregano Turkey Burger | 76 |
| Batty Bites | 76 |
| Slow Turkey Meatloaf | 76 |
| Easy Turkey Sloppy Joes | 77 |
| Roasted Turkey | 77 |
| Homemade Pan Sausage (Turkey) | 77 |
| Barbecue Cups | 78 |
| Rotini with Mock Italian Sausage | 78 |
| Turkey & Noodles | 78 |

## SEAFOOD AND FISH RECIPES ................. 79

| | |
|---|---|
| Baked Salmon | 79 |
| Cilantro-Lime Cod | 79 |
| Fish Sticks | 79 |
| Grilled Trout | 79 |
| Fish Tacos | 80 |
| Baked Fish | 80 |
| Easy low sodium Salmon with Lime and Herbs | 80 |
| Jollof Rice | 80 |
| Lemon Baked Fish | 81 |
| Crab with Linguine | 81 |
| Coconut Fish Dream | 81 |
| Three Way Macaroni Salad | 82 |
| Herb Topped Fish | 82 |
| Fish with Peppers | 82 |
| Baked Halibut | 82 |
| Broiled Garlic Shrimp | 83 |
| Scampi Linguini | 83 |
| Spanish Paella | 83 |
| Crab-Stuffed Shrimp | 83 |
| Tuna Veggie Salad | 84 |
| Shrimp Fajitas | 84 |
| Supreme of Seafood | 85 |
| Jambalaya | 85 |
| Shrimp Salad | 85 |

- Shrimp Quesadilla ............................................. 85
- Shrimp & Coconut Curry Noodle Bowl .................. 86
- Tuna Mayonnaise Pasta Salad .............................. 86
- Seafood Croquettes ............................................. 87
- Tuna-Noodle Skillet ............................................. 87
- Tuna Salad ........................................................... 87
- Baked Tuna .......................................................... 87
- Pasta Salad Nicosia ............................................. 88
- Salmon Veggie Salad ........................................... 88
- Salmon Salad ....................................................... 88
- Quesadilla of Crabs ............................................. 88
- Crab Salad ........................................................... 89
- Crab Cakes .......................................................... 89
- Citrus Relish ........................................................ 89
- Dilled Fish ........................................................... 90
- Zesty Lime Tilapia ............................................... 90
- Adobo Marinated Tilapia Tapas ........................... 90
- Leek, parsley and chive fishcakes ....................... 91
- Caribbean oven-baked salmon with vegetables ... 91
- Nathan Outlaw's baked sea bass ......................... 92
- Tropical fruit salsa and couscous ........................ 92
- Classic Spicy Shrimp and Linguine ..................... 93
- Caribbean lime shrimp salad ............................... 93
- Oven-Fried Fish ................................................... 94
- Trout Topped with Herb ...................................... 94
- Fresh & Fun Ceviche ........................................... 94
- Creamy Tuna Twist .............................................. 94
- Mediterranean Baked Trout ................................. 95
- Foil Baked Pimento Cod Fillets ........................... 95
- Shrimp-Stuffed Deviled Eggs .............................. 95
- Linguine with Garlic and Shrimp ......................... 96
- Easy Shrimp in Garlic Sauce (high protein) ........ 96
- Super Tuesday Shrimp ........................................ 96
- Shrimp Fried Rice ................................................ 97
- Creamy Shrimp and Broccoli Fettuccine ............. 97
- Honey Glazed Salmon ......................................... 97

## SALAD RECIPES .................................................. 99
- Apple Rice Salad ................................................. 99
- Cool Coconut Marshmallow Salad ...................... 99
- Cucumber Cups Stuffed with Buffalo Chicken Salad ............................................................................... 99
- Asian Pear Salad ................................................. 99
- Beet Salad ......................................................... 100
- Berry Wild Rice Salad ....................................... 100
- Buttermilk Herb Ranch Dressing ....................... 100
- Chinese Chicken Salad ..................................... 101
- Crunchy Quinoa Salad ...................................... 101
- Cowboy Caviar Bean and Rice Salad ............... 101
- Coleslaw with a Kick ......................................... 102
- Curry Chicken Salad ......................................... 102
- Curried Lacinato ................................................ 102
- Violet, Green Salad ........................................... 102
- Cool and Crispy Cucumber Salad ..................... 103
- Thai Salad with Corn ......................................... 103
- Tabbouleh .......................................................... 103
- Zesty lemon salad ............................................. 103
- Cabbage with Strawberries ............................... 104
- Strawberry Wedge Salad .................................. 104
- Blackberry Salad ............................................... 104
- Salad with Pear Vinaigrette and Toasted Sunflower Seeds ................................................ 104
- Greek-Style Couscous Salad ............................ 105
- Honey Dijon Cobb Salad .................................. 105
- Mediterranean Chickpea Side Salad ................ 106
- Dr. Pearl's Delicious Salad Dressing ................ 106
- Creamy Fruit Salad ........................................... 106
- Marinated Cucumber and Celery Salad ........... 106
- Mexican-Style Cucumber Salad ....................... 107
- Caribbean Carrot Salad .................................... 107
- Green Beans Salad ........................................... 107
- Rainbow Rice Noodle Salad ............................. 108
- Bow-Tie Pasta Salad ......................................... 108
- Three Sisters Salad ........................................... 108
- Strawberry & Lettuce Pasta Salad ................... 109
- Peach Quinoa Salad ......................................... 109
- Cucumber Watermelon Salad ........................... 109
- Wild Rice Salad ................................................. 110
- Fall Farro Salad ................................................. 110
- Winter Fennel and Citrus Salad ........................ 110
- Green Lentils and Jicama Salad ....................... 111
- Savory Citrus Salad .......................................... 111
- Riced Cauliflower Salad ................................... 111
- Summer Salad ................................................... 112
- Shrimp Salad with Cucumber Mint ................... 112
- Red Chili Mustard Vinegar ................................ 112
- Red Cabbage with Apples ................................ 112
- Purple and Gold Thai Coleslaw ........................ 113
- Pomegranate and Persimmon Salad ................ 113
- Raspberry Vinaigrette ....................................... 113
- Fire and Ice Watermelon Salsa ......................... 113
- Fruity Chicken Salad ......................................... 113
- Grilled Vegetable Pasta Salad .......................... 114
- Katy's Mango Salad .......................................... 114
- Lemony Shrimp & Couscous Salad .................. 114
- Kicking' Chicken Tacos ..................................... 115
- Pear and White Cheddar Salad ........................ 115
- Lemon Curry Chicken Salad ............................. 115
- Cottage Cheese Salad ...................................... 115
- Cranberry Frozen Salad .................................... 116

## MEAT RECIPES ................................................. 117
- Chili Con Carne ................................................. 117
- Grilled Marinated Beef Steak ............................ 117
- Meat Loaf ........................................................... 117
- Onion Smothered Steak .................................... 117
- Pork with Julienne Vegetables ......................... 118
- Salt-Free Pizza .................................................. 118
- Pork Pasties ...................................................... 118
- Barbecue Beef ................................................... 119
- Beef Casserole .................................................. 119
- Spicy Beef Stir-Fry ............................................ 119
- Beef Curry ......................................................... 120
- Slow Cooked Bavarian Pot Roast ..................... 120
- Roast Pork Loin with Sweet and Tart Apple Stuffing .............................................................. 121
- Pasta with Cheesy Meat Sauce ........................ 121
- Hawaiian-Style Slow-Cooked Beef ................... 122
- Stuffing of Tacos with Beef ............................... 122
- Spicy Barbecue Sauce ...................................... 122

| | |
|---|---|
| Fiesta Lime Tacos ................................................. 122 | Chicken and Corn Chowder ............................... 142 |
| Pork Steak .............................................................. 123 | Chicken and Dumplings ..................................... 142 |
| Spicy Lamb ............................................................. 123 | Chicken Seafood Gumbo .................................... 142 |
| Homemade Pan Sausage (Beef) ........................... 123 | Mediterranean Roasted Red Pepper Soup ........ 143 |
| Seasoned Pork Chops ........................................... 123 | Quick Mushroom Broth ...................................... 143 |
| Classic Beef Stroganoff with Egg Noodles ......... 124 | Simple Chicken Broth ......................................... 143 |
| Taco Stuffing ......................................................... 124 | Simple Soup Base ................................................ 144 |
| Open-Faced Steak & Onion Sandwich ............... 124 | Slow Cooker Gumbo ........................................... 144 |
| Parsley Burger ....................................................... 125 | Texas-Style Chili .................................................. 144 |
| Eggplant Casserole ............................................... 125 | Chilled Pea and mint soup ................................. 144 |
| Easy Beef Burgers ................................................. 125 | Vibrant carrot soup ............................................. 145 |
| Pork Chops with Herb Crust .............................. 125 | Creamy broccoli soup ......................................... 145 |
| Pork Carne ............................................................. 126 | Green Breakfast Soup ......................................... 145 |
| Jamaican Curried Goat ........................................ 126 | Vegetable Stew ..................................................... 146 |
| Mince with Basil ................................................... 126 | Cream of Corn Soup ........................................... 146 |
| Tortilla Beef Rollups ............................................ 126 | Chicken Tortilla Soup ......................................... 146 |
| Meat Pasties .......................................................... 127 | Lower Potassium Potato Soup ........................... 146 |
| Brewery Burger ..................................................... 127 | Rotisserie Chicken Noodle Soup ....................... 147 |
| Jamaican Beef Patties ........................................... 127 | Hearty Vegetable Soup ....................................... 147 |
| Chili Rice with Beef ............................................. 128 | Kidney-Friendly Cream of Mushroom Soup ... 147 |
| Cajun Pork Chops ................................................ 128 | Spring Vegetable Soup ........................................ 148 |
| Homemade Pan Sausage (Pork) .......................... 128 | Easy Low Sodium Pumpkin Soup ..................... 148 |
| Egg Fried Rice ....................................................... 128 | Mediterranean Soup Jar ..................................... 148 |
| Lamb Chops and Mustard Sauce ........................ 129 | Friendly Noodle Soup with Chicken ................ 148 |
| Spicy Pork Tenderloin ......................................... 129 | Kidney-Friendly Navy Bean Stew ..................... 149 |
| Hawaiian-Style Slow-Cooked Pulled Pork ........ 129 | Chicken Pot Pie Stew .......................................... 149 |
| Runzaa Tasty Meat and Bread Pocket ............... 130 | Beef and Cabbage Vegetable Soup .................... 149 |
| Sweet and Spicy Meatballs .................................. 130 | Chicken and White Bean Chili Stew ................ 150 |
| Slow Cook Chuck Roast ...................................... 130 | Chicken and Groundnut Stew ........................... 150 |
| Basic Meat Loaf .................................................... 131 | Potato Soup, Irish Baked .................................... 150 |
| Smothered Pork Chop ......................................... 131 | Ground Beef Soup ............................................... 151 |
| Black Bean Burger and Cilantro Slaw ............... 132 | Beef & Vegetable Soup ........................................ 151 |
| Cranberry Pork Roast .......................................... 132 | Beef Barley Stew .................................................. 151 |
| Beef Ribs ................................................................ 132 | Simple Beef Stew ................................................. 152 |
| Sukiyaki and Rice ................................................. 133 | Beef Tortilla Soup ................................................ 152 |
| Spicy Pork Chops with Apples ............................ 133 | Cream of Crab Soup ........................................... 152 |
| Beef Enchiladas .................................................... 133 | Côte d'Ivoire Fish ................................................ 153 |
| Chili Verde, Crock Pot ......................................... 134 | Winter minestrone .............................................. 153 |
| Hungarian Goulash .............................................. 134 | Turkey Paprikash ................................................. 153 |
| Italian Meatballs .................................................. 134 | Baked Cauliflower Soup ..................................... 154 |
| Beef Chops ............................................................ 135 | Simple Pork Stew ................................................ 154 |
| Herb Crusted Roast Leg of Lamb ....................... 135 | Cream of Prawn Soup ........................................ 154 |
| Herb-Crusted Pork Loin ..................................... 135 | Turkey Tortilla Soup ........................................... 154 |
| | Vibrant Potato soup ............................................ 155 |
| **SOUP & STEW RECIPES ............................. 137** | Simple Beef Broth ............................................... 155 |
| Baked Potato Soup .............................................. 137 | |
| Beef Barley Soup .................................................. 137 | **DRINK AND BEVERAGE RECIPES ........... 156** |
| Turkey Broth ........................................................ 137 | Apple Cup Cider ................................................. 156 |
| Thai Chicken Soup .............................................. 137 | Fresh Fruit Lassi .................................................. 156 |
| Renal-friendly cream of mushroom soup ......... 138 | Katie Shake .......................................................... 156 |
| Yogurt-Cucumber Soup ...................................... 138 | Chocolate Smoothie ............................................ 156 |
| Wild Rice Soup ..................................................... 139 | Apple Smoothie ................................................... 156 |
| Mushroom Stew with Creamy Polenta .............. 139 | Watermelon Bliss ................................................ 156 |
| Mushroom and Barley Soup ............................... 139 | Bahama Breeze .................................................... 157 |
| Minestrone Soup .................................................. 140 | Very Berry Goodness .......................................... 157 |
| Carrot Ginger Soup ............................................. 140 | Cran-tastic ............................................................ 157 |
| Butternut Squash and Cider Soup ..................... 140 | What a Peach ....................................................... 157 |
| Chestnut Celery Root Soup ................................ 141 | Easy Pineapple Protein Smoothie ..................... 157 |
| Yellow Lentil Stew ............................................... 141 | Mixed Berry Protein Smoothie .......................... 157 |
| Shiitake, Soba Noodles, and Miso Bowl ............ 141 | Kidney Nourishing Smoothie ............................ 158 |

- Blueberry Blast Smoothie .................... 158
- Four Ingredient Simple Blueberry Smoothie ......... 158
- Watermelon Summer Cooler .................... 158
- Lemonade .................................... 158
- Strawberry-Apple Smoothie ................... 158
- Easy No Milk Shake .......................... 159
- Berry Smoothie .............................. 159
- Lemon-Strawberry Punch ...................... 159
- Pineapple Lime Punch ........................ 159
- Berry yogurt smoothie ....................... 159
- Kidney friendly masala chai tea ............. 159
- Italian lemonade (distinctive kidney-friendly liquid refreshment) ......................... 160
- Pineapple coconut turmeric smoothie ......... 160
- Homemade kidney-friendly apple cider ........ 160
- Vegan Hot Chocolate ......................... 160
- Strawberry Cheesecake Smoothie .............. 161
- Aromatic Tea ................................ 161
- Watermelon Cooler ........................... 161
- Watermelon Lime Refresher ................... 161
- Coco Coffee Frappe .......................... 161
- Rose Hibiscus Limeade ....................... 161
- Mexican Coconut Drink ....................... 162
- Iced Tea with Mint .......................... 162
- Papaya Smoothie ............................. 162
- Strawberry Sesame Milkshake ................. 162
- Cherry Citrus Mocktail ...................... 163
- Pretty Pink Smoothie ........................ 163
- Green Kiwi Smoothie ......................... 163
- Fruity Baked Tea ............................ 163
- Homemade Rice Milk .......................... 164
- Fruit Julius ................................ 164
- Rhubarb Lemonade Punch ...................... 164
- Blueberry Punch ............................. 164
- Rhubarb Tea ................................. 164
- Every Berry Goodness ........................ 164
- Cranberry Blast Smoothie .................... 165
- Blueberry Protein Smoothie .................. 165
- Strawberry Blast Smoothie ................... 165
- Red Wine Vinaigrette ........................ 165
- Scarlet Frozen Fantasy ...................... 165
- Pineapple Bliss ............................. 165
- Peach Cobbler ............................... 166
- Coffee Creamer .............................. 166
- Party Punch ................................. 166
- Zippy Dip ................................... 166
- Lemon Apple Honey Smoothie .................. 166
- Berrylicious Smoothie ....................... 167

## SNACKS & SIDE RECIPES .................... 168
- BBQ Asparagus ............................... 168
- BBQ Corn on the Cob ......................... 168
- Low Salt Macaroni and Cheese ................ 168
- Cauliflower in Mustard Sauce ................ 168
- 60-Second Salsa ............................. 169
- Acorn Squash Baked with Pineapple ........... 169
- Alfredo Sauce ............................... 169
- Anytime Energy Bars ......................... 169
- Apple & Cherry Chutney ...................... 170
- BBQ Winter Squash ........................... 170
- Beef Jerky .................................. 170
- Brown Bag Popcorn ........................... 170
- Dry-Rubbed Barbecue Turkey Wings ............ 171
- Not Very Spicy Chipotle Wings ............... 171
- Cinnamon Biscotti ........................... 171
- Crispy Cauliflower Phyllo Cups .............. 172
- Sweet & Nutty Protein Bars .................. 172
- Homemade Herbed Biscuits .................... 172
- Oregano Salsa (canned) ...................... 173
- Tomatillo, Corn and Black Bean Chutney ...... 173
- Teriyaki Flavor Sauce ....................... 173
- Taco Seasoning .............................. 173
- Thai Lettuce Wraps .......................... 174
- Slovakian Sauerkraut and Egg Noodles ........ 174
- Cucumber Dill Cream Cheese Bites ............ 174
- Cinnamon Sugar Popcorn ...................... 174
- Sriracha Popcorn ............................ 175
- Cream Cheese and Tomatillo Spread ........... 175
- American Favorite Blend ..................... 175
- Low Sodium Deviled Eggs ..................... 176
- Strawberry Shortcake Chia Seed Pudding ...... 176
- Sweet Spice Cottage Cheese .................. 176
- Fruit Salsa ................................. 176
- Energy Bites ................................ 176
- Swiss Chard Crostini ........................ 177
- Cinnamon Scented Applesauce ................. 177
- Muhammara Dip ............................... 177
- Cinnamon Spiced Cornbread ................... 178
- Tangy Coleslaw .............................. 178
- Spiced Pepitas .............................. 178
- Watermelon Ice Cream ........................ 179
- Date Indulgence ............................. 179
- Easy Blueberry – Lemon Parfait .............. 179
- Gingerbread Christmas log ................... 179
- Traditional mince pies ...................... 180
- Easy baked pears ............................ 180
- Eton mess ................................... 181
- Crème brûlée ................................ 181
- Lemonade scones ............................. 181
- Chicken and Lime Salad Sandwich ............. 182
- Sunshine Carrots ............................ 182
- Overnight oats .............................. 182
- Roasted grape crostini with ricotta and balsamic reduction ................................... 182
- Sour candy grapes ........................... 182
- Raspberry pear sorbet ....................... 183
- Cherry brown butter bars .................... 183
- Grilled blackened tilapia ................... 183
- Honey garlic kebab marinade ................. 184
- Southern-fried okra ......................... 184
- Champ – Side Dish Irish Potato .............. 184

## DESSERT RECIPES .................... 185
- Strawberry Sorbet ........................... 185
- Triple Berry Protein Parfait ................ 185
- Sweet Cherry Cobbler ........................ 185
- Sugarless Pecan and Raisin Cookies .......... 186
- Spicy Raisin Cookies ........................ 186
- Crispy Butterscotch Cookies ................. 186
- Gooey, Carmel-Filled Butterscotch Cookies ... 187

- Dutch Apple Pancake .................................................. 187
- Butterscotch Apple Crisp ............................................ 187
- Low Sodium Pound Cake ............................................. 188
- Harvest Apple Cake with Cinnamon Yogurt Sauce ................................................................................. 188
- Easy Spicy Angel Cake ................................................ 188
- Easy Fruit Dip ............................................................. 188
- Chocolate Covered Strawberries ............................... 189
- Strawberry Pie ............................................................ 189
- Almond Pecan Caramel Corn ...................................... 189
- Apple Filled Crepes .................................................... 189
- Asian Pear Crisp ......................................................... 190
- Asian Pear Torte ......................................................... 190
- Apple Oat Shake ......................................................... 191
- Blueberry Squares ...................................................... 191
- Blueberry Whipped Pie .............................................. 191
- Molten Mint Chocolate Brownies ............................. 191
- Dried Cranberry Fruit Bars ....................................... 192
- Sunburst Lemon Bars ................................................. 192
- Filled Phyllo Pastries with Rustic Apple Cinnamon ................................................................................. 193
- Yellow Cake ................................................................. 193
- Tropical Fruit Salad with Basil Lime Syrup ............ 193
- Pineapple Pudding ...................................................... 194
- Old Fashioned Pound Cake ....................................... 194
- Vanilla Strudel ............................................................ 194
- Apple Muffins ............................................................. 195
- Cornbread Muffins ..................................................... 195
- Dessert Cups with Fresh Fruit .................................. 195
- Honey-Maple Trail Mix .............................................. 196
- Berry Oatmeal Muffins ............................................... 196
- Festive Raspberry Meringue Trifle .......................... 196
- Saskatoon Berry Pudding .......................................... 197
- Cherry filo pastry tarts .............................................. 197
- Reduced Sugar Carrot Cupcakes ............................... 198
- Christmas Turkey Crown with All the Trimmings 198
- Jam sponge cake .......................................................... 199
- Cornflake and ginger cookies ................................... 199
- Chocolate profiteroles with Chantilly cream ..... 199
- Meringue with mango & lime cream ....................... 200
- Chicken, leek & tarragon pie .................................... 200
- Christmas Cake ........................................................... 201
- Easter Cake .................................................................. 201
- Raspberry and passion fruit mousse ...................... 202
- Pineapple upside-down cake .................................... 202
- Pear crumble ............................................................... 202
- Shepherd's pie with swede & carrot mash ............ 203
- Jamaican Cornmeal Pie .............................................. 203
- Blackberry crumble .................................................... 204
- Chewy Lemon-Ginger-Coconut Cookies ................. 204
- Mini Pineapple Upside down Cakes ........................ 204
- Independence Day Jell-O Flag Layer Cup ............... 205
- Pineapple Cream Cake ............................................... 205
- Festive Cream Cheese Sugar Cookies ..................... 206
- Hot Fruit Compote ..................................................... 206

**4-WEEKS MEAL PLAN ............................... 207**
- Week 1 .......................................................................... 207
- Week 2 .......................................................................... 207
- Week 3 .......................................................................... 208
- Week 4 .......................................................................... 208

**CONCLUSION .............................................. 209**

# INTRODUCTION

**A renal diet is a low-phosphorus, low-protein, and low-sodium diet.** A renal diet emphasizes the value of eating high-quality food and keeping liquid consumption to a minimum.

To function properly, the body needs the right quantity of water. One of the most essential roles of the kidneys is to eradicate extra water from the body or to stock water when it is needed.

To decrease the excess in their tissue, people with impaired kidney function must adopt a kidney or renal diet. Consumed liquids and diets produce waste in the flesh. Kidney activity is compromised, and the kidneys are unable to properly filter or eliminate waste. Partaking in a renal diet can aid in maintaining kidney function and slow the progression of kidney disease.

For the body to function properly, certain substances in the blood and bodily fluids must be maintained in good proportion. Food provides minerals such as sodium (salt) and potassium, for example. However, they must remain at a certain amount. Extra nutrients like sodium and potassium are excreted in the urine while the kidneys are functioning properly. The kidneys also filter and help control other minerals like calcium and phosphate (which are needed for bone development, strength, and other functions).

Hormones, which are essential chemicals in the body, are generated by normal kidneys. As "messengers," these hormones pass across the bloodstream, controlling blood pressure, red blood cell production, and calcium balance.

Your kidneys help with the elimination of waste products from the body, such as urea and creatinine. Urea and other waste are generated as the body breaks down protein, often found in meat. Muscles produce creatinine, which is a waste substance. Urea and creatinine levels in the blood increase as kidney utility decreases. Creatinine levels in the blood are a clear indicator of how active the kidneys are. It is measured using a simple blood examination.

If you have chronic kidney disorder (CKD), it is imperative that you adjust your diet. Water restriction, a low-protein diet, restricting iodine, potassium, phosphate and other electrolytes, and consuming enough calories if you're losing weight are all potential strategies to improve your wellbeing.

You'll need to change your diet further if your kidney failure worsens or you need dialysis. This condition requires the use of a renal diet. When you're on dialysis for CKD, the renal diet aims to healthily maintain the body's electrolyte, nutrient, and fluid levels.

Dialysis patients must adhere to this diet in order to keep waste products from accumulating in their bodies. Fluid restriction is critical between dialysis treatments, and most dialysis patients urinate very little. Fat builds up in the body without urination, producing extra pressure on the heart and lungs.

To maintain a renal diet, sodium, protein, potassium, and phosphorus must both be screened. Check out our compilation of kidney-friendly recipes for a healthy lifestyle.

# YOUR FREE GIFT

To thank you for buying this book, I would like to offer you the book "Air Fryer Cookbook: 50 Delicious, Fast and Easy to Make Healthy Recipes" written by a very close friend of mine, Emily Finner, who kindly allowed me to share it with you.

Consuming excessive amounts of deep-fried food compromises your kidneys' ability to filter out harmful fats. Air-fried foods contain up to 80% less fat in comparison to foods that are deep-fried.

With this Air Fryer Cookbook you'll discover 50 delicious easy-to-make healthy recipes using your air fryer oven. If you don't have one yet, you can look through the recipes and maybe figure out that an air fryer oven would be a nice gift for you.

**FOLLOW THIS LINK**

**www.getYourAirFryerRecipes.com**

or

**SCAN THIS QR CODE**

**WITH YOUR MOBILE**

# UNDERSTANDING THE BASICS OF KIDNEY DISEASE

In the United States, over 26 million individuals have kidney failure. When the kidneys are compromised and unable to function properly, this condition develops. Diabetes, high blood pressure, and a number of other chronic (long-term) illnesses may all cause harm. Nerve injury, brittle bones, and malnutrition are causes that can lead to kidney disease.

The kidneys will cease functioning entirely if the disease worsens. This suggests a dialysis will be needed to restore kidney function. Dialysis is a procedure that uses a pump to disinfect and purify the blood. It will not heal kidney disease, but it will extend your life.

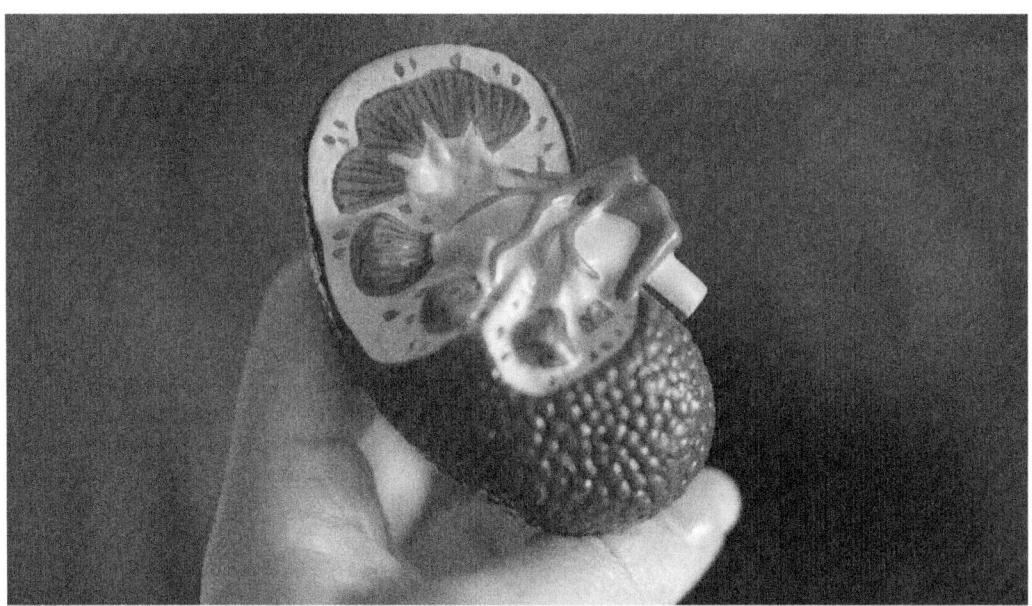

## Various Forms of Kidney Disease

**CKD (Chronic Kidney Disease).**

Chronic Kidney Disease is the most prevalent form of kidney disease. Persistent kidney failure is a chronic illness that does not get better over time. High blood pressure is the most common cause of this form.

Since high blood pressure places more strain on the glomeruli, it is worse for the kidneys. Glomeruli are thin blood vessels that filter blood in the kidneys. Gradually, the added strain weakens these receptors, causing kidney function to deteriorate.

A diabetic nephropathy is a common form of chronic kidney disease. Diabetes refers to a category of disorders marked by high blood sugar levels. When blood sugar levels increase, blood vessels in the kidneys are broken. This means that the kidneys aren't cleaning the blood well enough. When the body is overburdened by toxins, kidney dysfunction occurs.

**Kidney stones are a common ailment.**

Another common kidney condition is kidney stones. Minerals and other compounds in the blood crystallize in the kidneys, forming thick masses (stones). Normally, kidney stones migrate through the body during urination. While passing kidney stones may be excruciating, they seldom result in severe complications.

**Glomerulonephritis.**

Glomerulonephritis is the infection of the glomeruli. Glomeruli are tiny blood-collecting bodies found within the kidneys. Infections, medications, and congenital anomalies may all cause gliomaphritis (defects that appear at or shortly after birth). It continues to improve on its own.

**The polycystic kidney disease (PKD) damages the kidneys.**

Polycystic Kidney Syndrome is an inherited disorder in which the kidneys develop several cysts. These lumps will hinder the kidneys' ability to work, resulting in their failure. (It's worth noting that kidney cysts of this kind are usually mild and painless. A polycystic kidney disorder is a more serious condition.)

**Urinary tract diseases.**

Urinary tract infections (UTIs) are bacterial infections of the urinary tract that can affect any portion of the urinary system. The diseases of the urethra and bladder are the most common. They're normally dealt with right away and don't trigger any more welfare issues. This pathogen, on the other hand, will spread to the kidneys and cause damage if left untreated.

## Signs and Symptoms of Kidney Disease

Kidney disease is a condition that can often go unnoticed before the symptoms become serious. The following signs and symptoms are early indicators that you might be suffering from kidney failure:

- Sleeping trouble
- Tiredness
- Cramps and muscle contractions
- Struggle to focus
- Impoverished desire
- Puffiness around the eyes, in the morning
- Ankles / swollen feet
- A body that is oily, scaly
- Repeated urination, particularly at night

Important indications that kidney disease is progressing into kidney failure includes:

- Appetite deficit
- Nausea and sickness
- Shifts in the output of urine
- Retention of liquids
- Loss of libido

- Pericardium inflammation (a fluid-filled sac that shields the heart)
- Anemia (a loss in red blood cells)
- Sudden rise in levels of potassium (hyperkalemia)

## Various Kinds of Kidney Disorders and their Treatments

Kidney failure treatment typically focuses on the underlying cause of the issue. This ensures the doctor can make the process of checking your blood pressure, blood sugar, and cholesterol levels easy for you. To cure kidney failure, they should use a mixture of the following methods.

### Drugs and Prescriptions

The doctor can recommend angiotensin-converting enzyme (ACE) antagonists like lisinopril and Ramipril, as well as angiotensin receptors (ARB) antagonists like Irbesartan and Olmesartan. Several blood pressure medications can help delay the progression of kidney disease. Even if you don't have high blood pressure, your doctor can prescribe these medications to help keep your kidneys functioning properly.

Cholesterol drugs can also be beneficial (such as Simvastatin). This medication will help maintain kidney function by lowering blood cholesterol levels. Based on the signs, the doctor can also prescribe medications to reduce swelling and treat anemia (a drop in the number of Red Blood Cells).

### Changes in Diet and Lifestyle

Lifestyle changes are just as important as taking medications. Following a healthy lifestyle will help to reduce some of the major causes of kidney disease. Perhaps your doctor would recommend that you:

- Partake in the treatment of diabetes by insulin injections
- Reduce salt intake
- Cut back foods high in cholesterol
- Limit alcohol consumption
- Whole grains, herbs, and low-fat dairy items initiate a heart-healthy diet.
- Stop smoking
- Lose weight
- Physical health boost

### Dialysis and Kidney Infection

Dialysis is a type of blood filtration that is performed automatically. It's meant for those whose kidneys have failed or are about to fail. Dialysis is needed for the majority of patients with advanced kidney disease for the rest of their lives, or until a donor's kidney is available.

The two methods of dialysis that can be used are peritoneal dialysis and hemodialysis.

### Hemodialysis.

The blood is injected into a system that filters out waste materials and liquids during hemodialysis. Hemodialysis should be done in a hospital, at home, or at a dialysis center. Three sessions each week, lasting 3 to 5 hours, are sometimes arranged. Hemodialysis, however, may be done in more frequent, shorter sessions.

A few weeks before beginning hemodialysis, some patients will have surgery to establish an arteriovenous (AV) fistula. An AV fistula is created where an artery and a vein are connected just under the skin's surface, typically in the forearm. Due to a bigger blood vessel, hemodialysis treatment allows an increased volume of blood to circulate continuously into the bloodstream. As a result of this, there will be a higher quantity of blood pumped and purified. An arteriovenous graft (a looped and silicone tube) should be implanted and used for the same purpose where an artery and a vein cannot be attached.

The most common hemodialysis side effects are low blood pressure, muscle cramping, and itching.

**Peritoneal cavity dialysis.**

During peritoneal dialysis, the peritoneum (the membrane that surrounds the abdominal wall) takes the place of the kidneys. Dialysate, a stomach-shielding drug, is injected into a hose. The waste materials from the peritoneum make their way to the dialysate through the bloodstream. After that, the dialysate is extracted from the intestine.

Continuous ambulatory peritoneal dialysis, in which the stomach is filled and drained several times during the day, and continuous cycler-assisted peritoneal dialysis, in which an apparatus is used to move the fluid in and out of the stomach while the person is sleeping, are the two forms of peritoneal dialysis.

Viruses in the abdominal cavity, or in the region where the tube has been inserted, are the most frequent side effects of peritoneal dialysis. Weight gain and hernias may be possible side effects also. A hernia occurs as the intestine passes into a weak spot or a tear in the bottom abdominal wall.

## Best Long-Term Treatment for Kidney Disease

Kidney disease normally does not progress until it has been identified. Living a balanced lifestyle and following the doctor's recommendations are the easiest ways to improve kidney function. Kidney disease may get more serious over time. It's also likely that it'll cause kidney problems. If kidney failure is not treated, it can be fatal.

Kidney failure occurs when the kidneys are either partially or completely dysfunctional. Dialysis is needed to act as a working function for your kidneys in this stage by using a pump to remove waste from the blood. In certain cases, a kidney transplant may be recommended by the doctor.

## What Should Be Done in Order to Keep Kidney Failure at Bay?

Certain risk factors for kidney disease, such as age, race, and family history, are difficult to monitor. However, you can take the following steps to help avoid kidney disease:

- If you have diabetes, monitor your blood sugar
- Drink lots of water
- Blood pressure management
- Quit smoking
- Decreased consumption of salt
- For over-the-counter medications, be vigilant

Dosage recommendations for over-the-counter drugs should also be followed. You can potentially damage your kidneys if you take too much Bayer (aspirin) or ibuprofen (Advil, Motrin). Consult a specialist if the pain is not relieved by the normal dose of these drugs.

**Take an exam.**

Insist on a blood test from a doctor to check for kidney problems. In addition, kidney diseases should not manifest symptoms until they have advanced. A simple metabolic panel is a standard blood test that can be performed as part of a regular medical checkup (BMP). This examination shows the potential presence of creatinine or urea in the blood. Any contaminants spill into the bloodstream when the kidneys aren't working properly. A BMP can diagnose kidney issues early on, making them more manageable. If you have diabetes, heart disease, or elevated blood pressure, you should be checked on a regular basis.

**There are some additives that can be avoided.**

Kidney stones can be caused by a variety of chemicals in food, the following are examples of what can be avoided:

- Chicken and beef contain animal protein.
- An excessive amount of sodium.
- Citrus fruits like lemons, bananas, and grapefruits contain oxalate, a chemical also found in beets, lettuce, cocoa, and sweet potatoes.

**Make a request for calcium supplements.**

A correlation has been found between some calcium supplements and an increased risk of kidney stones. Before taking a calcium supplement, talk to the doctor.

# Fundamentals of Renal Diet

A diet that is low in protein, sodium, and phosphorus is known as a renal diet. A renal diet emphasizes the significance of consuming high-quality protein and limiting liquid intake. In certain patients, calcium and potassium would also need to be restricted. Given that each person's body is unique, it's important that each patient works with a renal dietitian to develop a diet that is tailored to their specific needs.

To reduce the amount of waste in their blood, people who have lost renal function must follow a kidney diet. Kidney function can be impaired, which causes the kidneys to be unable to filter or remove waste effectively. If there is an imbalance of electrolytes in a patient's blood, it can have a negative impact on their electrolyte levels. Maintaining a renal diet can help to enhance renal function and extend the onset of complete kidney disease.

## What is Renal Diet?

Appropriate nutrition is critical for renal health. Renal disease patients, in particular, must keep their potassium, sodium, and phosphorus intake under control.

Renal disorder patients can often need to manage a variety of nutrients. The information provided below will assist you with improving your eating habits.

Consult a doctor or a nutritionist on your specific dietary requirements.

### Role of Sodium

Sodium (sodium chloride) is a mineral that can be used in salt and is commonly used in food production. Although it takes time to get used to reducing salt consumption in your diet as it is one of the most commonly used seasonings. Salt/sodium restriction, on the other hand, is a useful tool in the treatment of kidney disease.

- Don't season rice with salt while you eat it.
- Don't use salt when boiling rice.

Begin to comprehend product labeling. Stop eating foods that have more than 300 mg salt per serving (600 mg for a complete frozen dinner). Avoid using salt-containing products with the first 4 to 5 ingredients on the product list.

Lunch must not include bacon, ham, hot dogs, sausages, meat, or nuggets, and regular condensed soup should be avoided. Consume only soups with signs indicating that the sodium level has been reduced–and only one cup, not the whole packet. "No extra salt" must be stated on canned vegetables. Flavored salts like onion salt, garlic salt, or seasoned salt should be avoided. Sea or kosher salt can also be avoided. Look for "lower salt used" options in your preferred treats, such as box mixes or peanut butter. Processed frozen meats that have been "in a solution" or that have been refrigerated or flavored should not be purchased. Typical offerings include pork chops, chicken breasts, steaks, pork tenderloin, and burgers.

### Role of Phosphorus

Phosphorus is another mineral that builds up in the blood when the kidneys aren't working properly. Calcium may be removed from your bones and accumulate in your blood vessels or skin as a result of an event. The bone condition would also become a problem, increasing the chances of developing a fracture.

Dairy products are the main source of phosphorus in the diet, so limit yourself to one cup of milk a day. If you use cheese or yogurt instead of powdered milk, you either need one glass or one ounce every day.

Phosphorus can be consumed in a variety of vegetables; Broccoli, dried beans, mushrooms, and brussels sprouts if limited to one cup a WEEK. The following cereals can be limited to one serving a week: oatmeal, wheat cereals, bran, and granola. White bread is better than whole-grain bread or crackers.

Soft drinks contain phosphorus, so only the translucent ones can be consumed. Mountain Dew (any kind), Dr. Pepper (any kind), colas, and root beers should all be avoided. Often prohibited are Hawaiian Punch, Fruit works, Cool iced tea, and Aquafina tangerine pineapple. Since alcohol contains phosphorus, it is best to eliminate all kinds.

**Role of Potassium**

Potassium is a chemical element that helps tissues function properly. High levels of potassium circulate through the bloodstream when the kidneys aren't working accordingly. This can cause irregularities in the way the heartbeats, and it may also lead to a heart attack. Potassium is mostly present in fruits and vegetables, as well as milk and meats. You'd have to avoid consuming some of them and limit the number of others.

**Potassium-rich foods to avoid include:**

- Melons like cantaloupe and honeydew (watermelon)
- Juice of prunes
- Oranges and juice with oranges
- Dried beans—all forms
- Bananas
- Winter squash
- Cooked greens, collards, spinach, kale, Swiss Chard
- Juice from grapefruit
- Pumpkin
- Tomatoes, tomato juice, or tomato sauce

Granola, bran cereals, molasses, "salt substitute" or "lite" sodium are also things to avoid.

To avoid eating too much potassium, eat a wide variety of low-potassium alternative vegetables and fruits every day.

# Foods to Avoid on Renal Diet

If you are on a renal diet, the items mentioned below should be avoided or used in moderation.

## 1. Soda in a dark color

Sodas contain additives that accommodate phosphorus in addition to sugar and calories, especially dark-colored sodas.

Phosphorus is often used in food and beverage processing to increase flavor, prolong shelf life, and avoid discoloration.

This extra phosphorus is absorbed more readily by the body than natural, animal and plant-based phosphorus.

Phosphorus in the form of chemicals isn't really bound to protein—with the exception of natural phosphorus—rather, it comes in the form of salt and is easily absorbed by the digestive tract.

In certain cases, additive phosphorus can be found in a product's ingredient list. Meat manufacturers, on the other hand, are not permitted to show the exact amount of phosphorus additives on the food label.

Although the amount of additive phosphorus varies depending on the type of beverage, most dark-colored sodas are expected to contain 50-100 mg per 200 ml serving. As a result, on a diet (renal), sodas, particularly dark sodas, must be shunned.

## 2. Avocado

Avocados are known for their heart-healthy fiber, fats, and antioxidants, as well as their other nutritional benefits. Avocados are usually a healthy count to a diet, but people with kidney disease must elude them.

Avocados have a high potassium content, so they are a good source of potassium. They contain a monstrous 727 mg (per cup) of potassium (150 g). That is double the potassium a banana of medium size has. One cup of avocado provides nearly 37% of the 2,000 mg potassium restriction.

Avocados, like guacamole, must be eluded on a renal diet, particularly if you've been advised to limit your potassium intake.

## 3. Foods in cans

Canned foods, such as soups, tomatoes, and beans, are often purchased due to their low cost and flexibility. Many canned foods, on the other hand, contain high amounts of sodium, which is added as a preservative to increase their shelf life.

Because of the sodium content in canned products, it is recommended that people with kidney disease prevent or limit their consumption. Low sodium or "no salt added" alternatives are normally better choices. Furthermore, draining and rinsing canned foods, such as canned beans and tuna, can lessen sodium content by 33 to 80 %, depending on the commodity.

To limit overall sodium consumption, it is normally safest to avoid, ban, or purchase low-sodium alternatives.

## 4. Bread made from whole wheat

Choosing the best bread for those with kidney failure can be difficult.

Whole wheat bread is a more nutritious alternative, due to its higher fiber quality. However, white bread is usually recommended over whole-wheat for people with kidney disease. This is due to the phosphorus and potassium content. The more bran and whole grains in the bread, the higher the phosphorus and potassium content.

For e.g., a 1-ounce (30-gram) serving of whole wheat bread contains about 57 mg phosphorus and 69 mg potassium. In addition, white bread contains just 28 mg of potassium and phosphorus. It's worth noting that most bread and bread products, whether white or whole wheat, contain relatively high levels of sodium. It is in your best interests to read the nutrient labels of various types of bread, choose a lower sodium substitute if possible, and keep track of your serving sizes.

To reiterate, when you are on a renal diet, it is best practice to favor white bread, and compare the food labeling in order to choose a brand that contains lower sodium.

## 5. Rice (brown)

Brown rice, like whole-wheat flour, is a whole grain with a higher potassium and phosphorus content than white rice. A cup of cooked brown rice contains 150 mg of phosphorus and 154 mg of potassium, while a cup of white rice contains just 69 mg of phosphorus and 54 mg of potassium (cooked).

White rice can be used in a renal diet to avoid an excessive intake of potassium and phosphorus, but only if the level is regulated and matched with other foods. Bulgur, pearled barley, buckwheat, and couscous are low-phosphorus grains that can be used as a substitute for brown rice.

## 6. Bananas

Bananas are known for their high potassium content. 1 medium banana contains 422 mg of potassium, despite being naturally low in sodium. If you eat a banana every day, sticking to a maximum potassium intake of 2,000 mg can be difficult.

Unfortunately, several other tropical fruits have high potassium levels as well. Pineapples, on the other hand, contain somewhat less potassium than most other tropical fruits and may be a more suitable yet delicious alternative.

On a renal diet, bananas are an unhealthy source of potassium and should be avoided.

## 7. Dairy products

Dairy products are high in proteins and vitamins. They're a good source of phosphorus and potassium, as well as a good source of protein. For e.g., 1 cup (240 ml) of whole milk contains 222 mg of phosphorus and 349 mg of potassium (18).

However, eating too much dairy in comparison to other phosphorus-rich foods can be detrimental to bone health in those with kidney disease. This could come as a surprise given that dairy and milk are both recommended for strong bones and muscles.

However, consuming too much phosphorus causes an excess of phosphorus in the blood, weakening the kidneys and forcing calcium out of the bones. This will weaken and shorten bones over time, increasing the chance of fractures or breaks. Dairy foods are also high in protein, 1 cup (240 ml) of milk contains about 8 g of protein.

It may be important to limit dairy consumption in order to avoid the accumulation of protein wastes in the blood. Dairy replacements, such as unenriched rice milk and almond milk, are lower in calcium, protein and potassium than the milk of cows, making them a safer milk supplement while on a diet.

Dairy items have a lot of potassium, phosphate and protein, so they can be avoided if you are on a diet (renal). Despite milk's calcium content (high), those with renal disease can experience bone loss due to its high phosphorus content.

## 8. Oranges and orange juice

While oranges and orange juice are probably best known for their vitamin C content, they are also high in potassium. One large orange has 333 mg of potassium (184 g). Furthermore, 1 cup of orange juice (240 ml) contains 473 mg of potassium. Oranges and orange juice can be avoided or restricted in the renal diet due to their potassium content. Apples, strawberries and cranberries, as well as their juices, are ideal substitutes for oranges and orange juice due to their lower potassium content.

## 9. Meats that have been processed

Processed meats have long been linked to chronic diseases and are widely regarded as unhealthy due to their preservative content. Salted, cured, roasted, or frozen meats are examples of processed meats. Pepperoni, bacon, jerky and sausage are only a few examples.

Processed meat usually contains large amounts of salt, which is used to improve taste and conserve flavor. As a result, if processed meats are a big part of your diet, maintaining your daily sodium intake under 2,000 mg can be difficult. In addition, processed meat is a good source of protein. If you've been told to keep track of your protein consumption, you'll need to exclude refined meats from your diet.

Processed meats are high in protein and salt and should be consumed in moderation on a renal diet.

## 10. Pickles, olives, and relish

Pickled or cured foods include pickles, relish, and processed olives. Significant amounts of salt are usually used during the pickling or curing period. A single pickle spear, for example, may contain over 300 mg of sodium. Similarly, 244 mg of sodium can be contained in 2 tablespoons of sweet pickle relish.

When processed olives are fermented and aged to make them less bitter, they also taste salty. 5 green pickled olives contain about 195 mg of sodium, which is a significant portion of the daily sodium intake in such a limited serving. Many supermarkets sell reduced-sodium pickles, olives, and relish, which have less sodium than regular versions.

Pickles, processed olives, and relish have a high salt level and should be avoided in the renal diet.

## 11. Apricots

Apricots are high in vitamins C and A, as well as fiber. Though they are still a good source of potassium. The potassium content in a cup of fresh apricots is 427 mg. Potassium is also even more abundant in dried apricots. Over 1,500 mg potassium can be found in a cup of dried apricots (30).

That means that 75 % of the 2,000 mg potassium restriction can be met with only one cup of dried apricots. On a renal diet, apricots, particularly dried apricots, should be avoided.

They also have over 400 mg of caffeine per raw cup and over 1,500 mg of caffeine per dry cup, adding another reason as to why they should be avoided.

## 12. Sweet Potatoes and Potatoes

Potatoes and sweet potatoes, which are rich in potassium, can be leached or soaked to reduce their potassium content.

The potassium content of potatoes can also be reduced by half by cutting them into small, thin parts and boiling them for at least ten minutes. It has been found that potatoes that have been submerged in water for at least four hours lowered the amount of potassium. A potato has less potassium in it before boiling than those that have not been soaked. This method is known as the "double cook operation" or "potassium leaching."

While cooking potatoes twice decreases their potassium content, it's crucial to note that this method doesn't remove it entirely. Potassium levels can still be high in double-cooked potatoes, so portion control is advised to keep potassium levels under control.

## 13. Tomatoes

Tomatoes are another potassium-rich food that may not be appropriate for a renal diet. They can be eaten raw or stewed, and sauces can be made from them, however the potassium content in a cup of tomato sauce is over 900 mg.

Tomatoes are widely used in some meals, which is unfortunate for those on a renal diet. Personal taste plays a big role in deciding on a potassium-free alternative. However, substituting tomato sauce for roasted red pepper sauce and consuming less potassium per meal can be just as delicious.

Tomatoes are another high-potassium snack to skip while you're on a renal diet.

## 14. Meals that are prepackaged, ready-to-eat, and ready-to-cook

Refined foods will add a significant amount of sodium to your diet. The most concentrated of all foods, packaged, premade and microwave meals, contain the highest sodium content.

Frozen pizza, instant noodles and microwaveable dinners are among the most important types to avoid. Maintaining a sodium level of up to 2,000 mg per day will be daunting if you consume heavily refined foods on a daily basis. Refined foods can be not only high in sodium, but they can also be poor in nutrients.

Packaged, instant, and premade meals are heavily processed diets with high sodium levels and nutritional deficiencies. These components should be kept to a minimum in a renal diet.

## 15. Swiss chard, spinach, and beet greens

Leafy green vegetables including Swiss chard, spinach and beet greens are rich in a variety of nutrients and minerals, including potassium. Potassium content in a cup ranges from 140mg to 290 mg when served fresh. The potassium content of leafy vegetables reduces when cooked to a smaller serving size, but it remains stable when cooked to larger serving size.

When fried, half a cup of raw spinach, for example, can be reduced to around a tablespoon. As a result, half a cup of raw spinach has far more potassium than cooked spinach. To stop excess potassium, new Swiss chard, spinach and beet greens are preferred overcooked.

However, since these foods are high in oxalates, which can increase the risk of kidney stones in people who are prone to them, you should restrict their consumption. Kidney stones can exacerbate renal tissue injury and make it difficult for the kidneys to function properly.

### 16. Raisins, dates and prunes, to name a few.

Dried fruits such as dates, raisins and prunes are all common. All of the nutrients, including potassium, are concentrated as fruits are dried. For e.g., 1 cup of dried prunes contains 1,274 mg of potassium, nearly 5 times the potassium content of 1 cup of prunes when fresh.

In addition, only 4 dates contain 668 mg of potassium (42). Because of the high potassium content of these famous dried fruits, it's best to stay away from them if you're on a renal diet.

### 17. Pretzels, popcorn and crackers

Pretzels, popcorn and crackers are examples of ready-to-eat snack foods that are low in protein and high in salt. It's normal to consume more than the prescribed portion size of these ingredients, resulting in higher-than-expected salt intake. Furthermore, if potatoes are used to produce chips, they will have a high potassium content. It is best to avoid consuming these when on a renal diet.

# Advantages of Renal Diet

To decrease the amount of excess in their blood, people with impaired kidney function must adopt a kidney or renal diet. Consumed liquids and diets contain waste that accumulates in the blood. Kidney activity is compromised and the kidneys are unable to properly filter or eliminate waste. Excess electrolyte levels in the blood may cause a patient's electrolyte levels to drop. A renal diet can help to maintain kidney function and slow the progression of kidney disease.

Kidneys are essential for good health. They are in charge of removing excess water, waste products, and other impurities from the blood. These chemicals are stored in the bladder and are only expelled when you urinate. The kidneys also regulate body salt, PH, and potassium levels. They produce hormones that regulate blood pressure and monitor red blood cell development. Vitamin D, which aids calcium digestion, is also found in the kidneys.

Kidney function can gradually deteriorate to the point that the kidneys are unable to function properly. An individual may require dialysis in this situation. Dialysis cleans the blood of waste and extra fat, and can aid in the healing of kidney disease, but it cannot cure it. Depending on the situation, a kidney transplant could be an alternative.

## 5 Benefits of Renal Diet

A renal diet is very much beneficial for everybody but especially for those who are suffering from kidney diseases. The following are five benefits one can achieve while on a renal diet:

- To balance the level of minerals, fluid, and electrolytes in your body during dialysis
- To restrict the accumulation of waste materials in the body when on dialysis
- To reduce weight and bad cholesterol, which further reduces the chances of many heart diseases
- To prevent kidney diseases like CKD, stones, etc.
- To facilitate better urination which will help in excreting out the extra waste materials from the body and prevent different urine diseases

It is not easy to follow any diet without proper planning and knowledge. This is where we've got you covered. In the upcoming chapters you will find detailed recipes of all varieties and as a bonus a complete four-week meal plan for your easiness.

# Breakfast Recipes

## Mexican Egg & Tortilla Skillet
*Time: 25 Mins, Serves: 4, Skill: Easy*

**Ingredients**
- Unsalted tortilla chips (6 oz.)
- Butter (2 tbsp)
- Low salt ketchup (1/4 cup)
- Chili powder (1 tsp)
- Green onions (2), sliced thin
- Eggs (8)

**Instructions**
- Whisk the eggs together in a mixing bowl until well combined.
- Combine the ketchup, cabbage, and chili powder with the egg mixture. Blend until it's almost completely smooth.
- In a pan, melt the butter, then add the tortilla chips and cook over medium heat until heated through.
- Stir in the egg mixture to the tortillas, and scramble until you reach the desired consistency. Serve right away on warm plates.

*Calories 143, Protein 24 g, Sodium 81 mg, Potassium 31 mg, Phosphorus 96 mg, Calcium 13 mg*

## Fresh Fruit Compote
*Time: 4 hours and 10 Mins, Serves: 2, Skill: Easy*

**Ingredients**
- Apple (1)
- Banana (1)
- Blackberries (1/2 cup)
- Strawberries (1/2 cup)
- Red raspberries (1/4 cup)
- Orange juice (1/2 cup)
- Blueberries (1/2 cup)
- Peaches (1/2 cup)

**Instructions**
- Fill a large tub halfway with orange juice.
- In a large mixing bowl, combine all of the fruit and gently toss to mix.
- Combine the fruit and the orange juice.
- Allow the mix to sit for 4 hours at room temperature when thawing frozen fruits.

*Calories 113, Protein 14 g, Sodium 8 mg, Potassium 4 mg, Phosphorus 9 mg, Calcium 13 mg*

## Burritos with Eggs and Mexican Sausage
*Time: 25 Mins, Serves: 4, Skill: Easy*

**Ingredients**
- Eggs, beaten (3)
- Flour tortillas (3)
- Chorizo (3 oz.)

**Instructions**
- In a skillet, fry the chorizo until it turns a dark brown color.
- Cook the eggs until they are cooked through.
- Fill the tortillas halfway with the filling, roll them to prevent the filling from leaking out, and fold the bottom edge in.

*Calories 130, Protein 27 g, Sodium 11 mg, Potassium 14 mg, Phosphorus 19 mg, Calcium 6 mg*

## Master Mix
*Time: 1 hour, Serves: 13, Skill: Hard*

**Ingredients**
- Cream of tartar (2 tsp)
- Baking soda (1 tsp)
- Milk powder (1 1/2 cups)
- Vegetable shortening (2 1/4 cups)
- Flour (8 1/2 cups)
- Baking powder (1 tbsp)

**Instructions**
- Mix the flour, tartar cream, baking soda, baking powder, and milk powder using a sifter.
- Use a pastry blender to break up the shortening while distributing it evenly through the mix.
- Keep refrigerated and dry in a large, airtight container.
- For 10 to 12 weeks, you'll be able to use it.

*Calories 135, Protein 20 g, Sodium 75 mg, Potassium 40 mg, Phosphorus 80 mg, Calcium 18 mg*

## Fig and Goat Cheese Quesadilla
*Time: 35 Mins, Serves: 4, Skill: Easy*

**Ingredients**
- Goat cheese (4 oz.)
- Fig jam (4 oz.)
- Whole-wheat tortillas, reduced sodium (4)

**Instructions**

- On a clean table or cutting board, lay out two tortillas.
- Using a thin layer of fig jam, spread it evenly across each tortilla.
- Spread the goat cheese chunks over the jelly. Place a fresh tortilla on top of each one and firmly press down.
- In a large iron skillet, heat oil over high heat. Cook each quesadilla for about 2 minutes, or until the bottoms are browned.
- Use the spatula to turn them and cook for a further 1 or 2 minutes. If necessary, lower the heat to avoid premature blackening on either side.
- Using a spatula, transfer each quesadilla to a plate. Eat each one after cutting it in half.

*Calories 300, Protein 13 g, Sodium 289 mg, Potassium 404 mg, Phosphorus 195 mg, Calcium 148 mg*

## Puffy Chili Rellenos Casserole
*Time: 55 Mins, Serves: 8, Skill: Easy*

**Ingredients**
- Large eggs (8)
- Milk (2/3 cup)
- Flour (1 cup)
- Baking powder, low sodium (1 tsp)
- Padilla peppers (8)
- Cheddar cheese (6 oz.), shredded
- Jack cheese (oz.), shredded
- Ricotta cheese (1 cup)

**Instructions**
- Preheat oven to 350°F.
- Roast the peppers. When cooked strip them of their skins.
- In a greased 9x13 tray, layer the cheddar and jack cheese and ricotta on the peppers.
- Blend the eggs, flour, milk, and baking powder until smooth in a blender, or food processor.
- Pour the mix over the peppers, cheese and ricotta, and bake for 30–40 minutes.
- Serve it immediately.

*Calories 145, Protein 24 g, Sodium 28 mg, Potassium 25 mg, Phosphorus 17 mg, Calcium 35 mg*

## Sudden Quiche
*Time: 1 hour and 20 Mins, Serves: 8, Skill: Hard*

**Ingredients**
- Eggs (6)
- Deep-dish frozen Pie shell (19")
- Grated cheese (4 oz.)
- 2 % or lower milk (1 cup)
- Total filling (2 cups)

**Instructions**
- Preheat oven to 350°F.
- In a large mixing bowl, whisk together the eggs, total filling, milk, and cheese (if the phosphorus is increased, use two ounces of cheese).
- The filling should be poured into a cold pastry shell.
- Bake for 45-60 minutes, or until a knife inserted in the center comes out clean.
- Allow a five-minute resting period.

*Calories 150, Protein 30 g, Sodium 70 mg, Potassium 35 mg, Phosphorus 80 mg, Calcium 14 mg*

## Spiced Applesauce Bread or Muffins
*Time: 1 hour 20 Mins, Serves: 12, Skill: Hard*

**Ingredients**
- Eggs (2)
- Flour (2 cups)
- Baking soda (1 tsp)
- Baking powder (1/2 tsp)
- Applesauce (1 1/2 cups)
- Brown sugar (1 cup)
- Vegetable oil (1/2 cup)
- Pumpkin pie spice (2 tsp)

**Instructions**
- Preheat oven to 350°F.
- Coat a muffin tin or a loaf pan with cooking spray.
- Combine the applesauce, oil, brown sugar, and eggs in a medium mixing cup.
- Combine the remainder of the ingredients in a separate medium mixing bowl.
- Stir in the applesauce mixture to the flour mixture until it is completely combined (do not overmix).
- The batter should be poured into a muffin tin or a loaf pan.
- Bake a loaf for 50-60 minutes if you're making one.
- Bake for about 20 minutes if you're making muffins.
- Probing it with a toothpick should yield a clear result, indicating that it is done.

*Calories 148, Protein 24 g, Sodium 81 mg, Potassium 31 mg, Phosphorus 46 mg, Calcium 13 mg*

## Mexican Brunch Eggs
*Time: 55 Mins, Serves: 8, Skill: Medium*

**Ingredients**
- Eggs, beaten (8)
- Toasted sliced bread (8)
- Chopped onion (1/2 cup)
- Garlic cloves (2), crushed
- Frozen corn (1 1/2 cups), thawed
- Cumin (1 1/2 tsp)
- Cayenne pepper (1/8 tsp)
- Margarine (2 tbsp)

**Instructions**
- In a large skillet, melt the margarine and sauté the onion and corn until soft.
- In a mixing bowl, whisk together the eggs, garlic, cumin, and cayenne pepper.
- Pour in the eggs (or egg substitute) and cook, stirring occasionally, over low heat until the eggs are fully cooked.
- Using a large platter, arrange the toast triangles.
- Place the egg mixture on the toast triangles.
- Serve quickly.

*Calories 130, Protein 32 g, Sodium 55 mg, Potassium 39 mg, Phosphorus 70 mg, Calcium 18 mg*

## Buckwheat Pancakes
*Time: 50 Mins, Serves: 10, Skill: Medium*

**Ingredients**
- Baking powder (2 tsp)
- Egg (1 large)
- Vanilla extract (1 tsp)
- Rice milk (1 3/4 cups)
- White vinegar (2 tsp)
- Butter, divided, for the skillet (2 tbsp)
- Buckwheat flour (1 cup)
- Flour (1/2 cup)
- Sugar (1 tbsp)

**Instructions**
- Pour the vinegar and rice milk into a mixing tub. Set the timer for it to sit for 5 minutes.
- Combine the buckwheat and all-purpose flour in a large mixing bowl. Add the sugar and baking powder and mix well.
- In a separate mixing bowl, whisk together the rice milk, egg, and vanilla extract. Then add the wet ingredients to the buckwheat mix and stir together.
- In a skillet over medium heat, melt the butter (1 and a half tablespoons). Toss the flour into the skillet with a 1/4-cup measuring cup. Cook the pancake for 2–3 minutes, or until tiny bubbles appear on the surface. On the backside, cook for 1-2 minutes more.
- Continue to cook the remaining batter in batches in the skillet, adding more butter as needed.

*Calories 140, Protein 25 g, Sodium 65 mg, Potassium 35 mg, Phosphorus 80 mg, Calcium 14 mg*

## 40-Second Omelet
*Time: 25 Mins, Serves: 1, Skill: Easy*

**Ingredients**
- Eggs (2)
- Water (2 tbsp)
- Filling (vegetables, meat, seafood) (1/2 cup)
- Unsalted butter (1 tbsp)

**Instructions**
- Combine the eggs and water in a mixing bowl and whisk until smooth.
- Melt the butter in a 10" omelet pan/frypan until a water drop sizzles.
- Pour the egg mixture into the pan, quickly spreading it out on the sides, and using an inverted pancake turner, carefully push cooked portions from the edges to the center, allowing uncooked portions to come into contact with the heated pan's surface. Tilt and move the pan as desired.
- If necessary, fill the omelet with 1/2 cup beef, vegetables, or seafood filling, placing the filling on the left side if you're right-handed and on the right side if you're left-handed.
- Invert the bottom half of the omelet onto a plate using the pancake turner.

*Calories 100, Protein 24 g, Sodium 81 mg, Potassium 31 mg, Phosphorus 96 mg, Calcium 13 mg*

## Apple Bran Muffins
*Time: 55 Mins, Serves: 12, Skill: Medium*

**Ingredients**
- Oil (2 tbsp)
- Whole wheat flour (2 cups)
- Scant buttermilk or sour milk (2 cups)

- Beaten egg (1)
- Molasses (1/2 cup)
- Wheat bran (1 1/2 cups)
- Baking soda (1 1/4 tsp)
- Nutmeg (1/2 tsp)
- Raisins (1/2 cup)
- Chopped nuts (1/2 cup)
- Orange juice (1)
- Orange rind (1 tbsp), grated
- Chopped apple (1 cup)

**Instructions**
- Preheat oven to 350°F.
- Toss the flour, bran, nutmeg, and baking soda together with a fork.
- In a large mixing bowl, combine the orange rind, raisins, apples, seeds, and nuts.
- Pour 1 cup of orange juice and 2 cups buttermilk into a two-cup measure.
- Combine the buttermilk mixture with the egg, oil, and molasses, and whisk together.
- With a few quick strokes, combine the liquid and dry ingredients.
- Pour two-thirds of the batter into greased muffin tins and bake for 25 minutes.

*Calories 145, Protein 20 g, Sodium 80 mg, Potassium 31 mg, Phosphorus 96 mg, Calcium 13 mg*

## Biscuits with Master Mix
*Time: 1 hour, Serves: 12, Skill: Medium*

### Ingredients
- Master Mix (3 cups)
- Water (2/3 cup)

### Instructions
- Preheat oven to 450°F.
- In a blender, thoroughly combine all the ingredients.
- Leave it to sit for 5 minutes.
- Knead the dough about 15 times on a well-floured surface.
- Roll out to a thickness of 1/2 inch and cut into 12 biscuits with a floured knife.
- Arrange 2" apart on a baking sheet that has not been greased.
- Bake for 10–12 minutes, or until golden brown.

*Calories 143, Protein 24 g, Sodium 81 mg, Potassium 31 mg, Phosphorus 96 mg, Calcium 13 mg*

## Bran Breakfast Bars
*Time: 1 hour 10 Mins, Serves: 6, Skill: Medium*

### Ingredients
- Whole wheat flour (1/2 cup)
- Oil (corn, safflower, or soybean) (1/3 cup)
- Pure bran (1 1/2 cups)
- Boiling water (1 cup)
- Oatmeal (1 cup)
- Chopped raisins or meds. dates, diced (1/3 cup)
- Sugar substitute (3 tbsp)

### Instructions
- Place the diced fruit in hot water.
- Allow to stand for 20 minutes—at the very least.
- In a big mixing bowl, combine the dry ingredients.
- Drain the berries, then add boiling water to the juice that has been drained, and blend with oil.
- Blend the mix for 1 minute.
- Pour in the dry ingredients right away and thoroughly combine.
- Remix after including the fruit.
- Layer the batter in a nonstick 8"x10" baking dish.
- Mark the cuttings in four narrow rows and six broad rows using your fingertips or a spatula to level them.
- In a preheated oven, bake for 22 minutes at 375°F.
- Cool it by putting it on a shelf.
- If you plan to keep it for more than two days, put it in the fridge or freeze it.

*Calories 120, Protein 25 g, Sodium 70 mg, Potassium 30 mg, Phosphorus 75 mg, Calcium 13 mg*

## Burritos Rapido's
*Time: 30 Mins, Serves: 4, Skill: Easy*

### Ingredients
- Eggs (8), beaten
- Corn tortillas (4)
- Canola or olive oil (1 1/2 tsp)
- Red bell pepper, diced (1/2)
- Green onions (scallions), (4)

### Instructions
- Heat the oil over medium heat in a medium frying pan.
- Cook, stirring occasionally, for 3 minutes, or until the bell pepper and green onion are soft.
- Before they are fully fried, add and scramble the eggs for about 5 minutes.

- Place two damp paper towels between the tortillas on a tray.
- Put the tortillas in the microwave for 2 minutes.
- Fill the soft tortillas halfway with the egg mixture.
- The tortillas should be rolled up and eaten.

*Calories 143, Protein 24 g, Sodium 81 mg, Potassium 31 mg, Phosphorus 96 mg, Calcium 13 mg*

## Stuffed Breakfast Biscuits
*Time: 40 Mins, Serves: 4, Skill: Easy*

### Ingredients
- Milk (3/4 cup)
- Eggs (4)
- Reduced-sodium bacon (8 0z.)
- Cheddar cheese (1 cup), shredded
- Scallions (1/4 cup), thinly sliced
- Flour (2 cups)
- Sugar (or honey) (1 tbsp)
- Baking soda (1/2 tsp)
- Lemon juice (1 tbsp)
- Softened unsalted butter (8 tbsp)

### Instructions
- Preheat oven to 425°F.
- Crisp up the bacon in a pan.
- Place the four ingredients in a mixing bowl and set aside. (Eggs, bacon, cheese, and scallions.)

The dough should be made as follows:
- Combine all of the dry ingredients in a big mixing cup.
- Break the unsalted butter into small pea-sized pieces with a fork or pastry knife.
- Make a "well" in the center of the dough and knead in the milk and lemon juice.
- Lightly flour the bottom and sides of muffin tins or line them with parchment paper.
- Fill muffin tins with a quarter-cup of the mixture.
- Bake for 10 to 12 minutes, or until golden brown.

*Calories 160, Protein 35 g, Sodium 85 mg, Potassium 40 mg, Phosphorus 80 mg, Calcium 18 mg*

## Easy Turkey Breakfast Burritos
*Time: 30 Mins, Serves: 8, Skill: Easy*

### Ingredients
- Canola oil (1/4 cup)
- Beaten eggs, scrambled (8)
- Diced onions (1/4 cup)
- Fresh bell peppers (red, yellow, or green) (1/4 cup), diced
- Seeded jalapeño peppers (2 tbsp)
- Turkey (1 lb.)
- Flour burrito shells (8 6-inch)
- Fresh scallions (2 tbsp), chopped
- Fresh cilantro (2 tbsp), chopped
- Chili powder (1/2 tsp)
- Smoked paprika (1/2 tsp)
- Shredded Monterey Jack and Cheddar cheese (1 cup)

### Instructions
- Sauté the meatloaf, onions, scallions, peppers, and cilantro in half of the oil until translucent, then season with the spices and turn off the heat.
- Add the remaining oil and scrambled eggs to another large sauté pan and heat over medium-high heat.
- Fill the burrito shells with equal parts vegetable and meatloaf mixture, cheese, and eggs, fold, and serve.

*Calories 213, Protein 100 g, Sodium 281 mg, Potassium 331 mg, Phosphorus 196 mg, Calcium 43 mg*

## Fluffy Homemade Buttermilk Pancakes
*Time: 35 Mins, Serves: 4, Skill: Easy*

### Ingredients
- Sugar (2 tbsp)
- Buttermilk (2 cups)
- Large eggs (2)
- Canola oil (1/4 cup)
- Flour (2 cups)
- Cream of tartar (1 tsp)
- Baking soda (1 1/2 tsp)

### Instructions
- Preheat the skillet to medium.
- In a large mixing bowl, combine the dry ingredients and whisk or spoon them into the buttermilk, egg, and oil mixture until completely moistened.
- Put one tbsp of canola oil in a skillet, then using a 1/3 measuring cup, scoop the pancake batter into the skillet. Each pancake should have a diameter of about 4 inches. Allow 2 inches between pancakes for quick flipping. Before all of the top

bubbles have vanished, rotate pancakes with a spatula.
- Serve immediately.

*Calories 135, Protein 70 g, Sodium 81 mg, Potassium 31 mg, Phosphorus 96 mg, Calcium 13 mg*

## Cheesesteak Quiche
*Time: 50 Mins, Serves: 6, Skill: Easy*

**Ingredients**
- Eggs, beaten (5)
- Cream (1 cup)
- Cooked prepared piecrust (1" x 9")
- Black pepper (1/2 tsp)
- Coarsely chopped Sirloin steak meat (1/2 lb.)
- Onions (1 cup), diced
- Canola oil (2 tbsp)
- Shredded pepper jack cheese (1/2 cup)

**Instructions**
- Cut the sliced sirloin into coarse pieces.
- Brown the sliced steak and onions in a sauté pan with the oil, then set aside to cool for 10 minutes before folding in the cheese and letting it rest.
- Whisk the eggs, cream, and black pepper in a large mixing cup until thoroughly combined.
- Spread the steak and cheese mixture on the bottom of the par-cooked piecrust, then top with the egg mixture and bake at 350°F for 30 minutes.
- Cover the cheesesteak quiche with foil and turn off the oven for 10 minutes before serving.

*Calories 150, Protein 55 g, Sodium 75 mg, Potassium 35 mg, Phosphorus 95 mg, Calcium 16 mg*

## Spicy Tofu Scrambler
*Time: 40 Mins, Serves: 5, Skill: Easy*

**Ingredients**
- Firm tofu (1 cup)
- Onion powder (1 tsp)
- Garlic powder (1/4 tsp)
- Olive oil (1 tsp)
- Red bell pepper (1/4 cup), chopped
- Green bell pepper (1/4 cup), chopped
- Clove garlic (1), minced
- Turmeric (1/8 tsp)

**Instructions**
- Sauté the garlic and bell peppers in olive oil in a medium-sized nonstick skillet.
- Before crumbling the tofu in the skillet, clean and rinse it. In a mixing cup, combine the remaining ingredients.
- Cook, whisking constantly until the tofu becomes a faint golden color, around 20 minutes on low-medium heat. The water in the mixture will evaporate.
- Serve immediately.

*Calories 400, Protein 19 g, Sodium 584 mg, Potassium 317mg, Phosphorus 177mg, Calcium 253mg*

## Southwest Baked Egg Breakfast Cups
*Time: 55 Mins, Serves: 12, Skill: Medium*

**Ingredients**
- Skim milk (1/2 cup)
- Eggs, beaten (2)
- Cumin (1/2 tsp)
- Black pepper (1/2 tsp)
- Cooking spray
- Rice (3 cups), cooked
- Cheddar cheese (4 oz.), shredded
- Green chilies (4 oz.), diced
- Pimentos (2 oz.), drained and diced

**Instructions**
- Combine the flour, 2 ounces cheese, chili, pimentos, eggs, cumin, milk, and pepper in a big mixing cup.
- Using nonstick cooking oil, coat muffin cups.
- Fill 12 muffin cups equally with the mixture. The remaining 2 ounces of melted cheese should be placed on top of each cup.
- Preheat the oven to 400 °F and bake for 15 minutes, or until the cake is baked.

*Calories 160, Protein 45 g, Sodium 90 mg, Potassium 40 mg, Phosphorus 100 mg, Calcium 20 mg*

## Summer harvest egg muffin cups
*Time: 45 Mins, Serves: 12, Skill: Medium*

**Ingredients**
- Eggs (8)
- Fresh herbs (1 tbsp)
- Whole stalk (3)
- Mayo (2 tsp)
- Brie (opt), small slices

- Vegetables (1 cup), diced small or shredded
- Oil (1 tsp)
- Lemon zest to taste (1 tsp)

**Instructions**

- In a small amount of oil, sauté the vegetables until they are slightly softened. Allow to cool. In a mixing cup, whisk together the eggs and mayonnaise.
- Combine the herbs and green sliced onions to the eggs and mayonnaise.
- Add the vegetables that have been cooked to the mix.
- Fill 12 muffin tins halfway with the mix.
- Serve with a small slice of brie on top (opt). (Silicon muffin tins are perfect since the muffins simply pop out. You may even create a 9x9 dish out of it, equivalent to a breakfast casserole.)
- Bake at 350°F for 20-25 minutes, or until the center of each muffin is firm. Sprinkle lemon zest on top of each muffin top.

*Calories 160, Protein 50 g, Sodium 90 mg, Potassium 75 mg, Phosphorus 96 mg, Calcium 20 mg*

## Smoky ham omelet
*Time: 25 Mins, Serves: 2, Skill: Easy*

**Ingredients**

- Eggs (4)
- Olive oil (1–2 tbsp)
- Garlic powder
- Onion powder
- Chives (opt)
- Chopped Red pepper (1/2 cup)
- Chopped Onion (1/3 cup)
- Chopped Low sodium ham (1/4 cup)
- Smoked paprika (1 tbsp)

**Instructions**

- Sauté the onion in a pan with the oil.
- Sauté until the onions are tender and transparent, and the sides are lightly charred, then add the red pepper. When the red pepper is slightly roasted, add the paprika and ham. Cook, stirring occasionally, for around 2 minutes, or until the paprika and ham are fragrant.
- In a dish, whisk the egg with a fork to create the omelet. Heat the pan over medium-low. When the pan is hot, drizzle one tablespoon of the oil into it and swirl it around to cover the pan.
- Set aside for 10 to 20 seconds after pouring in the egg mixture. Gently move the eggs to the center of the pan with a heat-safe spatula, then move the pan so that runny eggs have their spot. Repeat the operation until no more runny eggs are left to scoot over.
- Gently raise the omelet's underside from the skillet with the spatula. To make sure the omelet isn't stuck, move it forward and back a couple of times.
- Sprinkle on top, onion powder and garlic.
- Insert ham filling onto one side of the omelet and fold it over.
- Allow a few moments for it to cool before scooting it onto a plate.
- Serve with a sprinkling of chives on top.

*Calories 160, Protein 38 g, Sodium 81 mg, Potassium 36 mg, Phosphorus 96 mg, Calcium 13 mg*

## Toad in a Hole
*Time: 35 Mins, Serves: 4, Skill: Easy*

**Ingredients**

- Bell pepper (1 large)
- Freshly ground black pepper (1/4 tsp)
- Parmesan cheese (1/4 cup), grated
- Parsley (1/2 cup), chopped
- Eggs (4 Large)

**Instructions**

- Remove the seeds and split the bell peppers lengthwise into 4 1/2" thick rounds/rings.
- Gently coat the cast-iron skillet with cooking oil and heat it over medium heat.
- Cook for 2 minutes with the bell pepper rings in the skillet (so that the ring is visible).
- Turn the bell pepper and crack an egg into the center of each.
- Season the egg with pepper, and boil until the optimal quality is achieved (2-4 minutes).
- Finish with a parmesan cheese sprinkling.
- Add a sprig of minced parsley to the top of each egg.

*Calories 130, Protein 30 g, Sodium 75 mg, Potassium 35 mg, Phosphorus 90 mg, Calcium 15 mg*

## Eggs with Chiles
*Time: 40 Mins, Serves: 4, Skill: Easy*

**Ingredients**

- Eggs (8)

- Black pepper (1/8 tsp)
- Green chills (4 oz.), rinsed and diced
- Butter (2 tbsp)
- Onion, chopped (1/4 cup)
- Milk (2 tbsp)
- Water (2 tbsp)

**Instructions**
- Whisk together the eggs, milk, and water in a mixing cup.
- Combine the chilis and black pepper with the egg mix and set it aside.
- Melt butter in a pan over medium heat.
- In a pan, cook until the onion is tender.
- Pour the egg-chili mixture into the skillet and steam over low heat, stirring regularly.
- Scramble eggs slowly and softly; after cooking, extract the eggs from the pan when either moist or glossy; they can continue to cook after being extracted from the pan.

*Calories 170, Protein 45 g, Sodium 81 mg, Potassium 31 mg, Phosphorus 100 mg, Calcium 20 mg*

## Homemade Muesli
*Time: 55 Mins, Serves: 5, Skill: Medium*

**Ingredients**
- Coconut (unsweetened) (1/3 cup), shredded
- Shelled pumpkin seeds (3/4 cup)
- Dried cranberries (3/4 cup)
- Raisins (1/2 cup)
- Apples, dried (1 cup), finely chopped
- Dried apricots (1/2 cup), finely chopped
- Chia seeds (1/4 cup)
- Rolled oats (1 3/4 cups)
- Honey (1 1/2 tbsp)

**Instructions**
- In a big mixing cup, combine the dried apples and apricots.
- All of the ingredients can be mixed, including chia seeds, cranberries, pumpkin seeds, raisins, coconut, and oats.
- Mix all in until it's almost smooth.
- Mix in the honey until the paste is only mildly lumpy (but not sticky).
- It goes well with almond milk, daily yogurt, and non-dairy yogurt.

*Calories 150, Protein 36 g, Sodium 70 mg, Potassium 45 mg, Phosphorus 96 mg, Calcium 20 mg*

## Egg and Rice Muffins
*Time: 55 Mins, Serves: 6, Skill: Medium*

**Ingredients**
- Eggs (3 large)
- Whole milk (1/3 cup)
- Cumin (1/2 tsp)
- Rice (3/4 cup), cooked
- Pimentos (1 1/2 oz.)
- Green chilies (2 oz.), diced
- Shredded cheese (4 oz.), divided
- Black pepper (1/2 tsp)

**Instructions**
- Preheat the oven to 400°F.
- In a mixing dish, combine the cooked rice, 2 ounces of cheese, pimento, and the green chilies.
- Pour the batter into a 12-muffin tray that has been greased.
- Beat the eggs and milk, season with pepper and cumin.
- Fill the muffin tin with the batter.
- On top of the 12 muffins sprinkle the leftover cheese.
- Bake for 12-15 minutes, or until solid. Remove from pan and set aside to cool for 5 minutes before serving.

*Calories 180, Protein 40 g, Sodium 81 mg, Potassium 60 mg, Phosphorus 96 mg, Calcium 25 mg*

## Overnight Oatmeal of Blueberry Peanut Butter
*Time: 40 Mins, Serves: 4, Skill: Easy*

**Ingredients**
- Honey (2 tbsp)
- Chia seed (1 tbsp)
- Cinnamon (1 tsp)
- Old fashioned oats (2 cups)
- Almond milk (2 cups)
- Peanut butter granola (1/2 cup)
- Blueberries (1 cup)

**Instructions**
- In an airtight jar, combine the old-fashioned oats, chia seeds, honey, almond milk, and cinnamon.
- Combine all the ingredients and chill overnight.

- Spoon a one-cup helping of oatmeal (overnight).
- Add 2 tbsp of peanut butter granola & ¼ cup of fresh blueberries on the top of it.

*Calories 143, Protein 24 g, Sodium 81 mg, Potassium 31 mg, Phosphorus 96 mg, Calcium 23 mg*

## Asparagus and Swiss Cheese Frittata
*Time: 45 Mins, Serves: 4, Skill: Easy*

### Ingredients
- Eggs (3 large)
- Egg whites (5)
- Pepper (1/8 tsp)
- Butter (1 tbsp)
- Shallots (1/2 cup), chopped
- Parmesan cheese (2 tbsp), grated
- Heavy cream (1 tbsp)
- Swiss cheese (3 oz.), shredded, divided
- Asparagus (1/2 lb.), tough ends trimmed

### Instructions
- Preheat the oven to 350°F.
- After steaming for 3 - 4 minutes, thinly slice the crisp asparagus into 1/2" pieces on the diagonal.
- Melt butter in a 10" oven-safe pan over medium heat.
- Add the shallots and cook, stirring occasionally, for 4-5 minutes, or until golden.
- Add the steamed asparagus and season to taste with salt and pepper.
- Whisk together the eggs, egg whites, milk, grated cheese, salt, and pepper in a medium mixing cup.
- Stir in the Swiss cheese until it is fully included.
- Pour the egg mixture into the pan, covering the asparagus entirely, and cook for 4 minutes over medium heat, or when the edges start to set.
- Place the skillet in the oven for 16 to 18 minutes, or until the frittata is fully cooked.
- Serve directly after cutting into four identical wedges.

*Calories 226, Protein 24 g, Sodium 81 mg, Potassium 31 mg, Phosphorus 96 mg, Calcium 13 mg*

## Savory Egg Muffins
*Time: 1 hour 10 Mins, Serves: 12, Skill: Hard*

### Ingredients
- Olive oil (1 tbsp)
- Cloves of garlic (2), or to taste
- Mushrooms (1 cup), chopped
- Eggs (4)
- Red bell pepper (1 cup), chopped
- Green bell pepper (1), chopped
- Onion (1 cup), chopped
- Spinach (2 cups), chopped

### Instructions
- Preheat the oven to 350°F.
- Heat the oil, when hot add the peppers, and onion in a broad skillet until tender.
- After adding the spinach, garlic, and mushrooms, cook for a further two minutes.
- Crack the eggs into a mixing bowl and whisk them together.
- Stir in the cooked vegetables thoroughly.
- Pour into muffin cases with an even layer.
- Cook for a further 15-20 minutes in the oven, or until the eggs are fully cooked.

*Calories 200, Protein 30 g, Sodium 81 mg, Potassium 31 mg, Phosphorus 96 mg, Calcium 13 mg*

## Egg Sandwich
*Time: 25 Mins, Serves: 4, Skill: Easy*

### Ingredients
- Egg (1)
- Water (1 tbsp)
- A pinch of salt
- A pinch of black pepper
- Cheddar cheese (1 slice)
- Wheat bread (2 slices)
- Basil leaves (3 meds)
- Olive oil (1/2 tbsp)
- Tomato (2 slices)

### Instructions
- In a toaster or dry skillet, toast the bread and put it aside.
- Separate the basil leaves from the stems and position them in a separate bowl.
- Heat some olive oil in a small skillet over medium heat.
- After scrambling the eggs with water, season them with pepper and salt.
- Pour it into the skillet and cook the omelet in one layer without folding halfway around, then flip to cook the other side.

- Layering the ingredients: cheese on the warm bread slice, then the egg, with the sides rolled under for bread size fitting, then slices of tomatoes, basil leaves, then a second bread slice on top.
- When the sandwich is still tender, cut it diagonally in half and eat.

*Calories 180, Protein 28 g, Sodium 81 mg, Potassium 32 mg, Phosphorus 85 mg, Calcium 13 mg*

## Southern Style Grits
*Time: 55 Mins, Serves: 2, Skill: Medium*

**Ingredients**
- Water (1 cup)
- Milk (**1/3** cup)
- Salt (1/8 tsp)
- Butter (1 tbsp)
- Salt, to taste (optional)
- Stone-ground grits (**1/3** cup)
- Pepper, to taste (opt)

**Instructions**
- In a shallow saucepan, combine the grits, milk, salt, water, and half of the butter.
- Bring them to a boil, then reduce to low heat and simmer for 30 to 40 minutes, stirring continuously to avoid sticking.
- Add the remaining butter and season with salt and pepper to taste, if necessary.

*Calories 140, Protein 25 g, Sodium 81 mg, Potassium 31 mg, Phosphorus 96 mg, Calcium 13 mg*

## Quinoa Porridge
*Time: 30 Mins, Serves: 2, Skill: Easy*

**Ingredients**
- Quinoa (1/2 cup)
- Dried fruit chopped (2 tbsp)
- Nuts chopped (2 tbsp)
- Maple syrup (1/2 tbsp)
- Concord grapes, berries, or other fruit (opt) (1 tbsp)
- Crème Fraiche (opt) (1 tbsp)
- Water (1 cup)

**Instructions**
- Mix the quinoa and water in a medium saucepan.
- Simmer before the water heats, then add the dried fruit.
- Reduce the heat to low and simmer for 10-15 minutes, or until the quinoa is soft.
- Remove the pan from the heat and add the chopped nuts to it.
- To eat, split the mixture into two bowls and drizzle the maple syrup over each bowl's porridge; if necessary, apply sliced Concord grapes/fresh berries and crème Fraiche to each bowl for additional antioxidants (a spoonful).
- Stir thoroughly, before serving.

*Calories 200, Protein 35 g, Sodium 75 mg, Potassium 31 mg, Phosphorus 80 mg, Calcium 18 mg*

## German Pancake (Dutch Baby)
*Time: 25 Mins, Serves: 4, Skill: Easy*

**Ingredients**
- Eggs (2 large)
- Milk (**1/3** cup)
- Flour (1/2 cup)
- Vanilla (1/2 tsp)
- Butter (2 tbsp)
- Lemon (1/2)
- Nutmeg (1/4 tsp), freshly grated
- Powdered sugar (2 tbsp)

**Instructions**
- Preheat the oven to 425°F.
- In an oven-safe pan, melt the butter but do not brown it.
- In a medium mixing bowl, beat the eggs while the butter is warming up.
- Stir in the milk until it is combined.
- Then add the flour, nutmeg, and vanilla and whisk vigorously.
- Pour the mixture into the melted butter-filled pan.
- Bake for 15 minutes in the oven; do not open the oven door during this period.
- Take the dish out of the oven, break it into two servings, and plate each one individually.
- Squeeze the lemon over both halves.
- To serve, sprinkle powdered sugar through a sieve.

*Calories 175, Protein 26 g, Sodium 81 mg, Potassium 31 mg, Phosphorus 96 mg, Calcium 15 mg*

## Veggie Mug Omelet
*Time: 25 Mins, Serves: 1, Skill: Easy*

**Ingredients**
- Egg (1 large)

- Pepper (1/8 tsp)
- Water (1 tbsp)
- Tomato (1 tbsp), diced
- Cooking spray (1/8 tsp)
- Zucchini (1/4 cup), grated
- Cheddar cheese (1 tbsp), grated coarsely
- A pinch of salt (opt)

**Instructions**
- Spray a microwave-safe mug with cooking spray or lightly butter it.
- Crack an egg into a microwave-safe cup, season with pepper and salt, and whisk together until smooth.
- In a mixing dish, combine the tomato, zucchini, water, and grated cheese.
- In the mug, combine all of the ingredients.
- Microwave for 1 minute, swirl, and microwave for another minute, or until the egg mixture is set.
- Set aside for a few minutes to cool before serving.

*Calories 175, Protein 26 g, Sodium 81 mg, Potassium 31 mg, Phosphorus 96 mg, Calcium 15 mg*

## Huevos Rancheros
*Time: 35 Mins, Serves: 1, Skill: Easy*

**Ingredients**
- Eggs (2 large)
- Corn tortillas, 6-inches diameter (2)
- Avocado (2/3 ripe), sliced
- Olive (1 tbsp)
- Feta cheese (2 tbsp), crumbled
- Cilantro (1 tbsp), chopped

**Pico de Gallo:**
- Tomato (4 tbsp), chopped
- White onion (1/4 cup), chopped
- Cilantro leaves (1/4 cup), chopped
- Lime (1), juiced

**Instructions**
- In a pan, cook the olive oil over medium heat until it is hot.
- Break the eggs into the pan and cook until the whites are set and the yolk is golden brown.
- In a saucepan over low-medium heat, warm the corn tortillas one at a time.
- In a medium bowl, combine the tomato, cilantro leaves, onion, and lime juice to produce Pico de Gallo. Set it aside.
- Hot corn tortillas are put on individual plates and topped with a fried egg. Serve with Pico de Gallo and chopped avocado. Serve with feta cheese and cilantro crumbles on top.

*Calories 143, Protein 24 g, Sodium 81 mg, Potassium 150 mg, Phosphorus 96 mg, Calcium 13 mg*

## Cheddar Frittata
*Time: 35 Mins, Serves: 4, Skill: Easy*

**Ingredients**
- Eggs (8 large)
- Black pepper (1/4 tsp)
- Crushed red pepper flakes (1/4 tsp)
- Garlic cloves (2), minced
- Cheddar (1 oz.), shredded
- Olive oil (2 tbsp)
- Lacinato kale, tough stems removed and cut into ribbons (4 oz.)
- Kosher salt (1/4 tsp)

**Instructions**
- Preheat the oven to 350 °F.
- In a dish, whisk the eggs and put them aside.
- Heat the oil in an oven-safe skillet over medium heat, then add the kale, salt, red pepper, and black pepper, and cook, stirring regularly, until the kale starts to wilt, around 2 minutes. Add the garlic and cook for another 2 minutes then remove it from the heat.
- Pour the eggs into the pan, add the kale, and mix briefly, then bake for around 10 minutes, or until the eggs are set. Cut wedges into four equal portions and serve.

*Calories 180, Protein 26 g, Sodium 81 mg, Potassium 28 mg, Phosphorus 70 mg, Calcium 13 mg*

## Cherry Overnight Oats
*Time: 25 Mins, Serves: 1, Skill: Easy*

**Ingredients**
- Almond milk (1/2 cup)
- Honey (2 tsp)
- Cinnamon (1/8 tsp)
- Old fashioned rolled oats (1/2 cup)
- Sweet cherries (1/2 cup), pitted and halved

**Instructions**
- In a mason jar, mix all ingredients and swirl to combine.
- Cover it and keep it refrigerated overnight.

*Calories 175, Protein 24 g, Sodium 80 mg, Potassium 70 mg, Phosphorus 96 mg, Calcium 13 mg*

## Cheesy Scrambled Eggs with Fresh Herbs

*Time: 45 Mins, Serves: 4, Skill: Easy*

**Ingredients**
- Cream cheese, (1/2 cup)
- Rice milk (1/4 cup)
- Scallion (1 tbsp), green part only
- Fresh tarragon (1 tbsp), chopped
- Eggs (3)
- Egg whites (2)
- Black pepper, to taste
- Butter (2 tbsp)

**Instructions**
- Whisk together the eggs, cream cheese, egg whites, rice milk, tarragon, and scallions in a medium mixing bowl until smooth.
- In a big skillet, melt the butter over medium-high heat, stirring vigorously to cover the pan evenly.
- Pour in the egg mixture and simmer for around 5 minutes, or until the eggs are dense and the curds are creamy, stirring continuously. Serve with spice seasoning.

*Calories 180, Protein 75 g, Sodium 81 mg, Potassium 36 mg, Phosphorus 96 mg, Calcium 15 mg*

## Corn Pudding

*Time: 1 hour 15 Mins, Serves: 6, Skill: Medium*

**Ingredients**
- Butter, for greasing the baking dish
- Flour (2 tbsp)
- Eggs (3)
- Rice milk (3/4 cup), at room temperature
- Butter (3 tbsp), melted
- Light sour cream (2 tbsp)
- Granulated sugar (2 tbsp)
- Frozen corn kernels (2 cups), thawed
- Ener-G baking soda substitute (1/2 tsp)

**Instructions**
- Preheat the oven to 350 °F.
- Set aside an 8-x-8-inch baking dish that has been lightly greased with butter.
- Combine the flour and baking soda replacement in a mixing cup and set aside.
- Whisk together the eggs, butter, sour cream, rice milk, and sugar in a medium mixing cup.
- Add the flour mixture to the eggs and combine until smooth.
- Whisk the corn into the batter until it is thoroughly combined. Transfer to baking dish.
- Bake for around 40 minutes, or until the pudding is finished.
- Allow 15 minutes for the pudding to cool before serving warm.

*Calories 190, Protein 100 g, Sodium 75 mg, Potassium 60 mg, Phosphorus 96 mg, Calcium 13 mg*

## Curried Egg Pita Pockets

*Time: 35 Mins, Serves: 4, Skill: Easy*

**Ingredients**
- Eggs (3), beaten
- Butter (2 tsp)
- Curry powder (1 tsp)
- Ginger (1/2 tsp)
- Light sour cream (2 tbsp)
- Plain pita bread pockets (2), halved
- English cucumber (1/2 cup), julienned
- Scallion (1), both green and white parts chopped finely
- Watercress (1 cup), roughly chopped
- Red bell pepper (1/2), finely chopped

**Instructions**
- Whisk together the scallion, eggs, and red pepper in a mixing cup until well mixed.
- Melt the butter in a big nonstick skillet over medium heat.
- Pour the egg mixture into the skillet and cook, rotating the skillet but not stirring, for around 3 minutes, or until the eggs are set. Remove the eggs from the heat and place them on a plate to cool.
- Combine the curry powder, sour cream, and ginger in a mixing cup.
- Distribute the curry sauce evenly among the four pita bread slices, starting on the inner edge of one.
- Equally divide the cucumber halves and watercress.
- To serve, cut the eggs in half and divide the mixture equally.

*Calories 150, Protein 35 g, Sodium 81 mg, Potassium 40 mg, Phosphorus 96 mg, Calcium 13 mg*

## Chili Wheat Treats
*Time: 30 Mins, Serves: 2, Skill: Easy*

**Ingredients**
- Dash cayenne pepper
- Garlic powder (1/2 tsp)
- Spoon-size shredded wheat (4 cups)
- Margarine (1/2 cup)
- Chili powder (1 tbsp)
- Ground cumin (1/2 tsp)

**Instructions**
- Before baking, preheat the oven to 300 °F.
- In a 10" x 15" baking pan, dissolve the margarine.
- Combine the herbs in a separate dish. Evenly distribute the wheat and toss to cover.
- Preheat oven to 350°F and bake for 15 minutes, or until crisp. Keep in a pan with a lid.

*Calories 135, Protein 30 g, Sodium 81 mg, Potassium 31 mg, Phosphorus 96 mg, Calcium 13 mg*

## Country Biscuits and Gravy (Maple Crisp Bars)
*Time: 35 Mins, Serves: 2, Skill: Easy*

**Ingredients**
- Biscuits
- Flour (1 1/2 cups)
- Baking powder (2 tsp)
- Water (1/3 cup)
- Margarine (2 tbsp)
- Liquid non-dairy creamer (1/3 cup)
- Gravy
- Liquid non-dairy creamer (1 cup)
- Garlic powder (1/2 tsp)
- Pepper (1/2 tsp)
- Margarine (2 tbsp)
- Cornstarch (2 tbsp)
- Ground beef (6 oz.)
- Sage (1/2 tsp)
- Basil (1/2 tsp)

**Instructions**
- In a mixing cup, combine the baking powder and flour to create biscuits. To make the margarine look like a coarse meal, cut it into tiny bits. Add the water and creamer to make a dough.
- On a floured board, knead the dough 10 times. Roll out the dough and cut it into 8 biscuits. Bake until crispy on a greased baking sheet at 450°F for 10 to 12 minutes.
- In a mixing bowl, combine the ground beef and seasoning to create the sauce. Brown the beef in a pan over medium heat. Drain all of the water. Set the mixture aside. In the same utensil, melt the margarine on low heat.
- Whisk together the cornstarch and a quarter cup of creamer in a mug until smooth. Add it to the melted margarine and swirl vigorously over low heat before the paste thickens and bubbles.
- Add the beef and cook until it's well done. Serve with biscuits.

*Calories 165, Protein 30 g, Sodium 81 mg, Potassium 45 mg, Phosphorus 96 mg, Calcium 13 mg*

## Holiday Eggnog
*Time: 30 Mins, Serves: 2, Skill: Easy*

**Ingredients**
- Eggs (1/2 cup)
- Vanilla (1 1/2 tsp)
- Liquid (non-dairy) coffee creamer (1 1/2 cup)
- Sugar (2 tbsp)
- Nutmeg

**Instructions**
- Combine the first four ingredients in a high-powered blender or with an electric mixer until well mixed. Allow to cool.
- Add a pinch of nutmeg as a finishing touch.

*Calories 160, Protein 24 g, Sodium 81 mg, Potassium 31 mg, Phosphorus 96 mg, Calcium 13 mg*

## Ice Cream Sandwiches
*Time: 2 Hours 20 Mins, Serves: 4, Skill: Medium*

**Ingredients**
- Plain graham crackers (10)
- Lite cool whip (20 T), non-dairy

**Instructions**
- Graham crackers can be split in half.
- On one half, spread two teaspoons of cool whip.
- On top of the other component, put a cracker.
- Put the tray on top of it and freeze it for a few hours.
- Sandwiches are ready to serve once frozen.

*Calories 170, Protein 24 g, Sodium 81 mg, Potassium 31 mg, Phosphorus 96 mg, Calcium 13 mg*

## Onion Bagel Chips
*Time: 45 Mins, Serves: 4, Skill: Easy*

**Ingredients**
- Onion Powder (1/2 tsp)
- Plain bagels (4)
- Margarine (2 tbsp), melted

**Instructions**
- Using a knife, cut each bagel in half vertically. Cut 8 vertical slices from one half of the bagel, cut side down on a flat table. Repeat with the remaining bagels.
- Arrange the slices on a baking sheet in an even layer. Toss the onion powder and Margarine mixture on the bagels. Preheat the oven to 325 °F and bake for 20 minutes, or until golden brown and crisp. Remove the pan from the heat and set it aside to cool fully. Place in an airtight jar and keep refrigerated.

*Calories 175, Protein 30 g, Sodium 81 mg, Potassium 35 mg, Phosphorus 96 mg, Calcium 15 mg*

## Oriental Egg Rolls
*Time: 1 hour 5 Mins, Serves: 1, Skill: Medium*

**Ingredients**
- Cooked chicken (1 lb.), diced
- Vegetable oil (2 tbsps.)
- Bean sprouts (1/2 lb.)
- Shredded cabbage (1/2 lb.)
- Egg roll wrappers (20), 1 package
- Onion 1 medium (1 cup), chopped
- Garlic (1 clove), minced
- Low sodium soy sauce (1 tbsp)
- Oil for frying

**Instructions**
- Combine all ingredients in a large mixing bowl, except the wrappers and cooking oil, in a large mixing bowl. Allow to marinate for 30-minutes.
- Spoon the filling into the wrappers and fold according to the wrapper box instructions. Preheat the oil to 350°F.
- Fry the egg rolls until golden brown in hot oil (1 inch or more). Absorb extra moisture with paper towels.

*Calories 180, Protein 115 g, Sodium 81 mg, Potassium 31 mg, Phosphorus 96 mg, Calcium 18 mg*

## Snack Mix
*Time: 35 Mins, Serves: 4, Skill: Easy*

**Ingredients**
- Unsalted tiny pretzel twists (1 cup)
- Corn cereal squares (1 cup)
- Garlic powder (1/2 tsp)
- Onion Powder (1/2 tsp)
- Unsalted popped popcorn (3 cups)
- Parmesan cheese (1 tbsp)
- Rice cereal squares (1 cup)
- Margarine (1/3 cup), melted

**Instructions**
- In a mixing bowl, combine the cereals, pretzels, and popcorn. Melt the margarine and add the onion and garlic powder to it.
- Pour on top of the cereal mixture and roll to evenly distribute it.
- Add the cheese and mix well (parmesan).
- Bake for 7-10 minutes at 350°F. Keep the mix in an airtight container.

*Calories 155, Protein 60 g, Sodium 80 mg, Potassium 40 mg, Phosphorus 96 mg, Calcium 15 mg*

## Parmesan Cheese Spread
*Time: 4 hours 10 Mins, Serves: 4, Skill: Easy*

**Ingredients**
- Garlic powder (1/4 tsp)
- Cream cheese (3-oz), 1 package
- Parmesan cheese (2 tbsps.), grated
- Margarine (4 tbsps.), softened
- Dry white wine (1 tbsp)
- Dash of marjoram
- Dash of thyme
- Parsley (1 tbsp), minced

**Instructions**
- Mix all of the ingredients together well in a big mixing tub. Refrigerate for at least 4 hours.
- Serve with unsalted crackers, Melba bread, or celery stuffing to round out the meal.

*Calories 160, Protein 70 g, Sodium 81 mg, Potassium 60 mg, Phosphorus 96 mg, Calcium 13 mg*

## Spiced Pineapple Appetizer
*Time: 25 Mins, Serves: 4, Skill: Easy*

**Ingredients**
- Sugar (3 tbsps.)

- Garlic powder (1/8 tsp)
- White wine vinegar (1/4 cup)
- Crushed red pepper (1/4 tsp)
- Lime juice (2 tbsps.)
- Dijon mustard (1/2 tsp)
- Chunks of pineapple (20-oz), drained

**Instructions**
- In a saucepan, whisk together the sugar, vinegar, Dijon mustard, lime juice, seasoning, and garlic powder.
- Bring to a boil. Reduce the heat to low and cook for 3 minutes with the lid on.
- Combine the vinegar mixture with the pineapple in a cup and combine well. Serve with toothpicks to keep it soft.

*Calories 180, Protein 80 g, Sodium 81 mg, Potassium 50 mg, Phosphorus 96 mg, Calcium 13 mg*

## Popcorn Munch
*Time: 30 Mins, Serves: 6, Skill: Easy*

**Ingredients**
- Sweetened cereal-wheat puff (2 cups)
- Graham cracker cereal (2 cups)
- Unsalted popcorn (8 cups), popped

**Instructions**
- In a microwave-safe oven, combine the cereals and popcorn. Microwave on high for 1 and a half minutes or until hot. Set aside for 5 minutes to cool.
- Place the mix in an oven-safe pan and bake for six minutes at 350°F.
- Set aside for 5 minutes to cool before chopping into pieces.

*Calories 240, Protein 3 g, Sodium 118 mg, Potassium 35 mg, Phosphorus 47 mg, Calcium 5 mg*

## Fruit and Oat Pancakes
*Time: 35 Mins, Serves: 10, Skill: Easy*

**Ingredients**
- Rolled oats (1/2 cup)
- Baking powder (1/2 tsp)
- Flour (1 cup)
- Egg (1)
- One fruit cocktail can (8-oz), undrained
- Margarine (1 tbsp)
- Liquid non-dairy creamer (1/2 cup)

**Instructions**
- In a mixing pot, combine all ingredients except the margarine. In a skillet, melt the margarine.
- Pour around a quarter cup of batter per pancake into the skillet and cook over medium heat until the pancakes are dry and bubbly around the edges.
- Turn the pancakes with a spatula and cook until golden brown on the bottom.

*Calories 140, Protein 30 g, Sodium 81 mg, Potassium 31 mg, Phosphorus 96 mg, Calcium 13 mg*

## Three Pepper Quiche
*Time: 1 hour 25 Mins, Serves: 4, Skill: Medium*

**Ingredients**
- Margarine (1 tbsp)
- Eggs (4)
- Basil (1/2 tsp)
- Sweet red pepper (1), strips
- Cayenne pepper (1/8 tsp)
- Green pepper (1), strips
- Sweet yellow pepper (1), strips
- Water (1/2 cup)
- Liquid non-dairy creamer (1/2 cup)
- 19" pie shell, unbaked

**Instructions**
- In a skillet, melt the Margarine and sauté the pepper strips until soft but not limp. Combine the eggs or egg replacement, water, creamer, basil, and cayenne in a mixing cup.
- Arrange peppers on top of the unbaked pie crust. Pour the combination of eggs over the peppers.
- Preheat oven to 375°F and bake for 50-55 minutes, or until a knife inserted in the center comes out clean. Allow for a 10-minute rest period before serving.

*Calories 150, Protein 35 g, Sodium 75 mg, Potassium 45 mg, Phosphorus 90 mg, Calcium 15 mg*

## Cream Cheese Salad
*Time: 15 Mins, Serves: 4, Skill: Easy*

**Ingredients**
- Cream cheese (2 lb.)
- Crushed pineapple (6 oz), drained
- 1 carton of whipped cream (8-oz)
- Jell-O lime or raspberry (3-oz)

**Instructions**
- Combine the dry Jell-O and the cream cheese in a mixing dish.

- Add the pineapple that has been drained of its juices. Fold the milk into the mixture (whipped).
- Chill then serve.

*Calories 143, Protein 75 g, Sodium 81 mg, Potassium 45 mg, Phosphorus 96 mg, Calcium 18 mg*

## Cranberry Salad
*Time: 17 Mins, Serves: 4, Skill: Easy*

### Ingredients
- 2 raspberry packages (3-oz)
- Jell-O
- Whole cranberry sauce (1 can), not jellied
- Celery (1 cup), chopped
- Apples (1 cup), chopped & peeled
- Unsalted nuts (1/2 cup)

### Instructions
- Prepare Jell-O as directed on the box.
- Add the raspberry, apples, cranberry sauce, celery, and nuts while they are all cool and syrupy. Refrigerate until fully set.

*Calories 170, Protein 77 g, Sodium 81 mg, Potassium 45 mg, Phosphorus 96 mg, Calcium 15 mg*

## Strawberry Stuffing
*Time: 45 Mins, Serves: 3, Skill: Easy*

### Ingredients
- Tart apples (1 cup), diced, peeled
- Strawberries (1/2 cup), diced
- Celery (1/4 cup), chopped
- Poultry seasoning (1/4 tsp)
- Apple juice (1/4 cup)
- Bread crumbs (3 cups)
- Unsalted Margarine (2 tbsps.), melted

### Instructions
- Preheat the oven to 350 °F. In a mixing dish, combine all the ingredients, toss to mix thoroughly.
- Position it in a casserole dish that has been well greased. Bake for 30 minutes.

*Calories 155, Protein 24 g, Sodium 81 mg, Potassium 31 mg, Phosphorus 96 mg, Calcium 13 mg*

## Red Hot Jell-O Salad
*Time: 35 Mins, Serves: 5, Skill: Easy*

### Ingredients
- Apples (1 cup), chopped & peeled
- Cinnamon red hots (1/4 cup)
- Water (1/2 cup)
- Celery (1/2 cup), chopped
- Cherry (3 oz) 1 package
- Boiling water (1 cup)
- Jell-O

### Instructions
- Soak red hots overnight in water.
- Jell-O can be dissolved in boiling water.
- Pour the red-hot oil into the pan and stir until melted. Allow to cool before partially mounting.
- Blend in the celery, cherries, and apples thoroughly.
- Place in the refrigerator to chill before serving.

*Calories 155, Protein 70 g, Sodium 80 mg, Potassium 35 mg, Phosphorus 96 mg, Calcium 15 mg*

## Moroccan Couscous
*Time: 23 Mins, Serves: 6, Skill: Easy*

### Ingredients
- Margarine or olive oil (1/2 tbsp)
- Onion (2 tbsps.), chopped
- Dry couscous (2/3 cup)
- Water (1 cup)

### Instructions
- Cook the sliced onion in olive oil or margarine until tender.
- Bring the water to a boil in a saucepan.
- Blend in the onion and couscous thoroughly.
- Leave it to stand for 5 minutes.
- Before serving, fluff with a fork.

*Calories 150, Protein 40 g, Sodium 81 mg, Potassium 45 mg, Phosphorus 96 mg, Calcium 23 mg*

## Pasta with Pesto
*Time: 27 Mins, Serves: 4, Skill: Easy*

### Ingredients
- Dried basil (2 tbsps.)
- Olive oil (1/4 cup)
- Pasta (1 lb.), uncooked
- Fresh parsley (1/4 cup), chopped
- Parmesan cheese (1/4 cup), grated
- Clove of garlic (1), minced

### Instructions
- In a food processor or blender, combine all ingredients (except pasta). Blend until the mixture is almost smooth.

- Cook pasta according to box instructions in unsalted boiling water.
- Combine the drained pasta and the sauce in a large mixing bowl. Serve immediately.

*Calories 303, Protein 8 g, Sodium 47 mg, Potassium 170 mg, Phosphorus 145 mg, Calcium 92 mg*

## Crispy Fried Okra

*Time: 35 Mins, Serves: 2, Skill: Easy*

**Ingredients**
- 1 package frozen okra (16-oz), 1-inch segment
- Margarine (2 tbsp)
- Cornmeal (1/2 cup)
- Flour (1/2 cup)
- Beer/water (1 cup)
- Pepper (1/4 tsp)

**Instructions**
- Defrost the okra if frozen. In a mixing bowl, combine cornmeal, flour, and pepper. Break the margarine into the mixture until it becomes crumbly.
- After dipping the okra in water or cider, coat it in the cornmeal mixture.
- Place it on a baking sheet that has been greased. Preheat the oven to 350 °F and bake for 20 minutes, or until golden brown.
- Serve with toothpicks and low-sodium ketchup as a garnish.

*Calories 140, Protein 60 g, Sodium 80 mg, Potassium 55 mg, Phosphorus 96 mg, Calcium 13 mg*

# Vegetable Recipes

## Italian Eggplant Salad
*Time: 25 Mins, Serves: 4, Skill: Easy*

**Ingredients**
- Black pepper (1/4 tsp)
- Tomato (1 med), chopped
- Olive oil (3 tbsp)
- Eggplant (3 cups), cubed
- Onion (1 small), chopped
- White wine vinegar (2 tbsp)
- Garlic clove (1), chopped
- Oregano (1/2 tsp)

**Instructions**
- Put the eggplant in a pot of water that has been brought to a simmer.
- Bring the water to a boil and then reduce the heat.
- Cook for a further 10 minutes with the saucepan lid on.
- Drain the eggplants and place them in serving dishes with the onions and tomato.
- In a shallow dish, combine the garlic, oregano, vinegar, and black pepper.
- Combine the onions, tomato, and eggplant with the vinegar mixture.
- Drizzle a little oil over the eggplant mixture before serving.

*Calories 160, Protein 70 g, Sodium 81 mg, Potassium 45 mg, Phosphorus 96 mg, Calcium 15 mg*

## Carrots & Cabbage in Mustard Sauce
*Time: 55 Mins, Serves: 4, Skill: Easy*

**Ingredients**
- Olive oil (1 tbsp)
- Dijon mustard (2 tsp)
- Black pepper, to taste
- White-wine vinegar (1 tbsp+ 2tsp)
- Honey (1 tsp)
- Carrots (2 cups), shredded
- Cabbage (1 cup), shredded

**Instructions**
- In a mixing cup, combine the oil, honey, vinegar, and mustard.
- Add the pepper to taste, and mix well. Set the dressing aside.
- Bring a pot of water to a low boil, then add the carrots and cabbage.
- Cook until they begin to soften.
- Toss the veggies with the dressing after draining and chill for 45 minutes before eating.

*Calories 140, Protein 15 g, Sodium 81 mg, Potassium 14 mg, Phosphorus 36 mg, Calcium 13 mg*

## Pineapple Coleslaw
*Time: 1 hour 15 Mins, Serves: 3, Skill: Easy*

**Ingredients**
- Pineapple (8 oz.), drained
- Cabbage (2 cups), shredded
- Miracle Whip (1/4 cup)
- Pepper, to taste
- Onion (1/4 cup), chopped

**Instructions**
- In a large mixing cup, combine the cabbage, whip, pineapple, pepper, and onion.
- Chill for 60 minutes before serving.

*Calories 155, Protein 55 g, Sodium 85 mg, Potassium 40 mg, Phosphorus 90 mg, Calcium 13 mg*

## Basil Oil
*Time: 1 hour 10 Mins, Serves: 16, Skill: Hard*

**Ingredients**
- Vegetable oil (1 cup)
- Basil leaves (1 1/2 cups)

**Instructions**
- 1 1/2 cups basil leaves, washed and towel-dried.
- Combine the olive oil and basil leaves in a blender.
- In a skillet over medium heat, add the mix, cover, and steam for 4 minutes, stirring occasionally.
- Remove the pan from the heat and allow it to cool for 60 minutes.
- Strain the mixture into a container using a cheesecloth for around an hour.
- Make an effort to collect as much oil as possible.
- Remove the basil and refrigerate the oil for three months in an airtight container.

**Nutrients per serving**

*Calories 140, Protein 24 g, Sodium 81 mg, Potassium 31 mg, Phosphorus 96 mg, Calcium 13 mg*

## Black-Eyed Peas
*Time: 9 hours 40 Mins, Serves: 8, Skill: Hard*

**Ingredients**
- Black-eyed peas (2 cups), dried
- Curry powder (1/2)
- Water or low-sodium vegetable stock (3 1/2 cups)
- Onion (1), chopped
- Cayenne pepper (1 pinch)
- Ginger (1/2 tsp)
- Thyme (1/2 tsp)
- Celery (1 cup), diced
- Smoked turkey (optional) (12 oz.)
- Garlic cloves (6), chopped

**Instructions**
- Fill a large mixing bowl halfway with water, add the peas, cover, and soak for at least 8 hours.
- After 8 hours, drain the excess water and rinse it with cold water.
- In a pot, mix the peas, pepper, ginger, curry powder, thyme, garlic, onion, celery, vegetable oil, and stock.
- Over a strong flame, bring the mixture to a simmer.
- Reduce the heat to low and cover, stirring occasionally, for more than 90 minutes, or until the peas have tendered.

*Calories 160, Protein 35 g, Sodium 80 mg, Potassium 35 mg, Phosphorus 96 mg, Calcium 13 mg*

## Blasted Brussels Sprouts
*Time: 45 Mins, Serves: 6, Skill: Medium*

**Ingredients**
- Parmesan Cheese (4 tbsp)
- Fruit flavored vinegar (1/4 cup)
- Olive oil (1-2 tbsp)
- Brussels Sprouts (2 cups), one stalk

**Instructions**
- Break the Brussels sprouts first.
- In a dish, combine the olive oil and sprouts.
- Place the sprouts on a baking sheet that has been greased.
- Preheat oven to 450 °F and bake the tray for 10 minutes.
- Garnish with parmesan cheese and citrus vinegar.

*Calories 160, Protein 55 g, Sodium 85 mg, Potassium 40 mg, Phosphorus 96 mg, Calcium 13 mg*

## Kidney friendly Pico de Gallo
*Time: 25 Mins, Serves: 3, Skill: Easy*

**Ingredients**
- Purple Onion (1/2)
- Jicama (1 cup)
- Sugar (1 tbsp)
- Garlic cloves (6)
- Pinch of salt (1)
- Lime juice (1/4 cup)
- Peppers (2 cups)

**Instructions**
- Combine the bell pepper, lime juice, garlic, onion, sugar, jicama, and salt in a food processor.
- After applying the salsa to a serving dish, serve with your desired main.

*Calories 200, Protein 115 g, Sodium 81 mg, Potassium 45 mg, Phosphorus 96 mg, Calcium 15 mg*

## Roasted tomatillo salsa
*Time: 45 Mins, Serves: 8, Skill: Medium*

**Ingredients**
- Lime juice (1/4 cup)
- Cilantro (1 bunch)
- Water (1/4 cup)
- Tomatillos (17)
- Head garlic (1)
- Jalapenos (3)

**Instructions**
- Start by slicing the tomatillos.
- In a greased baking pan, mix the tomatillos, jalapenos, and garlic.
- To simmer in water, put them in the oven for 15 minutes.
- In a processor, puree the cooked tomatillo mixture with lime juice and cilantro until creamy.
- After pouring the mixture into the serving dish, serve with tacos.

*Calories 180, Protein 60 g, Sodium 81 mg, Potassium 45 mg, Phosphorus 96 mg, Calcium 13 mg*

## Kidney Friendly Beans
*Time: 1 hour and 30 Mins, Serves: 6, Skill: Easy*

**Ingredients**
- Cider vinegar (2 tbsp)
- Garlic (4 cloves)
- Ground pepper (1/2 tsp)

- Raw lima beans (1 cup)
- Onion (1 1/2 cups)
- White rice (1 cup)
- Oil (3 tbsp)
- Honey (1 tbsp)
- Jalapeno peppers (2)
- Salt (1/4 tsp)
- Smoked paprika (1/2 tsp)

**Instructions**
- Cook for 60 minutes in a cooker with rice, 5 cups water, and beans, according to the cooker's instructions.
- In a saucepan, heat the oil and add the sliced onions. Cook until the onions are smooth and transparent.
- Combine the honey, salt, paprika, jalapenos, pepper, and vinegar in a mixing cup.
- When the rice and beans are done, combine them with the garlic, sautéed onions, and seasoning mix. Serve with a sprinkling of chives on top.

*Calories 155, Protein 45 g, Sodium 81 mg, Potassium 40 mg, Phosphorus 96 mg, Calcium 13 mg*

## Sweet Korean lentils
*Time: 35 Mins, Serves: 4, Skill: Easy*

**Ingredients**
**Sauce:**
- Sesame oil (1 tsp)
- Coconut amino's (1/4 cup)
- Brown sugar (2 tbsp)
- Fresh ginger (1)
- Garlic cloves (2)
- Red pepper (1/2 tsp)
- Water (2 cups)

**Lentils:**
- Yellow Onion (1/2)
- Olive oil (1 tbsp)
- Green onions (2)
- Red lentil (1 cup)

**Instructions**
- Water, garlic, sugar, sesame oil, coconut amino, ginger, and red pepper can all be mixed in a skillet. Set aside once combined.
- In a large pot, heat the oil over high heat and sauté the onions for 5 minutes.
- Combine the sauce and lentils in a pan and carry to a boil.
- Cover the pan and reduce the flame to low.
- Allow 10 minutes for the sauce to boil.
- Lentils can be served in baking dishes with green onions strewn on top.

*Calories 170, Protein 60 g, Sodium 85 mg, Potassium 30 mg, Phosphorus 92 mg, Calcium 15 mg*

## Chickpea sunflower sandwich
*Time: 50 Mins, Serves: 4, Skill: Easy*

**Ingredients**
**Garlic Herb Sauce:**
- Dried dill (1 tsp)
- Lemon juice (1 tbsp)
- Prepared hummus (1/4 cup)
- Garlic cloves (2)

**Chickpeas Sandwich:**
- Water for thinning the sauce
- Sunflower seeds (1/4 cup)
- Chickpeas (15 oz.)
- Maple syrup (1 tbsp)
- Vegan mayonnaise (3 tbsp)
- Fresh dill (2 tbsp)
- Dijon mustard (1/2 tsp)
- Red onion (1/4 cup)
- Wheat bread (8 slices)
- Pepper pinch (1)

**Optional Toppings:**
- Sliced lettuce, onion, tomato

**Instructions**
- Combine the lemon, garlic, hummus, and dill in a small bowl. Set it aside for the time being. It's time to begin preparing the garlic sauce.
- Chickpeas can be finely crushed in a large mixing cup.
- Combine Maple syrup, dill, sunflower seeds, mustard, black pepper, mayonnaise, and red onions.
- Place the bread slices on a plate and butter them.
- On the bread strips, spread the chickpea filling and then drizzle with the garlic sauce. Put the second slice of bread on top of the first.

Calories 143, Protein 24 g, Sodium 81 mg, Potassium 40 mg, Phosphorus 96 mg, Calcium 13 mg

## Kidney-friendly balsamic vinaigrette
*Time: 15 Mins, Serves: 4, Skill: Easy*

**Ingredients**
- Balsamic vinegar (1/4 cup)
- Honey (2 tbsp)
- Poppy seed (1 tsp)
- Garlic clove (1)
- Dijon mustard (1 tbsp)
- Oil (canola) (3/4 cup)
- Black pepper (1/2 tsp)

**Instructions**
- In a blender or food processor, combine the black pepper, poppy seed, honey, oil, vinegar, mustard, and garlic for 5 minutes to produce an emulsified mixture.

*Calories 140, Protein 35 g, Sodium 81 mg, Potassium 31 mg, Phosphorus 96 mg, Calcium 13 mg*

## Easy chia seed pudding
*Time: 4 hours and 15 Mins, Serves: 4, Skill: Easy*

**Ingredients**
- Chia Seeds (1/2 cup)
- Cinnamon (1/4 tsp)
- Vanilla Extract (1 tsp)
- Maple Syrup (1/4 cup)
- Rice Milk (1 1/2 cups)

**Instructions**
- Combine the maple syrup, rice milk, chia seeds, cinnamon, and vanilla in a mason jar.
- Cover the bottle with plastic wrap and place it in the refrigerator for 4 hours.

*Calories 155, Protein 35 g, Sodium 81 mg, Potassium 55 mg, Phosphorus 90 mg, Calcium 13 mg*

## Herb pesto
*Time: 10 Mins, Serves: 4, Skill: Easy*

**Ingredients**
- Lemon juice (2 tbsp)
- Garlic cloves (2)
- Parsley leaves (1/2 cup)
- Basil leaves (1 cup)
- Olive oil (1/4 cup)
- Oregano leaves (1/2 cup)

**Instructions**
- In a processor, combine basil, garlic, parsley, and oregano for three minutes.
- Combine with the olive oil and lemon juice in a mixing bowl. Keep the mixture in an airtight container in the refrigerator for up to one week.

*Calories 300, Protein 8 g, Sodium 45 mg, Potassium 177 mg, Phosphorus 125 mg, Calcium 82 mg*

## Smoothie bowl
*Time: 20 Mins, Serves: 1, Skill: Easy*

**Ingredients**
- Blueberries (1 tbsp), fresh
- Unsweetened coconut (1 tbsp), shredded
- Protein powder (2 tbsp)
- Banana (1/2)
- Strawberries (1/2 cup), frozen
- Blueberries (3/4 cup), frozen
- Water (1/4 cup)
- Coconut milk (3 tbsp)
- Honey (1 tsp)

**Instructions**
- In a high-powered blender, combine the banana, strawberries, water, blueberries, coconut milk, protein powder, and honey to make a smooth sorbet.
- Put the sorbet into a cup and top with fresh berries and coconut before ready to consume.

*Calories 180, Protein 150 g, Sodium 81 mg, Potassium 55 mg, Phosphorus 96 mg, Calcium 13 mg*

## Irish colcannon
*Time: 35 Mins, Serves: 6, Skill: Easy*

**Ingredients**
- Diced onion (1)
- Black pepper, to taste
- Garlic (2 cloves), minced
- Sea salt, to taste
- Olive oil (3 tbsp)
- Parsnips (3), sliced
- Kale (1 cup), chopped
- Russet potato (1/2)
- Green cabbage (1 cup), shredded
- Green peas (1 1/2 cups)

**Instructions**
- In a pot, bring water to a boil before adding the potatoes and parsnips and cooking for 15 minutes.

- Drain the vegetables and set aside the cooking liquid in the pot.
- In a mixing bowl, combine two teaspoons olive oil, the vegetables, and one-third of the cooking water.
- Add the kale and cabbage to the remaining cooking water, in the same pot where the vegetables were frying.
- Cook until the kale and cabbage are soft, around 5 minutes.
- Take the kale and cabbage from the water, drain them and put them in a container with a seal.
- In a skillet over medium heat, heat the olive oil and roast the garlic and onion for a few minutes.
- In a large mixing bowl, combine the garlic and onion, then add the peas and stir well.
- Place the parsnip and potato mixture first on the serving tray, followed by the vegetables, and season with salt, and black pepper.

*Calories 170, Protein 160 g, Sodium 81 mg, Potassium 45 mg, Phosphorus 96 mg, Calcium 15 mg*

## Vegan shortbread cookies
*Time: 55 Mins, Serves: 8, Skill: Medium*

**Ingredients**
- Coconut oil (1/4 cup)
- Dried cranberries (1/8 cup), chopped
- Baking soda (1/8 tsp)
- Unbleached flour (1 cup)
- Dried apricots (1/8 cup), chopped
- Powdered sugar (1/2 cup)
- Non-dairy yogurt (2 1/2 tbsp)
- Vanilla extract (1 tsp)
- Pecans (1/8 cup), chopped
- Cardamom (1 tsp), ground
- Pastry wheat flour (1/2 cup)
- Salt (1/4 teaspoon)

**Instructions**
- Preheat the oven to 325 °F.
- Whisk together yogurt, sugar, and coconut oil, then include cardamom and vanilla to produce a creamy and smooth mixture.
- In a mixing cup, add the flour, salt, and baking soda.
- In a mixing bowl, combine the flour mix and coconut oil mix. To produce a dough, mix the ingredients together with a spoon.
- Combine the nuts and fruits in the dough. Thoroughly knead the dough.
- Make a log out of the dough.
- After covering the logs with parchment paper, place them in the freezer for 30 minutes.
- Cut the logs after they've been frozen and put them in a baking tray lined with parchment paper.
- Bake the cake for 20 minutes, or until baked through.
- Keep in an airtight container after baking.

*Calories 155, Protein 100 g, Sodium 90 mg, Potassium 45 mg, Phosphorus 90 mg, Calcium 18 mg*

## Asparagus medley
*Time: 40 Mins, Serves: 5, Skill: Easy*

**Ingredients**
- Farfalle pasta (2 cups), cooked
- Black pepper, to taste
- Cilantro leaves (1/2 cup), chopped
- Asparagus (2 cups), ends discarded
- Cumin (1 tbsp)
- Ears corn (1 1/3 cups)
- Chickpeas (1/2 cup)
- Non-dairy yogurt (6 tbsp)
- Fresh spinach (1 1/2 cups), opt
- Water (1 cup)
- Olive oil (4 tbsp)
- Dill (1 cup), chopped
- Divided lemon juice (4 tbsp)
- Mint leaves (1/2 cup), chopped
- Sumac (1/2 tbsp), opt
- Shallot (1), thinly sliced
- Sea salt, to taste

**Instructions**
- To start, cook the pasta as directed on the box. Place it aside in a covered dish to keep it warm.
- In a mixing bowl, combine mint, cilantro, two teaspoons lemon juice, olive oil, black pepper, dill, and salt.
- Heat the olive oil in a pan and cook the shallots for 2 minutes.
- After two minutes of cooking, add the cumin, chickpeas, corn, black pepper, and asparagus.
- Cook, stirring regularly, for 7 minutes.
- Thoroughly add and combine the spinach.

- Allow it to simmer for 3 minutes on a low heat setting.
- Mix in the pasta thoroughly.
- Remove the pan from the fire and combine it with the herbs and vegetables. Squeeze in some lemon juice if desired, and serve with yogurt and sumac.

*Calories 180, Protein 100 g, Sodium 85 mg, Potassium 70 mg, Phosphorus 95 mg, Calcium 20 mg*

## Crepes with passion fruit
*Time: 1 hour and 5 Mins, Serves: 4, Skill: Hard*

**Ingredients**
**For crepes:**
- Butter (1 1/2 tbsp)
- Unbleached flour (1 cup)
- Oat milk (1 1/4 cups)
- Large eggs (2)

**For sauce:**
- Sugar (1/2 cup)
- Passion fruit, the pulp (3/4 cup)

**Instructions**
- In a mixing bowl, whisk together the eggs, milk, and flour. Set the bowl aside.
- In a saucepan, combine the sugar and fruit pulp.
- Over medium heat, bring the fruit pulp mixture to a simmer.
- Reduce the heat to low and continue to cook until the liquid has been reduced to half its original volume. Set it aside for the time being.
- In a crepe tray, melt half a tablespoon of butter over high heat, then pour in crepe batter and spread it out. Cook for about 1 ½ minutes on one side. Cook for another 45 seconds after flipping the crepe.
- When the crepe is finished, transfer it to a serving plate and top it with a spoonful of sauce before folding it in half and serving.

*Calories 175, Protein 110 g, Sodium 85 mg, Potassium 55 mg, Phosphorus 95 mg, Calcium 20 mg*

## Vegan bread
*Time: 1 hour 10 Mins, Serves: 6, Skill: Medium*

**Ingredients**
- Flax seeds (4 tbsp), ground
- Salt (1/8 tsp)
- Vanilla extract (1 1/2 tsp)
- Baking soda (1 tsp)
- Bananas (47 grams)
- Agave nectar (2 tbsp)
- Vegetable oil (1/3 cup)
- Applesauce (1/2 cup)
- Sugar (1/2 cup)
- Whole wheat flour (1 1/2 cups)

**Instructions**
- Crush the bananas in a mixing bowl and stir in the vegetable oil, cinnamon, vanilla, sugar, flaxseeds, agave nectar, applesauce, and baking soda. The contents of the bowl should be well combined.
- Finally, combine the flour with the other ingredients and mix well.
- Bake the batter for 60 minutes at 350 °F in a greased baking tray.

*Calories 143, Protein 70 g, Sodium 81 mg, Potassium 150 mg, Phosphorus 96 mg, Calcium 13 mg*

## Vegetable broth
*Time: 1 Hour, Serves: 2, Skill: Medium*

**Ingredients**
- Carrots (2 cups), chopped
- Water (8 cups)
- Olive oil (2 tbsp)
- Dried thyme (1/2 tsp)
- Onions (2 1/2 cups), chopped
- Garlic (4 cloves), peeled
- Fresh Italian parsley (1/4 cup)
- Celery (2 cups), stalks
- Black peppercorns (1 tsp)
- Bay leaves (2)

**Instructions**
- In a pan, heat the oil and add the garlic, carrots, onions, and celery.
- Cook, stirring regularly, for 5 minutes over medium heat.
- In a dish, combine the peppercorns, bay leaves, parsley, and thyme. Cover the pot halfway with water and bring to a boil over high heat.
- When the liquid starts to boil, reduce the flame to low and cover.
- Cook on low heat for 30 minutes.
- Strain the contents of the container with a strainer. The solids can be thrown out; however, the liquid should be saved.
- Place it in freezer storage containers.

*Calories 180, Protein 70 g, Sodium 81 mg, Potassium 80 mg, Phosphorus 96 mg, Calcium 13 mg*

## Festive Cranberry Stuffing
*Time: 45 Mins, Serves: 2, Skill: Easy*

**Ingredients**
- Apple juice (1/4 cup)
- Stale bread (3 cups)
- Poultry seasoning (1/4 tsp)
- Raw cranberries (1/2 cup)
- Tart apples (1 cup), peeled
- Celery (1/4 cup), chopped
- Unsalted butter (2 tablespoons)

**Instructions**
- Combine stale bread, sliced apple tart, apple juice, celery, cranberries, poultry seasoning, and butter in a large mixing bowl.
- Bake for 30 minutes at 350 °F in a preheated oven after pouring the batter into a greased casserole dish.

*Calories 150, Protein 80 g, Sodium 81 mg, Potassium 70 mg, Phosphorus 96 mg, Calcium 13 mg*

## Everyday Spanish style beans
*Time: 45 Mins, Serves: 3, Skill: Easy*

**Ingredients**
- Mexican oregano (1 tsp)
- Oil (1 tbsp)
- Water (2 cups), divided
- Cilantro (1/2 cup), chopped
- Cumin (1/4 teaspoon)
- Tomato paste (2 tbsp)
- Black pepper, to taste
- Onion (1/2 medium), diced
- Butternut squash (1/2 cup), diced
- Garlic (2 cloves), minced
- Rinsed low-sodium pink kidney beans (2 cans)
- Bell pepper (1 med), diced
- Salt (1/2 teaspoon)

**Instructions**
- In a medium-sized skillet, heat the oil and sauté the garlic and onion for 3 minutes.
- Blend in the squash and green bell pepper until smooth. Fill the skillet with one cup of water.
- Cook, stirring continuously, for 5 minutes.
- Add the kidney beans, cilantro, cumin, and oregano.
- Apply a cup of water and the tomato paste. Enable 15 minutes for the sauce to boil before seasoning salt and pepper.
- Serve with rice.

*Calories 160, Protein 70 g, Sodium 81 mg, Potassium 80 mg, Phosphorus 96 mg, Calcium 15 mg*

## Simple Puerto Rican sofrito
*Time: 35 Mins, Serves: 2, Skill: Easy*

**Ingredients**
- Culantro (6 leaves), opt
- Cilantro (1 bunch)
- Garlic cloves (10), chopped
- Green pepper (1), chopped
- Salt (1 tsp)
- Aja peppers (5)
- Spanish Onion (1), chopped

**Instructions**
- To start, in a blender, puree the onions.
- Combine the green bell pepper, garlic, culantro, dulce pepper, cilantro, and salt in the blender with the onions.
- In an airtight jar, freeze the sofrito.
- Add two teaspoons of sofrito when you are making rice, peas, or soups.

*Calories 143, Protein 24 g, Sodium 81 mg, Potassium 31 mg, Phosphorus 96 mg, Calcium 13 mg*

## Glazed Green Beans
*Time: 25 Mins, Serves: 4, Skill: Easy*

**Ingredients**
- Green beans (1½ lb.)
- Juice (1/2 lemon)
- Oil (1 tbsp)
- Water (12 cups)
- Black pepper (opt)

**Sauce:**
- Water (1 tbsp)
- Oil (1 tsp)
- Honey (1 tbsp)
- Garlic (1 clove), minced

**Instructions**
- Bring the water to a low boil in a stockpot.
- Mix in the beans and steam for three minutes.
- Remove the beans from the pot and set them aside to clean.

- In a mixing bowl, combine one teaspoon of oil, honey, and garlic. Add water to make a paste. Set it aside for the time being.
- In a skillet, heat one tablespoon of oil over low heat. Toss the beans in.
- Cook for 3 minutes while coating the beans in the sauce continuously.
- In a baking dish, toss the cooked beans with a squeeze of lemon juice and a sprinkle of seasoning.

*Calories 160, Protein 95 g, Sodium 80 mg, Potassium 70 mg, Phosphorus 96 mg, Calcium 15 mg*

## Broccoli blossom
*Time: 25 Mins, Serves: 2, Skill: Easy*

**Ingredients**
- Tarragon (1/4 tsp)
- Onion powder (1/4 tsp)
- Ground black pepper, to taste
- Oil (1 tbsp)
- Toasted English muffin (1)
- Onion (1/4 cup), chopped
- Water (3 tbsp)
- Ground red pepper, to taste
- Red cabbage (1 cup), chopped
- Garlic powder (1/4 tsp)
- Broccoli (1/2 cup), chopped
- Parmesan cheese (2 tbsp), grated

**Instructions**
- In a skillet over medium heat, heat the oil, then add the vegetables and cook for 3 minutes.
- Half-fill the skillet with water and position it over a burner to steam for 5 minutes.
- After 5 minutes, apply the spices and simmer for another 2 minutes.
- Place the vegetables on top of the muffins, serve with parmesan cheese.

*Calories 180, Protein 96 g, Sodium 75 mg, Potassium 55 mg, Phosphorus 96 mg, Calcium 15 mg*

## Spicy Kenyan Greens
*Time: 35 Mins, Serves: 4, Skill: Easy*

**Ingredients**
- Turnip greens (10 oz.), chopped
- Pepper (2 tsp)
- Greens collards (1 lb.), chopped
- Butter (2 tbsp)
- Water (1 cup)
- Yellow onion (1), chopped
- Jalapeño pepper (1)
- Olive oil (2 tbsp)
- Tomatoes (3 medium), chopped
- Salt (1/2 tsp)
- Coconut milk (1 can)
- Peanuts, to garnish

**Instructions**
- In a skillet, combine the water, onions, jalapeno pepper, one tablespoon of olive oil, and black pepper.
- Over a medium flame, bring the water to a simmer.
- When the mixture starts to boil, sweep in the greens thoroughly. The cooking time is 3 minutes.
- After 3 minutes of frying, strain the mixture and put it aside to cool.
- Melt the butter in a skillet and apply the olive oil.
- Combine the tomatoes, coconut milk, cooked greens, and onions in a skillet and cook for 5 minutes over medium heat.
- Season with salt and pepper to taste.
- To serve, drizzle peanuts over the fried green mixture.

*Calories 190, Protein 100 g, Sodium 80 mg, Potassium 70 mg, Phosphorus 96 mg, Calcium 13 mg*

## Pasta with peas and lemon
*Time: 35 Mins, Serves: 4, Skill: Easy*

**Ingredients**
- Parmesan cheese (1/4 oz.)
- Juiced lemon (1)
- Frozen peas (10 oz.)
- Black pepper (1/4 tsp)
- Short pasta (any) (8 oz.)
- Kosher salt (1/4 tsp)

**Instructions**
- Bring a pot half full of water to a boil.
- Lower the heat so the water is at a simmer and then add the peas.
- Remove the peas from the pot when cooked and set them aside.
- Cook pasta for 10 minutes in a large pot.
- In a mixing bowl, combine the cheese, lemon juice, salt, peas, black pepper, and mash with a fork.

- Strain the spaghetti and toss it in with the mixture. Using a serving spoon even out the pasta and pea mixture.

*Calories 145, Protein 45 g, Sodium 81 mg, Potassium 85 mg, Phosphorus 96 mg, Calcium 13 mg*

## Coconut curry cauliflower
*Time: 37 Mins, Serves: 4, Skill: Easy*

**Ingredients**
- Olive oil (2 tbsp)
- Lime juice (1/2 lime)
- Cauliflower (1/2 medium)
- Coconut milk (13 1/2 oz.)
- Kosher salt (1/4 tsp)
- Cilantro (1/4 cup), chopped
- Curry paste (1 tsp)

**Instructions**
- In a pan, heat the oil and add the salt and cauliflower. The cooking time is 7 minutes.
- Pour the coconut milk and curry paste over the cauliflower and cover the pan.
- Set the timer for 10 minutes to boil.
- Season with salt and pepper to taste and garnish with lime juice and cilantro.

*Calories 170, Protein 80 g, Sodium 70 mg, Potassium 60 mg, Phosphorus 96 mg, Calcium 15 mg*

## Red lentil stew
*Time: 1 hour 10 Mins, Serves: 6, Skill: Medium*

**Ingredients**
- Jalapeño pepper (1), diced
- Turmeric (1/2 tsp)
- Ginger (1 tbsp), grated
- Fresh cilantro leaves (1/4 cup)
- Water (4 cups)
- Coconut oil (3 tbsps.)
- Cumin seeds (1/2 tsp)
- White rice (4 cups), cooked
- Onion (1), diced
- Coriander seeds (1/2 tsp)
- Russet potato (1), diced
- Red lentils (1 cup)
- Spinach leaves (2 cups)
- Lemon juice (1/2 tsp)

**Instructions**
- In a low-heat pot, cook the jalapeno, onion, and spices for around 10 minutes in hot coconut oil.
- After 10 minutes, add the salt and ginger and continue to cook for another 5 minutes.
- Add the lentils and water.
- Enable the mixture to simmer for a few minutes.
- Place the potatoes in the pot and bring it to a boil.
- After covering the water, allow it to simmer for 20 minutes.
- Once the sauce has simmered, add the cilantro, lemon juice, and spinach. Stir until wilted. Serve with lemon juice and a pinch of cayenne pepper to taste.

*Calories 150, Protein 90 g, Sodium 81 mg, Potassium 70 mg, Phosphorus 96 mg, Calcium 15 mg*

## Vegetable curry
*Time: 45 Mins, Serves: 5, Skill: Easy*

**Ingredients**
- Mustard seeds (1 tsp)
- Coconut milk (1 can)
- Chili flakes (1/2 tsp)
- Piece of ginger (1)
- Fennel seeds (1 tsp)
- Cumin seeds (1 tsp)
- Black peppercorns (1/4 tsp)
- Coriander seeds (1 tsp)
- Carrot (61 g), diced
- Basmati rice (2 cups)
- Coconut oil (1 tbsp)
- Turmeric (1 tsp)
- Onion (70 g), quartered
- Green peas (1 cup)
- Cauliflower (1 1/2 cups)

**Instructions**
- Follow the package instructions for cooking the rice.
- In a small saucepan, heat the spices for 2 minutes over medium heat.
- In a mixing bowl, combine the coconut oil with all the vegetables. Sauté for 3 minutes.
- Add the chili flakes, turmeric, and ginger, cook for 6 minutes over a low flame.
- In a blender, combine the cooked spice mixture with the onions and process to produce a paste.

- In a saucepan, bring coconut milk to a simmer. Add the spice paste and mix thoroughly.
- After including the cooked vegetables and spice mixture to the coconut milk, boil for 10 minutes.
- Serve the vegetable curry with your desired accompaniment.

*Calories 145, Protein 110 g, Sodium 81 mg, Potassium 90 mg, Phosphorus 96 mg, Calcium 15 mg*

## Stuffed Poblano pepper
*Time: 35 Mins, Serves: 4, Skill: Easy*

### Ingredients
- Poblano peppers (5 medium)
- Garlic (2 cloves), minced
- Pecans (1/3 cup), chopped
- Red peppers (1/2 cup)
- Olive oil (3 tbsp)
- Water (2 cups)
- Celery (2), diced
- Quinoa (1 cup)
- Onion (1), diced
- Carrots (2), diced
- Canned chipotle (1 tbsp), minced
- Canned sodium peas (1 cup)

### Instructions
- Strip the seeds from the poblano pepper by splitting it lengthwise. Don't remove the stem.
- Heat water in a pot and add the quinoa, bring to a boil and simmer until cooked. Set it aside for the time being.
- Cook the carrots, onion, and celery for 8 minutes in a skillet with olive oil.
- After adding the garlic, cook for a further minute.
- Add the quinoa, chipotle, pecans, red pepper, and peas.
- Fill the poblanos with the quinoa mixture and put them on a parchment-lined baking dish.
- Bake for thirty minutes at 375°F in a preheated oven.

*Calories 170, Protein 110 g, Sodium 85 mg, Potassium 65 mg, Phosphorus 90 mg, Calcium 13 mg*

## Vegetarian Egg Fried Rice
*Time: 25 Mins, Serves: 5, Skill: Easy*

### Ingredients
- Fresh ginger (1 tbsp)
- Garlic (2 cloves)
- Yellow onion (1 cup)
- Carrots (2 medium)
- Green peas (1/2 cup)
- Extra-firm tofu (1 cup)
- Green onions (2)
- Large eggs (6)
- Cilantro (1/2 cup)
- Soy sauce, reduced sodium (1 tbsp)
- Canola oil (3 tbsps.)
- Dry mustard (1/4 tsp)
- Rice (4 cups), cooked

### Instructions
- Garlic and ginger root should be peeled and grated. Dice and combine the tofu and yellow onion together in a shallow bowl. Carrots should be peeled and sliced along with the green onions and cilantro.
- Beat the eggs in a pan and cook them like an omelet. Remove the fried eggs, cut them into small pieces and set them aside.
- Heat the oil in a pan over low heat. Add the ginger, yellow onion, garlic, carrots, tofu, peas, and dry mustard.
- As the carrots soften, add the rice, cut eggs, and soy sauce. Remove from the heat and stir in the remaining ingredients.
- Before serving, garnish with cilantro and green onions.

*Calories 343, Protein 15 g, Sodium 238 mg, Potassium 350 mg, Phosphorus 230 mg, Calcium 83 mg*

## Tempeh Pita Sandwiches
*Time: 20 Mins, Serves: 4, Skill: Easy*

### Ingredients
- Tempeh (8 oz.)
- Balsamic vinegar (2 tbsps.)
- Sesame oil (2 tbsps.)
- Onion (1 small)
- Bell pepper, red (1)
- Mayonnaise (4 tsp)
- Pita bread (2 pieces), 6-inch size
- Mushrooms (1/2 cup)

### Instructions
- Cut the tempeh into 12 parts. Thinly slice the bell pepper, onion, and mushrooms.

- Heat 1 tablespoon of sesame oil in a large skillet over medium heat. Fry the sliced tempeh for 3 to 4 minutes on either side, until golden brown. After applying the balsamic vinegar, cook for a further minute, then turn them over and cook for another minute. Remove the Tempeh from the skillet.
- Melt the remaining sesame oil over low heat. Add the bell pepper, mushrooms, and onion and cook until they are tender.
- Cut the pita in half to create a pocket. Spread 1 tablespoon of mayonnaise on each half. Place 1/4 of the vegetable blend and 3 slices of tempeh in each half of the pita. Serve immediately.

*Calories 130, Protein 110 g, Sodium 81 mg, Potassium 95 mg, Phosphorus 96 mg, Calcium 13 mg*

## Vegetable Crumble

*Time: 45 Mins, Serves: 6, Skill: Medium*

**Ingredients**
- Crème Fraiche half fat (200ml)
- Plain flour (2 tbsp)
- Wholegrain mustard (1 tsp)
- Vegetable stock low salt (400ml)
- Celeriac (450g)
- Sweet potatoes (3 /180g approx.)
- Medium carrots (3/180g approx.)
- Leeks (2/140g approx.)
- Frozen peas (200g)
- Dried sage (1 tsp)

**Crumble**
- Butter (150g)
- Plain flour (200g)
- Ground almonds (50g)
- Italian hard cheese (40g)
- Flaked almonds (25g)

**Instructions**
- Preheat the oven to 190°C and boil a large pot of water. Peel and dice the sweet potatoes, celeriac, and carrots. Following that, the leeks should be cleaned, dried, and sliced.
- Add the vegetables & frozen peas to the boiling water. Boil for 10-15 minutes before removing and discarding the water.
- Add the drained vegetable mix to the dry saucepan. Cook on low heat for 5 minutes.
- In a mixing bowl, combine the crème Fraiche, flour, and mustard. Before the vegetables have thickened, stir the mix into them, then add the sage. After that, switch off the heat.
- To make the crumble use the tip of your fingers to rub the butter, flour, & ground almonds together until they bear a resemblance to breadcrumbs. Grate the parmesan and combine it with the flaked almonds in the crumble mix.
- Half-fill an oven-safe dish with the vegetable filling. Bake for 30 to 35 minutes, or until it is golden brown at the top.
- Serve.

*Calories 250, Protein 150 g, Sodium 90 mg, Potassium 100 mg, Phosphorus 96 mg, Calcium 25 mg*

## Vegetable Frittata

*Time: 35 Mins, Serves: 4, Skill: Easy*

**Ingredients**
- Eggs (6)
- Soft cheese (35g)
- Oregano (1 tsp), dried
- Olive oil (1 tbsp)
- Onion (1)
- Garlic (1 clove)
- Red bell pepper (1)
- Carrot (1)
- Tender stem broccoli (100g)
- Peas (100g), fresh/frozen
- Black pepper (1/2 tsp)

**Instructions**
- Preheat the oven to 220 °F. Peel and chop the carrot and boil it with the broccoli for around 5 minutes, or until it is soft, and then set it aside. Peel the onion and finely chop it, then deseed and chop the red pepper before peeling the garlic clove.
- In a mixing bowl, combine the egg, cheese, black pepper, and herbs. After that, heat the oil in a frying pan, add the onion, and after 5 minutes, crush and add the garlic. After adding the sliced carrot and bell pepper, cook for another minute. Add the broccoli, cook for a further minute. Now is the time to include the peas.
- Before pouring the egg mixture over the vegetables, finish whisking it. Stir until the mixture is uniformly spread in the pan. On the stovetop, cook for 1-2 minutes, or until the frittata's edge/corners are lighter in color.

- Place in the oven for 8-10 minutes. Pull the frittata out from the oven when it has set or has a slight jiggle in the middle. Enable it to cool for 5 minutes in the pan before slicing it neatly.

*Calories 160, Protein 100 g, Sodium 81 mg, Potassium 60 mg, Phosphorus 96 mg, Calcium 13 mg*

## Bulgur Vegetable Salad
*Time: 20 Mins, Serves: 4, Skill: Easy*

### Ingredients
- Bulgur (1 cup), cooked
- Black pepper, to taste
- Broccoli (1 cup), chopped
- Cauliflower (1 cup), chopped
- Red bell pepper (1), diced
- Scallion (1), chopped
- Fresh basil leaves (2 tbsp), chopped
- Lemon juice & zest (1)
- Olive oil (1 tbsp)

### Instructions
- In a mixing bowl, combine all the ingredients.
- Toss them one more time before serving.

*Calories 160, Protein 100 g, Sodium 81 mg, Potassium 70 mg, Phosphorus 96 mg, Calcium 13 mg*

## White bean veggies burgers
*Time: 30 Mins, Serves: 4, Skill: Easy*

### Ingredients
- Lemon juice (1 tsp)
- White beans (1 cup)
- Black pepper, to taste
- Garlic powder (1 tsp)
- White rice (1 cup), cooked
- Dried thyme (2 tsp)
- Onion (1/2), chopped
- Corn (1/2 cup)
- Red bell pepper (1/2 cup) chopped
- Chipotle pepper (1/2 tsp)
- All-purpose flour (1/3 cup)
- Egg (1)
- Extra virgin olive oil (2 tsp)

### Instructions
- In a pan, mash the beans with a masher.
- Add the corn, garlic powder, chipotle pepper, lemon juice, egg, rice, onion, thyme, flour, black pepper, and bell pepper.
- Produce patties with the bean mixture then set aside.
- Heat the olive oil in a skillet over low heat.
- Fry patties for 5 minutes on either side, or until golden brown on both ends. Then serve.

*Calories 200, Protein 140 g, Sodium 90 mg, Potassium 70 mg, Phosphorus 96 mg, Calcium 15 mg*

## German braised cabbage
*Time: 35 Mins, Serves: 4, Skill: Easy*

### Ingredients
- Caraway seed (1/2 tsp)
- Apple cider vinegar (3 tbsp)
- Dry mustard (1/2 tsp)
- Olive oil (1 tbsp)
- Chopped pear (1)
- Red cabbage (5 cups), shredded
- Sweet onion (1/4), chopped
- Sugar (1 tbsp)

### Instructions
- Cook the onion, cabbage, and pear for 10 minutes in a hot skillet over a high flame.
- Combine the mustard, sugar, vinegar, and caraway seed in a mixing bowl.
- Stir the mustard mixture into the cabbage mixture and thoroughly combine them.
- Simmer for 5 minutes.

*Calories 150, Protein 120 g, Sodium 80 mg, Potassium 70 mg, Phosphorus 96 mg, Calcium 15 mg*

## Greek couscous salad
*Time: 30 Mins, Serves: 5, Skill: Easy*

### Ingredients
- Couscous (3 cups), cooked
- Feta cheese (1/4 cup)
- Cherry tomatoes (1 cup)
- English cucumber (1), diced
- Scallion (1), chopped
- Lemon juice (1 tbsp)
- parsley (2 tbsp), chopped
- Slices of black olives (1/2 cup)
- Balsamic vinegar (2 tbsp)

### Instructions
- Combine the tomatoes, olives, mustard, cucumber, lemon juice, scallion, parsley, couscous, vinegar, and feta cheese in a large mixing bowl.

*Calories 160, Protein 50 g, Sodium 81 mg, Potassium 70 mg, Phosphorus 96 mg, Calcium 13 mg*

## Citrus Orzo salad
*Time: 25 Mins, Serves: 4, Skill: Easy*

**Ingredients**
**Dressing**
- Parmesan cheese (2 tbsp), grated
- Red pepper flakes (1/4 tsp)
- Lime Juice (2 tbsp)
- Olive oil (1/4 cup)
- Lime zest (1/2 lime)
- Oregano (2 tbsp), chopped

**Salad**
- Orzo pasta (3 cups), cooked
- Yellow bell pepper (1), diced
- Red bell pepper (1), diced
- Red onion (½), chopped
- Zucchini (1), diced

**Instructions**
- In a bowl combine the lemon juice, parmesan cheese, olive oil, oregano, lime zest and juice, and flakes, then set it aside.
- In a separate bowl, combine the broccoli, orzo, zucchini, red, and yellow bell peppers.
- Toss the salad with the prepared sauce, mix, and serve.

*Calories 120, Protein 80 g, Sodium 81 mg, Potassium 45 mg, Phosphorus 90 mg, Calcium 13 mg*

## Vegetable Biriyani
*Time: 1 Hour, Serves: 4, Skill: Easy*

**Ingredients**
- Curry powder (1/2 tsp)
- Water (2 1/4 cups)
- Olive oil (2 tbsp)
- Basmati rice (1 cup)
- Cardamom (1/2 tsp), ground
- Coriander seeds (1/2 tsp)
- Cumin seeds (1/2 tsp)
- Carrot (1), diced
- Garlic cloves (2), minced
- Sweet onion, (1/2), chopped
- Coriander (1 tsp), ground
- Cumin (1/2 tsp), ground
- Turmeric (1/4 tsp), ground
- Green beans (1 cup)
- Cauliflower florets (2 cups)
- Cilantro leaves, for garnish (1/4 cup), chopped

**Instructions**
- Heat one tablespoon of extra-virgin olive oil in a pan on a medium-high heat.
- After adding the cumin, curry powder, and coriander, cook for 30 minutes.
- For the rice, bring 1 and 3/4 cups of water to a boil.
- Reduce the heat to low and simmer, covered, for 12 minutes.
- Remove the pan from the heat after 12 minutes and set it aside.
- Cook the onion for 8 minutes over medium heat in the curry paste mixture.
- After adding the garlic, cook for one minute.
- After adding the cardamom, turmeric, coriander, and cumin cook for another minute.
- Cook the carrots, cauliflower, and beans for 3 minutes.
- Pour about 2/3 cup of water into the skillet and fry, covered, for 10 minutes.
- Stir the rice mixture into the vegetables to combine them.
- Serve with cilantro as a garnish.

*Calories 180, Protein 110 g, Sodium 85 mg, Potassium 80 mg, Phosphorus 90 mg, Calcium 16 mg*

## Lettuce falafel wrap
*Time: 35 Mins, Serves: 4, Skill: Easy*

**Ingredients**
- Red onion (2), chopped
- Lemon juice (1)
- Cumin (2 tsp), ground
- Tortillas (4)
- Lettuce (6 oz.)
- Flour (3/4 cup)
- Chickpeas (15 oz.)
- Canola oil (2 tbsp)
- Garlic cloves (2), minced
- Yogurt (1/4 cup)
- Black pepper, to taste
- Cucumber (1), chopped

**Instructions**
- Wash lettuce in hot water to wilt it.

- Drain the water from the lettuce and combine it with the rice, chickpeas, and cumin in a blender.
- Shape patties out of the blended mixture and set aside.
- Heat one tablespoon of olive oil in a skillet over medium heat and cook patties for 3 minutes on either side.
- Blend the garlic, pepper, lemon juice, and yogurt in a mixing cup.
- On each tortilla, layer falafel, cucumber, onions, and green salads, then drizzle with the yogurt mixture.

*Calories 170, Protein 100 g, Sodium 81 mg, Potassium 60 mg, Phosphorus 96 mg, Calcium 13 mg*

## Roasted root vegetables
*Time: 40 Mins, Serves: 6, Skill: Easy*

**Ingredients**
- Rosemary (1 tsp), chopped
- Turnips (1 cup), chopped
- Parsnips (1 cup), chopped
- Rutabaga (1 cup), chopped
- Extra-virgin olive oil (1 tbsp)
- Black pepper, to taste

**Instructions**
- Combine the olive oil, rutabaga, turnips, rosemary, and parsnips in a mixing bowl.
- Spread the mixture out on the baking sheet.
- Season with pepper and bake for 25 minutes in a preheated oven at 400 °F.

*Calories 190, Protein 110 g, Sodium 75 mg, Potassium 45 mg, Phosphorus 96 mg, Calcium 13 mg*

## Broccoli Salad
*Time: 25 Mins, Serves: 4, Skill: Easy*

**Ingredients**
- Small florets of broccoli (4 cups)
- Sesame seeds (2 tbsp)
- Carrot (1 large), grated and peeled
- Red cabbage (1 1/2 cups), thinly sliced
- Raisins (1/4 cup)
- Scallions (4), thinly sliced

**For Dressing:**
- Apple cider vinegar (1 tbsp)
- Basil (1 tbsp), dried
- Mayonnaise (2 1/2 tbsp)
- Garlic powder (1 tsp)
- Pinch of cayenne pepper

**Instructions**
- Combine the grated carrots, broccoli florets, sliced cabbage, raisins, sesame seeds, and sliced scallions in a large mixing bowl. Toss them together thoroughly to merge.
- Combine the mayonnaise, apple cider vinegar, garlic powder, cayenne pepper, and basil in a small mixing bowl or mixing cup. In a big mixing bowl, add all the ingredients and pour over the vegetables.
- Toss the vegetables in the dressing to coat them.
- Chill for 30 minutes before tossing the salad and serving.

*Calories 160, Protein 80 g, Sodium 81 mg, Potassium 60 mg, Phosphorus 90 mg, Calcium 13 mg*

## Parmesan Zucchini & Squash
*Time: 40 Mins, Serves: 4, Skill: Easy*

**Ingredients**
- Parmesan cheese (4 tsp), grated
- Margarine (1 tbsp)
- Zucchini & squash (1 1/2 cups), thinly sliced
- Onion (1/4 cup), chopped
- Red bell pepper (1/2 c), chopped
- Black pepper (1/4 tsp)
- Water (1 tbsp)

**Instructions**
- Over medium heat, preheat a nonstick skillet.
- In a mixing bowl, combine the vegetables, black pepper, water, and margarine.
- Simmer for 3 minutes in the skillet with the lid on.
- Remove the lid, turn the heat up to medium-high, & stir fry until the ingredients are smooth and crisp.
- Serve with a sprinkling of grated Parmesan cheese as a finishing flourish.

*Calories 160, Protein 90 g, Sodium 75 mg, Potassium 70 mg, Phosphorus 96 mg, Calcium 13 mg*

## Zucchini Cake
*Time: 1 Hour and 20 Mins, Serves: 6, Skill: Hard*

**Ingredients**
- Eggs (4)
- Vegetable oil (1 1/2 cups)
- Baking powder (1 tsp)
- Cinnamon (1 tsp)

- Brown sugar (1/2 cup)
- White sugar (1/2 cup)
- Molasses (2 tbsp)
- Raw zucchini (3 cups), grated
- Flour (3 cups)
- Baking soda (1 tsp)
- Nuts (1/4 cup, opt), chopped

**Instructions**
- Beat the eggs in a separate container.
- Add the sugars, molasses, zucchini, and vegetable oil.
- Blend until fully smooth.
- Add and combine the baking soda, salt, cinnamon, and baking powder.
- Add nuts to the mix if necessary.
- In a greased and floured 9 x 13-inch pan, bake for 1 hour at 347°F.

*Calories 180, Protein 140 g, Sodium 81 mg, Potassium 70 mg, Phosphorus 96 mg, Calcium 15 mg*

## Ratatouille
*Time: 50 Mins, Serves: 4, Skill: Easy*

**Ingredients**
- Zucchini squash (2 cups)
- Garlic (4 cloves)
- Tomatoes (1 cup), canned
- Olive oil (2 tbsps.)
- Fresh oregano (1 tbsp)
- Fresh rosemary (1 tbsp)
- Fresh basil (1 tbsp)
- Parmesan cheese (8 tbsps.), grated
- Fresh sage (1 tbsp)
- Onion (2 cups)
- Yellow crookneck squash (3 cups)
- Yellow bell pepper (1)
- Eggplant (1 medium)
- Green bell pepper (1)
- Carrots (2 medium)
- Red bell pepper (1)
- Black pepper (1 tbsp)
- Fresh thyme (1 tbsp)

**Instructions**
- Thinly dice the eggplant, squash, peppers, onions, and carrots. Garlic cloves should be minced before being used. Combine the olive oil, black pepper, ginger, basil, and carrots in a saucepan.
- Cook for 2 minutes before adding the remaining vegetables (except the tomatoes).
- Cook, stirring often, for 10 to 15 minutes, or until the vegetables are half tender.
- In a large mixing bowl, thoroughly combine the tomatoes and parmesan cheese.
- Cook on low heat for about 30 minutes with the lid closed. Serve immediately.
- Freeze the rest of the Ratatouille in 1–2 cup halves. Reheat it in the microwave for a quick lunch later.

*Calories 160, Protein 80 g, Sodium 75 mg, Potassium 90 mg, Phosphorus 96 mg, Calcium 13 mg*

## Veggie Strata
*Time: 2 Hours and 20 Mins, Serves: 2, Skill: Hard*

**Ingredients**
- Sourdough bread, 1/2-inch-thick slices (7 slices)
- Raw mushrooms (1 cup)
- Onion (1 cup)
- Unsalted margarine (1 tbsp)
- Red bell peppers (1 cup)
- Tabasco hot sauce (1 tsp)
- Large eggs (7)
- Fresh lettuce leaves (15)
- Tarragon vinegar (1/4 cup)
- Worcestershire sauce (1 tsp)
- Half & half creamer (1 3/4 cup)
- Black pepper (1/2 tsp)
- Sharp cheddar cheese (1 oz.), shredded

**Instructions**
- Cut the bread into little cubes. Place it on the baking tray and bake at 225°F for 15 minutes. Turn them and bake for another 15 minutes, or until crisp and dried on the other side.
- Cut the mushrooms, bell peppers, and onion into small pieces.
- Heat the margarine in a small saucepan and sauté the mushrooms, red peppers, and onions.
- Using cooking mist, spray a 9" square baking dish. Half of the bread squares, accompanied by half of the vegetable mixture, should be arranged in a single layer in the dish. On top of this layer, arrange the lettuce leaves.
- Place the remaining bread and vegetables on top of the first layer.
- Combine the eggs, vinegar, half-and-half creamer, black pepper, Worcestershire sauce, and hot sauce

in a mixing bowl. Evenly distribute it over the bread.
- Refrigerate it for 1 hour or overnight, wrapped with plastic wrap.
- Enable 20 minutes for the strata to come to room temperature after being removed from the fridge.
- Preheat the oven to 350 °F. Remove the plastic wrap and bake for 50 minutes.
- Remove from the oven and sprinkle cheddar cheese on top. Bake for 10 minutes longer, or until a knife inserted in the center comes out clean.
- Serve with a sweet sauce and broken into nine squares.

*Calories 180, Protein 90 g, Sodium 80 mg, Potassium 60 mg, Phosphorus 96 mg, Calcium 13 mg*

## Carrot Cake
*Time: 1 Hour, Serves: 6, Skill: Easy*

### Ingredients
- Pineapple, canned (1 cup), crushed
- Baking powder (1 tsp)
- Cinnamon (2 tsp), ground
- Eggs (2)
- Granulated sugar (1 cup)
- Vegetable oil (1/2 cup)
- Carrots (1 1/2 cups), grated or shredded
- Nutmeg (1/4 tsp)
- Vanilla extract (1 tsp)
- All-purpose flour (2 cups)
- Ground cloves (1/4 tsp)
- Baking soda (2 tsp)

### Instructions
- Preheat the oven to 375 °F.
- In a mixing bowl, whisk together the egg, oil, and sugar.
- Add the carrots and vanilla extract. Mix the ingredients together until they form a smooth mixture.
- Add the remaining ingredients and mix well.
- Pour the batter into a 9" x 13" cake pan that has been oiled and floured.
- Bake for at least 30 minutes. Leave it to cool for 10 minutes before removing it from the pan.
- Use icing or whipped cream to decorate (optional).

*Calories 150, Protein 80 g, Sodium 90 mg, Potassium 70 mg, Phosphorus 96 mg, Calcium 25 mg*

## Roasted Red Pepper, Vegan Provolone Cheese Sandwiches
*Time: 1 Hour and 5 Mins, Serves: 4, Skill: Easy*

### Ingredients
- Olive oil (1 tbsp)
- Red bell peppers (2 medium)
- Basil leaves, fresh
- Sandwich rolls (2), whole-grain
- Vegan cheese (8)
- Daiya cheese, provolone-style (4 slices)

### Instructions
- Using a paper towel, wash and dry the red peppers. On the stove, two burners should be lit. Place each pepper on the burners with tongs. Turn the peppers as one side starts to turn purple. Continue turning and frying the peppers until they are blackened. It will take about 5-7 minutes.
- Place the peppers in a paper bag with tongs and seal it. Allow 5 to 8 minutes to cool.
- Break all of the rolls in half lengthwise.
- Half-fill a small cup of olive oil. Apply the oil to the inside of each sandwich bun.
- Cover the bottom half of each roll with Daiya cheese (2 slices). In a toaster oven, toast it. Toasted cheese should start to melt after a few minutes. Place the rolls aside after removing them from the toaster.
- Put the red peppers on a plate after removing them from the bag. With your hands, scrape the blackened skin off the pepper's exterior.
- After cutting the stem, slice the open peppers, use a paper sheet to discard of the seeds and any excess water. Cut the peppers in half.
- To make a sandwich, spread two halved peppers on each half of the bun, sprinkle with fresh basil leaves, and top with the other half.

*Calories 145, Protein 110 g, Sodium 81 mg, Potassium 60 mg, Phosphorus 96 mg, Calcium 20 mg*

## Spicy Chickpeas (Chana Masala)
*Time: 1 Hour and 5 Mins, Serves: 6, Skill: Medium*

### Ingredients
- Canned chickpeas (30 oz.)
- Onion (1 medium)
- Garlic (3 cloves)
- Fresh ginger (1 tbsp)
- Canola oil (2 tbsp)

- Fresh cilantro (1/4 cup)
- Chili powder (1 tsp)
- Garam masala (1 tsp)
- Canned tomatoes (8 oz.), diced, unsalted
- Coriander powder (1 tsp)
- Lemon wedges (4)
- Turmeric (1 tsp), ground

**Instructions**
- Mince the ginger and garlic, and chop the onion and cilantro. Drain and rinse the canned chickpeas.
- In a pan, heat the oil and cook the ginger, onion, and garlic for 3 minutes.
- Add the tomatoes and continue to cook for 3 to 4 minutes more.
- Add the coriander powder, chili powder, garam masala, and turmeric, and cook for an additional minute.
- Pour half a cup of water into the pot with the chickpeas. Allow 10 to 15 minutes to cook on low heat.
- Garnish with a lemon wedge and chopped cilantro. Serve with rice and naan bread as desired.

*Calories 180, Protein 90 g, Sodium 81 mg, Potassium 55 mg, Phosphorus 96 mg, Calcium 13 mg*

## Four Ingredient Vegetable Broth
*Time: 50 Mins, Serves: 4, Skill: Medium*

**Ingredients**
- Beans (1 can), drained and rinsed
- Tomatoes (1 can), diced
- Corn (1 can), drained and rinsed
- Refried beans (1 can)

**All ingredients are fat-free, with no salt added, 14.4 oz. cans.**

**Instructions**
- In a pan, mix all ingredients and whisk to combine the refried beans.
- Cook until done on low heat, then serve.

*Calories 143, Protein 24 g, Sodium 81 mg, Potassium 31 mg, Phosphorus 96 mg, Calcium 13 mg*

## Honeyed Carrots & Leeks
*Time: 12 Mins, Serves: 2, Skill: Easy*

**Ingredients**
- Leeks (1/2 cup), sliced
- Baby carrots (1 lb.), washed
- Brown sugar (1 tsp), granulated
- Olive oil (1 tsp)
- Honey (1 tbsp)
- Lemon juice (2 tbsp)
- Lemon (1), zested

**Instructions**
- Mix the leeks, carrots, sugar, oil, 2 tablespoons of lemon juice, lemon zest and honey in a medium saucepan.
- Cover and bring to a boil for 5 minutes.
- Remove the cover and cook for a further 2 minutes.

*Calories 140, Protein 100 g, Sodium 81 mg, Potassium 80 mg, Phosphorus 96 mg, Calcium 13 mg*

## Rice O'Brien
*Time: 1 Hour and 25 Mins, Serves: 4, Skill: Hard*

**Ingredients**
- Water (1 1/2 cups)
- Red pepper (1/4 tsp)
- Black pepper (1/2 tsp)
- Thyme or rosemary (1/2 tsp)
- Rice (1 cup), uncooked
- Onion (1/2 cup), thinly sliced or chopped
- Green pepper (1/4 cup), chopped
- Carrots (1/4 cup), shredded
- Lemon juice (1 tbsp)
- Margarine (1 tbsp)

**Instructions**
- Combine all the ingredients in a big saucepan of boiling water.
- Bring to a boil in a sealed pan for 15 minutes (do not stir).
- Fluff the rice with a fork after removing it.

*Calories 160, Protein 100 g, Sodium 81 mg, Potassium 70 mg, Phosphorus 96 mg, Calcium 13 mg*

## Steamed Asparagus
*Time: 1 Hour, Serves: 2, Skill: Medium*

**Ingredients**
- Lemon juice (1 tbsp)
- Fresh asparagus spears (12)
- Margarine (2 tbsps.), melted (unsalted)
- Water (2 cups)

**Instructions**
- Squeeze the juice of a lemon into a margarita bottle.

- Bring the water to a low boil.
- Place the asparagus in a steamer over a skillet of water that is simmering.
- After the asparagus turns light green, steam it for a further 2 minutes.
- Remove the asparagus from the pan and drizzle the margarine and lemon juice over it. Serve immediately.

*Calories 145, Protein 80 g, Sodium 81 mg, Potassium 50 mg, Phosphorus 95 mg, Calcium 13 mg*

## Macaroni Salad
*Time: 1 Hour, Serves: 4, Skill: Medium*

### Ingredients
- Hard-boiled, shelled eggs (3), chopped
- Mayonnaise (1/2 cup)
- Celery (1/2 cup), chopped
  Dry mustard (1 tsp)
- Paprika
- Black pepper
- Macaroni (3 cups), cooked
- Pimentos (1/4 cup)
- Onion (1/2 cup), chopped
- Green pepper (1/2 cup), chopped

### Instructions
- Clean the fried macaroni thoroughly with cold water.
- Except for the black pepper and paprika, toss the macaroni with the remaining ingredients. Get a thorough mixture.
- Finish with a sprinkling of paprika and black pepper.
- Serve.

*Calories 170, Protein 90 g, Sodium 81 mg, Potassium 50 mg, Phosphorus 96 mg, Calcium 15 mg*

## Fried Onion Rings
*Time: 40 Mins, Serves: 4, Skill: Easy*

### Ingredients
- Vegetable oil (1/2 cup), for frying
- Plain cornmeal (3/4 cup)
- All-purpose flour (1/4 cup)
- Sugar (1 tsp)
- Onions (4 medium)
- Egg (1), beaten
- Water (1/4 cup)

### Instructions
- In a mixing cup, combine the flour, sugar, and cornmeal; set aside.
- Create rings out of the onions by peeling them and chopping them crosswise into 14" thick strips.
- Combine the beaten egg and water in a mixing bowl.
- Dip the rings in the egg wash before covering them in the cornmeal mix.
- Fry rings in hot vegetable oil for 3-5 minutes, turning once, until golden brown.
- Drain on paper towels and serve right away.

*Calories 145, Protein 80 g, Sodium 81 mg, Potassium 60 mg, Phosphorus 96 mg, Calcium 13 mg*

## Baked Yellow Squash
*Time: 1 Hour and 10 Mins, Serves: 3, Skill: Medium*

### Ingredients
- Margarine or butter (2 tbsp.), melted
- Lemon juice (1 tbsp.)
- Thyme (3/4 tsp)
- Black pepper (1/8 tsp)
- Yellow squash (2 cans), sliced
- Onion (1 medium), chopped
- Celery stalk (1 small), chopped
- Bell pepper (1 large), chopped

### Instructions
- Preheat oven to 175 °F.
- In a large skillet, sauté all the ingredients in margarine, except the lemon juice, until the onions are translucent, stirring occasionally.
- Squeeze the lemon juice into the mixture.
- In a casserole dish, position the sautéed mixture.
- Bake for 30 minutes, then serve.

*Calories 180, Protein 70 g, Sodium 81 mg, Potassium 50 mg, Phosphorus 96 mg, Calcium 15 mg*

## Yellow Squash & Green Onions
*Time: 50 Mins, Serves: 4, Skill: Medium*

### Ingredients
- Yellow straight neck or crook neck squash (2 cups), washed and sliced
- Black pepper (1 tsp)
- Butter or margarine (2 tbsp.)
- Green onion (1 cup), chopped

**Instructions**
- Cook the squash slices for 15 minutes or until tender, then rinse.
- Heat the butter in a frying pan and sear the onions until they are soft.
- Toss in the squash and a pinch of black pepper.
- Bring to a boil for 5 minutes over low heat, sealed, before reheating the dish.

*Calories 143, Protein 60 g, Sodium 81 mg, Potassium 50 mg, Phosphorus 96 mg, Calcium 13 mg*

# Poultry Recipes

## Chicken Veronique
*Time: 40 Mins, Serves: 4, Skill: Easy*

**Ingredients**
- Pepper (1/4 tsp)
- Water (1/2 cup)
- Orange marmalade (2 tbsp)
- Bay leaf (1)
- Flour (1 tbsp)
- Halved white grapes (1 cup)
- Pepper (1/4 tsp)
- Unsalted Margarine (6 tbsp)
- White wine (1/4 cup)
- Parsley (1 tsp)
- 1 chicken breast (4oz.)

**Instructions**
- In a mixing cup, whisk together the flour and 1/4 teaspoon of pepper. Using a thin dusting of flour, gently cover the chicken. In a pan, sauté the chicken in margarine until golden brown.
- Place the remaining components, except for the grapes, in the skillet. Bring to a simmer then add the chicken. Cook for 25 minutes, or until the chicken is cooked through.
- Remove the chicken from the skillet and set aside. Cook the remaining components for a further 2 minutes, stirring continuously, while adding the grapes.
- To serve, drizzle the sauce on top of the chicken.

*Calories 200, Protein 150 g, Sodium 81 mg, Potassium 50 mg, Phosphorus 96 mg, Calcium 13 mg*

## Grilled Chicken Sesame
*Time: 1 Hour 10 Mins, Serves: 4, Skill: Medium*

**Ingredients**
- Sesame seeds (1 tbsp), toasted
- Sherry (1 tbsp)
- Ginger (2 tsp), grated
- Honey (2 tbsp)
- Soy sauce (1 tbsp), low in salt
- Skinned, boned chicken breast (4, 4oz. each) (halves)
- Vegetable spray

**Instructions**
- In a mixing bowl, combine the ingredients (first 5).
- Flatten chicken pieces with a rolling pin or mallet to 1/4-inch thickness.
- Using the vegetable spray, coat the grill. Grill the chicken for 4 minutes on either side over medium-hot coals, basting often with the soy sauce mixture.
- Place the mixture in a serving bowl.

*Calories 170, Protein 160 g, Sodium 81 mg, Potassium 70 mg, Phosphorus 96 mg, Calcium 20 mg*

## Lemon Tarragon Chicken
*Time: 1 Hour and 20 Mins, Serves: 4, Skill: Medium*

**Ingredients**
- Dried tarragon (1/2 tsp), crushed
- Dry sherry (3 tbsp)
- Chicken broth (1 3/4 cups), without salt
- Hot cooked noodles
- Flour (1/3 cup)
- Sour cream (1/4 cup)
- Margarine (2 tbsp)
- Lemon pepper seasoning (1/2 tsp)
- Boneless chicken breast halves (8 medium without skin, about 1 1/2 lb.)
- Cloves of garlic (2), minced
- Fresh mushrooms (2 cups), halved

**Instructions**
- Melt the margarine in a 12-inch skillet over medium heat. Toss in the chicken, onions, tarragon, garlic, sherry, mushrooms, and lemon pepper.
- Cook, turning once, for 10 to 12 minutes, or until the chicken is no longer pink. Using a slotted spoon, cut the chicken and mushrooms.
- In a screw-top bowl, blend the chicken broth and flour until well mixed. Toss the ingredients into the skillet.
- Cook and mix over medium-high heat until the sauce is thick and bubbly. In a mixing dish, pour about ½ cup of the skillet mixture and whisk in the sour cream.
- Add the chicken and mushrooms to the same skillet.
- Bring to a low boil, then reduce to low heat (remember not to boil).
- Mix with hot fried noodles and serve.

*Calories 143, Protein 110 g, Sodium 81 mg, Potassium 40 mg, Phosphorus 96 mg, Calcium 13 mg*

## Oven-Fried Chicken
*Time: 1 Hour 35 Mins, Serves: 2, Skill: Hard*

**Ingredients**
- Shortening (1/4 cup)
- Margarine (1/4 cup)
- Flour (1/2 cup)
- Paprika (1 tsp)
- Pepper (1/2 tsp)
- Onion Powder (1/2 tsp)
- Broiled fryer chicken (1 3-lb.), cut up

**Instructions**
- Preheat the oven to 425 °F. Clean the chicken and pat it dry. In a 13" x 9" x 2" baking tray, heat the shortening and margarine. Combine the flour, pepper, paprika, and onion powder in a medium mixing dish. Using the flour mixture, coat the chicken parts thoroughly.
- Cook for 30 minutes, exposed, with skin side down in liquid shortening.
- Cook for around 30 minutes, or until the chicken's thickest parts are tender.

*Calories 143, Protein 115 g, Sodium 81 mg, Potassium 40 mg, Phosphorus 96 mg, Calcium 13 mg*

## Slow Chicken Meatloaf
*Time: 9 hours and 25 Mins, Serves: 6, Skill: Hard*

**Ingredients**
- Mustard (1 tsp), prepared
- Chicken, boneless (1 ½ lb.), grounded
- Brown sugar (1/4 cup)
- Egg (1 medium), beaten
- Vegetable oil (1 tbsp)
- Oats (1/2 cup)
- Garlic clove (1), minced
- Onion (1/2 cup), diced
- Balsamic vinegar (1 tbsp)
- Black pepper (1/2 tsp)

**Instructions**
- Combine the vegetable oil, ground chicken, oats, egg, sugar, onion, black pepper, and garlic in a loaf tin and blend well.
- Shape a "sling" for the meatloaf by wrapping two sheets of baking paper across the bottom and sides of the crockpot. Using the baking paper, cover the meatloaf.
- Toss the meatloaf with a mixture of butter, mustard, and vinegar.
- Cook for 8 hours on low heat.
- When it's finished, raise the four strips of baking paper and clear them from the crockpot.
- Dismantle it and cut it into servings.

*Calories 170, Protein 120 g, Sodium 81 mg, Potassium 31 mg, Phosphorus 96 mg, Calcium 13 mg*

## Barley-Rice Pilaf
*Time: 1 Hour and 25 Mins, Serves: 3, Skill: Medium*

**Ingredients**
- Yellow onion (1 small), chopped
- Barley (1/3 cup)
- Pepper (1/8 tsp)
- Margarine (1 tbsp)
- Chicken broth (2 cups), low in sodium
- Carrot (1), peeled & chopped fine
- Stalk celery (1), chopped fine
- White rice (1/3 cup)
- Dried thyme (1/2 tsp)

**Instructions**
- In a saucepan over low heat, melt the margarine, then add the onion and cook until soft, around 5 minutes.
- Add the rice and barley and bring to a boil for 1 minute.
- Add the remaining ingredients and reduce to a low heat.
- Decrease the heat to low and simmer for 15 minutes, sealed, or until the liquid is gone.

*Calories 160, Protein 130 g, Sodium 81 mg, Potassium 40 mg, Phosphorus 96 mg, Calcium 14 mg*

## Chicken Cabbage Stir Fry
*Time: 1 Hour and 20 Mins, Serves: 4, Skill: Medium*

**Ingredients**
- Chicken breast halves (3)
- Vegetable oil (1 tsp)
- Low sodium soy sauce (1 tbsp)
- Green cabbage (3 cups), shredded
- Cornstarch (1 tbsp)
- Ground ginger (1/2 tsp)
- Garlic powder (1/4 tsp)
- Water (1/2 cup)

## Instructions

- Remove the chicken breasts from the package and cut them into strips.
- Heat the oil in a pan.
- Cook the chicken strips over medium-high heat, rotating periodically, until finished.
- Add the cabbage. Cook for 2 minutes, or until the cabbage is crunchy-tender.
- In a mixing cup, blend the cornstarch and seasonings; add the soy sauce and water and whisk until smooth.
- Toss the sauce with the cabbage and chicken combination.
- Cook for 1 minute, or until the sauce has thickened and the chicken has been fully covered.

*Calories 150, Protein 110 g, Sodium 85 mg, Potassium 45 mg, Phosphorus 96 mg, Calcium 13 mg*

## Chicken Salad

*Time: 1 Hour and 20 Mins, Serves: 4, Skill: Medium*

### Ingredients

- Chicken breasts (4), boneless & skinless
- Mayonnaise of Duke (3/4 cup)
- Red grapes (1 cup), seedless and cut in half
- Celery (1/4 cup), chopped
- Red onion (1/4 cup), chopped finely
- Salt (1/4 tsp)
- Black pepper (1/8 tsp)

### Instructions

- Combine the chicken with some water in a pot. (Chicken must be covered with water.)
- Cook the chicken for 25 minutes over medium heat, then leave to cool.
- Chop the chicken into small pieces.
- Combine the grapes, chicken, celery, mayonnaise, and onions in a bowl.
- Finish with a pinch of black pepper.

*Calories 170, Protein 140 g, Sodium 81 mg, Potassium 45 mg, Phosphorus 96 mg, Calcium 16 mg*

## Rice Pilaf

*Time: 1 Hour and 40 Mins, Serves: 3, Skill: Hard*

### Ingredients

- Wild rice (1/4 cup)
- White rice (1 cup)
- Onions (1/2 cup), chopped
- Garlic cloves (1-2), minced
- Fresh parsley (2 tbsp), finely chopped
- Black pepper (1-2 tsp.), ground
- Chicken stock or broth (3 c), low sodium
- Olive oil or unsalted butter (2 tsp)
- Orzo pasta (1/4 cup)

### Instructions

- Preheat oven to 175 °F.
- Bring the chicken stock to a low boil in a saucepan.
- In a pan, gently sauté the garlic and onions in butter until they tend to caramelize.
- Add the rice and orzo and sauté until it starts to brown.
- Add the chicken stock, parsley, and black pepper.
- Boil with the cover on for 30 minutes.
- Serve with a fork to fluff it up.

*Calories 150, Protein 100 g, Sodium 81 mg, Potassium 45 mg, Phosphorus 96 mg, Calcium 13 mg*

## Turkey Nuggets with Honey Mustard

*Time: 1 Hour and 40 Mins, Serves: 8, Skill: Hard*

### Ingredients

- Low-fat milk, 1%, (2 tbsps.)
- Egg (1 large)
- Mayonnaise (1/2 cup)
- Yellow mustard (1 tbsp)
- Honey (1/3 cup)
- Turkey breasts (1 lb.), boneless
- Worcestershire sauce (2 tsp)
- Cornflakes (3 cups)

### Instructions

- Mix the mustard, mayonnaise, honey, and Worcestershire sauce in a small cup; when the nuggets are finished, chill the sauce and use it as a dipping sauce.
- Preheat the oven to 400 °F.
- Cut the breasts into 36 pieces of similar dimensions.
- Crumble the cornflakes and place the crumbs in a large zip lock bag.
- Whisk the egg and milk together in a tiny mixing cup; dunk the little turkey parts in the whisked egg, then shake them in a Ziplock bag to cover them in cornflake crumbs.

- On a baking tray covered with nonstick cooking spray, bake the nuggets for 15 minutes, or until tender.

*Calories 160, Protein 110 g, Sodium 81 mg, Potassium 40 mg, Phosphorus 96 mg, Calcium 13 mg*

## Turkey Salad

*Time: 1 Hour and 10 Mins, Serves: 4, Skill: Easy*

**Ingredients**
- Turkey breast (4), boneless & skinless
- Mayonnaise of Duke (3/4 cup)
- Red grapes (1 cup), seedless and cut in half
- Celery (1/4 cup), chopped
- Red onion (1/4 cup), chopped finely
- Salt (1/4 tsp)
- Black pepper (1/8 tsp)

**Instructions**
- Combine the turkey with some water in a pot. (Turkey must be covered with water.)
- Cook the turkey for 25 minutes in water over medium heat, then leave to cool.
- Chop the turkey into small pieces.
- Combine the grapes, turkey, celery, mayonnaise, and onions in a big mixing bowl.
- Finish with a pinch of black pepper.

*Calories 140, Protein 115 g, Sodium 18 mg, Potassium 24 mg, Phosphorus 16 mg, Calcium 13 mg*

## Easy Gravy

*Time: 40 Mins, Serves: 4, Skill: Easy*

**Ingredients**
- Chicken or beef broth (2 cups), low sodium
- Black pepper (1/2 tsp)
- Paprika (1/2 tsp)
- Garlic powder (1/2 tsp)
- Onion powder (1/2 tsp)
- Corn starch (1/3 cup)

**Instructions**
- Combine all the ingredients in a large mixing bowl, making sure there are no lumps, then pour it into the saucepan.
- Simmer, stirring continuously, over medium heat until the sauce has thickened.
- Serve over pasta, potatoes, or beef.

*Calories 140, Protein 100 g, Sodium 81 mg, Potassium 55 mg, Phosphorus 96 mg, Calcium 13 mg*

## Curry Chicken

*Time: 1 Hour and 5 Mins, Serves: 4, Skill: Medium*

**Ingredients**
- Dry thyme (1/2 tsp)
- Lemon juice (1/4 cup)
- Onion (1 medium), chopped
- Curry powder (2 tsp)
- Black pepper (1/2 tsp)
- Garlic clove (1 medium), chopped (optional)
- Water (1 cup)
- Chicken (1 whole), cut in small parts, skin removed
- Vegetable or olive oil (2 tbsps.)

**Instructions**
- After cleaning the chicken, soak it with lemon juice.
- Mix the seasonings in a bowl and rub onto the chicken.
- Marinate the seasoned chicken overnight in the refrigerator.
- Heat the oil in a saucepan and brown the seasoned chicken.
- Add a splash of water to the marinating bowl to preserve marinade.
- Pour the remaining marinade over the browned chicken and cook on low heat until the chicken is tender, about 20 minutes.
- Quickly serve over hot rice.

*Calories 170, Protein 150 g, Sodium 81 mg, Potassium 40 mg, Phosphorus 96 mg, Calcium 13 mg*

## Stuffing of Tacos with Chicken

*Time: 1 Hour and 10 Mins, Serves: 4, Skill: Medium*

**Ingredients**
- Taco shells
- Ground red pepper (1/2 tsp)
- Vegetable oil (2 tbsp)
- Italian seasoning (1 tsp)
- Lean ground chicken (1 1/4 lb.)
- Onion powder (1 tsp)
- Tabasco sauce (1/2 tsp)
- Black pepper (1/2 tsp)
- Garlic powder (1 tsp)
- Nutmeg (1/2 tsp)

## Instructions

- Heat the oil in a big skillet and add the ground chicken and the remaining ingredients.
- Cook until all the components, including the beef, are cooked through and fully mixed.
- Fill each taco shell with 4 tablespoons of beef.

*Calories 160, Protein 100 g, Sodium 81 mg, Potassium 45 mg, Phosphorus 96 mg, Calcium 13 mg*

## Chicken and Summer Vegetable Kebabs

*Time: 1 Hour and 40 Mins, Serves: 4, Skill: Hard*

### Ingredients

- Peach jam (1 tbsp)
- Olive oil (2 tbsps.)
- Bell pepper, red (1)
- Onion (1 medium)
- Lemon juice (2 tbsps.)
- Salt (1/4 tsp)
- Herb seasoning blend (1 tsp)
- Zucchini (1 medium)
- Chicken thighs (1lb.), boneless, skinless
- Summer squash, yellow (1 medium)

### Instructions

- To make the marinade, microwave the peach jam for 10-15 seconds in a shallow microwave-safe dish. In a spice seasoning bowl, whisk together the olive oil, lemon juice, and salt until well mixed.
- Rinse the chicken thighs and dry them with a paper towel before cutting each boneless thigh into four sections and storing them in a zip-lock bag.
- Brush the boneless bits with half of the marinade (the other half will be used on the vegetables). To marinate, seal the zip-lock bag and place it in the refrigerator.
- To produce kebabs, cut the vegetables into small parts, put them in a container, and add the remaining marinade over the vegetables, mixing to coat them.
- Using skewers, thread the chicken and vegetables together (8 tiny or 4 wide skewers).
- Place the skewers on a hot, medium grill and cook, covered, for 12 to 15 minutes, rotating the skewers halfway through to ensure even cooking.

*Calories 150, Protein 120 g, Sodium 81 mg, Potassium 50 mg, Phosphorus 96 mg, Calcium 15 mg*

## Chicken Nuggets with Honey Mustard

*Time: 1 Hour and 50 Mins, Serves: 8, Skill: Hard*

### Ingredients

- Low-fat milk, 1% (2 tbsp)
- Egg (1 large)
- Mayonnaise (1/2 cup)
- Yellow mustard (1 tbsp)
- Honey (1/3 cup)
- Chicken breasts (1 lb.), boneless
- Worcestershire sauce (2 tsp)
- Cornflakes (3 cups)

### Instructions

- Mix the mustard, mayonnaise, honey, and Worcestershire sauce in a small cup; when the nuggets are finished, chill the sauce and use it as a dipping sauce.
- Preheat the oven to 400 °F.
- Cut the breasts into 36 pieces of similar dimensions.
- Crumble the cornflakes and place the crumbs in a large zip-lock bag.
- Whisk the egg and milk together in a tiny mixing cup; dunk the little chicken parts in the whisked egg, then shake them in a Ziplock bag to cover them in cornflake crumbs.
- On a baking tray covered with nonstick cooking spray, bake the nuggets for 15 minutes, or until tender.

*Calories 160, Protein 130 g, Sodium 81 mg, Potassium 40 mg, Phosphorus 96 mg, Calcium 13 mg*

## Easy Chicken and Pasta Dinner

*Time: 1 Hour 35 Mins, Serves: 4, Skill: Medium*

### Ingredients

- Chicken breast (5 oz.), cooked
- Olive oil (1 tbsp)
- Red bell pepper (1/2 cup)
- Zucchini (1 cup)
- Pasta, any shape (2 cups), cooked
- Low-sodium Italian dressing (3 tbsp)

### Instructions

- Peel and thinly slice the zucchini and bell pepper.
- In a large skillet, heat the olive oil and cook the peppers and zucchini until soft and crispy, then move to a serving dish.

- Cut the chicken into small strips using a sharp knife.
- Heat the cooked pasta and chicken strips separately in the microwave.
- Toss the pasta with the dressing and eat alongside the sautéed vegetables and chicken strips.

*Calories 150, Protein 110 g, Sodium 81 mg, Potassium 40 mg, Phosphorus 96 mg, Calcium 13 mg*

## Herb-Roasted Chicken Breasts

*Time: 4 hours and 45 Mins, Serves: 4, Skill: Hard*

**Ingredients**
- Herb and garlic seasoning blend, Mrs. Dash (2 tbsp)
- Black pepper (1 tsp), freshly ground
- Olive oil (1/4 cup)
- Chicken breasts (1 pound), skinless, boneless
- Onion (1 medium)
- Garlic cloves (1–2)

**Instructions**
- In a mixing bowl, chop the garlic and onion and merge with the seasoning, ground pepper, and olive oil.
- Add the chicken breasts to the marinade, cover, and set aside for 4 hours, or overnight at a low temperature.

**Instructions for baking**
- Preheat the oven to 350 °F.
- Position the marinated chicken in a baking dish lined with foil.
- Pour the remaining marinade over the chicken breasts and bake for 20 minutes at 350°F, with an additional 5 minutes under the broiler to brown them.

*Calories 160, Protein 120 g, Sodium 70 mg, Potassium 70 mg, Phosphorus 96 mg, Calcium 13 mg*

## Indian Chicken Curry

*Time: 1 Hour 45 Mins, Serves: 4, Skill: Medium*

**Ingredients**
- Onions (2 medium)
- Ginger root (1" cube)
- Vegetable oil (5 tbsp)
- Chicken drumsticks (small, 1-1/2 lb.)
- Whole cumin seeds (3/4 tsp)
- Bay leaves (2)
- Cinnamon stick (1)
- Salt (3/4 tsp)
- Whole peppercorns (1/4 tsp)
- Garam masala (1/2 tsp)
- Tomato (1 medium)
- Garlic (2 cloves)
- Cayenne pepper (1 1/2 tsp)

**Instructions**
- Strip the chicken skin and peel the tomato. Mince the garlic, onion, and ginger root.
- Heat the oil in a big, broad pot over medium-high heat and add the cumin seeds, bay leaves, cinnamon stick, and peppercorns, continuously stirring.
- Whisk in the garlic, ginger, and onion until brown specks form on the onion, around 3 minutes.
- Add the chicken, cayenne pepper, tomato, salt, and 14 cups of water to the pot and bring to a boil, continuously stirring.
- Cover the pot tightly, turn down the heat to a minimum, and simmer for around 25 minutes, or until the chicken is tender and juicy, stirring occasionally.
- Remove the cover and reduce the heat to medium-low, season with garam masala, and cook for around 5 minutes, stirring regularly, to reduce the amount of oil.

*Calories 150, Protein 115 g, Sodium 81 mg, Potassium 31 mg, Phosphorus 96 mg, Calcium 13 mg*

## Chicken Stir-Fry

*Time: 1 Hour 30 Mins, Serves: 6, Skill: Medium*

**Ingredients**
- Red chili pepper (1/4 tsp), ground, or to taste
- Parsley (optional garnish)
- Soy sauce (2 tsp), reduced-sodium
- Cornstarch (2 tbsp), separated
- Sugar (1/2 tsp)
- Sesame oil (1/4 tsp)
- Egg (1 large), beaten
- Water (2 tbsp), separated
- Chicken breast (12 oz.), sliced
- Canola oil (3 tbsp), separated
- Onions (1 cup), sliced
- Bell pepper, green (1), sliced
- Sherry (1 tbsp)

**Instructions**

- Whisk together 1 large egg, 1 tablespoon cornstarch, 1 tablespoon water, 1 tablespoon canola oil, and the chicken in a deep mixing bowl; set aside for 20 minutes.
- In a small dish, mix the remaining water and cornstarch and set aside.
- In a skillet, heat 2 tablespoons of oil and add the marinated meat mixture, frying until it browns.
- Toss in the green bell peppers and chili peppers in the skillet with the sherry and stir-fry for 1 minute before including the sugar, sesame oil, and soy sauce.
- Until it thickens, stir in the remaining cornstarch and water combination, then serve.

*Calories 253, Protein 20 g, Sodium 408 mg, Potassium 386 mg, Phosphorus 184 mg, Calcium 49 mg*

## Low sodium instant pot turkey chili
*Time: 1 Hour and 35 Mins, Serves: 4, Skill: Medium*

**Ingredients**
- Turkey (1 lb.), ground
- No Salt Added Pinto Beans (1 can, 15 oz.)
- Fresh black ground pepper (1 tbsp)
- Cayenne pepper (1/2 tsp)
- No Added Salt Green Chilies and Diced Tomatoes (1 can, 10 ounces)
- No Salt Added Tomato Sauce (1 can 8 oz.)
- Herb-Ox Sodium Free Chicken broth (1 packet, 1.2 oz.)
- Water (1/2 cup)
- Onion (1), diced
- Green pepper (1), diced
- Yellow pepper (1), diced
- Powdered chili (2 tbsp)

**Instructions**
- Preheat the Instant Pot to sauté, then insert the ground turkey to brown for 3-5 minutes.
- Cook for another 3 minutes after adding the onions and sliced peppers.
- Fill the instant pot halfway with water and a packet of chicken broth. Combine the chili powder and pepper in a large mixing bowl. Fold the sliced tomatoes and washed beans in gently.
- Close the vent, lock the cover, and set the timer to "chili" for 40 minutes. Allow the pressure to naturally subside (NPR). Remove the cap and carefully prepare the ingredients before serving.

*Calories 143, Protein 100 g, Sodium 81 mg, Potassium 60 mg, Phosphorus 96 mg, Calcium 13 mg*

## Chicken Fried Rice
*Time: 1 Hour 50 Mins, Serves: 6, Skill: Hard*

**Ingredients**
- Garlic (2 cloves)
- Soy sauce, reduced sodium (1 tbsp)
- Fresh ginger (1 tbsp)
- Carrots (2 medium)
- Green peas (1/2 cup)
- Rice (4 cups), cooked
- Yellow onion (1 cup)
- Green onions (2)
- Cilantro (1/2 cup)
- Chicken (500 gm), boil and shredded.
- Dry mustard (1/4 tsp)
- Canola oil (3 tbsp)

**Instructions**
- Shred the garlic and ginger root. The yellow onion can be chopped into tiny sections. Carrots should be peeled and sliced. Cilantro and green onions may be sliced.
- Heat the oil in a pan over low heat. With the ginger, yellow onion, and garlic, combine the carrots, boiled and shredded chicken, peas, and dried mustard.
- When the carrots are tender, add the rice and soy sauce. Remove from the heat and mix in the remaining ingredients.
- Garnish with green onions and cilantro before serving.

*Calories 160, Protein 120 g, Sodium 81 mg, Potassium 45 mg, Phosphorus 96 mg, Calcium 13 mg*

## Chicken Waldorf salad
*Time: 40 Mins, Serves: 4, Skill: Easy*

**Ingredients**
- Miracle Whip (1/2 cup)
- Chicken (8 oz), cooked & cubed
- Ginger (1/2 tbsp), ground, optional
- Apple (1/2 cup), chopped
- Raisins (2 tbsp)
- Celery (1/2 cup), chopped

**Instructions**
- Mix all ingredients together carefully.

- It's best to keep it in the fridge for a few hours to allow the flavors to meld.

*Calories 180, Protein 120 g, Sodium 90 mg, Potassium 70 mg, Phosphorus 100 mg, Calcium 20 mg*

## Chicken Casserole
*Time: 40 Mins, Serves: 4, Skill: Easy*

### Ingredients
- Water (350ml)
- Carrots (2 medium), peeled and sliced
- Vegetable oil (1 tbsp)
- Salt (1/4 tsp)
- Fresh parsley (1 tbsp), chopped
- Onion (1 medium), chopped
- Lean chicken (1 kg)
- White pepper (1/4 tsp)

### Instructions
- Fry the onion in a skillet with vegetable oil.
- Add the chicken and cook until it is golden colored.
- Add the water and carrots, and proceed to cook until the chicken is tender.
- Cook, stirring occasionally until the carrots and meat are completely cooked.
- Season with pepper, salt, and finely chopped parsley.

*Calories 331, Protein 20 g, Sodium 125 mg, Potassium 386 mg, Phosphorus 216 mg, Calcium 71 mg*

## Turkey Waldorf salad
*Time: 40 Mins, Serves: 4, Skill: Easy*

### Ingredients
- Mayonnaise (1/4 cup)
- Cooked turkey breast (12 oz.), unsalted
- Apple juice (2 tbsp)
- Celery (1 cup)
- Red apples (3 medium)
- Onion (1/2 cup

### Instructions
- Cut the turkey into cubes. Dice the apples and celery and finely slice the onion.
- In a medium mixing bowl, combine the turkey, apple, celery, and onion.
- In a mixing cup, add the mayonnaise and apple juice. Stir all together until it's well blended.
- Refrigerate before serving.

*Calories 200, Protein 101 g, Sodium 81 mg, Potassium 90 mg, Phosphorus 95 mg, Calcium 13 mg*

## Chicken Stew
*Time: 1 Hour 35 Mins, Serves: 8, Skill: Medium*

### Ingredients
- Chicken broth, low-sodium (2, 10 1/2-oz cans)
- Black pepper (1/4 tsp)
- Frozen carrots (1 10-oz bag)
- Dried basil (1//4 tsp)
- Sliced okra (1 10-oz bag), frozen
- Onions (1 cup), sliced
- Vegetable oil (3 tbsps.)
- Chicken breast (2 lbs.), cut into bite-size pieces
- All-purpose flour (2 tbsps.)
- Garlic cloves (2), minced
- Green peppers (3/4 cup)

### Instructions
- In a pot on medium-high heat, pour in the oil and fry the meat.
- Take the chicken out of the pan and set it aside.
- Sauté the garlic, onion, and pepper together in the pan.
- Cook for 2 to 3 minutes after applying the flour, stirring often. Add the chicken broth.
- Continue to cook until the chicken and broth have reached a boil.
- Cook for about 10 minutes then add the black pepper, carrots, and basil and cover it in foil. When the gravy cooks, it will thicken.
- After adding the okra, cook for another 5-10 minutes.
- Arrange on a bed of steaming white rice.

*Calories 195, Protein 115 g, Sodium 115 mg, Potassium 90 mg, Phosphorus 96 mg, Calcium 20 mg*

## Salisbury Steak
*Time: 1 Hour 30 Mins, Serves: 4, Skill: Medium*

### Ingredients
- Onion (1 small), chopped
- Black pepper (1 tsp)
- Green pepper (1/2 cup), chopped
- Egg (1)
- Chopped steak, or lean ground beef (1 lb.)
- Vegetable oil (1 tbsp)
- Water (1/2 cup)

- Corn starch (1 tbsp)

**Instructions**

- Combine the meat, onion, black pepper, egg, and green pepper in a mixing bowl. Once mixed, shape into patties.
- In a pan, heat the oil, then add the patties and sear on all sides.
- After including half of the water, boil for 15 minutes. Remove the patties from the pan and set them aside.
- Combine the beef drippings, remaining water, and corn starch in a pan. Stir the gravy to thicken it as its heating.
- Pour the sauce over the patties and serve right away.

*Calories 200, Protein 100 g, Sodium 81 mg, Potassium 40 mg, Phosphorus 96 mg, Calcium 13 mg*

## Special Pizza

*Time: 1 Hour and 30 Mins, Serves: 6, Skill: Medium*

**Ingredients for crust:**

- Active dry yeast (1 tbsp)
- Vegetable shortening (2 tbsp)
- Granulated sugar (1 tbs)
- All-purpose flour (2 cups)
- Water (1 cup)

**Ingredients for Pizza:**

- Onions (1/2 cup), diced
- Italian seasoning (1 tbsp)
- Chili powder (1 tbsp)
- Garlic powder (1/2 tbsp)
- Lean ground beef, chicken or turkey (1/2 lb.)
- Green peppers (1/2 cup), diced
- Italian seasoning (1/2 tsp)
- Sharp cheddar cheese (4 oz), reduced-fat, grated
- Tomato paste (1/4 cup)
- Onion powder (1/2 tbsp)
- Vegetable oil (1/2 cup)

**Instructions**

- Preheat the oven to 425 °F.
- In a frying pan, brown the meat of your choice in vegetable oil. In a mixing dish, combine the powdered onion, Italian seasoning, and garlic.
- Cook until the meat is brown, then add the powder.
- Drain the fat by rubbing the meat on paper towels. Combine the chili powder, tomato paste and Italian seasoning to prepare the pizza sauce.
- In a bowl, combine and knead the dry yeast, vegetable shortening, sugar, flour, & water to make the crust. Leave it to rest.
- Once the dough has rested, stretch it evenly over the pizza plate with both hands.
- Spread the sauce evenly over the pizza dough and sprinkle half a cup of cheese on top.
- Bake for 15-20 minutes in a preheated oven.
- Take it out of the oven and sprinkle the leftover cheese, meat of your choice, green peppers, and onions on top.
- Return it to the oven for a final 10 minutes.

*Calories 140, Protein 80 g, Sodium 81 mg, Potassium 45 mg, Phosphorus 90 mg, Calcium 20 mg*

## Homemade Pan Sausage (Chicken)

*Time: 1 Hour 20 Mins, Serves: 6, Skill: Easy*

**Ingredients**

- Ground sage (2 tsp)
- Fresh lean chicken (1lb.), ground
- Granulated sugar (2 tsp)
- Ground black pepper (1 tsp)
- Ground red pepper (1/2 tsp)
- Basil (1 tsp), optional
- Cooking spray

**Instructions**

- Preheat the oven to 350 °F and pulverize the chicken.
- To make sausages, mix all of the ingredients thoroughly.
- To produce a patty, take two teaspoons of the meat mixture and shape it into a sausage.
- Transfer sausages to an ovenproof dish and bake until cooked through.

*Calories 201, Protein 115 g, Sodium 81 mg, Potassium 90 mg, Phosphorus 96 mg, Calcium 13 mg*

## Basic Chicken Loaf

*Time: 1 hour and 40 Mins, Serves: 4, Skill: Medium*

**Ingredients**

- Lean chicken (1lb.), ground, boneless
- Green bell pepper (1/2 cup), diced
- Water (1/4 cup)
- Egg white (1)

- Lemon juice (1 tbsp)
- Plain bread crumbs (1/2 cup)
- Onion powder (1/2 tsp)
- Italian seasoning (1/2 tsp)
- Onions (1/2 cup), chopped
- Black pepper (1/4 tsp)

**Instructions**
- Preheat the oven to 200ºF.
- Squeeze the juice of a lemon onto the poultry.
- Mix the remaining components in a dish.
- Gently fold in the meat.
- Cook the loaf in a skillet for 45 minutes.

*Calories 210, Protein 120 g, Sodium 90 mg, Potassium 45 mg, Phosphorus 80 mg, Calcium 13 mg*

## Stir Fry Meal
*Time: 40 Mins, Serves: 4, Skill: Easy*

**Ingredients**
- Frozen stir fry vegetables (1 10-oz. package)
- Low sodium soy sauce (1/2 tbsp)
- Rice (2 cups), cooked
- Cooking oil (2 tbsp)
- Chicken breasts (2 medium), cut in bite-size pieces

**Instructions**
- Heat the oil in a 9x10' pan on high heat.
- Add the chicken.
- Add the vegetables and toss to combine.
- Mix thoroughly with the soy sauce.
- Lower the heat to medium-high and roast, uncovered, for 3 to 5 minutes, or until the chicken is ready. Stirring occasionally.
- Serve with rice.

*Calories 145, Protein 100 g, Sodium 81 mg, Potassium 70 mg, Phosphorus 90 mg, Calcium 15 mg*

## New Orleans-Style Rice Dressing
*Time: 1 Hour and 5 Mins, Serves: 6, Skill: Easy*

**Ingredients**
- Vegetable oil (2 tbsp)
- Green peppers (1/4 cup), chopped
- Celery (1/4 cup), chopped
- Lean turkey (1lb.), ground
- Cayenne pepper (1/2 tsp)
- All-purpose flour (2 tbsp)
- Garlic clove (1), chopped
- Onion (1/4 cup), chopped
- Rice (2 cups), cooked
- Green onions (1/4 cup), chopped
- Chicken broth (1 cup), low sodium

**Instructions**
- Preheat oven to 175 ºF.
- Heat the oil in a pan, add the meat, and cook until browned over medium heat.
- Remove the meat from the pan and dry it on a paper towel.
- In a pan, brown the flour to create a thick roux.
- Add the celery, onions, garlic and peppers and cook until they are tender. Apply the roux to the meat.
- Fill the dish halfway with fried rice and turkey.
- Gently drizzle in a tiny volume of low sodium broth until the mixture is moist. Add water if the mixture is too dry.
- Put half a gallon of water into a 12-quart baking dish.
- Cook for 20 minutes.

*Calories 150, Protein 80 g, Sodium 81 mg, Potassium 31 mg, Phosphorus 96 mg, Calcium 13 mg*

## Fajitas
*Time: 1 hour and 30 Mins, Serves: 6, Skill: Medium*

**Ingredients**
- Dry cilantro (1/2 tsp)
- Flour tortillas (4)
- Vegetable spray
- Vegetable oil (2 tbsp)
- Raw chicken strips (1 1/2 lb.), peeled and deveined
- Chili powder (2 tsp)
- Cumin (1/2 tsp)
- Lemon or lime juice (2 tbsp)
- Green and red pepper (1/4), sliced lengthwise
- White onion (1/2), sliced lengthwise

**Instructions**
- Preheat the oven to 300ºF.
- Heat the vegetable oil in a non-stick pan over medium heat.
- Add the seasonings, lemon or lime juice, and chicken; simmer for 5 to 10 minutes, until meat is tender.
- In a pan, roast the onion and pepper for 1 to 2 minutes.

- Take it off the heat and add the coriander.
- Bake the tortillas covered in foil in the oven. Cook for a maximum of 10 minutes.
- Spoon the tortilla mix into each tortilla, fold as desired and serve.

*Calories 343, Protein 24 g, Sodium 281 mg, Potassium 331 mg, Phosphorus 196 mg, Calcium 23 mg*

## White Bread Dressing
*Time: 1 hour and 10 Mins, Serves: 4, Skill: Easy*

**Ingredients**
- Garlic powder (1/4 tsp)
- Chicken broth (1/4 cup), unsalted
- Margarine (2 tbsp)
- Onions (1/4 cup), chopped
- Plain bread crumbs (1 1/2 cups) or 3 slices bread, crumbled
- Celery (1/4 cup), chopped
- Poultry seasoning (1 tsp)

**Instructions**
- In a small saucepan, melt the margarine. Toss in the onions and cook until they go tender.
- Add celery, poultry seasoning, chicken broth, and garlic powder.
- Add the bread crumbs, stirring continuously to avoid burning them.
- Place the mixture in a small baking dish.
- Preheat the oven to 375 °F and bake for 30 minutes.
- Add a little water if the dressing is too hard.

*Calories 190, Protein 110 g, Sodium 81 mg, Potassium 40 mg, Phosphorus 96 mg, Calcium 13 mg*

## Cornbread Dressing
*Time: 1 hour and 35 Mins, Serves: 5, Skill: Medium*

**Ingredients for cornbread:**
- Plain cornmeal (2 cups)
- All-purpose flour (1 1/2 cups)
- Sugar (1/4 cup)
- Baking powder (1/2 tsp)
- Water (2 1/2 cups)
- Egg (1)
- Vegetable oil (2 tbsp)

**Ingredients for dressing:**
- Chicken parts and giblets (2 cups)
- Water (4 cups)
- Onion (1 cup), chopped
- Celery (1/2 cup), chopped
- Green peppers (1/2 cup), chopped
- Black pepper (1 tsp)
- Poultry seasoning (1 tsp)
- Onion powder (1 tsp)
- Sage (1 tsp)

**Instructions for cornbread:**
- Preheat oven to 410 °F.
- Combine the sugar, flour, cornmeal, and baking powder in a mixing bowl.
- Add the water, egg, and oil and beat together to form a smooth dough.
- Place it on a greased 9" x 9" square baking dish.
- Bake until the color changes to a golden-brown.
- Set aside to cool.

**Dressing recommendations:**
- Put the chicken parts and giblets in a big pot of boiling water after washing them.
- Combine the celery, green pepper, onion, and black pepper in a separate pot with water and bring to a boil.
- Simmer for 30 minutes, or until vegetables are soft.
- Set aside two cups.
- Drain the meat once it is cooked, and allow it to cool.
- Remove the meat from the bone and whisk together the remaining dressing components.
- Add all components with two cups of chicken broth to keep the mixture moist.
- Spread the mixture onto the baking sheet to bake.
- Bake until golden brown at 410°F.

*Calories 210, Protein 115 g, Sodium 90 mg, Potassium 46 mg, Phosphorus 92 mg, Calcium 15 mg*

## Giblet Gravy
*Time: 40 Mins, Serves: 4, Skill: Easy*

**Ingredients**
- All-purpose flour (1 tbsp)
- Chicken broth (2 cups)
- Poultry liver or giblets (1-2 boiled), chopped
- Hard-boiled egg (1), sliced or chopped

**Instructions**
- Combine 1 tablespoon of flour with the broth and steam until fluffy.

- In a saucepan, boil the remaining broth over low heat, stirring continuously.
- In a dish, combine the giblets and the egg.
- Stir continuously until the desired thickness is achieved (approximately 5 minutes).

*Calories 180, Protein 130 g, Sodium 85 mg, Potassium 65 mg, Phosphorus 90 mg, Calcium 13 mg*

## Herb Rice Casserole

*Time: 1 hour and 35 Mins, Serves: 2, Skill: Medium*

**Ingredients**
- Parsley flakes (1/2 tsp)
- Vegetable oil (1 tbsp)
- Fresh green onions (3), chopped
- White rice (1 cup), uncooked
- Chicken stock (2 cups), unsalted
- Green bell pepper (1/4 cup), chopped
- Chives (1 tbsp)

**Instructions**
- Preheat oven to 175 °F.
- Combine all the ingredients in a casserole dish ensuring they are thoroughly mixed.
- Bake for 45 to 50.

*Calories 190, Protein 115 g, Sodium 70 mg, Potassium 80 mg, Phosphorus 90 mg, Calcium 13 mg*

## Crunchy Chicken Nuggets

*Time: 1 hour and 25 Mins, Serves: 4, Skill: Medium*

**Ingredients**
- Seasoning salt (1/4 tbsp)
- Egg whites (2)
- Melted margarine or butter (1 tbsp)
- Ranch dressing (1 tbsp), reduced-fat, for dipping
- Water (1 tbsp)
- Ready-to-eat crispy rice cereal (2 1/2 cups)
- Paprika (1 1/2 tbsp)
- Chicken breasts (1lb.), boneless, skinless
- Garlic powder (1/8) tbsps.)
- Onion powder (1/8 tbsp)

**Instructions**
- Mix the egg whites and water in a dish.
- Combine the paprika, crispy rice cereal, powdered onion, salt, and powdered garlic on a large sheet of wax paper.
- Split the chicken into 1 1/2-inch pieces.
- Brush the white egg mixture on all sides of the chicken. Roll the chicken in the cereal blend.
- Place a baking sheet on top of an ungreased baking tin in a single layer. Brush the sheet with a smear of melted butter, then in a single layer add the chicken on top.
- Preheat oven to 450°F and bake for 12 minutes, or until no longer pink in the center.
- Serve immediately with a dipping sauce (reduced-fat ranch dressing).

*Calories 200, Protein 125 g, Sodium 85 mg, Potassium 55 mg, Phosphorus 80 mg, Calcium 15 mg*

## Fiesta Lime Fajitas

*Time: 1 hour and 20 Mins, Serves: 4, Skill: Medium*

**Ingredients**
- Lime Seasoning Blend, Mrs. Dash Fiesta (4 tbsp)
- Olive oil (2 tbsp)
- Drumettes of chicken (1lb.)

**Instructions**
- Preheat the oven to 350 °F.
- Drizzle a little olive oil over the chicken drumettes.
- Sprinkle Lime Seasoning Blend, Mrs. Dash Fiesta on all sides of the chicken.
- Bake for 30 minutes, or until the chicken is fully cooked.
- Serve with tortillas or rice.

*Calories 180, Protein 100 g, Sodium 85 mg, Potassium 55 mg, Phosphorus 80 mg, Calcium 15 mg*

## Chicken Tikka

*Time: 1 hour and 30 Mins, Serves: 4, Skill: Hard*

**Ingredients**
- Lemon juice (1 tsp)
- Natural yogurt, low in fat (3 tbsp)
- Curry paste (1 tbsp)
- Chicken breasts (2), boneless, skinless

**Instructions**
- Combine the yogurt and curry paste in a mixing dish.
- Add the chicken and lemon juice and combine well.
- Refrigerate for 1 hour, or overnight if you have time, to encourage the flavors to infuse.
- Place the coated chicken under a preheated grill for around 20 minutes, or until the juices flow clear when pierced with a knife.

- Serve as the main course with boiled rice and a side salad, or as a sandwich in a tortilla wrap of sliced lettuce.

*Calories 199, Protein 100 g, Sodium 80 mg, Potassium 45 mg, Phosphorus 90 mg, Calcium 15 mg*

## Chicken Vegetable Salad

*Time: 40 Mins, Serves: 4, Skill: Easy*

**Ingredients**
- Green pepper (1/2 cup), finely chopped
- Pimentos (3 tbsp), diced
- Celery (1/2 cup), finely diced
- Salad dressing or light mayonnaise (1/2 cup)
- Cooked chicken (1 1/2 cups), diced
- Lemon juice (1 tbsp)
- Onions (1/2 cup), finely chopped

**Instructions**
- In a large mixing bowl, combine the green pepper, onions, chicken, celery, and pimento.
- In a mixing cup, combine the mayonnaise and lemon juice. Pour the sauce over the chicken and vegetable mix.
- Combine all components, seal, and place in the refrigerator to cool before serving.

*Calories 180, Protein 110 g, Sodium 81 mg, Potassium 40 mg, Phosphorus 96 mg, Calcium 13 mg*

## Chicken'N Rice

*Time: 1 hour and 40 Mins, Serves: 4, Skill: Hard*

**Ingredients**
- Onion powder (1 tbsp)
- Garlic powder (1/2 tbsp)
- Bay leaves (1 tbsp), crushed, optional
- Rice (1 cup), uncooked
- Chicken parts (1 lb.)
- Vegetable oil (1 tbsp)
- Black pepper (1 tbsp)
- Water (4 cups)
- Poultry seasoning (1 tbsp)
- Onion (1/2 cup), chopped

**Instructions**
- Cover the chicken parts with water and add the poultry seasoning, black pepper, onion and garlic powder, and bay leaves. Place the mix in the oven. Cook until the chicken is fully tender.
- Strip the skin and meat from the bone and set aside two cups of the meat and broth.
- Combine the rice, olive oil, two cups of broth, and chicken meat in a pot. Bring it to a low boil over medium heat.
- Simmer on low heat for 20-25 minutes. Until eating, reheat it.

*Calories 170, Protein 100 g, Sodium 80 mg, Potassium 65 mg, Phosphorus 96 mg, Calcium 13 mg*

## Lemon Chicken

*Time: 1 hour and 15 Mins, Serves: 4, Skill: Medium*

**Ingredients**
- Poultry seasoning (1/4 tbsp)
- Chicken (2 1/2 lb.), cut as desired
- Crushed corn flakes (1 cup)
- Vegetable oil (4 tbsp)
- Black pepper (1 tbsp)
- Lemon juice (1 tbsp)
- All-purpose flour (1 cup)

**Instructions**
- Preheat the oven to 400 °F.
- Wash and dry the chicken parts vigorously before brushing with lemon juice.
- Mix together the cornflakes, black pepper, flour, and poultry seasoning in a bowl.
- Use vegetable oil to grease a baking sheet (about 1 inch deep).
- Toss the chicken with the other ingredients in a bag, starting with the larger pieces. Make sure to coat them thoroughly.
- Place the coated chicken in a baking dish.
- Cook for 20-30 minutes on each side in a preheated oven.

*Calories 180, Protein 105 g, Sodium 100 mg, Potassium 70 mg, Phosphorus 90 mg, Calcium 13 mg*

## Stuffed Green Peppers

*Time: 1 hour and 45 Mins, Serves: 6, Skill: Hard*

**Ingredients**
- Green peppers (6 small), seeded with tops removed
- Vegetable oil (2 tbsp)
- Rice (1 1/2 cups), cooked
- Ground lean beef, turkey, or chicken (1/2 lb.)
- Sugar (1/2 tbsp)
- Onions (1/4 cup), chopped
- Italian seasoning (2 tbsp)
- Paprika

- Celery (1/4 cup), chopped
- Lemon juice (2 tbsp)
- Black pepper (1 tbsp)
- Celery seed (1 tbsp)

**Instructions**
- Preheat the oven to 325 °F.
- Heat the oil in a saucepan. Add your choice of meat.
- Stir in the celery and onions after the meat has browned.
- Mix all ingredients in a saucepan except the paprika and green peppers. Switch off the heat. Combine all components in a mixing bowl.
- Fill the peppers with the mixture. Place in a dish, sealed or foil-coated. Bake in the oven for 30 minutes. Sprinkle the paprika over the top when serving.

*Calories 140, Protein 80 g, Sodium 81 mg, Potassium 45 mg, Phosphorus 85 mg, Calcium 13 mg*

## Chicken Salad Delight
*Time: 1 hour and 30 Mins, Serves: 4, Skill: Easy*

**Ingredients**
- Chicken (2 cups), diced
- Lemon juice (1 tbsp)
- Dry mustard (1 tbsp)
- Mayonnaise (1/2 cup)
- Celery (1/3 cup), chopped
- Black pepper (1/4 tbsp)
- Parsley (1 tbsp), dried, optional
- Fresh onion (1/4 cup), chopped
- Fresh green pepper (1/4 cup), chopped

**Instructions**
- Combine the chicken, parsley, onion, celery, green pepper, and lemon juice in a big mixing bowl.
- Combine the vinegar, black pepper, mustard, and mayonnaise in a mixing dish. After that, pour in the chicken mixture and thoroughly combine the ingredients.

*Calories 160, Protein 125 g, Sodium 70 mg, Potassium 65 mg, Phosphorus 96 mg, Calcium 13 mg*

## Jalapeno Pepper Chicken
*Time: 1 hour and 20 Mins, Serves: 4, Skill: Medium*

**Ingredients**
- Vegetable oil (3 tbsp)
- Black pepper (1/4 tbsp)
- Chicken (2-3 lbs.). skin and fat removed
- Ground nutmeg (1/2 tbsp)
- Jalapeño peppers (2 tsp), finely seeded and chopped
- Onion (1), sliced into rings
- Chicken bouillon (1 ½ cups), Low sodium

**Instructions**
- Heat the oil in a big skillet and brown the chicken parts, then set them aside.
- Add the onion rings to the hot oil and cook until they are translucent. Add the bouillon and bring to a low boil, stirring often.
- Season the chicken with nutmeg and black pepper and return it to the skillet. Simmer for 35 minutes, covered, or until the chicken is tender.
- Cook for about a minute after adding the jalapeno peppers.

*Calories 190, Protein 110 g, Sodium 90 mg, Potassium 45 mg, Phosphorus 80 mg, Calcium 15 mg*

## Easy low sodium Lemon chicken
*Time: 1 hour and 40 Mins, Serves: 4, Skill: Hard*

**Ingredients**
- Chicken breasts (4), boneless, skinless, 1/2-inch thickness
- Fresh ground black pepper (1/2 tsp)
- Lemon juice (2 tbsp)
- Vegetable oil (1 tbsp)
- Lemon (1), sliced
- White wine (1/3 cup)
- Dried oregano (2 tbsp)

**Instructions**
- Preheat a frying pan for around 2 minutes on medium/high heat. In a mixing cup, combine the oil, white wine, and lemon juice.
- In a pan, toss the chicken breasts in with half of the oregano and half of the pepper, and steam for 3-4 minutes. After flipping the breasts and inserting the remaining oregano and pepper, cook for 3-4 minutes more. According to an instant-read thermometer, the internal temperature must be 165 °F. Remove the chicken from the pan and set it aside.
- Add the lemon slices to the liquid in the skillet and heat for a few minutes, or before the lemons start to caramelize. Reduce the heat to low heat and

continue to cook until the mixture has cooled to around half its original temperature.
- Place the chicken on a plate and serve it with the sauce and lemons.

*Calories 175, Protein 145 g, Sodium 90 mg, Potassium 60 mg, Phosphorus 95 mg, Calcium 16 mg*

## BBQ Chicken Pita Pizza
*Time: 1 hour and 35 Mins, Serves: 8, Skill: Hard*

**Ingredients**
- Barbecue sauce (3 tbsp), low-sodium
- Pita bread (2), 6-1/2-inch size
- Garlic powder (1/8 tbsp)
- Chicken (4 oz.), cooked
- Purple onion (1/4 cup)
- Feta cheese (2 tbsp), crumbled

**Instructions**
- Preheat the oven to 350 °F.
- Spray a baking sheet with nonstick cooking spray and spread out two pitas on it.
- Take 1-1/2 tbsp of barbecue sauce and distribute it evenly over each pita
- Peel and chop the onion and scatter the pieces over the pitas.
- Place chicken cubes on pita bread.
- Brush feta cheese and garlic powder on top of the pitas.
- Bake in the oven for 11 to 13 minutes.

*Calories 160, Protein 115 g, Sodium 75 mg, Potassium 50 mg, Phosphorus 90 mg, Calcium 15 mg*

## Curried Turkey and Rice
*Time: 1 hour and 30 Mins, Serves: 4, Skill: Hard*

**Ingredients**
- Vegetable oil (1 tbsp)
- Chicken broth (1 cup), low sodium
- White rice (2 cups), cooked
- Turkey breast (8 x 1lb.), cut into cutlets
- Sugar (1 tbsp)
- Onion (1), chopped
- Margarine (1 tbsp), unsalted
- Creamer (1/2 cup), non-dairy
- Curry powder (2 tbsp)
- Flour (2 tbsp)

**Instructions**
- In a large skillet, heat the oil. Toss in the turkey. Cook, rotating once, for about 10 minutes, or until it is no longer pink. Put the turkey on a platter. Cover it in foil.
- In the same skillet, melt the margarine. Add the onion and curry powder. Cook, stirring occasionally, for 5 minutes.
- In a mixer, combine the broth, non-dairy creamer, and sugar. Continually stir until the paste thickens.
- Place the turkey back into the skillet. Cook for around 2 minutes, or until the turkey is completely cooked.
- Serve on a bed of white rice.

*Calories 150, Protein 105 g, Sodium 80 mg, Potassium 45 mg, Phosphorus 90 mg, Calcium 14 mg*

## Polynesian Turkey Kabobs
*Time: 1 hour and 35 Mins, Serves: 4, Skill: Hard*

**Ingredients**
- Egg (1)
- Onion (1/4 cup), chopped
- Ginger (1 tsp), ground
- Garlic clove (1), crushed
- Pineapple chunks in juice (1 x 20-oz can), drained and reserving 1/3 cup juice
- Red pepper (1 large), cut into 22 pieces
- Green pepper (1 large), cut into 23 pieces
- Reserved pineapple juice (1/3 cup)
- Ground raw turkey (1 lb.)
- Unsalted crackers (1/3 cup), crushed five crackers
- Margarine (2 tbsp), melted
- Orange marmalade (2 tbsp)
- Ginger (1 1/2 tsp), ground

**Instructions**
- Combine the egg, onion, ground raw turkey, garlic clove, crackers and ginger in a mixing bowl. Make meatballs from them (30).
- Place the meatballs, pineapple pieces and peppers onto 15 x 8" wooden skewers. Then place them on a baking sheet and bake for 30 minutes (broiler).
- Combine the margarine, pineapple juice, marmalade, and ginger in a mixing cup. Using a brush, brush the kabobs. Broil for 20 minutes, rotating once, and basting with sauce at 4 inches from the heat source.

*Calories 180, Protein 125 g, Sodium 85 mg, Potassium 40 mg, Phosphorus 96 mg, Calcium 13 mg*

## Turkey Fajitas
*Time: 5 hours 15 Mins, Serves: 4, Skill: Hard*

**Ingredients**
- Lime juice (2 tbsp)
- Fresh cilantro (2 tbsp), chopped
- Garlic (1/4 tsp), minced
- Light sour cream (1/2 cup)
- Flour tortillas, 7-inch (10)
- Red onion (1 tbsp), chopped
- Pepper (1/4 tsp)
- Garlic clove (1), minced
- Boneless turkey breast (1 lb.)
- Chili powder (1 tsp)
- Fresh coriander (1 tbsp), chopped
- Oil (1 tbsp)
- Lettuce (3 cups), shredded

**Instructions**
- Combine the turkey, pepper, 1 minced garlic clove, chili powder, lime juice, 1 tablespoon cilantro, and oil in a mixing bowl.
- Cover and marinate in the refrigerator for 3 hours or more.
- In a cup, mix the chili, 2 teaspoons cilantro, onion, and 1/4 teaspoon garlic to make the salsa. Allow for it to sit for 1 hour.
- Broil the turkey for 10 minutes on either side, 6 inches away from the heat source. Chop the strips into small pieces.
- When the turkey is cooking, wrap the tortillas in foil and steam them for 8 minutes in the oven.
- To serve, wrap fluffy tortillas around the turkey, salsa, lettuce, and sour cream.

*Calories 347, Protein 26 g, Sodium 261 mg, Potassium 321 mg, Phosphorus 186 mg, Calcium 25 mg*

## Oregano Turkey Burger
*Time: 25 Mins, Serves: 4, Skill: Easy*

**Ingredients**
- Oregano (1/4 tbsp)
- Slender ground turkey (1 lb.)
- Black pepper (1/4 tbsp)
- Ground thyme (1/4 tbsp)
- Lemon juice (1 tbsp)

**Instructions**
- Mix all the ingredients thoroughly.
- Shape into 4 small patties about ¾ inches thick.
- Prepare in a skillet or broiler tray that is thinly greased.
- Broil for 10 to15 minutes, once rotated, about 3" from the flame.

*Calories 155, Protein 111 g, Sodium 75 mg, Potassium 55 mg, Phosphorus 85 mg, Calcium 14 mg*

## Batty Bites
*Time: 1 hour and 20 Mins, Serves: 6, Skill: Medium*

**Ingredients**
- Wheat bread slices (12)
- Smoked turkey (1/2 lb.), sliced
- Catalina dressing

**Instructions**
- Using a bat-shaped cookie cutter, carve two bat-shaped bats out of a slice of bread.
- Stack two turkey bits together to create bat-shaped cutouts.
- Repeat for the remaining turkey.
- Split the turkey into half of the bread forms (double-stacked).
- Drizzle 1 tablespoon dressing over the turkey and cover with the remaining bread cutouts.

*Calories 155, Protein 120 g, Sodium 90 mg, Potassium 45 mg, Phosphorus 80 mg, Calcium 15 mg*

## Slow Turkey Meatloaf
*Time: 4 hours 20 Mins, Serves: 6, Skill: Hard*

**Ingredients**
- Mustard (1 tsp), prepared
- Turkey, 93% lean (1 1/2 lbs.), ground
- Brown sugar (1/4 cup)
- Egg (1 medium), beaten
- Vegetable oil (1 tbsp)
- Oats (1/2 cup)
- Garlic clove (1), minced
- Onion (1/2 cup), diced
- Balsamic vinegar (1 tbsp)
- Black pepper (1/2 tsp)

**Instructions**
- Combine the vegetable oil, ground turkey, oats, egg, onion, black pepper, and garlic in a loaf tin and blend well.
- Shape a "sling" for the meatloaf by wrapping two sheets of baking paper across the bottom and sides of the crockpot. Using the baking paper, cover the meatloaf.

- Toss the meatloaf with a mixture of sugar, mustard, and vinegar.
- Cook for 8 hours on low heat.
- When it's finished, raise the four strips of baking paper and clear them from the crockpot.
- Dismantle it and cut it into little parts.

*Calories 140, Protein 100 g, Sodium 80 mg, Potassium 55 mg, Phosphorus 96 mg, Calcium 13 mg*

## Easy Turkey Sloppy Joes
*Time: 1 hour 10 Mins, Serves: 6, Skill: Easy*

**Ingredients**
- Red onion (1/2 cup)
- Hamburger buns (6)
- Brown sugar (2 tbsp).
- Bell pepper green (1/2 cup)
- Turkey, 7% fat, (1-1/2 lb.), ground
- Chicken grilling seasoning blend (1 tbsp)
- Worcestershire sauce (1 tbsp)
- Tomato sauce (1 cup), low-sodium

**Instructions**
- Chop the bell pepper and onion into tiny bits.
- Combine the vegetables and ground turkey in a wide skillet and cook over medium-high heat until the turkey is completely cooked. Ensure that the solution does not evaporate.
- In a shallow dish, combine the grilling spices, tomato sauce, brown sugar, and Worcestershire sauce.
- Combine the meat and sauce in a large mixing bowl. Reduce the heat to low and cook for another ten minutes.
- Fill burger buns with 6 parts of turkey mixture and serve.

*Calories 180, Protein 120 g, Sodium 95 mg, Potassium 115 mg, Phosphorus 100 mg, Calcium 13 mg*

## Roasted Turkey
*Time: 4 hours and 40 Mins, Serves: 8, Skill: Hard*

**Ingredients**
- Poultry seasoning (1 tsp)
- Fresh thyme (4 sprigs)
- Turkey stock (1 cup), low-sodium, from turkey giblets
- Fresh parsley (4 sprigs)
- Turke (12 pounds), fresh or frozen - avoid self-basting
- Fresh rosemary (4 sprigs)
- Unsalted butter (1/2 cup)
- Fresh sage (4 sprigs)

**Instructions**
- Defrost the turkey in the fridge for 3 days before roasting if you are not using fresh produce. Check the plastic wrap on the turkey to determine the cooking time.
- Preheat the oven to 425 °F.
- Remove the collar and giblet pocket from the cavity of the turkey. Using a tap wash the turkey.
- Dry it with clean paper towels after soaking it with cool water.
- Using the thumbs, remove the turkey breast skin and drumsticks. Rub poultry seasoning under the surface of the turkey. Place rosemary, parsley, sage, and thyme sprigs between the skin and the turkey meat.
- Put a meat thermometer into the thickest section of the thigh.
- Rub the turkey breast with butter or oil, and position it on a shelf in a roasting pan. Aluminum foil may be used to partly cover it. After baking for 30 minutes or more, decrease the heat to 325 °F.
- After 10 to 15 minutes, begin whisking the giblet supply and pan juices into the turkey. During the last 30 minutes of preparation, remove the foil from the roasting pan. Cook for 3 to 4 hours, or before an instant-read thermometer reads 165 °F.
- Let the roasted turkey sit for 30 minutes before carving.

*Calories 160, Protein 105 g, Sodium 70 mg, Potassium 65 mg, Phosphorus 96 mg, Calcium 17 mg*

## Homemade Pan Sausage (Turkey)
*Time: 55 Mins, Serves: 4, Skill: Easy*

**Ingredients**
- Ground sage (2 tsp)
- Cooking spray
- Fresh lean turkey (1lb.), ground
- Granulated sugar (2 tsp)
- Ground black pepper (1 tsp)
- Ground red pepper (1/2 tsp)
- Basil (1 tsp), optional

**Instructions**
- If possible, buy turkey already ground, if not you will have to do this yourself.

- In a large mixing bowl, combine all the ingredients to form a sausage.
- Take measurements using two teaspoons of the turkey mixture and produce individual sausages.
- Fry in a skillet or bake in the oven until cooked through.

*Calories 170, Protein 115 g, Sodium 85 mg, Potassium 75 mg, Phosphorus 80 mg, Calcium 18 mg*

## Barbecue Cups
*Time: 25 Mins, Serves: 4, Skill: Easy*

**Ingredients**
- Low-fat refrigerator biscuits (1- 10-ounce package)
- Lean ground turkey (3/4 lb.)
- Garlic powder (dash)
- Spicy barbecue sauce (1/2 cup)
- Onion flakes (2 tbsp)

**Instructions**
- Combine the barbecue sauce, garlic powder flakes, and turkey in a mixing bowl. Make a rigorous mix.
- Press each biscuit into the muffin tin by flattening it.
- Spoon the turkey mixture into the center of the biscuit cup.
- Place in the oven until cooked through.

*Calories 190, Protein 110 g, Sodium 75 mg, Potassium 65 mg, Phosphorus 96 mg, Calcium 14 mg*

## Rotini with Mock Italian Sausage
*Time: 1 hour and 30 Mins, Serves: 4, Skill: Medium*

**Ingredients**
- Rotini pasta (4 oz.), uncooked
- Lean ground turkey (3/4 lb.)
- Red pepper (1/4 tsp), crushed
- Tomato paste (3 tbsp)
- Unsalted can of tomatoes (190 grams), chopped
- Parmesan cheese (2 tbsp), grated
- Onion (1 cup), chopped
- Garlic clove (1), minced
- Celery (1/2 cup), chopped
- Italian seasoning (3/4 tsp)
- Fennel seeds (1/4 tsp)

**Instructions**
- Prepare the rotini pasta according to the package instructions. Drain.
- Brown the turkey in a nonstick skillet over medium heat, stirring to crumble it. Using a paper towel, absorb the excess liquid.
- Combine the garlic, onion, seasonings, and celery with the turkey in the skillet. Cook for 3 minutes, stirring continuously.
- Add the tomatoes and tomato paste. Cook for 15 minutes on low heat, partly sealed.
- Serve on rotini with a sprinkling of cheese.

*Calories 170, Protein 100 g, Sodium 86 mg, Potassium 45 mg, Phosphorus 80 mg, Calcium 15 mg*

## Turkey & Noodles
*Time: 1 hour and 10 Mins, Serves: 2, Skill: Easy*

**Ingredients**
- Fresh lean turkey (2 lb.), ground
- Green onions (1/2 cup), chopped
- Green pepper (1/2 cup), chopped
- Black pepper (1 tbsp)
- Italian seasoning (1 tbsp)
- Dry elbow macaroni (2 cups)
- Olive or vegetable oil (1 tbsp)

**Instructions**
- Cook the macaroni in 4 cups of boiling water in a medium microwave. Enable it to boil for 5 minutes, or until the required tenderness is reached. Drain and set aside.
- Melt the vegetable oil in a big skillet over low heat. Cook, stirring periodically until the ground turkey is cooked through.
- In a large mixing cup, combine the onions, green peppers, black pepper, Italian seasoning, and baked macaroni. Make a rigorous mix.
- Boil, covered, before the desired temperature is reached, or warm for 5 minutes until serving.

*Calories 190, Protein 115 g, Sodium 90 mg, Potassium 55 mg, Phosphorus 100 mg, Calcium 15 mg*

# SEAFOOD AND FISH RECIPES

## Baked Salmon
*Time: 1 hour and 5 Mins, Serves: 4, Skill: Easy*

**Ingredients**
- Canned pimento (1/4 cup)
- Mayonnaise (1/2 cup)
- Salmon (14 oz.), no salt, drained
- Onion (2/3 cup), chopped
- Plain bread crumbs (1/4 cup)
- Green pepper (1/4 cup), diced
- Grated parmesan cheese (2 tsp)
- Non-stick cooking spray

**Instructions**
- Preheat the oven to 347 °F.
- Spray a baking tray with nonstick cooking spray.
- Combine the onion, mayonnaise, salmon, pimento, and pepper in a mixing bowl.
- Fill a baking jar halfway with the salmon mixture. On top, sprinkle bread crumbs and Parmesan cheese.
- Bake for 20 minutes, or until the topping is light brown (or until completely heated).

*Calories 120, Protein 105 g, Sodium 40 mg, Potassium 45 mg, Phosphorus 65 mg, Calcium 14 mg*

## Cilantro-Lime Cod
*Time: 40 Mins, Serves: 2, Skill: Easy*

**Ingredients**
- Fresh cilantro (1/2 cup), sliced
- Cod fillets (1 lb.)
- Mayonnaise (1/2 cup)
- Lime juice (2 tbsps.)

**Instructions**
- Blend the lime juice, mayonnaise, and sliced cilantro in a mixing cup. 1/4 cup sauce may be split and set aside in a bowl to pair with the cod.
- Drizzle the remaining mayonnaise mixture over the fish.
- Coat a skillet in cooking spray and heat on medium-high. Cook for about 8 minutes, turning once until the cod fillets are damp but firm.
- Toss with the cilantro-lime sauce leftover and serve.

*Calories 160, Protein 110 g, Sodium 65 mg, Potassium 40 mg, Phosphorus 35 mg, Calcium 20 mg*

## Fish Sticks
*Time: 55 Mins, Serves: 4, Skill: Easy*

**Ingredients**
- Cooking spray
- Tilapia fillets (3 x 1 lb.), cut into 1/2 by 3" strips
- Whole wheat, panko dry breadcrumbs (1 cup), or plain
- Plain cereal flakes, or whole grain (1 cup)
- Lemon pepper (1 tbsp)
- Salt (1/4 tbsp)
- Garlic powder (1/2 tbsp)
- Paprika (1/2 tbsp)
- All-purpose flour (1/2 cup)
- Egg whites (2 large), beaten

**Instructions**
- Preheat the oven to 450 °F.
- Spray a baking sheet with cooking spray and put it on a wire rack.
- In a food processor, add breadcrumbs, lemon pepper, cereal flakes, paprika, garlic powder, and salt.
- Blend or refine the paste until it is finely ground. Enable to cool in a shallow dish.
- In a second shallow dish, pound the egg whites, and in a third shallow dish, sift the flour.
- Dredge each fish strip in flour, then dip it in the egg and coat all sides in the breadcrumb mix.
- Place the rack that has been prepared into place. Before cooking, spray both sides of the breaded fish with cooking spray.
- Bake for 10 minutes, or until crisp and golden brown.

*Calories 180, Protein 120 g, Sodium 70 mg, Potassium 60 mg, Phosphorus 35 mg, Calcium 25 mg*

## Grilled Trout
*Time: 1 hour and 20 Mins, Serves: 2, Skill: Medium*

**Ingredients**
- Lemon pepper (1 tsp), salt free
- Paprika (1/2 tsp)
- Rainbow trout fillets (2 lb.)
- Salt (1/2 tsp)
- Cooking oil (1 tbsp)

## Instructions
- Preheat the grill to medium-high.
- Generously oil all sides of the trout fillets. Combine the spices in a bowl. Both fillets should be vigorously rubbed in the spices.
- Place the seasoned trout fillets on the preheated grill, skin side down. Grill for 4 minutes.
- Cook, flipping the fillets halfway through, for 3 to 5 minutes, or until the fish flakes easily with a fork.

*Calories 190, Protein 135 g, Sodium 70 mg, Potassium 45 mg, Phosphorus 50 mg, Calcium 20 mg*

## Fish Tacos
*Time: 1 hour and 5 Mins, Serves: 4, Skill: Easy*

### Ingredients
- Garlic powder (1 tbsp)
- Lemon juice (1/4 cup)
- Fish fillets (12-16 x 1 lb.), your desired fish
- Crackers (20) unsalted tops, crushed finely
- Butter or margarine (1/4 cup), unsalted
- Dill (2 tbsp)

### Instructions
- Preheat the oven to 400 °F.
- In a mixing cup, combine the crackers, lemon juice, dill, and garlic.
- Melt the margarine or butter in a saucepan.
- Dip the fish in melted butter, then roll it in the crumb mixture.
- In a baking tray, bake the fish for 8-10 minutes, or until flaky.

*Calories 155, Protein 110 g, Sodium 50 mg, Potassium 45 mg, Phosphorus 36 mg, Calcium 23 mg*

## Baked Fish
*Time: 1 hour and 10 Mins, Serves: 4, Skill: Medium*

### Ingredients
- Garlic powder (1 tbsp)
- Paprika (1 1/2 tbsp)
- Green pepper (1/4 medium)
- Parmesan cheese (2 tbsp)
- Trout fillets (4x oz.)
- Lemon (1 small)
- Black pepper (1 1/2 tbsp)
- Onion (1 small)

### Instructions
- Preheat the oven to 375 °F.
- Place the fish in an oiled baking tray or on aluminum foil.
- Season the fish with black pepper, garlic powder, and paprika on both sides.
- Thinly slice the green peppers and arrange them on top of the fish. Slice the onion into rings and place them on top of the fish.
- Squeeze the lemon over the trout and serve.
- Bake in the preheated oven for 30 minutes.
- Put the fried cod on a bed of parmesan cheese. Serve immediately.

*Calories 155, Protein 140 g, Sodium 70 mg, Potassium 52 mg, Phosphorus 35 mg, Calcium 18 mg*

## Easy low sodium Salmon with Lime and Herbs
*Time: 40 Mins, Serves: 4, Skill: Easy*

### Ingredients
- Fresh dill weed (2 tbsp), or, (1 teaspoon), dried & crumbled
- Limes (2)
- Fresh salmon fillets (4)
- Fresh thyme (12 sprigs)

### Instructions
- Place two salmon fillets on a big sheet of aluminum foil, and another one on top of the other (use enough foil to wrap carefully across the fillets with space to spare). Squeeze 1 lime over the salmon, and gently rub them with dill weed.
- Cut the second lime into thin slices and layer it on top of the fish slices. Place thyme sprigs on top and carefully fold the aluminum foil over them.
- Grill the pouches for 12-15 minutes, rotating once every 7 minutes, over medium heat. The fish will flake with a fork when it is cooked.

*Calories 180, Protein 125 g, Sodium 40 mg, Potassium 55 mg, Phosphorus 70 mg, Calcium 26 mg*

## Jollof Rice
*Time: 1 hour and 20 Mins, Serves: 2, Skill: Medium*

### Ingredients
- Long-grain white or brown rice (100g)
- Vegetable oil (1 tbsp)
- Garlic clove (1), chopped
- Onion (1), minced
- Stock cube (1/2), reduced salt
- Chili pepper (1), minced

**Instructions**
- Bring the rice to a boil and cook for 5 minutes.
- Clean and drain it with cold water to remove any lingering starch.
- Return the rice to a boil with the stock cube in 200 ml/3/4 pints cold water.
- Add the onions, vegetable oil, garlic, and chili pepper.
- Cook for 30 to 40 minutes, or until the water has evaporated completely.
- Serve with white fried cod and a selection of side salads.

*Calories 165, Protein 112 g, Sodium 35 mg, Potassium 45 mg, Phosphorus 80 mg, Calcium 30 mg*

# Lemon Baked Fish

*Time: 1 hour and 30 Mins, Serves: 2, Skill: Easy*

**Ingredients**
- Dried rosemary (1 pinch)
- Black pepper (1 pinch)
- White boneless fish fillets (4 x 100g)
- Rind of lemon (1), grated
- Lemon juice (2 tbsp)
- Butter/margarine (1 tbsp), reduced-salt

**Instructions**
- Preheat the oven to 425 °F.
- Arrange the fish on a single sheet in a baking dish. Rub the butter/margarine, grated lemon rind, lemon juice, rosemary, & seasoning on the fish fillets.
- Cover the fish in foil & bake for 25 mins, or before it flakes easily when measured with a fork.
- Serve with boiled/mashed potatoes/rice and a boiled vegetable of your choosing.

*Calories 190, Protein 124 g, Sodium 60 mg, Potassium 40 mg, Phosphorus 61 mg, Calcium 18 mg*

# Crab with Linguine

*Time: 1 hour, Serves: 6, Skill: Easy*

**Ingredients**
- Parsley (1 cup)
- Water (2-1/2 quarts)
- Linguine (12 oz.)
- Olive oil (2 tbsp)
- Garlic (2)
- Lemon juice (1 tbsp)
- Black pepper (1/4 tsp)
- Raw crabs (3/4 lb.)

**Instructions**
- Remove the meat from the crab shells.
- Chop the parsley into small sections.
- Linguine should be cooked in a large pot until tender.
- Slice and split the garlic cloves while the pasta is heating. In a frying pan over medium heat, toast the cloves, stirring occasionally, until the garlic darkens and softens. Remove the garlic cloves from the flames and peel the outer layer.
- In a frying pan, heat the olive oil, then add the sliced garlic. When roasted, garlic should be golden brown. You may cut cloves in half or leave them whole.
- Add the parsley and crab and cook for 1 to 2 mins, or until the crabs become pinkish.
- After boiling the pasta, there should be around 1 cup of liquid leftover. Toss together the pasta, crab, and garlic in the pan. After adding all of the ingredients together, add the reserved cup of liquid.
- Season with black pepper and lemon juice to taste. Serve right away.

*Calories 155, Protein 112 g, Sodium 70 mg, Potassium 42 mg, Phosphorus 65 mg, Calcium 25 mg*

# Coconut Fish Dream

*Time: 40 Mins, Serves: 4, Skill: Easy*

**Ingredients**
- Turmeric (1/2 tbsp), ground
- Cod fillet (450g), cut into large chunks without skin
- Onion (1), chopped and grated
- Coconut milk (300 ml or 1/2-pint), reduced fat
- Garam masala (1/4 tsp)
- Cumin seeds (1 tbsp)
- Margarine/butter (3 tsp), low salt
- Vegetable oil (1 tbsp)
- Green chilies (3), chopped
- Red chili powder (1/2 tbsp)
- Coriander (2 handfuls), chopped

**Instructions**
- Heat the oil and margarine/butter in a saucepan over low heat.
- Add the onion and cumin seeds, and cook until the onion is tender. Add the green chilies, chili

powder, and ground turmeric. Mix together thoroughly.
- Once the sauce is vivid and the oil has spread, add a pinch of garam masala and whisk in the coconut milk. Add the cod and cook for a further 12-15 minutes.
- Garnish with a sprinkling of coriander before eating.
- Serve with rice and a spoonful of green salad.

*Calories 170, Protein 145 g, Sodium 70 mg, Potassium 45 mg, Phosphorus 70 mg, Calcium 19 mg*

## Three Way Macaroni Salad
*Time: 40 Mins, Serves: 6, Skill: Easy*

**Ingredients**
- Tuna fish (1 can)
- Hard-boiled eggs (4), chopped
- Sweet onion (1/2 cup)
- Macaroni (8 oz.), dry
- Celery (1/2 cup.), chopped
- Red bell pepper (1/2 cup)
- Mayonnaise (3/4 cup.), low-fat
- Fresh chives (2 tbsp), cut fine
- Black pepper (1/4 tsp), fresh ground
- Cider vinegar (1 tbsp)

**Instructions**
- Prepare macaroni as directed on the box.
- Add the remaining ingredients to a large mixing bowl.
- Combine all the ingredients thoroughly.
- Toss the "Macaroni" with the egg salad.
- Throw in the tuna to create Tuna Salad with "Macaroni."

*Calories 143, Protein 4 g, Sodium 182 mg, Potassium 63 mg, Phosphorus 36 mg, Calcium 6 mg*

## Herb Topped Fish
*Time: 45 Mins, Serves: 4, Skill: Easy*

**Ingredients**
- Mayonnaise (1/2 cup)
- Sour cream (1/2 cup)
- Fresh ground pepper, to your taste
- Salmon (24 oz.), 8 x 1-1/2-inch-thick pieces
- Chives (4 tbsp), chopped
- Parsley (2 tbsp), chopped
- Parmesan cheese (1/4 cup), grated
- Onion powder (1/2 tsp)
- Dry mustard (1/2 tsp)
- Dried dill (1/2 tsp)

**Instructions**
- Butter a baking tray and place the uncooked fish fillets in it. Hand-blend the remaining ingredients.
- Arrange the mixture on top of the fillets. Bake for 20 minutes at 350°F or until the fish flakes.

*Calories 165, Protein 125 g, Sodium 45 mg, Potassium 56 mg, Phosphorus 70 mg, Calcium 17 mg*

## Fish with Peppers
*Time: 45 Mins, Serves: 4, Skill: Easy*

**Ingredients**
- Chicken broth (1/2 cup), low in sodium
- Green pepper (1/2), cut into rings
- Garlic powder (1 tsp)
- Lemon pepper (1/2 tsp)
- Tomato sauce (1/4 cup), without salt, low sodium
- White fish fillets (1 1/2 lb.)
- Capers (1 tsp)
- Oil (2 tbsp)
- Red pepper (1/2), cut into rings

**Instructions**
- Cut the fish into four-inch chunks. Sprinkle lemon pepper and garlic powder on top.
- Fry the fish in oil in a skillet over medium heat for 5 minutes, turning regularly.
- Add the capers, broth, peppers, and tomato sauce. Reduce the heat to low and simmer for 10 minutes, sealed.
- Cook for an additional 5 minutes, or before the fish flakes quickly with a fork and the peppers are tender.

*Calories 165, Protein 105 g, Sodium 52 mg, Potassium 30 mg, Phosphorus 71 mg, Calcium 16 mg*

## Baked Halibut
*Time: 45 Mins, Serves: 2, Skill: Easy*

**Ingredients**
- Halibut steaks (1 1/2 lb.)
- Lemon slices (dipped in paprika)
- Mayonnaise (1/4 cup)
- Bread crumbs (3/4 cup)

**Instructions**
- Cut the steaks from the center bone and split them into serving-size pieces.

- Using mayonnaise, cover them completely. Roll the halibut in bread crumbs then place them in a baking dish that has been buttered.
- Place the lemon slices on top.
- Bake in a preheated oven for 15 minutes, or until the fish flakes easily when inspected with a fork. Serve immediately.

*Calories 180, Protein 120 g, Sodium 54 mg, Potassium 44 mg, Phosphorus 60 mg, Calcium 20 mg*

## Broiled Garlic Shrimp
*Time: 1 hour, Serves: 4, Skill: Medium*

**Ingredients**
- Pepper (1/8 teaspoon)
- Margarine (1/2 cup), unsalted, melted
- Lemon juice (2 tsp)
- Shrimp in shells (1 lb.)
- Fresh parsley (1 tbsp), chopped
- Onion (2 tbsp), chopped
- Garlic clove (1), minced

**Instructions**
- Preheat the broiler in the oven. Wash, dry, and peel the shrimp. Combine the margarine, lemon juice, onion, garlic, and pepper in a baking dish.
- Add the shrimp and cover with a lid.
- Cook for 5 minutes under the broiler. Broil for another 5 minutes on the other side.
- Serve on a tray with the pan juices diluted. Serve with a parsley garnish.

*Calories 140, Protein 104 g, Sodium 55 mg, Potassium 35 mg, Phosphorus 25 mg, Calcium 30 mg*

## Scampi Linguini
*Time: 1 hour, Serves: 4, Skill: medium*

**Ingredients**
- Olive oil (1 tbsp)
- Dry linguini (4 oz.)
- Garlic clove (1), minced
- Dry white wine (1/4 cup)
- Basil (1/2 tsp)
- Lemon juice (1 tbsp)
- Fresh parsley (1 tbsp), chopped
- Shrimp (1/2 lb.), peeled and cleaned

**Instructions**
- In a skillet, heat the oil. Add the garlic and shrimp.
- Cook until the shrimp turns yellow, stirring regularly.
- Add the white wine, lemon juice, parsley, and basil.
- Continue to cook for another 5 minutes. Meanwhile, cook the linguini in a pot of boiling water until tender (unsalted). Drain all of the water.
- Apply the shrimp and any leftover sauce to the linguini and serve.

*Calories 160, Protein 130 g, Sodium 25 mg, Potassium 49 mg, Phosphorus 61 mg, Calcium 21 mg*

## Spanish Paella
*Time: 1 hour 15 Mins, Serves: 2, Skill: Medium*

**Ingredients**
- Red bell pepper (1/3 cup), chopped
- Green onion (1/3 cup), sliced
- Garlic cloves 2, minced
- Pepper (1/4 tsp)
- Chicken breast (1/2 lb.), boneless and skinless, cut into 1/2-inch piece
- Water (1/4 cup)
- Chicken broth (10-1/2-oz can), low in salt
- Medium-size shrimp (1/2 lb.), peeled & cleaned
- Frozen green peas (1/2 cup)
- Ground saffron (a dash)
- White rice, instant (1 cup), uncooked

**Instructions**
- In a two-quart casserole dish, combine the first three ingredients and cover with the lid. Microwave for 4 to 5 minutes on heavy.
- Combine the shrimp and the remaining ingredients in the casserole dish. Cover and cook for 3 and 1/2 to 4 1/2 minutes on warm, or until the shrimp turns pink.
- Add the rice and mix thoroughly. Cook for 5 minutes, or until the rice is tender.

*Calories 180, Protein 135 g, Sodium 58 mg, Potassium 42 mg, Phosphorus 75 mg, Calcium 20 mg*

## Crab-Stuffed Shrimp
*Time: 1 hour 20 Mins, Serves: 10, Skill: Medium*

**Ingredients**
- Crab meat (6 oz.)
- Jumbo shrimp (12), raw and shelled with tails on
- Hot sauce (3 drops)
- Black pepper (1/8 tsp)
- Dry bread crumbs (1/4 cup)
- Butter (3 tbsp), unsalted

- Parsley (1 tsp)
- Celery (1)
- Onion (1)
- Green bell pepper (1)
- Lemon juice (1/4 tsp)
- Garlic powder (1/8 tsp)

**Instructions**

- Preheat the oven to 450 °F.
- Prepare the parsley, bell pepper, onion, celery, and crab meat by peeling and thinly dicing them.
- Toss the prepared ingredients with breadcrumbs, lemon juice, garlic powder, hot sauce and season with black pepper in a mixing bowl.
- Coat a baking dish with nonstick cooking spray.
- Remove the shrimp from the shell, rinse it, and pat it off. (This recipe calls for frozen shrimp, which should be thawed before using.)
- Using a sharp knife, cut a 1/2"-wide pocket from the tail around the middle of the shrimp's inner curved side, leaving 1/2 " at the top. Do not strike the back of a shrimp. Enlarge the cut with your finger.
- Use around 2-1/2 teaspoons crab mixture per shrimp. Stretch it out to fill it. Arrange the shrimp on a baking dish.
- Drizzle the shrimp with molten butter. Preheat the oven to 350 °F and bake for 10 to 12 minutes. Be careful not to overcook them.
- Garnish with melted unsalted butter, if needed. Dietary Analysis.

*Calories 144, Protein 106 g, Sodium 70 mg, Potassium 44 mg, Phosphorus 60 mg, Calcium 30 mg*

## Tuna Veggie Salad
*Time: 45 Mins, Serves: 4, Skill: Easy*

**Ingredients**

- Bell pepper, red (1/2 cup)
- Red wine vinegar (2 1/2 tbsp)
- Green onions (1/4 cup)
- Zucchini (1 cup)
- Garlic clove (1)
- Green bell pepper (1/2 cup)
- Black pepper (1/8 tsp)
- Tuna (5 oz. can), packed in water
- Fresh basil (1/4 cup)
- Olive oil (1 tbsp)

**Instructions**

- Cut the zucchini into thin slices and dice the bell peppers. Slice the green onions and basil. The garlic cloves must be minced.
- Put 3/4 cup of water into a medium saucepan.
- Steam the zucchini slices and diced bell peppers in a steamer basket over boiling water. (10 minutes of boiling the water and 10 minutes of steaming the zucchini.)
- Remove the vegetables from the heat and place them in a medium serving bowl.
- Combine the green onions, basil, and tuna in a mixing bowl.
- To make the dressing, combine the oil, vinegar, black pepper, and garlic in a sturdy container and shake vigorously.
- Toss the veggies and tuna mixture with the seasoning.
- Serve immediately.

*Calories 145, Protein 102 g, Sodium 46 mg, Potassium 48 mg, Phosphorus 49 mg, Calcium 25 mg*

## Shrimp Fajitas
*Time: 45 Mins, Serves: 2, Skill: Easy*

**Ingredients**

- Vegetable oil (2 tbsp)
- Dry cilantro (1/2 tsp)
- Flour tortillas (4)
- Vegetable spray
- Raw shrimp (1 1/2 lb.), peeled and deveined
- Chili powder (2 tsp)
- Cumin (1/2 tsp)
- Lemon or lime juice (2 tbsp)
- Green and red pepper (1/4), sliced lengthwise
- White onion (1/2), sliced lengthwise

**Instructions**

- Preheat the oven to 300°F.
- In a nonstick tray, heat the vegetable oil over low heat.
- Add the seasonings, lemon or lime juice, and shrimps. Cook for 5 to 10 minutes, or until tender.
- Add the onion and pepper and roast for 1 to 2 minutes.
- Remove the pan from the heat and stir in the coriander.
- Bake the tortillas after arranging them on the foil. Cook for a maximum of 10 minutes.

- Divide the mixture among the tortillas, wrap them and serve.

*Calories 343, Protein 24 g, Sodium 281 mg, Potassium 331 mg, Phosphorus 196 mg, Calcium 23 mg*

## Supreme of Seafood
*Time: 40 Mins, Serves: 4, Skill: Easy*

### Ingredients
- Bread crumbs (1 cup)
- Crabmeat (1 cup), cooked - boiled
- Shrimp (1 cup) cooked - boiled
- Green pepper (4), chopped
- Celery (1 cup), chopped
- Green onions (2), chopped
- Black pepper (1/2 tsp)
- Green peas (1/2 cup), frozen
- Mayonnaise (1/2 cup)

### Instructions
- Preheat the oven to 375 °F.
- Combine all ingredients except the bread crumbs in a mixing bowl.
- Pour the mixture into a casserole dish that has been greased with oil.
- Apply a sprinkling of bread crumbs to the top.
- Bake the casserole for 30 minutes.

*Calories 155, Protein 109 g, Sodium 58 mg, Potassium 62 mg, Phosphorus 45 mg, Calcium 18 mg*

## Jambalaya
*Time: 1 hour and 35 Mins, Serves: 4, Skill: Hard*

### Ingredients
- Onion (2 cups)
- Beef broth (2 cups), low-sodium
- Butter or trans-fat free margarine (1/2 cup)
- Bell pepper (1 cup)
- Garlic cloves (2)
- Raw shrimp (2 lb.)
- Converted (parboiled) white rice (2 cups), uncooked
- Black pepper (1/2 tsp)
- Canned tomato sauce (8 oz.), low-sodium

### Instructions
- Preheat the oven to 350 °F.
- Chop the bell pepper, onion, and garlic into tiny bits. The shrimp should be peeled and deveined.
- Add all of the products to a mixing bowl to combine (except the butter).
- Uniformly spread the mixture into a 9 x 13-inch baking dish.
- Split up the butter into little bits and spread them over the mixture.
- Wrap foil around the dish and secure it.
- Bake for 1 hour and 15 minutes.

*Calories 170, Protein 115 g, Sodium 70 mg, Potassium 65 mg, Phosphorus 60 mg, Calcium 30 mg*

## Shrimp Salad
*Time: 1 hour and 20 Mins, Serves: 3, Skill: Hard*

### Ingredients
- Green pepper (1 tbsp), chopped
- Onion (1 tbsp), chopped
- Tabasco or hot sauce (1/8 tbsp)
- Mayonnaise (2 tbsp)
- Chili powder (1/2 tbsp)
- Lemon juice (1 tbsp)
- Shrimp (1 lb.), chopped, boiled, & deveined
- Hard-boiled egg (1), chopped
- Lettuce, shredded or chopped (optional)
- Celery (1 tbsp), chopped
- Mustard dry (1/2 tbsp)

### Instructions
- In a mixing bowl, combine all ingredients except the lettuce and thoroughly blend.
- Chill in the refrigerator for 30 minutes before serving.
- Serve in a lettuce-covered dish or on a sandwich.

*Calories 160, Protein 100 g, Sodium 42 mg, Potassium 45 mg, Phosphorus 55 mg, Calcium 18 mg*

## Shrimp Quesadilla
*Time: 40 Mins, Serves: 4, Skill: Easy*

### Ingredients
- Flour tortillas (2), burrito size
- Sour cream (2 tbsp)
- Salsa (4 tsp)
- Cumin (1/4 tbsp), ground
- Raw shrimp (5 oz.)
- Cilantro (2 tbsp)
- Cheddar cheese
- Lemon juice (1 tbsp)

- Jalapeno (2 tbsp), shredded
- Cayenne pepper (1/8 tbsp)

**Instructions**

- Devein and remove the shell from the shrimp then rinse and break into tiny sections. Finely chop the cilantro.
- In a zip-lock pan, combine the lemon juice, cilantro, cumin, and cayenne pepper to make the marinade. Allow the shrimp parts to marinate for 5 minutes.
- Put the shrimp marinade in a pan over medium heat. Before the shrimp turns orange, stir-fry it for 1-2 minutes. Remove the shrimp from the pan and set aside, leaving the marinade.
- Whisk together the sour cream and marinate it in a skillet.
- In a wider microwave or pan, prepare the tortillas. Two teaspoons of salsa should be placed on each tortilla. 1 tablespoon of cheese and 1/2 of the shrimp mixture on top.
- Drizzle 1 tablespoon sour cream over the shrimp marinade mixture. Before withdrawing the tortilla from the plate, fold it in half and flash fry it.
- Divide each tortilla into four parts. Garnish with cilantro and a lemon slice, then serve.

*Calories 165, Protein 104 g, Sodium 60 mg, Potassium 50 mg, Phosphorus 45 mg, Calcium 18 mg*

## Shrimp & Coconut Curry Noodle Bowl

*Time: 35 Mins, Serves: 4, Skill: Easy*

**Ingredients**

- Lime juice (1 tbsp)
- Coconut oil (2 tbsp)
- Honey (2 tsp)
- Onion (1), diced
- Summer squash or zucchini (2), diced
- Water (1/2 cup)
- Sweet corn kernels ears (2)
- Garlic cloves (2), minced
- Ginger (1 tbsp), minced
- Soy sauce (1 tbsp), low sodium
- Basil or roughly chopped cilantro (1/4 cup)
- Rice noodles (8 oz.)
- Thai red curry paste (2 to 3 tbsp)
- Coconut milk (1 can), full fat
- Chopped green onions or sliced jalapeño pepper (opt. for topping)
- Shrimp (12), sautéed with a pinch of pepper & salt in olive oil (extra virgin)

**Instructions**

- Prepare the rice noodles as directed on the box.
- Melt the coconut oil in a large skillet. Add the onion, cook for 5 minutes over high flame. Cook for another 5 minutes or so after adding the zucchini, garlic, corn, and ginger, until they begin to soften.
- Add the curry paste and simmer for an additional minute.
- In a mixing cup, add coconut milk, soy sauce, water, and honey. It is optional to include additional ingredients. Add some sautéed shrimp to the mix. Continue to simmer for another 5 minutes until the mixture thickens. Add more water if the sauce gets too thick.
- Remove the skillet from the heat source. Adjust the quantity of lime zest and juice to taste, and use either cilantro or basil.
- Divide the noodles among bowls and top with the curry sauce to eat. For an additional topping sprinkle with green onions and jalapeno peppers.

*Calories 140, Protein 102 g, Sodium 40 mg, Potassium 45 mg, Phosphorus 35 mg, Calcium 25 mg*

## Tuna Mayonnaise Pasta Salad

*Time: 40 Mins, Serves: 2, Skill: Easy*

**Ingredients**

- Tuna (one can 200g or 8oz.), in spring water
- Spring onions (2), chopped
- Sweetcorn (2 tbsp), canned
- Mayonnaise (2 tbsp), reduced in fat
- White pepper/black pepper
- Pasta (90 gm or 3 oz.)
- Parsley or coriander, chopped

**Instructions**

- Prepare the pasta as directed on the box. After draining it, put it in a dish.
- Drain the tuna and combine it with pasta, spring onions, parsley, and sweetcorn in a large mixing bowl.
- Add in the mayonnaise and mix until it is evenly coated.
- Add salt and pepper to taste.

- Before eating, toss in any remaining parsley.

*Calories 165, Protein 115 g, Sodium 52 mg, Potassium 54 mg, Phosphorus 70 mg, Calcium 17 mg*

## Seafood Croquettes

*Time: 1 hour and 30 Mins, Serves: 4, Skill: Hard*

**Ingredients**
- Water-packed salmon or tuna (1 can 14.75-oz.)
- Cracker crumbs or plain bread crumb (1/2 cup), unsalted
- Cooking spray or vegetable oil (1) tbsp
- Crab meat (1 lb.), frozen or fresh
- Regular mayonnaise (1/4 cup)
- Egg whites (2)
- Ground mustard (1/2 tbsp)
- Onion (1/4 cup), chopped
- Lemon juice (2 tbsp), optional
- Black pepper (1/2 tbsp)

**Instructions**
- Drain the canned salmon or tuna.
- In a medium bowl, mix all the ingredients except the oil. Ensuring you mix it rigorously.
- Split the mixture into eight balls and flatten each one to produce patties.
- Heat the vegetable oil in a skillet.
- Slowly lower the patties into the boiling oil.
- Softly brown the patties on both sides. If the patties are fried in grease, drain them on paper towels when cooked.

*Calories 150, Protein 108 g, Sodium 65 mg, Potassium 60 mg, Phosphorus 45 mg, Calcium 20 mg*

## Tuna-Noodle Skillet

*Time: 40 Mins, Serves: 4, Skill: Easy*

**Ingredients**
- Green peas (1/2cup), frozen and thawed
- Vegetable cooking spray
- Water (2/3 cup)
- Onion (2 tbsp), minced
- Curry powder (1/4 tbsp)
- Fresh parsley, chopped (optional)
- Black pepper (1/4 tbsp)
- Tuna with water (1-9 1/4-oz.), sapped
- Cream of mushroom soup (1 10 3/4-oz. can)
- Rotini hot (2 cups), cooked without fat or corkscrew pasta, salt

**Instructions**
- Gently brush a nonstick wok in cooking spray and heat on medium.
- Cook the onion until it is soft.
- Combine the water, curry powder, pepper, and soup in a bowl and mix well before pouring into the wok.
- Add the fried rotini, peas, and tuna. Steadily stir for 10 minutes on low heat.
- Garnish with parsley if desired.

*Calories 175, Protein 120 g, Sodium 40 mg, Potassium 50 mg, Phosphorus 59 mg, Calcium 18 mg*

## Tuna Salad

*Time: 25 Mins, Serves: 2, Skill: Easy*

**Ingredients**
- Celery (1/4 cup), chopped
- Red pepper (1/4 cup), chopped
- Honey Mustard by Ken's (2 tbsp)
- Canned tuna (12 oz.), low sodium
- Red onion (1/4 cup), chopped

**Instructions**
- Cut the red pepper, celery, and red onion into fine bits.
- In a mixing bowl, combine the honey mustard and tuna.

*Calories 180, Protein 130 g, Sodium 54 mg, Potassium 45 mg, Phosphorus 60 mg, Calcium 25 mg*

## Baked Tuna

*Time: 40 Mins, Serves: 4, Skill: Easy*

**Ingredients**
- Non-stick cooking spray
- Canned tuna in water (14 oz.), no salt, drained
- Onion (2/3 cup), chopped
- Green pepper (1/4 cup), diced
- Pimento (1/4 cup), canned
- Mayonnaise (1/2 cup)
- Parmesan cheese (2 tsp), grated
- Plain bread crumbs (1/4 cup)

**Instructions**
- Preheat the oven to 175 °F.
- Using nonstick cooking oil, coat a baking sheet.
- Combine the onion, tuna, pimento, mayonnaise, and pepper in a large mixing bowl.

- Fill a baking sheet halfway with the tuna mixture. Top the mixture with the bread crumbs and Parmesan cheese.
- Bake for 20 minutes, or until the topping is light brown (or until completely heated).

*Calories 160, Protein 103 g, Sodium 35 mg, Potassium 45 mg, Phosphorus 60 mg, Calcium 22 mg*

## Pasta Salad Nicosia
*Time: 40 Mins, Serves: 4, Skill: Easy*

### Ingredients
- Dry mustard (2 tsp)
- Small shell macaroni (4 cups), cooked
- Olive oil (1/3 cup)
- Green onions (5), chopped, including tops
- Pepper (1/4 tsp)
- Fresh green beans (2 cups), cut into 1-inch pieces
- Fresh parsley (1 tbsp), Chopped
- Basil (1 tsp)
- Tuna (1x 7-3/4-oz. can), in water, drained
- Olive oil (1 tbsp)
- Lemon juice (1/2 cup)

### Instructions
- In a mixing cup, toss the macaroni with 1 tablespoon of olive oil and set aside. To blanch the green beans, place them in boiling water for 2 minutes. Then chill in cool running water and strain using a colander. Drain all of the water.
- Combine the beans, lemon juice, 1/3 cup olive oil, parsley, mustard, and basil in a mixing bowl. Add the tuna, pepper, green onions, and macaroni.
- Toss, then wrap and allow to cool for 1 to 2 hours or more.

*Calories 173, Protein 4 g, Sodium 189 mg, Potassium 68 mg, Phosphorus 30 mg, Calcium 7 mg*

## Salmon Veggie Salad
*Time: 45 Mins, Serves: 4, Skill: Easy*

### Ingredients
- Garlic clove (1)
- Green onions (1/4 cup)
- Zucchini (1 cup)
- Green bell pepper (1/2 cup)
- Black pepper (1/8 tsp)
- Salmon (5 oz. can), packed in water
- Olive oil (1 tbsp)
- Red wine vinegar (2-1/2 tbsp)
- Red bell pepper (1/2 cup)
- Fresh basil (1/4 cup)

### Instructions
- Cut the zucchini into thin slices and dice the bell peppers. Slice the green onions and basil. The garlic cloves need to be minced.
- Put 3/4 cup of water into a medium saucepan.
- Steam the zucchini slices and diced bell peppers in a steamer basket over boiling water in a saucepan. (10 minutes of boiling water and 10 minutes of steaming broccoli.)
- Remove the vegetables from the heat and drain them to catch some liquid that might have escaped.
- Combine the green onions, basil, and salmon in a mixing bowl. Add the vegetables and mix thoroughly.
- To make the dressing, combine the oil, vinegar, black pepper, and garlic in a sturdy container and shake vigorously.
- Toss the veggies and tuna mixture with the seasoning and serve.

*Calories 149, Protein 104 g, Sodium 25 mg, Potassium 45 mg, Phosphorus 51 mg, Calcium 19 mg*

## Salmon Salad
*Time: 30 Mins, Serves: 2, Skill: Easy*

### Ingredients
- Ken's Honey Mustard Dipping Sauce (2 tbsp)
- Celery (1/4 cup), chopped
- Red onion (1/4 cup), chopped
- Red pepper (1/4 cup), chopped
- Canned salmon (12 oz.), low sodium

### Instructions
- Chop the celery, red pepper & red onion into small bits.
- Mix it with honey mustard and salmon and serve.

*Calories 155, Protein 115 g, Sodium 41 mg, Potassium 35 mg, Phosphorus 54 mg, Calcium 21 mg*

## Quesadilla of Crabs
*Time: 40 Mins, Serves: 4, Skill: Easy*

### Ingredients
- Flour tortillas 02 (burrito size)
- Sour cream (2 tbsp)
- Salsa (4 tsp)
- Ground cumin (1/4 tbsp)

- Crab (5 oz.)
- Cilantro (2 tbsp)
- Cheddar cheese
- Lemon juice (1 tbsp)
- Jalapeno (2 tbsp), shredded
- Cayenne pepper (1/8 tbsp)

**Instructions**
- Rinse the crabs and cut into tiny sections. Finely chop the cilantro.
- In a zip-lock pan, combine the lemon juice, cilantro, cumin, and cayenne pepper to make the marinade. Allow the crabs to marinate for 5 minutes.
- Put the crab marinade in a pan over medium heat. Before the crab turns orange, stir-fry it for 1-2 minutes. Remove the crab from the pan and set aside, leaving the marinade.
- Whisk together the sour cream and the remaining marinade in the pan.
- In a wider microwave or pan, prepare the tortillas. Two teaspoons of salsa should be placed on each tortilla. 1 tablespoon of cheese and 1/2 of the crab mixture on top.
- Drizzle 1 tablespoon sour cream over the crab marinade mixture. Fold the tortilla in half and fry it.
- Divide each tortilla into four parts. Garnish with cilantro and a lemon slice and serve.

*Calories 160, Protein 108 g, Sodium 70 mg, Potassium 45 mg, Phosphorus 60 mg, Calcium 18 mg*

## Crab Salad
*Time: 40 Mins, Serves: 4, Skill: Easy*

**Ingredients**
- Crab (1 lb.), boiled, chopped and deveined
- Dry mustard (1/2 tsp)
- Lettuce, chopped or shredded (optional)
- Hard-boiled egg (1), chopped
- Celery (1), chopped
- Green pepper (1), chopped
- Onion (1), chopped
- Mayonnaise (2 tbsp)
- Lemon juice (1 tsp)
- Chili powder (1/2 tsp)
- Tabasco or hot sauce (1/8 tsp)

**Instructions**
- Add all ingredients (except lettuce) to a mixing bowl and combine.
- Allow it to cool in the refrigerator for 30 minutes.
- Serve in a sandwich or as a salad on a bed of lettuce, if needed.

*Calories 155, Protein 100 g, Sodium 58 mg, Potassium 45 mg, Phosphorus 49 mg, Calcium 25 mg*

## Crab Cakes
*Time: 30 Mins, Serves: 4, Skill: Easy*

**Ingredients**
- Garlic powder (1 tsp)
- Egg (1), egg substitute or egg white optional
- Green or red pepper (1/3 cup), finely chopped
- Crackers (1/3 cup), low sodium
- Mayonnaise (1/4 cup), reduced-fat
- Dry mustard (1 tbsp)
- Crushed red pepper or black pepper (1 tsp)
- Lemon juice (2 tbsp)
- Vegetable oil (2 tbsp)

**Instructions**
- In a mixing bowl, combine all the ingredients.
- Shape patties by dividing the mixture into 6 spheres.
- Heat the vegetable oil in a medium-hot pan or a 347 °F oven.
- In a hot pan, cook the patties for 4 to 5 minutes.
- Serve immediately.

*Calories 180, Protein 105 g, Sodium 45 mg, Potassium 50 mg, Phosphorus 40 mg, Calcium 18 mg*

## Citrus Relish
*Time: 45 Mins, Serves: 8, Skill: Easy*

**Ingredients**
- White vinegar (1/4 cup)
- Sugar (2-4 tbsps.)
- Small lemons, kumquats, or limes (2 lbs.)
- Glass jars
- Mustard seed (1/4 cup)

**Instructions**
**Pickled Fruit**
- At the end of each fruit's stem, create a cross.
- Place them in glass jars and cover them with vinegar.
- Apply 2 teaspoons of mustard seed to each jar. Cover with lids.

- Allow it to stay at room temperature for around a month before making the relish and serving it.

**Citrus Relish**
- Mix the fruit and sugar in a small frying pan, adjust the sweetness as required.
- Shake the pan often over medium heat for 5-10 minutes, or before the mixture cooks and the fruit becomes glossy and translucent.
- It may be eaten hot or cold.
- Use remaining pickling vinegar in salad dressings or to marinate chicken or fish.

*Calories 155, Protein 80 g, Sodium 33 mg, Potassium 35 mg, Phosphorus 25 mg, Calcium 25 mg*

# Dilled Fish
*Time: 55 Mins, Serves: 6, Skill: Medium*

**Ingredients**
- Dill weed (1/2 tsp)
- Mustard powder (1/4 tsp)
- Lemon Juice (4 tsp)
- Pepper (a dash)
- Onion, freeze-dried (1 tsp), instant, minced
- Firm white fish (1 1/2 lbs.), fresh

**Instructions**
- Preheat the oven to 475°F.
- Clean the fish by rinsing and drying it.
- Put it in a baking dish.
- Add 2 teaspoons of honey mustard, onion, pepper, and dill weed.
- Pour some lemon juice over the fish to give some zing.
- Bake for 17-20 minutes, uncovered.

*Calories 160, Protein 118 g, Sodium 60 mg, Potassium 32 mg, Phosphorus 45 mg, Calcium 30 mg*

# Zesty Lime Tilapia
*Time: 40 Mins, Serves: 4, Skill: Easy*

**Ingredients**
- Julienned carrots (1 cup)
- Lime peel (2 tsp), zest, grated
- Tilapia (16 oz.)
- Ground black pepper (1 tsp)
- Green onions (1/2 cup), sliced
- Julienned celery (3/4 cup)
- Orange juice (4 tsp)

**Instructions**
- Preheat the oven to 450 °F.
- Combine the celery, carrots, lime zest, and green onions in a shallow bowl.
- Cut the tilapia into four pieces that are similar in size. Tear 4 big foil squares don't coat them with nonstick spray.
- Arrange 14 vegetables slightly off-center on each sheet of foil, then top with tilapia and 1 teaspoon of orange juice squirted on each one; season with freshly ground black pepper.
- Fold the foil over the end, crimp the edges, and place the foil packets on a baking sheet to form a pouch or envelope. Cook for about 12 minutes (if the fish is thick, 3-5 minutes longer). When the fish is finished, easily cut it with a fork.
- Remove the fish from the foil pouches and put them directly on plates. Be cautious when opening due to the steam.

*Calories 140, Protein 103 g, Sodium 40 mg, Potassium 35 mg, Phosphorus 50 mg, Calcium 25 mg*

# Adobo Marinated Tilapia Tapas
*Time: 1 hour, Serves: 4, Skill: Hard*

**Ingredients**
- Nonstick cooking spray
- Wonton wrappers (48), small
- Tilapia filets (6 x 3-oz.)

**Adobo Sauce:**
- Oregano (1 tbsp)
- Spanish paprika (3 tbsp)
- Olive oil (1/4 cup), extra-virgin
- Black pepper (1 tsp)
- Fresh cilantro (3 tbsp), chopped
- Red wine vinegar (1/2 cup)
- Red pepper flakes (1 tsp)

**Slaw Mix:**
- Fresh garlic (1 tbsp), chopped
- Mayonnaise (1/2 cup)
- Slaw mix cabbage (4 cups), fresh, shredded
- Lemon juice (1/4 cup)
- Cilantro leaves (1/4 cup), fresh, rough cut
- Green scallions (1/4 cup), fresh, sliced thin on the bias

**Instructions**
- Preheat the oven to 400 °F.
- In a mixing cup, combine all of the adobo ingredients and set aside.

- Marinate the fish fillets for 30 minutes in half a cup of adobe sauce.
- Coat a baking sheet tray loosely with nonstick cooking spray and bake the fish for 15 minutes at 400°F, turning halfway through. Remove the dish from the oven and put it on a plate to cool.
- In a medium mixing cup, add the mayonnaise, ginger, leftover adobo sauce, cilantro, and scallions. Toss in the cabbage and mix until it is uniformly coated.
- Brush a mini muffin tin with nonstick cooking spray. Using one wonton wrapper to cover the muffin cups.
- Bake the crispy wontons for 5 minutes at 350 °F, then cut them from the tray.
- Divide the fish between the wontons (break or split into 48 pieces) and cover with equivalent quantities of the slaw mixture. Serve with a garnish of cilantro berries.

*Calories 170, Protein 130 g, Sodium 45 mg, Potassium 40 mg, Phosphorus 46 mg, Calcium 25 mg*

## Leek, parsley and chive fishcakes

*Time: 1 hour 10 Mins, Serves: 6, Skill: Hard*

**Ingredients**
- Potatoes (3 medium)
- Salmon (100g), skinless and boneless
- Pollock (100g), skinless and boneless
- Zest of lemon (1 small)
- Fresh parsley (1 tbsp)
- Fresh chives (1 tbsp)
- Leek (1)
- Freshly ground black pepper
- Eggs (2), beaten
- Plain flour (4oz.)
- Panko/ white breadcrumbs (6oz.), fresh
- Veggie oil (3 tbsp)
- Salad leaves, mixed (80g)

**Instructions**
- Preheat oven to 428 °F. To begin, peel and dice the potatoes into small pieces. Then mash them after boiling them for 20-30 mins in plenty of water until tender. Fry the leeks until soft in 1 tbsp of oil after cleaning, slicing, and trimming them.
- Steam, poach or bake the fish until flaky and golden brown. Remove it from the liquid with a slotted spatula and set it aside in a cup.
- Mash the potatoes, lemon zest, flaked cod, leeks, black pepper, and spices together in a large mixing bowl. From the fishcake mixture, form eight small balls with wet hands. By lightly pressing them, you can make fishcakes.
- Using flour, egg, and breadcrumbs, coat each fishcake. After that, pour the remaining oil onto the baking tray and place the fishcakes on top, flipping them over to coat all sides.
- Preheat the oven to 350 °F, and bake the cookies for 20 mins, or until golden brown. Toss with mixed salad leaves before serving.

*Calories 145, Protein 105 g, Sodium 55 mg, Potassium 40 mg, Phosphorus 60 mg, Calcium 18 mg*

## Caribbean oven-baked salmon with vegetables

*Time: 1 hour 15 Mins, Serves: 4, Skill: Hard*

**Ingredients**
- Salmon fillets (4/120g approx.)
- Lemon (1)
- Spring onions (2), trimmed
- Scotch bonnet pepper (1)
- Garlic cloves (3)
- Fresh thyme/ lemon thyme (a handful)
- Fresh coriander (a Handful)
- Fresh basil (a Handful)
- Celery (1 stalk)
- White cabbage (250g)
- Green pepper (1/2)
- Red pepper (1/2)
- Yellow pepper (1/2)
- Carrot (1)
- Vegetable oil (2 tbsp)
- Onion (1 large), peeled and chopped
- Celery stalk (1), chopped

**Instructions**
- To make the Caribbean green seasoning, blend the spring onions, scotch bonnet, coriander, thyme, garlic, basil, celery, and onion in a food processor. Half-fill the trout bowl. Cleaning with lemon is a good idea. Add 2 tablespoons of salt and pepper. If you have the time, put it in the fridge overnight, or for an hour before cooking.
- Preheat the oven to 350 °F. Place the fish in a greased baking dish and drizzle it with oil. After wrapping it in foil, cook for 20 mins. Bring a large

saucepan of water to a boil. The first step in preparing the vegetables is slicing the celery, peppers, white cabbage, and carrot.

- Cook for another 10 mins, or until the fish is slightly browned, after removing the foil after 20 mins. Boil all of the sliced vegetables in plenty of water for about 10 mins, or until they're slightly soft, before draining, while the fish is in the oven for the last 10 mins.
- Heat 2 tablespoons of oil in a pan, sauté the boiled vegetables for 3 mins, then season with a pinch of Caribbean seasoning.
- Serve the fish on a bed of sautéed vegetables.

*Calories 143, Protein 106 g, Sodium 40 mg, Potassium 35 mg, Phosphorus 48 mg, Calcium 20 mg*

## Nathan Outlaw's baked sea bass

*Time: 55 Mins, Serves: 4, Skill: Medium*

Ingredients

- Sea Bass fillets (4/70-80g)
- Red peppers (2)
- Dill (3 tsp), chopped
- Spring onions (6)
- Tarragon (3 tsp), chopped
- Fennel seeds (1 tsp)
- Broccoli florets (250g)
- White wine (100ml)
- Green beans (120g)
- White wine vinegar (100ml)
- Olive oil (50ml)
- Shallots (4)
- New potatoes (200g), washed
- Carrots (2 large)
- Smoked paprika (1 tsp)
- Caster sugar (50g)
- Pepper, to taste

Instructions

- Preheat the oven 400°F. Cook the potatoes until they are soft in a pan with boiling water. Before slicing them in half, drain it and set it aside until it is cool enough to handle. After being cored and deseeded, peppers should be cut into wide strips. Peeling and slicing carrots is required. After halving and peeling the shallots, trim the ends of spring onions.
- In a roasting tray, toss together the shallots, red peppers, carrots, and spring onions. Sprinkle the fennel seeds on top, then whisk together the wine, sugar, white wine vinegar, and half of the olive oil until smooth. After adding the new potatoes, top with paprika. After placing the tray on the stove, cook for 5 mins on medium heat.
- Roast, stirring halfway through, for 20-25 mins. Drizzle a small amount of water into the dish if it appears dry. In the meantime, in a large saucepan, heat the water to a boil. Then, on the flesh of the fish, sprinkle the pepper.
- Place the fish on top of the vegetables after 20-25 mins. Return the fish to the oven for another 8 mins, or until done. Cook the broccoli and green beans for 6-8 mins in boiling water.
- Remove the tray from the oven and drizzle the remaining olive oil and chopped herbs over it. Drain and serve with boiled broccoli and green beans.

*Calories 190, Protein 140 g, Sodium 70 mg, Potassium 45 mg, Phosphorus 60 mg, Calcium 25 mg*

## Tropical fruit salsa and couscous

*Time: 45 Mins, Serves: 4, Skill: Easy*

**Ingredients**

- Fillets (4/ 100g approx.)
- Olive oil (4 tbsp), extra virgin
- Vanilla pod (1), seeds only
- Tropical fruit salsa
- Pineapple (175g), fresh
- Mango (175g), fresh
- Papaya (175g), fresh
- Red chili (1/2)
- Red onion (1 tbsp)
- Lime (1/2)
- Ground black pepper
- Couscous (200g)
- Boiling water (200ml)
- Mango vinegar
- Mango (75g)
- White wine vinegar (30ml)
- Water (30ml)
- White sugar (110g)
- Root ginger (1/2 tsp)

**Instructions**

- Before making mango vinegar, peel, dice, and destone the mangos. Combine the sugar, water, and vanilla seeds in a saucepan and bring to a boil.

Add another 2 mins to the boil time. Remove it from the heat and add the mango and wine vinegar to it. Blend until smooth in a blender.

- Before chopping them into 0.5cm cubes, peel, destone, deseed, or core the fruits. The red chili should be deseeded and chopped, and the red onion should be peeled and finely diced. Now is the time to peel the root ginger and chop the coriander. After that, combine all the ingredients in a mixing bowl and stir well. Pour half of the water into a couscous measuring cup.
- Set aside for 5-10 mins after covering the couscous in boiling water. Ascertain that the frying pan is extremely hot. Brush the fish with olive oil and lime juice and season with freshly ground black pepper. Sear the fish for about 5 mins on each side until cooked through over high heat. After you take it off the heat, set it aside.
- Fluff the couscous with a fork before serving. In a mixing bowl, whisk together the mango vinegar and the tropical salsa. Make a small mound of salsa in the middle of each plate. On top of the salsa mounds, serve the fish fillets.

*Calories 170, Protein 132 g, Sodium 40 mg, Potassium 25 mg, Phosphorus 45 mg, Calcium 22 mg*

## Classic Spicy Shrimp and Linguine
*Time: 55 Mins, Serves: 4, Skill: Medium*

**Ingredients**
- Linguine (8 oz.)
- Red pepper (1/2 tsp)
- Shrimp (24)
- Olive oil (4 tbsp)
- Garlic (2 tsp)
- Black pepper (1/2 tsp)
- Paprika (1 tsp)
- Broccoli florets (4 cups)
- Basil (1 tsp)
- Oregano (1/2 tsp)
- Parmesan cheese (2 tbsp)
- Lemon wedges (4)

**Instructions**
- When boiling the linguine, follow the package directions.
- In a bowl combine 2 tablespoons of Extra virgin olive oil, shrimp, garlic, half the paprika, and half the black pepper.
- In a skillet, cook the shrimp until they are pink and opaque, about 5 mins.
- Combine the broccoli with 1/4 cup water in a microwave-safe bowl. Cover and microwave for 4–5 mins on high.
- After draining, return the pasta to the pot. In a mixing bowl, combine the rest of the olive oil, paprika, black pepper, oregano, and basil. Add a sprinkling of parmesan cheese for a finishing touch.
- After the broccoli and shrimp have been cooked, toss them in the seasoning mixture.
- On a serving dish, layer the shrimp and broccoli over the pasta. Sprinkle with red pepper flakes and freshly squeezed lemon juice.

*Calories 155, Protein 100 g, Sodium 35 mg, Potassium 20 mg, Phosphorus 45 mg, Calcium 25 mg*

## Caribbean lime shrimp salad
*Time: 35 Mins, Serves: 8, Skill: Easy*

**Ingredients**
**Salad**
- Broccoli slaw (6 cups)
- Pineapple (1 cup), tidbits
- Mandarin orange (1 cup)
- Garlic powder (1/2 tsp)
- Cranberries (1/2 cup)
- Cilantro (1/2 cup)
- Green onions (1)
- Mini shrimp (1–2 cups)

**Honey lime dressing**
- Honey (1/4 cup)
- Apple cider vinegar (1/4 cup)
- Lime juice (1/8 cup)
- Canola oil (1/2 cup)
- Onion (2 tbsp)

**Instructions**
- Toss the salad ingredients together in a large mixing bowl.
- Combine the dressing components in a mixer or food processor.
- Pour the dressing over the salad and toss to combine. As a final touch, little tortilla strips may be added.

*Calories 140, Protein 105 g, Sodium 65 mg, Potassium 40 mg, Phosphorus 50 mg, Calcium 21 mg*

## Oven-Fried Fish
*Time: 45 Mins, Serves: 8, Skill: Easy*

**Ingredients**
- Eggs (2)
- Water (1 tbsp)
- Paprika (1 tsp)
- Garlic powder (1/2 tsp)
- Cornmeal (1 cup)
- Lemon
- Creole seasoning (1 tbsp)
- Garlic powder (1/2 tsp)
- Onion powder (1/2 tsp)
- Black pepper (1/2 tsp)
- Cayenne pepper (1/2 tsp)
- Oregano (1/2 tsp)
- Thyme (1/2 tsp)
- Canola oil (3 tbsp)
- Whitefish fillets (1 1/2 lb.)

**Instructions**
- Preheat oven to 400°F. A 9×13-inch ceramic baking dish should be butter-coated.
- Before splitting the fillets in half lengthwise, dry the fish with a clean towel on all sides.
- In a shallow mixing cup, beat the eggs with paprika, water, and garlic powder. In a separate dish, blend the seasoning mixture and cornmeal.
- After dipping the fish in the egg mixture, carefully coat one portion at a time in the cornmeal mixture. Place the coated fish on a baking sheet. For the remaining fish, repeat the procedure.
- Cook for 15 mins, or until the fish is golden brown and cooked through. Flip once halfway through.
- With a pinch of citrus, serve promptly.

*Calories 150, Protein 110 g, Sodium 40 mg, Potassium 35 mg, Phosphorus 55 mg, Calcium 20 mg*

## Trout Topped with Herb
*Time: 45 Mins, Serves: 4, Skill: Easy*

**Ingredients**
- Mayonnaise (1/2 cup)
- Sour cream (1/2 cup)
- Fresh ground pepper, to your taste
- Trout (8/ 24 oz.), 1-1/2-inch-thick pieces
- Chives (4 tbsp), chopped
- Parsley (2 tbsp), chopped
- Parmesan cheese (1/4 cup), grated
- Onion Powder (1/2 tsp)
- Dry mustard (1/2 tsp)
- Dried dill (1/2 tsp)

**Instructions**
- Butter a baking tray and place the uncooked trout fillets in it. Hand-blend the remaining ingredients.
- Arrange the mixture on top of the fillets. Bake for 20 minutes at 350°F or until the fish flakes.

*Calories 145, Protein 102 g, Sodium 55 mg, Potassium 25 mg, Phosphorus 40 mg, Calcium 16 mg*

## Fresh & Fun Ceviche
*Time: 45 Mins, Serves: 6, Skill: Easy*

**Ingredients**
- Shrimp (12)
- Green onions (2)
- Olive oil (1 tbsp)
- Yellow banana pepper (1 medium)
- Hot chili pepper (1 small)
- Cilantro (2 tbsp)
- Lime juice (3 tbsp)
- White vinegar (2 tbsp)
- Garlic powder (1 tsp)
- Pineapple (1 cup)

**Instructions**
- Remove the frozen shrimp's tails and toss them out. Chop the rest into bite-size bits.
- Put the green onions, strawberries, peppers, and cilantro in a food processor and pulse until coarsely chopped. A chunky appearance is important.
- Toss in the lime juice, vinegar, and garlic.
- On a serving platter, combine the lettuce, olive oil, and sliced shrimp.
- The fresh pineapple's core should be removed. In a food processor, pulse all the ingredients until they are coarse. Along with the shrimp and vegetables, add the pineapple to the plate. It is necessary to combine the ingredients. Refrigerate for at least 30 mins before serving.

*Calories 150, Protein 110 g, Sodium 35 mg, Potassium 25 mg, Phosphorus 40 mg, Calcium 25 mg*

## Creamy Tuna Twist
*Time: 25 Mins, Serves: 4, Skill: Easy*

**Ingredients**
- Mayonnaise (3/4 cup)

- Celery pea size (1/2 cup)
- Dill weed (1 tbsp)
- Vinegar (2 tbsp)
- Shell macaroni (1 1/2 cups)
- Tuna (6 1/2 oz.)
- Peas (1/2 cup)

**Instructions**

- Mix the macaroni shells, mayonnaise, and vinegar thoroughly in a mixing bowl.
- Combine the remaining ingredients in a mixing bowl and stir until well combined.
- Refrigerate for a few hours, covered.

*Calories 143, Protein 4 g, Sodium 182 mg, Potassium 63 mg, Phosphorus 36 mg, Calcium 6 mg*

## Mediterranean Baked Trout

*Time: 1 hour and 15 Mins, Serves: 4, Skill: Medium*

**Ingredients**

- Pitted Kalamata olives (1/4 cup)
- Lemon (1)
- Fennel bulb (1/2 large)
- Onion (1/2 large)
- Virgin olive oil (2 tbsp)
- McCormick (4 tsp)
- Trout butterflied fillets rainbow (2)
- Panko breadcrumbs (1/4 cup)

**Instructions**

- Preheat the oven to 400ºF and place the baking rack in the middle. Line a baking sheet with greased aluminum foil.
- In a bowl combine 1 teaspoon of Mediterranean Spiced Sea Salt, tossed with sliced onion and fennel until evenly coated. Arrange the ingredients evenly on the prepared baking tray. Bake the fennel for 10 mins, or until tender and caramelized.
- Place the trout fillets on top of the baking sheet once it has been removed from the oven. Add the Panko breadcrumbs and 3 teaspoons of salt (per butterflied fillet 2 tbsp). Halved lemon slices, and sliced olives should be arranged around the fish.
- Return to the oven for another 5 mins of baking, then broil for another 3-5 mins, or until the breadcrumbs are golden brown and the fish is cooked. Breadcrumbs will burn if they are baked for too long. Cut the fillets in half after taking them out of the oven. Serve immediately after dividing vegetables among serving plates and topping with fish.

*Calories 170, Protein 135 g, Sodium 60 mg, Potassium 40 mg, Phosphorus 35 mg, Calcium 16 mg*

## Foil Baked Pimento Cod Fillets

*Time: 55 Mins, Serves: 4, Skill: Medium*

**Ingredients**

- Cod fillets (12 oz.)
- Black pepper (1/2 tsp)
- Pimento peppers (4 oz.)
- Olive oil (1 tbsp)
- Lemon (1)
- Salt (1/4 tsp)

**Instructions**

- Preheat the oven to 350ºF.
- Cover the baking dish with two wide sheets of heavy-duty aluminum foil.
- Thinly sliced lemon slices should be used to cover half of each sheet of foil.
- Arrange 2 cod fillets (approx. 6oz. per foil) on top of the lemon slices.
- Season with salt and pepper to taste on each fillet.
- Drizzle olive oil over each fillet after scattering the diced pimentos on top.
- Fold the foil corners inwards to seal the cod. Bake for 20 mins. To serve, take the fillets out of the foil and place them on a plate.

*Calories 140, Protein 100 g, Sodium 40 mg, Potassium 25 mg, Phosphorus 34 mg, Calcium 20 mg*

## Shrimp-Stuffed Deviled Eggs

*Time: 50 Mins, Serves: 6, Skill: Medium*

**Ingredients**

- Eggs (6 large), boiled
- Black pepper (1/4 tsp)
- Shrimp (1/2 cup)
- Mustard (1/2 tsp)
- Mayonnaise (1-1/2 tbsp)
- Lemon juice (1/2 tsp)

**Instructions**

- Cut the boiled eggs in half lengthwise with a knife. Remove the yolks and place them in a cup with care.
- Finely cut the shrimp and blend in a mixing bowl with the egg yolks, mayonnaise, mustard, lemon juice, and seasoning. Mix thoroughly.

- Position the shrimp and yolk mixture in the egg white halves and serve.

*Calories 155, Protein 115 g, Sodium 52 mg, Potassium 34 mg, Phosphorus 47 mg, Calcium 22 mg*

## Linguine with Garlic and Shrimp

*Time: 40 Mins, Serves: 6, Skill: Easy*

**Ingredients**
- Parsley (1 cup)
- Water (2-1/2 quarts)
- Linguine (12 oz.)
- Olive oil (2 tbsp)
- Garlic (2)
- Lemon juice (1 tbsp)
- Black pepper (1/4 tsp)
- Raw shrimp (3/4 lb.)

**Instructions**
- Remove the shrimp's shells and devein them. Chop the parsley into small sections.
- Pasta should be cooked in a large pot until tender.
- Slice and split the garlic cloves while the pasta is heating. In a frying pan over medium heat, toast the cloves, stirring occasionally. It's ready to use as the garlic darkens and softens. Remove the garlic cloves from the flames and peel the flesh down.
- In a frying pan, heat the olive oil, then add the sliced garlic. When roasted, garlic should be golden brown. You may cut cloves in half or leave them whole.
- Add the parsley and shrimp and cook for 1 to 2 mins, or until the shrimp becomes pinkish.
- After boiling the pasta, there should be around 1 cup of liquid leftover. Toss together the pasta, shrimp, and garlic in a pan. After adding all of the ingredients together, add the reserved cup of liquid.
- Season with black pepper and lemon juice to taste. Serve immediately.

*Calories 165, Protein 120 g, Sodium 25 mg, Potassium 28 mg, Phosphorus 35 mg, Calcium 28 mg*

## Easy Shrimp in Garlic Sauce (high protein)

*Time: 45 Mins, Serves: 4, Skill: Medium*

**Ingredients**
- Bowtie pasta (8 oz.)
- Basil (2 tbsp)
- Black pepper (1/8 tsp)
- Butter (3 tbsp)
- Garlic cloves (3)
- Onion (1/4 cup)
- Raw shrimp (1 lb.)
- Whipped cream cheese (1/2 cup)
- Creamer (1/4 cup)
- White wine (1/4 cup)

**Instructions**
- Clean, devein, and peel the shrimp.
- Place the pasta in a pot of boiling water to cook.
- When the pasta is heating, finely mince the garlic and onion. Melt butter in a skillet over medium heat. After introducing the onion, shrimp, and garlic, cook for 1 minute. Cook until the shrimp becomes brown, around 1 or 2 mins after inserting it (do not overcook).
- Once the pasta has been cooked for 12 minutes, drain it.
- Remove the shrimp from the pan and set it aside. Reduce the temperature. In a skillet, combine the cream cheese, onion, garlic, and butter to make a sauce.
- Combine the half-and-half creamer and the remaining ingredients in a mixing bowl and stir well. Include the wine until the mixture is almost smooth. Place the shrimp in the sauce to re-cook.
- Drain the pasta and divide it into four bowls to eat. On top, place the garlic sauce and shrimp. Add a touch of black pepper and 1/2 tablespoon of fresh basil, chopped.

*Calories 164, Protein 109.5 g, Sodium 40 mg, Potassium 25 mg, Phosphorus 45 mg, Calcium 20 mg*

## Super Tuesday Shrimp

*Time: 45 Mins, Serves: 4, Skill: Medium*

**Ingredients**
- Pasta (4 oz.)
- Onion (2 tbsp)
- Feta cheese (1/4 cup)
- Sun dried tomatoes (1/4 cup), in oil
- Garlic cloves (2)
- Olive oil (1 tbsp)
- Shrimp (12 oz.)
- Peapods (8 oz.)

**Instructions**
- Clean, devein, and peel the shrimp.

- Cook the pasta according to instructions.
- Finely mince the garlic and onion, and sauté until lightly brown.
- Add the sun-dried tomatoes, shrimp and peapods.
- Stir occasionally until the shrimp changes color and the peapods reach their desired texture (still slightly crunchy).
- Drain the pasta and mix it with the shrimp. To serve, sprinkle with feta cheese.

*Calories 155, Protein 104 g, Sodium 45 mg, Potassium 29 mg, Phosphorus 75 mg, Calcium 21 mg*

## Shrimp Fried Rice

*Time: 1 hour and 25 Mins, Serves: 4, Skill: Hard*

**Ingredients**
- White long-grain rice (4 cups)
- Salt (1/4 tsp)
- Onion (3/4 cup)
- Garlic clove (1)
- Ginger root (1 tbsp)
- Scallions (3 tbsp)
- Peanut oil (5 tbsp)
- Black pepper (3/4 tsp)
- Shrimp (1/2 cup)
- Peas and carrots (1 cup)
- Eggs (4), beaten

**Instructions**
- Dice the onions and scallions and finely cut them. Garlic and ginger can be finely diced.
- Heat 1 tablespoon of oil in a large nonstick skillet over medium-high heat. Add the onions to the skillet.
- Add 1/2 teaspoon fresh black pepper and cook for around 2 mins, or until the onion is tender.
- Add the scallions, garlic, and ginger to the pan and cook for about a minute.
- Add the shrimp and cook until well cooked.
- Heat the carrots and peas then add them to the skillet. Add the shrimp to the vegetable mixture.
- Using another skillet, add 2 tablespoons of oil and the eggs and scramble them. In a mixing bowl, combine the eggs, peas, and shrimp.
- Reheat the skillet, 1 tbsp oil should be applied. Add 4 cups cooked corn, dipped in oil.
- Season the rice with salt and pepper in a pot of boiling water, then set aside for 2 mins without stirring.
- Then, when constantly stirring, apply the shrimp, and eggs to the rice. Warm it up before serving.

*Calories 200, Protein 125 g, Sodium 70 mg, Potassium 35 mg, Phosphorus 40 mg, Calcium 25 mg*

## Creamy Shrimp and Broccoli Fettuccine

*Time: 1 hour 10 Mins, Serves: 3, Skill: Hard*

**Ingredients**
- Fettuccine (4 oz.)
- Broccoli florets (1-3/4 cup)
- Shrimp (3/4 lb.)
- Garlic clove (1)
- Cream cheese (10 oz.)
- Garlic powder (1/2 tsp)
- Lemon juice (1/4 cup)
- Peppercorns (3/4 tsp)
- Creamer (1/4 cup)
- Red bell pepper (1/4 cup)

**Instructions**
- Boil the pasta, omitting the salt.
- Add the broccoli after 3 mins of boiling. Drain all excess moisture.
- In a large nonstick pan, cook the shrimp until thoroughly cooked. Add garlic for 2 to 3 mins on medium heat.
- Add the cream cheese, half-and-half, garlic powder, lemon juice, and peppercorns. 2 mins of preparation. Mix thoroughly.
- Toss the shrimp and pasta together. If desired, add the bell pepper.

*Calories 140, Protein 103 g, Sodium 43 mg, Potassium 29 mg, Phosphorus 32 mg, Calcium 19 mg*

## Honey Glazed Salmon

*Time: 1 hour, Serves: 4, Skill: Hard*

**Ingredients**
- Garlic Ginger Glaze
- Sesame oil
- Honey (3 tbsp)
- Soy sauce (4 tbsp)
- Rice vinegar (4 tbsp)
- Freshly cracked black pepper

- Salmon fillet skinned (1 lb.)
- Garlic cloves (3-4)
- Ginger (1/2 inch), grated

**Instructions**

- In a saucepan, whisk together 3 tablespoons of sugar, 1 tablespoon of sesame oil, 4 tablespoons of Soy sauce, 3-4 garlic cloves, 4 tablespoons of rice vinegar, and 1/2-inch grated ginger. Cook for about 10 mins, stirring continuously until the sauce has reduced and thickened.
- Season all sides of the salmon fillets with freshly cracked black pepper. Cook the salmon in a skillet over high heat with a few teaspoons of oil until crispy on both sides, around 5-6 mins per side, protected with a lid in between.
- Drizzle the salmon fillet with the honey glaze. While it's still hot, serve as soon as possible.

*Calories 205, Protein 104 g, Sodium 90 mg, Potassium 70 mg, Phosphorus 50 mg, Calcium 20 mg*

# SALAD RECIPES

## Apple Rice Salad
*Time: 25 Mins, Serves: 4, Skill: Easy*

**Ingredients**
- Olive oil (1 tbsp)
- Honey (2 tsp)
- Brown/ Dijon mustard (2 tsp)
- Orange peel (1 tbsp), finely shredded
- Garlic powder (1/4 tsp)
- Chilled cooked rice of any kind (2 cups)
- Apples (2 medium), chopped
- Balsamic vinegar (2 tbsp)
- Celery (1 cup), thinly sliced
- Shelled sunflower seeds (2 tbsp), unsalted

**Instructions**
- Combine the honey, olive oil, orange peel, and garlic powder in a mixing cup and set aside.
- Combine the rice, celery, apples, and sunflower seeds in a large mixing bowl. Toss to ensure it is well combined.
- Toss the rice salad mixture with the seasoning until it is well seasoned.
- Serve immediately, or refrigerate for up to 24 hours.

*Calories 93, Protein 24 g, Sodium 11 mg, Potassium 31 mg, Phosphorus 46 mg, Calcium 23 mg*

## Cool Coconut Marshmallow Salad
*Time: 35 Mins, Serves: 6, Skill: Easy*

**Ingredients**
- Dried coconut (1 cup), shredded
- Fruit cocktail (15 oz.), drained
- Fruit-flavored marshmallows (8.8 oz.)
- Sour cream (2 cups)

**Instructions**
- In a mixing bowl, combine all the ingredients.
- Chill the salad for an hour before eating if you like it creamy. Chill the salad overnight if you want it molded.

*Calories 113, Protein 35 g, Sodium 21 mg, Potassium 33 mg, Phosphorus 96 mg, Calcium 17 mg*

## Cucumber Cups Stuffed with Buffalo Chicken Salad
*Time: 45 Mins, Serves: 8, Skill: Easy*

**Ingredients**
- Mayonnaise (1/2 cup)
- Blue cheese crumbs (1/4 cup)
- Lemon juice (2 tbsp)
- Fresh garlic (1 tbsp), chopped
- Fresh chives (2 tbsp), chopped
- Chicken breast (3 cups), diced or shredded
- Black pepper (1/2 tsp)
- Smoked paprika (1 tsp)
- Italian seasoning (1/2 tsp)
- Cayenne pepper (1 tsp)
- Hot sauce (2 tbsp)
- Seedless cucumbers (2 large), sliced into 1-inch pieces
- Fresh parsley (1/4 cup), chopped, for garnish

**Instructions**
- Except for the chicken and cucumbers, combine all the ingredients in a medium-sized mixing bowl.
- Add the chicken and stir until it is fully coated. Set aside for 30 minutes in the refrigerator.
- Take it out of the fridge and spoon an equivalent amount (about 1-2 teaspoons) onto each cucumber slice.

*Calories 152, Protein 29 g, Sodium 51 mg, Potassium 46 mg, Phosphorus 116 mg, Calcium 23 mg*

## Asian Pear Salad
*Time: 25 Mins, Serves: 4, Skill: Easy*

**Ingredients**
- Walnuts or pecans (1/2 cup)
- Green leaf lettuce (6 cups)
- Asian pears (4), peeled, cored & diced
- Stilton or blue cheese (2 oz.)
- Pomegranate seeds (1/2 cup)
- Sugar (1/2 cup)
- Water (1/2 cup)
- Serve with oil and vinegar dressing

**Instructions**
- In a nonstick container, dissolve the sugar in water.

- Heat until the mixture has thickened into syrup.
- Stir in the nuts.
- Crush the nuts on aluminum foil or parchment paper and set aside.
- In a bowl, place the lettuce.
- Add the pears, pomegranate nuts, and cheese and mix.
- Serve with an oil-and-vinegar sauce and a sprinkling of nuts.

*Calories 134, Protein 44 g, Sodium 85 mg, Potassium 71 mg, Phosphorus 76 mg, Calcium 33 mg*

## Beet Salad

*Time: 1 hour 20 Mins, Serves: 4, Skill: Medium*

**Ingredients**
- Chilled beets (4), roasted, peeled, and diced
- Walnuts or pecans (1/2 cup)
- Leaf lettuce (1)
- Fresh basil (1/4 cup), chopped fine
- Fruit or herb vinegar (1/2 cup)
- Olive oil (2 tbsp)
- Stilton or blue cheese (2-3 oz.)

**Instructions**
- Preheat the oven to 400 °F.
- Roast beets for 45 minutes, or until tender.
- Dice and peel the beets once they have cooled.
- In a saucepan, add the nuts, water, and sugar. Boil the fluid, stirring constantly until most of the liquid bubbles have vanished.
- Pour the nuts onto aluminum foil or parchment paper. Separate the nuts when they are still light.
- Enable the components to cool before storing it at room temperature.
- Make a bed of lettuce.
- Combine the beets, balsamic vinegar, basil, and olive oil in a mixing cup.
- Sprinkle it on the bed of lettuce, adding the nuts and cheese on top.

*Calories 36, Protein 1 g, Sodium 3 mg, Potassium 120 mg, Phosphorus 20 mg, Calcium 35 mg*

## Berry Wild Rice Salad

*Time: 1 hour and 30 Mins, Serves: 8, Skill: Medium*

**Ingredients**.
- Water (2 cups)
- Collard greens (1 cup), lightly steamed
- Onion (1/2 cup), chopped
- Mixed berries (2 1/2 cups)
- Blueberries (1/4 cup)
- Lemon juice (2 tbsp)
- Wild rice (1 cup)
- Fresh mint (1/4 cup), chopped
- Olive oil (1 tbsp)
- Sour cream (1/2 cup), reduced-fat

**Instructions**
- Pour the water and rice into a large saucepan.
- Bring to a boil, then reduce to low heat, cover, and simmer for 45-55 minutes, or until all the liquid is absorbed.
- Fill a broad mixing bowl halfway with rice and add the steamed greens, onions, and berries.
- To create a full mix, add all the ingredients in a blender.
- Combine all the dressing ingredients, excluding the sour cream, in a food processor or blender and blend until smooth, adding more liquid if desired.
- Whisk the sour cream until it is completely combined.
- Toss the rice salad in the dressing until it is evenly coated.
- Serve immediately, or cover and store in the refrigerator for later usage.

*Calories 139, Protein 24 g, Sodium 28 mg, Potassium 43 mg, Phosphorus 66 mg, Calcium 13 mg*

## Buttermilk Herb Ranch Dressing

*Time: 40 Mins, Serves: 2, Skill: Easy*

**Ingredients**
- Milk (1/2 cup)
- Vinegar (2 tbsp)
- Fresh chives (1 tbsp), chopped
- Dill (1 tbsp)
- Mayonnaise (1/2 cup)
- Oregano Leaves (1 tbsp), chopped
- Garlic powder (1/4 tsp)

**Instructions**
- Combine the mayonnaise, milk, and vinegar in a medium mixing cup.
- Add 1/4 teaspoon of garlic powder, fresh chives, oregano leaves, and dill.
- Come them together.

- Refrigerate for at least 1 hour to allow flavors to develop.
- To serve, drizzle the dressing on top of a salad.

*Calories 71, Protein 5 g, Sodium 71 mg, Potassium 122 mg, Phosphorus 65 mg, Calcium 53 mg*

## Chinese Chicken Salad
*Time: 55 Mins, Serves: 8, Skill: Medium*

**Ingredients**
- Olive oil (3 tbsp)
- Sesame seeds (2 tbsp)
- Cooked chicken or turkey (2 cups), diced
- Head cabbage (1/2), shredded and chopped
- Green onions (4), diced
- Sugar or Splenda (1/4 cup)
- Ramen noodles (2 packages)
- Sesame oil (1 tbsp)
- White wine vinegar or rice vinegar (1/2 cup)

**Instructions**
- While the ramen noodles are still in the bag, crush them into smaller pieces.
- Remove the seasoning packets from the packages and discard them.
- Warm 1 tablespoon of extra-virgin olive oil in a skillet.
- Add the noodles and sesame seeds.
- When golden brown, remove from the heat.
- In a mixing bowl, combine the chicken/turkey, cabbage, and green onions, then add the sesame seeds and ramen noodles.
- In a separate dish, combine the sesame seed, starch, 2 teaspoons olive oil, and vinegar.
- Drizzle the dressing over the salad.

*Calories 43, Protein 12 g, Sodium 81 mg, Potassium 113 mg, Phosphorus 55 mg, Calcium 13 mg*

## Crunchy Quinoa Salad
*Time: 45 Mins, Serves: 8, Skill: Easy*

**Ingredients**
- Water (2 cups)
- Cucumbers (1/2 cup), seeded and diced
- Quinoa (1 cup), rinsed
- Green onions (3), chopped
- Fresh mint (1/4 cup), chopped
- Lemon rind (1 tbsp), zest
- Olive oil (4 tbsp)
- Parmesan cheese (1/4 cup), grated
- Head Boston or Bibb lettuce (1/2)
- Leaf parsley (1/2 cup), chopped
- Lemon juice (2 tbsp)

**Instructions**
- Rinse the quinoa under cold running water until it is clean.
- Toast the quinoa for 2 minutes in a skillet over medium-high heat, stirring periodically. Stir in 2 cups of water and bring to a boil, then reduced to low heat, covered, and simmer for 8-10 minutes. Allow a couple of minutes of cooking before fluffing with a fork.
- Combine the mint, parsley, zest, lemon juice, and olive oil with cucumbers, and onions. Toss the quinoa into the blend (cooled).
- Cover lettuce cups halfway with the mixture and top with parmesan cheese.

*Calories 36, Protein 11 g, Sodium 3 mg, Potassium 120 mg, Phosphorus 20 mg, Calcium 35 mg*

## Cowboy Caviar Bean and Rice Salad
*Time: 40 Mins, Serves: 6, Skill: Easy*

**Ingredients**
- Rice (3 cups), cooked
- Lime juice (1/4 cup)
- Olive or canola oil (1/2 cup)
- Brown sugar (2 tbsp)
- Dijon mustard (1 tbsp)
- Black pepper (1/2 tsp)
- Red bell pepper (1/2 cup), diced
- Black beans (1/2 cup), drained and rinsed
- Jalapeño (1), seeded and diced
- Cilantro (1/2 cup), chopped
- Fresh or frozen corn (1/2 cup), cooked

**Instructions**
- Until serving, leave the corn and rice to cool.
- To produce the dressing, combine the lime juice, oil, mustard, brown sugar, and black pepper in a mixing cup.
- Mix the remaining ingredients in a separate measuring cup.
- Toss the salad and corn and rice with the dressing and mix them thoroughly.
- Until serving, chill for 1 hour.

*Calories 46, Protein 12 g, Sodium 3 mg, Potassium 120 mg, Phosphorus 20 mg, Calcium 35 mg*

## Coleslaw with a Kick
*Time: 45 Mins, Serves: 10, Skill: Easy*

**Ingredients**
- Cider vinegar (2 tsp)
- Granulated sugar (3 tbsp)
- Fresh dill (2 tsp), chopped
- Bag coleslaw mix with carrots (1 lb.)
- Mayonnaise (1 cup)
- Horseradish (1 tbsp)

**Instructions**
- Combine the mayonnaise, vinegar, sugar, horseradish, and dill in a mixing cup.
- Whisk together with the coleslaw components until well mixed.
- Allow it to cool in the refrigerator for 1 hour. Allowing it to cool overnight enhances the flavor.

*Calories 71, Protein 5 g, Sodium 71 mg, Potassium 122 mg, Phosphorus 65 mg, Calcium 53 mg*

## Curry Chicken Salad
*Time: 35 Mins, Serves: 8, Skill: Easy*

**Ingredients**
- Chicken or turkey (2 cups), cooked
- Green onions (4), chopped
- Celery stalks (3), chopped
- Nuts (1/2 cup)
- Raisins (1/2 cup)
- Mayonnaise (1 1/2 cups)
- Curry powder (1 tsp)
- Mango Chutney such as Major Grey (1/2 cup)

**Instructions**
- To render the dressing, blend mayonnaise, curry powder, and chutney in a mixing dish.
- Mix the chicken, green onions, nuts, raisins, and celery in a cup, and add the dressing.
- Enable to cool in the refrigerator overnight to improve the flavor.

*Calories 43, Protein 2 g, Sodium 81 mg, Potassium 129 mg, Phosphorus 16 mg, Calcium 13 mg*

## Curried Lacinato
*Time: 40 Mins, Serves: 4, Skill: Easy*

**Ingredients**
- Oil (1 tbsp)
- Yellow onion (1/2), sliced
- Curry powder or Garam masala (1 tsp)
- Turmeric (1 tsp)
- Lacinato or other kale (4 cups), sliced lengthwise and then chopped
- Water or low sodium broth (1/2 cup)
- Rice vinegar (1/4 cup)
- Sesame seeds (2 tbsp)

**Instructions**
- Remove the rough kernel from the kale and clean it. Cut into long strips crosswise every 3 inches until chopping them.
- Sauté the onion in a skillet until it is translucent. Allow for a minute or two of roasting time when you add the curry powder and turmeric.
- In a big pot, combine the kale with the chicken broth or water. Keep an eye on it. Add 1/4 cup of water if it requires more liquid.
- Before the kale turns light green and wilts, cover and stir. If you overcook it, it will become black.
- After extracting the kale from the pot, only the juices remain. Add the rice vinegar, sesame seeds, and soy sauce to the remaining juices. Stir constantly until the sesame seeds pop and the sauce thickens.
- Mix in the sesame oil until smooth, then pour over the kale and serve.

*Calories 300, Protein 19 g, Sodium 353 mg, Potassium 390 mg, Phosphorus 270 mg, Calcium 80 mg*

## Violet, Green Salad
*Time: 35 Mins, Serves: 4, Skill: Easy*

**Ingredients**
- Sugar snap peas or frozen peas (1 cup)
- Pear (1)
- Goat cheese (3 oz)
- Chive flowers, violets, or edible flowers (1 oz)
- Plain or Greek plain yogurt (1/4 cup)
- Pomegranate molasses (1/4 cup)
- Spring greens (4 cups)
- Cucumber (1)
- Lemon juice (2 tbsp)
- Fresh parsley (1/4 cup)
- Nuts (1/4 cup), optional
- Olive oil (1/2 cup)
- Mustard (1 tsp)
- Allspice (1 pinch)

**Instructions**
- Cut the greens into bite-sized sections.
- Cucumbers can be split into discs, then quarted.
- To use frozen peas, split the pods in thirds and thaw at room temperature for around half an hour.
- In a mixing dish, combine the diced pear and greens.
- If you have some remaining goat cheese, blend it with the chives and break it into 1/2-inch pieces.
- Combine the yogurt, lemon juice, molasses, parsley, allspice, olive oil, and mustard in a food processor or mixer.
- In a big mixing dish, combine the salad and the dressing.
- For a dazzling show, scatter goat cheese, spices, and nuts around the surface.

*Calories 300, Protein 13 g, Sodium 289 mg, Potassium 404 mg, Phosphorus 195 mg, Calcium 148 mg*

## Cool and Crispy Cucumber Salad
*Time: 25 Mins, Serves: 4, Skill: Easy*

**Ingredients**
- Fresh ground black pepper, to taste
- Fresh cucumber (2 cups)
- Italian or Caesar salad dressing (2 tbsp)

**Instructions**
- Combine the cucumber and salad dressing in a medium-size bowl with a lid.
- Give it a good shake.
- To serve, season with black pepper. It can be stored in the refrigerator until ready to use.
- Serve the food to your guests.

*Calories 83, Protein 4 g, Sodium 81 mg, Potassium 121 mg, Phosphorus 39 mg, Calcium 13 mg*

## Thai Salad with Corn
*Time: 40 Mins, Serves: 6, Skill: Easy*

**Ingredients**
- Limes (2), zest, juice
- Red onion (1/2), chopped
- Cilantro (1/2 cup), chopped
- Head cabbage (1/2), shredded
- Carrot (1/2 cup), shredded
- Garlic cloves (2), minced
- Thai sweet chili sauce (2-3 tbsp)
- Sweet corn kernels (1/2 cups)

**Instructions**
- In a small bowl, whisk all the ingredients together.
- It can be stored in the fridge for up to 24 hours.

*Calories 81, Protein 14 g, Sodium 51 mg, Potassium 126 mg, Phosphorus 31 mg, Calcium 16 mg*

## Tabbouleh
*Time: 55 Mins, Serves: 8, Skill: Medium*

**Ingredients**
- Warm water (1 cup)
- Pepper (1/8 tsp)
- Vegetable or olive oil (3 tbsp)
- Lemon juice (3 tbsp)
- Cucumber (1/2 med), seeded & chopped
- Parsley (1/2 cup), chopped
- Bulgur wheat (1 cup)
- Green onion (2 tbsp), finely chopped
- Fresh mint (1 tbsp), finely chopped

**Instructions**
- Combine the bulgur and warm water in a mixing bowl.
- Enable to rest for 30 minutes.
- Add the parsley, cucumber, mint, pepper, and green onion.
- In a mixing cup, combine the lemon juice and oil.
- Combine it with the bulgur mixture & toss well.
- Cover and leave to rest for an hour.
- If needed, serve with yogurt in a lettuce-lined dish.

*Calories 113, Protein 8 g, Sodium 54 mg, Potassium 39 mg, Phosphorus 26 mg, Calcium 11 mg*

## Zesty lemon salad
*Time: 35 Mins, Serves: 2, Skill: Easy*

**Ingredients**
Salad:
- Peppers (1 cup), finely diced
- Onion (1/4 cup), finely diced
- Radish (1/4 cup), finely diced
- Fresh parsley or mint (1/4 cup), chopped
- Cucumber (1 cup), finely diced

**Zesty Lemon Dressing:**
- Lemon (1/2), squeezed
- White or Apple cider vinegar (1 Tbsp)
- Extra virgin olive oil (1 Tbsp)
- Clove of garlic (1/2), minced, more to taste
- Salt and pepper, to taste

**Instructions**
- Drain, split, and combine all vegetables in a serving bowl.
- Combine all the dressing ingredients in a mixing bowl and toss with the vegetables.
- Serve.

*Calories 71, Protein 11 g, Sodium 31 mg, Potassium 110 mg, Phosphorus 61 mg, Calcium 12 mg*

# Cabbage with Strawberries
*Time: 30 Mins, Serves: 6, Skill: Easy*

**Ingredients**
- Olive or vegetable oil (2 tbsp)
- Cider vinegar (1/4 cup)
- Brown sugar (2 tbsp)
- Fresh Strawberries (1 cup)
- Green Cabbage (1 small)
- Onion (1), coarsely chopped

**Instructions**
- Sauté the onion in the oil in a wide skillet until softened (nearly 5 minutes).
- Add the vinegar, cinnamon, and sugar; combine the strawberries and cabbage.
- Bring to a boil, then reduce to low heat, cover, and simmer until the cabbage wilts, around 15 minutes.

*Calories 83, Protein 2 g, Sodium 74 mg, Potassium 122 mg, Phosphorus 82 mg, Calcium 13 mg*

# Strawberry Wedge Salad
*Time: 45 Mins, Serves: 4, Skill: Easy*

**Ingredients**
- Chipotle powder (1/4 tsp) salt-free
- Olive oil (3 tbsp)
- Sour cream (1/2 cup)
- Freshly ground black pepper
- Dill (a handful), finely chopped
- Head of butter lettuce, leaves washed and separated
- Strawberries (1 cup), washed and halved
- Garlic powder (1/4 tsp), salt-free

**Instructions**
- Preheat the oven to 375 °F.
- Combine the strawberries, 1 tablespoon of oil, garlic, and chipotle powder in a cup. Mix the strawberries softly with your hands so they are evenly covered. Then, using parchment paper, fill an oven sheet with strawberry slices in a single coat and roast the mixture for 12 to 15 minutes.
- To produce the dressing, in a separate cup, whisk together the sour cream, pepper, the remaining two tablespoons of oil, and one tablespoon of water. Blend the milky dressing with a fork or a brush until it has thickened. If it's already too dense, include a splash of water before the perfect quality is reached. Then, include the remainder of the greens, including the dill and giving it another gentle whirl.
- For a family-style meal, place the leaves on individual plates or a large serving platter. Finish with the chipotle strawberry and the dressing drizzled over.

*Calories 112, Protein 14 g, Sodium 51 mg, Potassium 130 mg, Phosphorus 91 mg, Calcium 6 mg*

# Blackberry Salad
*Time: 40 Mins, Serves: 4, Skill: Easy*

**Ingredients**
- Blackberries (1/2 cup), fresh
- Feta cheese (2 tbsp)
- Bacon (2 tbsp), cooked
- Green onion stalks (2)
- Almonds (5–6), toasted
- Balsamic vinaigrette (1/4 c)
- Lettuce (4 cups), fresh

**Instructions**
- Layer the lettuce, green onion, and blackberries in a dish.
- Toss to mix the dressing and the salad. The crumbled bacon may be topped with feta cheese.
- Serve immediately.
- Alternatively, combine all the fresh ingredients in a mixing bowl and include the bacon, feta, and dressing just before serving.

*Calories 81, Protein 14 g, Sodium 251 mg, Potassium 326 mg, Phosphorus 131 mg, Calcium 9 mg*

# Salad with Pear Vinaigrette and Toasted Sunflower Seeds
*Time: 30 Mins, Serves: 2, Skill: Easy*

**Ingredients**
- Pear (1/2 medium), very ripe, cored, and diced
- Cider vinegar (2 tsp)
- Olive oil (1/4 cup)

- Mint leaves 1/2 tbsp), roughly chopped
- Iceberg lettuce (3 cups), fresh
- Sunflower seeds (2 tbsp), raw

**Instructions**

- In a serving bowl, position the cleaned and dried lettuce.
- Preheat a medium-sized skillet over medium-high heat. Sunflower seeds may be strewn around a hot, dry skillet.
- When toasting the seeds, keep stirring until they turn a light brown color.
- Set them aside.
- Combine the diced pear (1/2 cup), vinegar, olive oil, and mint leaves in a mixer or an immersion blender cylinder. Set aside any of the leftover pear pieces.
- At a medium speed, cutting up a pear takes around 15 seconds.
- To make a smooth, emulsified sauce, increase the pace to 30 seconds or more.
- Check for seasoning and add more vinegar if necessary.
- Half of the sauce can be added to the lettuce.
- Scatter the remaining diced pear and toasted sunflower seeds on top.

*Calories 181, Protein 34 g, Sodium 210 mg, Potassium 316 mg, Phosphorus 113 mg, Calcium 19 mg*

## Greek-Style Couscous Salad

*Time: 40 Mins, Serves: 6, Skill: Easy*

**Ingredients**

**Dressing:**

- Red wine vinegar (2 tbsp)
- Extra virgin olive oil 1/4 cup)
- Fresh lemon juice (2 tbsp)
- Dijon-style mustard (2 tbsp)
- Honey (2 tsp)
- Garlic (2 tsp), minced
- Dried oregano 1/2 tsp)
- Dried parsley (1/2 tsp), chopped
- Black pepper (1/8 tsp)

**Salad:**

- Water (1 1/2 cups)
- Israeli or pearl couscous (1 cup)
- Olive oil (1 tsp)
- Canned chickpeas (3/4 cup), drained and rinsed
- Seedless cucumber (1/2 cup, chopped)
- Black olives (**1/3** cup), sliced
- Red onion (1/4 cup), drained and finely diced
- Italian parsley (1/4 cup), chopped
- Feta cheese (3 oz.), crumbled

**Instructions**

**For Dressing Instructions**

- Combine the vinegar, lemon juice, honey, garlic, mustard, oregano, parsley, pepper, and salt in a mixing cup.
- When whisking, drizzle in the olive oil gently. Cover and keep refrigerated until ready to serve. This will yield a quarter cup of dressing.

**Salad preparation Instructions**

- Bring water to a boil in a medium saucepan over high heat. Reduce the heat to low and add the couscous to the pan.
- Cover and cook for about 10 minutes, or until the water is absorbed. Remove from the heat and set aside for 2-3 minutes, insulated.
- Toss the couscous with olive oil to prevent it from sticking together.
- Stir in the chickpeas, cucumber, onion, olives, and parsley after the couscous has cooled. To mix, kindly swirl the ingredients together.
- Season to taste right before serving. Toss in the cheese and gently mix. Drizzle the dressing over the top.

*Calories 73, Protein 4 g, Sodium 21 mg, Potassium 121 mg, Phosphorus 61 mg, Calcium 23 mg*

## Honey Dijon Cobb Salad

*Time: 40 Mins, Serves: 4, Skill: Easy*

**Ingredients**

**Salad:**

- Eggs (4)
- Blue cheese crumbles (2 oz.)
- Romaine lettuce (8 cups)
- Cucumber (1)
- Red onion (1/2)

**Dressing:**

- Olive oil (2 tbsp)
- White wine vinegar (4 tbsp)
- Honey (2 tbsp)
- Dijon mustard (2 tsp)

**Instructions**

Salad:
- To create the salad's base, cut the Romain lettuce, cucumber, and red onion.
- Place the eggs in a layer in a saucepan to produce hard-boiled eggs.
- Carry the water to a simmer, surrounding the eggs by at least 1 inch.
- Take it off the heat, cover it, and set it aside for around 15 minutes.
- Wash the eggs in cold water and peel off the shells.
- Toss the boiled eggs with the remainder of the salad after splitting them in half.
- Add blue cheese crumbles on top.

Decorative elements:
- Blend the olive oil, cinnamon, white wine vinegar, and Dijon mustard in a mixing cup.
- When preparing to serve, drizzle about two teaspoons over each salad serving.

*Calories 102, Protein 6 g, Sodium 29 mg, Potassium 112 mg, Phosphorus 61 mg, Calcium 3 mg*

## Mediterranean Chickpea Side Salad
*Time: 25 Mins, Serves: 4, Skill: Easy*

**Ingredients**
- Cucumber (1)
- Red onion (1/2)
- Feta cheese (2 oz.)
- Olive oil (1 tbsp)
- Chickpeas (15 1/2 oz.)
- Red wine vinegar (2 tbsp)
- Dried oregano (1 tsp)
- Fresh or dried parsley (1 tsp)
- Lemon juice (1 tbsp)

**Instructions**
- Drain the chickpeas.
- Thinly dice the cucumber & red onion.
- In a medium mixing bowl, combine the chickpeas, cucumbers, and red onion.
- Break up the feta into little pieces and toss it into the bowl.
- Add the olive oil, lemon juice, and red wine vinegar with a whisk to combine.
- Sprinkle oregano and parsley on top.

*Calories 73, Protein 19 g, Sodium 29 mg, Potassium 141 mg, Phosphorus 61 mg, Calcium 3 mg*

## Dr. Pearl's Delicious Salad Dressing
*Time: 55 Mins, Serves: 10, Skill: Medium*

**Ingredients**
- Dijon mustard (1/8 cup)
- Garlic (1/2 tsp), minced
- Sugar (1/2 tbsp)
- Rice seasoned vinegar (3/8 cup)
- Canola oil (3/4 cup)

**Instructions**
- To thoroughly mix the products, shake them vigorously for 30 seconds to 1 minute in a sealable container or large Mason jar.
- Drizzle the dressing over a salad and serve. Store the leftovers in the fridge.

*Calories 73, Protein 14 g, Sodium 81 mg, Potassium 121 mg, Phosphorus 66 mg, Calcium 10 mg*

## Creamy Fruit Salad
*Time: 25 Mins, Serves: 4, Skill: Easy*

**Ingredients**
- Peaches (2 medium), diced
- Plain Greek yogurt (1 cup)
- Brown sugar cinnamon (2 tsp), to taste
- Lemon (1), juiced
- Strawberries (1 cup), cut in quarters, lengthwise
- Blueberries (1 cup)

**Instructions**
- In a medium mixing cup, combine all the berries.
- In a small cup, combine the yogurt, lemon juice, and brown cinnamon sugar. To create a full mix, add all the ingredients in a blender.
- Toss the fruit and yogurt mixture together. Combine the products, sample, and change the seasoning as required.
- Refrigerated leftovers can be stored for up to 2 days.

*Calories 132, Protein 4 g, Sodium 21 mg, Potassium 191 mg, Phosphorus 163 mg, Calcium 11 mg*

## Marinated Cucumber and Celery Salad
*Time: 35 Mins, Serves: 4, Skill: Easy*

**Ingredients**
- Celery (1 1/2 cup), thinly sliced
- Shallot (2 tbsp), minced
- Parsley (1/2 cup), chopped
- Green olives (3 oz.), chopped

- Apple cider vinegar (1 tbsp)
- Lemon juice (2 tbsp)
- Cucumber (2 cups), halved lengthwise and thinly sliced
- Lemon zest (1 tbsp)
- Extra virgin olive oil (1 tbsp)
- Salt (1/8 tsp)
- Black pepper (1/8 tsp)

**Instructions**
- In a large mixing bowl, add all the ingredients and combine.
- Serve cold or at room temperature.

*Calories 130, Protein 27 g, Sodium 11 mg, Potassium 14 mg, Phosphorus 19 mg, Calcium 6 mg*

## Mexican-Style Cucumber Salad
*Time: 45 Mins, Serves: 4, Skill: Easy*

**Ingredients**
- Red onion (1/2 small), thinly sliced
- Lime juice (2)
- Mexican oregano (1/2 tsp)
- Cucumber (1 large), peeled and sliced

**Instructions**
- Gently blend the cucumber and red onion in a medium mixing cup. In another mixing cup, combine the lime juice and oregano.
- Cover and set aside for at least 30 minutes to allow flavors to merge.
- Combine the two together.
- Serve cold or at room temperature. Leftovers may be stored in the refrigerator for up to 3 days.

*Calories 143, Protein 24 g, Sodium 81 mg, Potassium 31 mg, Phosphorus 96 mg, Calcium 13 mg*

## Caribbean Carrot Salad
*Time: 40 Mins, Serves: 6, Skill: Easy*

**Ingredients**
- Water (12 cups)
- Carrots (10 oz.), shredded
- Pineapple (8 oz.), drained

**Dressing:**
- Lime Juice (1)
- Vegetable oil (1 tbsp)
- Honey (1 tbsp)
- Clove of garlic (1), minced
- Dijon mustard (1/2 tsp)
- Ginger (1/2 tsp)
- Pinch of allspice or nutmeg

**Instructions**
- Bring a stockpot of water to a boil with the shredded carrots. Cook the carrots for 3 minutes after they've been boiled, just before they're soft. Turn off the heat and move the carrots to a dish and set aside.
- In a cup, mix together the lime juice, honey, garlic, ginger, oil, sugar, and nutmeg or allspice to create the salad dressing.
- Combine the cooled carrots and drained pineapple in a mixing dish.
- Kindly fold the pineapple and carrots into the dressing.
- Chill for at least an hour before serving.
- Keep leftovers refrigerated for up to 4 days.

*Calories 50, Protein 21 g, Sodium 182 mg, Potassium 94 mg, Phosphorus 119 mg, Calcium 6 mg*

## Green Beans Salad
*Time: 30 Mins, Serves: 4, Skill: Easy*

**Ingredients**
- Oil (1 tbsp)
- Lemon juice (1/2)
- Black pepper, freshly ground, to taste
- Water (12 cups)
- Green beans (1 1/2 lb.), rinsed and ends trimmed

**Sauce:**
- Honey (1 tbsp)
- Water (1 tbsp)
- Garlic clove (1 large), minced
- Oil (1 tsp)

**Instructions**
- Get the stockpot's water to a low boil and add the beans. Cook for 3 minutes, or until the beans are light green in color. Be cautious not to overcook them.
- Remove and rinse the beans for 1 minute in cold water. Place the dried beans in a big mixing bowl after they have cooled.
- To create a sauce, blend the honey, garlic, water, and 1 teaspoon of oil in a mixing cup.
- Heat 1 tablespoon of oil in a wide skillet over low heat. Swirl the beans in the oil. Continue to stir for about 3 minutes after adding the sauce. Green beans that are finished will be bright green and crisp-tender.

- Switch to a serving bowl.
- Now add some pepper (black) and lime juice to enhance the taste.
- Serve and enjoy.

*Calories 150, Protein 17 g, Sodium 82 mg, Potassium 194 mg, Phosphorus 219 mg, Calcium 16 mg*

## Rainbow Rice Noodle Salad
*Time: 45 Mins, Serves: 5, Skill: Easy*

**Ingredients**
**Salad:**
- Red bell pepper (1 cup), chopped
- Purple cabbage (1 cup), shredded
- Carrots (1 cup), shredded
- Edamame (1 cup), shelled
- Sesame seeds (2 tbsp)
- Thai Kitchen rice noodles (6 oz.)
- Cucumber (1 cup), chopped

**Dressing:**
- Olive oil (1/2 cup)
- Sesame oil (3 tbsp)
- Soy sauce (2 tsp)
- Honey (1 1/2 tbsp)
- Rice wine vinegar (1/4 cup)
- Garlic (1 tbsp), minced

**Instructions**
- Bring a pot of water to a boil and cook the rice noodles as directed on the package. Put aside after draining and rinsing with cool water.
- Combine the diced vegetables and fried rice noodles in a large mixing bowl.
- Combine the olive oil, soy sauce, butter, sesame oil, rice vinegar, and minced garlic in a mixing cup. To emulsify the mixture, shake it vigorously in a packed container, or combine it for a few seconds in a blender or food processor.
- Toss the noodles and vegetables in the dressing to combine.
- Sprinkle sesame seeds on top, and serve.

*Calories 43, Protein 14 g, Sodium 93 mg, Potassium 311 mg, Phosphorus 169 mg, Calcium 9 mg*

## Bow-Tie Pasta Salad
*Time: 55 Mins, Serves: 8, Skill: Medium*

**Ingredients**
- Onion (2 tbsp), minced
- Bow-tie pasta (farfalle) (2 cups), cooked
- Celery (1/4 cup), chopped
- Green bell pepper (2 tbsp), chopped
- Carrot (2 tbsp), shredded

**Dressing:**
- Black pepper (1/8 tsp), freshly grounded
- Mayonnaise (2/3 cup)
- Sugar (1/2 tsp)
- Fresh-squeezed lemon juice (1 tbsp)

**Instructions**
- In a mixing bowl, combine the pasta, bell pepper, celery, carrot, and onion.
- Mix together the black pepper, sugar, mayonnaise, and lemon juice in a separate cup until smooth.
- Toss the pasta and vegetables with the dressing. Combine all the ingredients in a big mixing bowl and cover them fully. Serve immediately.

*Calories 103, Protein 4 g, Sodium 119 mg, Potassium 321 mg, Phosphorus 162 mg, Calcium 10 mg*

## Three Sisters Salad
*Time: 45 Mins, Serves: 6, Skill: Easy*

**Ingredients**
- Basil leaves (5 sprigs)
- Olive oil (2 tbsp)
- Zucchini (1 medium)
- Corn (15 oz.), drained
- White navy beans (1 cup), drained and rinsed
- Cherry or grape tomatoes (15), halved
- Lemon (1)
- A pinch of pepper
- A pinch of salt

**Instructions**
- Using a grater or a shredding tool, shred the zucchini and place in a mixing bowl.
- To render a flat bottom, break the end of a corn ear off. By laying the corn on its flat bottom, take the kernels off the cob. Fill the mixing cup halfway with corn. Rinse and add the corn to the zucchini.
- Throw in the drained beans and tomatoes. To create a full mix, add all the ingredients in a blender.
- Detach the leaves from the roots of the basil. Pile 4-5 leaves on top of each other, roll lengthwise and cut into ribbons. The basil ribbons should be tied to the cup.

- Squeeze the lemon over the top of the olive oil in the mixing bowl. To create a full mix, add all the ingredients in a blender.
- Season to taste with salt and pepper, if necessary.

*Calories 150, Protein 17 g, Sodium 82 mg, Potassium 194 mg, Phosphorus 219 mg, Calcium 16 mg*

## Strawberry & Lettuce Pasta Salad

*Time: 30 Mins, Serves: 4, Skill: Easy*

### Ingredients
- Water (12 cups)
- Honey (1 tsp)
- Pasta (1/2 lb.)
- Strawberries (1/2 pint)
- Lettuce leaves (3 cups)
- Walnuts (1/3 cup), chopped
- Cheese (1/3 cup), crumbled
- Pomegranate or balsamic vinegar (2 tbsp)
- Virgin olive oil (1/4 cup)
- Pinch of black pepper

### Instructions
- Bring water to a boil in a large pot with half a teaspoon of salt and a tablespoon of olive oil. Cook for around 8 minutes after adding the pasta.
- Slice strawberries and split them in half or thirds, based on how large they are.
- Strain the pasta and put it aside to cool in a sieve.
- In a serving basket, combine the salad, cooled pasta, sliced strawberries, chopped almonds, and feta.
- In a cup, add the vinegar, sugar, olive oil, and black pepper. Combine the foods with a fork or a brush.
- In a mixing cup, add all the salad ingredients. Once more, combine well and chill.

*Calories 130, Protein 32 g, Sodium 55 mg, Potassium 39 mg, Phosphorus 70 mg, Calcium 18 mg*

## Peach Quinoa Salad

*Time: 25 Mins, Serves: 4, Skill: Easy*

### Ingredients
- Arugula or mesclun (3 cups)
- Beets (1/4), shredded
- Carrot (1), shredded
- Red bell pepper (1/2), sliced in rings
- Yellow/orange bell pepper (1/2), sliced in rings
- Red onion (1/2), sliced thinly
- Peach (1), sliced
- Water (2 cups)
- Quinoa (1 cup)
- Blueberries/ cherries (1 cup)

**Dressing:**
- Lemon (1)
- Olive oil (1/4 cup)
- Honey (2 tsp)

### Instructions
- In a medium saucepan, bring water to a boil. Insert the quinoa and cook for around 10 minutes, or until it has consumed all the oil. Spread out to cool on a serving platter. Arrange the arugula over the quinoa.
- Toss the greens with shredded beets and carrots.
- Arrange the shredded vegetables in a circle shape with the bell pepper loops.
- Place the sliced onion on top of the other vegetable.
- Arrange the peach slices in a decorative pattern along the platter's sides.
- As a finishing flourish, scatter the blueberries/cherries on top of the salad.
- In a cup, mix together all the ingredients to create the dressing.
- Right before serving, drizzle the dressing over the salad.

*Calories 129, Protein 27 g, Sodium 211 mg, Potassium 124 mg, Phosphorus 119 mg, Calcium 26 mg*

## Cucumber Watermelon Salad

*Time: 30 Mins, Serves: 4, Skill: Easy*

### Ingredients
- Red onion (1/2 small), thinly sliced
- Olive oil (2 tbsp)
- Balsamic vinegar (1 tbsp)
- Watermelon (4 cups), diced
- Cucumber (2 cups), diced
- Feta cheese (2 oz.), crumbled
- Black pepper (1/2 tsp)

### Instructions
- Add all the ingredients in a mixing cup and mix well.
- Serve immediately.

*Calories 73, Protein 4 g, Sodium 21 mg, Potassium 121 mg, Phosphorus 61 mg, Calcium 23 mg*

# Wild Rice Salad
*Time: 1 hour 20 Mins, Serves: 8, Skill: Medium*

**Ingredients**
- Olive oil (1 tbsp)
- Walnuts (2/3 cup), chopped
- Celery rib (4 inches), sliced
- Scallions (4), thinly sliced
- Raisins (2/3 cup)
- Red apple (1 medium), semi-tart, cored and diced
- Pomegranate seeds (1/2 cup)
- Wild rice (1 cup)
- Water (2 cups)
- Lemon zest (1/2 tbsp)
- Lemon juice (3 tbsp)
- Black pepper, freshly ground, to taste
- Olive oil (1/3 cup)
- Sea salt (1/2 tsp)

**Instructions**
- Clean the wild rice in a strainer of cold water.
- In a medium saucepan, mix it with oil, water, and salt if appropriate. Carry to a boil, then drop to low heat to sustain a gentle simmer.
- Cook for 50 minutes, or until the rice is tender and the liquid has evaporated. If necessary, apply more water after the rice kernels have burst to achieve a soft texture.
- In a large mixing cup, combine the walnuts, scallions, raisins, celery, apples, pomegranate seeds, and lemon zest.
- In a container with a tight-fitting cap, mix the lemon juice, olive oil, and pepper and shake vigorously.
- Toss the apple mixture with half of the dressing and toss well.
- Set the rice aside to cool until it's just mildly moist.
- Serve with the leftover dressing and the fruit combination in a cup or on a lettuce bed at room temperature.

*Calories 172, Protein 41 g, Sodium 215 mg, Potassium 521 mg, Phosphorus 84 mg, Calcium 18 mg*

# Fall Farro Salad
*Time: 1 hour 10 Mins, Serves: 5, Skill: Medium*

**Ingredients**
- Cranberries (1/2 cup), dried
- Smoked Mozzarella cheese (1/2 cup), cubed
- Scallions (2), chopped, white and green parts
- Italian parsley (1/2 cup), minced
- Mint leaves (1/4 cup), minced
- Olive oil (3 tbsp)
- Farro (1 1/2 cups)
- Water (3 cups)
- Walnuts (1/4 cup), chopped
- Lemon juice (2 tsp), or to taste
- A pinch of sugar
- Black pepper, freshly ground, to taste
- A pinch of sea salt

**Instructions**
- Cover the farro with water in a large saucepan.
- Carry to a simmer, then turn down to low.
- Cook for 30 minutes, or until the potatoes are soft and the lid is tightly closed. (If the farro is pearlized, the cooking time can be reduced.)
- After draining for 10 minutes, set aside to cool.
- In a broad mixing bowl, add cooled farro, cranberries, cheese, almonds, scallions, mint, parsley, lemon juice, olive oil, and a pinch of sugar.
- Season to taste with salt and pepper, if necessary. Serve.

*Calories 190, Protein 4 g, Sodium 93 mg, Potassium 231 mg, Phosphorus 82 mg, Calcium 13 mg*

# Winter Fennel and Citrus Salad
*Time: 40 Mins, Serves: 4, Skill: Easy*

**Ingredients**
**Dressing:**
- Dill (1 tbsp)
- Dijon mustard (1/2 tsp)
- Honey (1/2 tsp)
- Black pepper (1/8 tsp), freshly ground
- Lemon juice (1 tbsp)
- Olive oil (3 tbsp)

**Salad:**
- Fennel (2 cups), thinly sliced, hard bottom
- Red onion (70g), thinly sliced
- Arugula (2 cups)
- Dill (2 tbsp), minced
- Orange (139g)
- Hazelnuts (1 tbsp), toasted

**Instructions**
- To create the dressing, mix together all the ingredients in a container and cover tightly.

- Giving it a good shake to ensure optimal mixing.
- In a small serving bowl, combine the onion, arugula, fennel, and dill to make the salad. To keep a smooth mix, keep stirring.
- Split the orange into tiny rounds by peeling and dicing it. Add it to the bowl and arrange it with the other ingredients in a visually appealing manner.
- Drizzle the salad with the sauce. Softly toss the citrus rounds together in a pattern.
- Sprinkle the salad with toasted hazelnuts and serve.

*Calories 103, Protein 4 g, Sodium 81 mg, Potassium 431 mg, Phosphorus 196 mg, Calcium 11 mg*

## Green Lentils and Jicama Salad
*Time: 45 Mins, Serves: 5, Skill: Easy*

**Ingredients**
- Lentils (1 cup)
- Thyme sprigs (4)
- Bay leaf (1)
- Water
- Onion (1 medium), diced
- Carrot (1 medium), diced
- Jicama (2 cups), diced
- Cilantro (1/2 cup), chopped
- Sea salt
- Canned salt-free beets (1 cup), drained and diced

**Dressing**
- Lemon (1), zested and half juiced
- Shallot (3 tbsp), chopped
- Garlic cloves (2), minced
- Olive oil (1/4 cup)

**Instructions**
- Combine the carrots and onion, as well as the thyme, lentils, and bay leaf, in a saucepan. Fill the saucepan halfway with water, enough to cover the lentils with 3/4" of water.
- Cook for 20-25 minutes, or until vegetables are soft but not overcooked, over medium heat.
- When the lentils are frying, make the dressing by whisking all the ingredients together thoroughly in a mixing bowl.
- In a big serving bowl, mix the beets and jicama.
- Remove the twigs of thyme and bay leaf from the fried lentils, drain out the extra moisture, and toss the lentils with the beets and jicama.

- Allow to cool slowly before filling the cup halfway with dressing and stirring thoroughly.
- Garnish with lemon zest and cilantro, if needed.

*Calories 143, Protein 24 g, Sodium 41 mg, Potassium 39 mg, Phosphorus 126 mg, Calcium 13 mg*

## Savory Citrus Salad
*Time: 40 Mins, Serves: 4, Skill: Easy*

**Ingredients**
- Extra-virgin olive oil (2 tbsp)
- Kalamata olives (1/4 cup), pitted and halved
- Fresh rosemary (2 tbsp), roughly chopped
- White wine or champagne vinegar (1 tbsp)
- Red onion (2 tbsp), sliced
- Pomegranate seeds (2 tbsp)
- Sea salt (1/4 tsp)
- Lime (20 oz.), peeled and pith removed

**Instructions**
- Break the lime into rounds by chopping them crosswise.
- Arrange lime slices on a platter.
- Heat the oil in a small skillet over medium-high heat for around 1 minute before reducing the heat to medium.
- Add the olives and rosemary to the skillet and cook, stirring regularly, for around 2 minutes, or until the rosemary is mildly sizzling but still fresh.
- Take the pot off the heat and drain the contents into a shallow bowl.
- Immediately pour in the vinegar and toss in the onion slices.
- Drizzle the limes with the dressing combination.
- If necessary, season with salt.
- Serve with pomegranate seeds as a garnish.

*Calories 123, Protein 29 g, Sodium 91 mg, Potassium 221 mg, Phosphorus 261 mg, Calcium 19 mg*

## Riced Cauliflower Salad
*Time: 35 Mins, Serves: 6, Skill: Easy*

**Ingredients**
- Pomegranate seeds (1/2 cup)
- Almonds (1/2 cup), sliced or chopped
- Mint (1/2 cup), chopped
- Chickpeas (1 cup)
- Cranberries (1/2 cup), dried, sweetened
- Cauliflower (4 1/2 cups), riced
- Lemon (1), zested

- Lemons (2), juiced
- Olive oil (1/4 cup)

**Instructions**
- Cut the core and leaves from the cauliflower florets and grate them on the wide whole side of a box grater.
- In a big salad bowl, position the riced cauliflower.
- Toss in the pomegranate, mint, almonds, cranberries, chickpeas, and lemon zest.
- Toss the salad with lemon juice and olive oil, gently mixing all ingredients.
- Serve with crisp bread or as a side salad for lunch.

*Calories 143, Protein 24 g, Sodium 81 mg, Potassium 31 mg, Phosphorus 96 mg, Calcium 13 mg*

## Summer Salad
*Time: 40 Mins, Serves: 4, Skill: Easy*

**Ingredients**
- Head bibb or butter lettuce (1 small), torn
- Strawberries (6-8), sliced
- Purple onion (1 small), sliced in rings
- Sugar (1 tsp)
- Slivered almonds (1/4 cup), toasted
- Parmesan cheese (1/4 cup), shredded
- Olive oil (1/4 cup)
- Balsamic vinegar (2 tbsp)
- Pepper (1/8 tsp)

**Instructions**
- Toss all the salad ingredients together in a salad dish.
- Mix the dressing ingredients in a jar: olive oil, balsamic vinegar, sugar, and pepper; cover and shake gently until completely mixed.
- Toss the salad with the dressing to coat it.
- Immediately serve.

*Calories 49, Protein 14 g, Sodium 22 mg, Potassium 122 mg, Phosphorus 62 mg, Calcium 3 mg*

## Shrimp Salad with Cucumber Mint
*Time: 30 Mins, Serves: 6, Skill: Easy*

**Ingredients**
- Fresh mint leaves (1 cup)
- Lemon juice (2 tbsp)
- Olive oil (3 tbsp)
- Cucumber (1/2), seeded, diced
- Lemon zest (1)
- Med shrimp (2 lb.), cleaned
- Pepper, to taste

**Instructions**
- Blanch the shrimp for 3 minutes in boiling water, then drain and put aside.
- In a blender or food processor, combine the mint and lemon juice and pulse to coarsely chop the mint.
- Drizzle in the olive oil after pureeing the mint until it is finely sliced.
- Combine the shrimp, mint blend, cucumber, zest, and pepper in a bowl and serve.

*Calories 323, Protein 44 g, Sodium 381 mg, Potassium 531 mg, Phosphorus 61 mg, Calcium 33 mg*

## Red Chili Mustard Vinegar
*Time: 35 Mins, Serves: 8, Skill: Easy*

**Ingredients**
- Pepper
- Chili powder (1 tbsp)
- Red wine vinegar (1/4 cup)
- Olive oil (1/2 cup)
- Dijon mustard (2 tbsp)
- Shallots (1 tbsp), chopped

**Instructions**
- Combine the mustard, pepper, chili powder, shallots, and vinegar in a mixing cup.
- Drizzle in the oil steadily until it emulsifies.
- To taste, apply more chili powder or seasoning.

*Calories 73, Protein 4 g, Sodium 21 mg, Potassium 121 mg, Phosphorus 61 mg, Calcium 23 mg*

## Red Cabbage with Apples
*Time: 30 Mins, Serves: 6, Skill: Easy*

**Ingredients**
- Olive or vegetable oil (2 tbsp)
- Cider vinegar (1/4 cup)
- Brown sugar (2 tbsp)
- Green apple (1)
- Head red cabbage (1 small)
- Onion (1), coarsely chopped

**Instructions**
- Sauté the onion in the oil in a wide skillet until softened (nearly 5 minutes).
- Mix in the vinegar, sugar, and pepper;
- Add the apple and cabbage.
- Bring to a boil, then reduce to low heat, cover, and simmer until the cabbage wilts, around 15 minutes.

*Calories 139, Protein 4 g, Sodium 181 mg, Potassium 131 mg, Phosphorus 196 mg, Calcium 13 mg*

## Purple and Gold Thai Coleslaw
*Time: 25 Mins, Serves: 3, Skill: Easy*

**Ingredients**
**Dressing:**
- Light soy sauce (1 1/2 tbsp)
- Brown sugar (3 tbsp)
- Ginger (2 tbsp), peeled and minced
- Garlic (1/2 tbsp), minced
- Peanut butter (5 tbsp)
- Rice vinegar (5 tbsp)
- Canola oil (5 tbsp)

**Slaw:**
- Red cabbage (7 cups)
- Yellow pepper (2 cups), sliced or chopped
- Green onions (3/4 cup), sliced
- Fresh cilantro (1/2 bunch)

**Instructions**
- In a mixing bowl, combine all the dressing components.
- Add the slaw ingredients and the dressing in a wide mixing bowl. Combine thoroughly, and serve.

*Calories 73, Protein 41 g, Sodium 221 mg, Potassium 92 mg, Phosphorus 218 mg, Calcium 12 mg*

## Pomegranate and Persimmon Salad
*Time: 45 Mins, Serves: 12, Skill: Easy*

**Ingredients**
- Mixed salad greens (6 cups)
- Dried basil leaves (2 tbsp)
- Raspberry vinegar (1/4 cup)
- Olive oil (2 tbsp)
- Fresh persimmons (2-3)
- Goat cheese (8 oz.), crumbled
- Pomegranate seeds (1/2 cup)
- Pecans or cashews (1/2 cup), chopped

**Instructions**
- Clean the greens. In the salad spinner, rinse well or spin.
- Toss oil with pomegranate seeds, vinegar, nuts, basil.
- Peel and chop the persimmons and layer them on the top of the greens with goat cheese (crumbled).
- Chill before serving.

*Calories 280, Protein 15 g, Sodium 219 mg, Potassium 304 mg, Phosphorus 105 mg, Calcium 108 mg*

## Raspberry Vinaigrette
*Time: 10 Mins, Serves: 6, Skill: Easy*

**Ingredients**
- Raspberry vinegar (1/2 cup)
- Oil (1/4 cup)
- Dijon mustard (1 tsp)
- Sugar (1 tbsp)
- Mint leaves (1/4 cup), chopped

**Instructions**
- In a bowl, combine all the ingredients.

*Calories 93, Protein 21 g, Sodium 92 mg, Potassium 29 mg, Phosphorus 128 mg, Calcium 13 mg*

## Fire and Ice Watermelon Salsa
*Time: 25 Mins, Serves: 6, Skill: Easy*

**Ingredients**
- Green bell pepper (1 cup), chopped
- Lime juice (2 tbsp)
- Cilantro (1 tbsp), chopped
- Green onion (1 tbsp), chopped
- Jalapeño (2 meds), seeded and minced
- Garlic clove (1), crushed
- Watermelon (3 cups), chopped

**Instructions**
- In a large mixing bowl, combine all the ingredients and mix thoroughly.
- Chill for at least an hour before serving.
- Serve with chicken or seafood as a sauce or a dip.

*Calories 33, Protein 4 g, Sodium 29 mg, Potassium 22 mg, Phosphorus 29 mg, Calcium 22 mg*

## Fruity Chicken Salad
*Time: 35 Mins, Serves: 8, Skill: Easy*

**Ingredients**
- Apple (1), cubed
- Raisins (3/4 cup)
- Sour cream (1/2 cup)
- Mayonnaise (1/4 cup)
- Rice vinegar (1 tsp), unseasoned
- Sugar (2 tsp)
- Chicken breasts (2 cups), cooked
- Almonds (1 cup), sliced
- Celery stalk (1), chopped
- Green onion (1), chopped

- Seedless grapes (2 cups)
- Chinese five-spice blend (1/2 tsp)

**Instructions**
- Combine the chicken, celery, green onion, almonds, grapes, apples, and raisins in a big mixing bowl.
- Blend the sour cream, rice vinegar, mayonnaise, sugar, and Chinese 5-Spice in a separate cup.
- In a mixing bowl, combine the chicken and the dressing.

*Calories 173, Protein 27 g, Sodium 129 mg, Potassium 221 mg, Phosphorus 361 mg, Calcium 23 mg*

## Grilled Vegetable Pasta Salad
*Time: 45 Mins, Serves: 8, Skill: Easy*

**Ingredients**
- Lemon juice (1/4 cup)
- Olive oil (1/4 cup)
- Black pepper (1/2 tsp)
- Rotini (12 oz.), uncooked
- Zucchini (2 medium), sliced
- Head anise fennel (1), sliced
- Mushrooms (8), quartered
- Garlic cloves (2), minced
- Gijon mustard (1 tbsp)
- Red onion (1 medium), sliced
- Fresh basil leaves (2 tbsp), shredded
- Fresh thyme (1 tbsp)
- Fresh parsley (1 tbsp), chopped

**Instructions**
- To produce the dressing, whisk together all the ingredients in a big mixing bowl.
- In a large mixing bowl, combine all the vegetables. Pour half of the dressing over the vegetables and toss to evenly coat them. Allow the vegetables to marinate while the pasta cooks according to the package directions. Rinse the rotini in cold water.
- Preheat the oven to broil, or fire up the grill in the meantime, using a greased broiler tray whether using the microwave or a barbecue bowl if using the grill.
- Place the vegetables on a broiling pan or a hot grill basket and cook until golden brown, stirring every 4-5 minutes to ensure even browning. Move to a serving bowl with the pasta and any leftover dressing, as well as the fresh herbs, and serve after tossing.

*Calories 93, Protein 2 g, Sodium 129 mg, Potassium 121 mg, Phosphorus 69 mg, Calcium 17 mg*

## Katy's Mango Salad
*Time: 25 Mins, Serves: 4, Skill: Easy*

**Ingredients**
- Fresh cilantro (3-4 tbsp), chopped
- Jalapeño pepper (1), seeded, finely chopped
- Mangos (2 large), diced
- Red peppers (2), diced
- Juice from limes (2)
- Honey (2 tbsp)

**Instructions**
- In a mixing cup, combine all the ingredients and chill for 1 hour.

*Calories 73, Protein 4 g, Sodium 21 mg, Potassium 121 mg, Phosphorus 61 mg, Calcium 23 mg*

## Lemony Shrimp & Couscous Salad
*Time: 25 Mins, Serves: 4, Skill: Easy*

**Ingredients**
- Water (1 1/2 cups)
- Fresh lemon juice (3 tbsp)
- Olive oil (1 tbsp)
- Parmesan cheese (1/2 cup), grated
- Couscous (1 cup), uncooked
- Shrimp (1 lb.), cooked
- Red pepper (1 1/2 cups), diced
- Green onions (1/4 cup), sliced
- Fresh basil (1/2 cup), chopped
- Chicken broth (1/4 cup), low-salt

**Instructions**
- Bring the water to a low boil.
- Stir in the couscous.
- Once cooked, cover it with plastic wrap and set it aside for 5 minutes.
- Then fluff with a fork.
- In a mixing cup, combine the couscous, shrimp, green onions, peppers, and basil.
- Add the broth, olive oil, vinegar, lemon juice, and salad dressing.
- Toss gently to cover.
- Add a sprinkling of grated cheese on top.

*Calories 134, Protein 41 g, Sodium 113 mg, Potassium 118 mg, Phosphorus 263 mg, Calcium 11 mg*

## Kicking' Chicken Tacos
*Time: 25 Mins, Serves: 6, Skill: Easy*

**Ingredients**
- Green onions (2), sliced
- Cilantro (1/2 cup), chopped
- Chicken breasts (1 lb.), skinless and boneless
- Taco seasoning (1 1/2 tsp), without salt
- Lime (1), juiced
- Corn tortillas (8)
- Iceberg lettuce (1 cup), chopped or shredded
- Sour cream (1/4 cup)

**Instructions**
- Boil the water and cook the chicken for 20 minutes.
- Shred the chicken or thinly slice it into bite-size pieces.
- In a mixing bowl, combine the chicken, lime juice, and Mexican seasoning.
- Fill the tortillas with lettuce and chicken.
- Add sour cream, cilantro, green onions, or other garnishes if desired.

*Calories 79, Protein 24 g, Sodium 22 mg, Potassium 189 mg, Phosphorus 291 mg, Calcium 23 mg*

## Pear and White Cheddar Salad
*Time: 30Mins, Serves: 2, Skill: Easy*

**Ingredients**
Salad
- Thick white bread (1 slice)
- Organic leaves (60g), mixed & freshly washed
- Ripe pears (2 medium)
- Juice of lemon (1/4)
- Cherry tomatoes (60g)
- Cheddar cheese mature white (60g)

Salad dressing
- Rapeseed oil (1 tbsp)
- Olive oil (2 tbsp)
- Golden syrup (1 tsp)
- Wholegrain mustard (1 level tsp)
- Brown sugar (a pinch)
- Balsamic vinegar (2 tbsp)

**Instructions**
- In a lidded bowl, add the vinegar, rapeseed and olive oil, mustard, golden syrup, and sugar; shake vigorously until the mixture is thick and smooth. Refrigerate.
- To make croutons, first cut the bread into pieces, then heat 1 tablespoon of oil in a frying pan and fry the bread cubes until golden brown and crunchy, then keep warm in the oven until ready to serve.
- Quarter cherry tomatoes and peel, root, and slice pears; clean and prepare 4 salad leaf parts on plates / in tiny containers; drizzle lemon juice over pear slices.
- Arrange croutons and cherry tomatoes on top of the cheese cubes or crumbles, and drizzle the sauce over the salad.

*Calories 73, Protein 10 g, Sodium 21 mg, Potassium 221 mg, Phosphorus 91 mg, Calcium 22 mg*

## Lemon Curry Chicken Salad
*Time: 25 Mins, Serves: 4, Skill: Easy*

**Ingredients**
- Vegetable oil (1/4 cup)
- Celery (1/2 cup), sliced
- Frozen lemonade concentrate (1/4 cup), thawed
- Ground ginger (1/4 tsp)
- Curry powder (1/4 tsp)
- Garlic powder (1/8 tsp)
- Chicken (1 1/2 cups), cooked and diced
- Grapes (1 1/2 cups), halved

**Instructions**
- Combine the lemonade concentrate, oil, and spices in a big mixing cup.
- Gently toss in the remaining ingredients.
- Serve after 1 hour marinating.

*Calories 43, Protein 22 g, Sodium 121 mg, Potassium 310 mg, Phosphorus 196 mg, Calcium 19 mg*

## Cottage Cheese Salad
*Time: 30 Mins, Serves: 4, Skill: Easy*

**Ingredients**
- 1 package Jell-O (3-oz), lime or raspberry
- Whipped cream (8-oz), 1 carton
- Creamed cottage cheese (2 lb.)
- Pineapple (6-oz.), 1 can juice packed, drained, crushed

**Instructions**
- Combine the dry Jell-O and the cheese in a mixing dish.
- Add the pineapple that has been drained of its juices. Add the cream into the mixture.

- Let it chill.

*Calories 143, Protein 24 g, Sodium 89 mg, Potassium 21 mg, Phosphorus 196 mg, Calcium 43 mg*

## Cranberry Frozen Salad

*Time: 25 Mins, Serves: 4, Skill: Easy*

**Ingredients**
- Vanilla extract (1/2 teaspoon)
- Cranberry sauce (16 oz.), 1 can
- Cream cheese (8 oz.), 1 package
- Whipping cream (1/2 pint)

**Instructions**
- Melt the cream cheese with a blender.
- In this order, add the whipping cream, vanilla, and cranberry sauce.
- Using a pastry container, pipe it into a 9" x 9" baking tray.
- Freeze.
- To serve, cut the frozen salad into squares.

*Calories 73, Protein 11 g, Sodium 91 mg, Potassium 120 mg, Phosphorus 22 mg, Calcium 2 mg*

# Meat Recipes

## Chili Con Carne
*Time: 1 hour and 45 Mins, Serves: 2, Skill: Hard*

**Ingredients**
- Garlic powder (1 tsp)
- Ground cumin (1/2 tsp)
- Water (1/4 liter.)
- Lean ground beef (1 lb.)
- Onion (1 cup), chopped
- Green pepper (1/2 cup), chopped
- Chili powder (2 tbsp)
- Paprika (1/2 tsp)

**Instructions**
- Brown the beef in a pot. Drain all unnecessary fat. Add the green pepper and onion.
- Continue to cook until the onion is translucent. After including the remaining ingredients, cook for 1 hour and 30 minutes.
- measure the chili and add enough water to create 5 cups before serving.

*Calories 367, Protein 36 g, Sodium 232 mg, Potassium 321 mg, Phosphorus 96 mg, Calcium 13 mg*

## Grilled Marinated Beef Steak
*Time: 8 hours and 30 Mins, Serves: 4, Skill: Hard*

**Ingredients**
- Garlic cloves (2), minced
- Pepper (1/4 tsp)
- Chuck steak (1 1/2 lb.)
- Beer (12 oz.), 1 can
- Green onion (1/2 cup), sliced
- Green pepper (1/4 cup), chopped
- Vinegar (2 tbsp)
- Teriyaki sauce (1 tbsp)
- Sugar (2 tbsp)

**Instructions**
- Put the steak in a bowl. Place the remaining ingredients over the steak and mix well.
- Marinate in the refrigerator for 6 to 8 hours, stirring once or twice to enable the essences to absorb.
- Drain and put aside the steak marinade.
- Broil the steak for 15 to 20 minutes over medium coals, coating it often with the reserved marinade.

*Calories 548, Protein 30 g, Sodium 1344 mg, Potassium 561 mg, Phosphorus 96 mg, Calcium 65 mg*

## Meat Loaf
*Time: 1 hour and 20 Mins, Serves: 4, Skill: Hard*

**Ingredients**
- Dry mustard (1/4 tsp)
- Nutmeg (1/4 tsp)
- Onions (2 tbsp)
- Eggs (2), beaten
- Milk (3/4 cup)
- Bread crumbs (2/3 cup)
- Ground beef (1 1/2 lbs.)
- Sage (1/2 tsp)
- Mushrooms (1/2 cup), fresh, sliced

**Topping**
- Ketchup (1/4 cup), without salt
- Brown sugar (2 tbsp)
- Cheddar cheese (1/4 cup), shredded

**Instructions**
- In a mixing tub, combine all the meatloaf ingredients and pat onto a pan.
- Preheat oven to 350°F and bake for 1 hour. Enable the grease to drain after extracting them from the oven.
- Toss the topping ingredients together and scatter over the meatloaf.
- Bake for 5 minutes, or before the cheese starts to melt.

*Calories 372, Protein 18.2 g, Sodium 334.6 mg, Potassium 120 mg, Phosphorus 68 mg, Calcium 25 mg*

## Onion Smothered Steak
*Time: 1 hour and 35 Mins, Serves: 4, Skill: Hard*

**Ingredients**
- Vinegar (1 tbsp)
- Garlic clove (1), minced
- Flour (1/4 cup)
- Bay leaf (1)
- Dried thyme (1/4 tsp), crushed
- Round steak (1 1/2 lb.), 3/4" thick
- Oil (2 tbsp)
- Pepper (1/8 tsp)
- Water (1 cup)

- Onions (3), sliced

**Instructions**
- Cut the steak into 8 separate halves with a sharp knife. Pound the flour and pepper onto the steak with your fingers.
- Brown the meat in oil in a skillet (both sides). Put it on a plate and set it aside.
- In a skillet, combine the garlic, vinegar, bay leaf, and thyme. Simply get it to low heat.
- Put the meat in the middle of the mixture and top with the sliced onions. With the cover down, cook for an hour.

*Calories 518, Protein 30 g, Sodium 544 mg, Potassium 510 mg, Phosphorus 161 mg, Calcium 55 mg*

## Pork with Julienne Vegetables
*Time: 35 Mins, Serves: 2, Skill: Easy*

**Ingredients**
- Garlic clove (1), minced
- Lemon juice (2 tbsp)
- Julienne zucchini (2 cups), strips
- Dry white wine (1/3 cup)
- Julienne summer squash (1 cup), strips
- Red bell pepper (1/2 cup), strips
- Pepper (1/8 tsp)
- Pork cutlets (2)
- Flour (1/2 cup)

**Instructions**
- Cut each cutlet to a thickness of 1/4 inch. In a mixing bowl, combine the flour and seasonings.
- Dredge the cutlets in the flour. In a wide skillet with 2 tablespoons of olive oil, cook the cutlets for 5 minutes on either size. Place on a warm serving platter.
- Toss the pan with the wine and lemon juice. Heat it until it reduces. Then stir in 1 tablespoon of margarine.
- Drizzle the sauce on top of the cutlets. Combine the vegetables and 1 tablespoon of margarine in a saucepan.
- Cook for 3 to 4 minutes over high heat, stirring constantly.
- Serve the pork with vegetables on top.

*Calories 191, Protein 20.9 g, Sodium 152.5 mg, Potassium 31 mg, Phosphorus 96 mg, Calcium 13 mg*

## Salt-Free Pizza
*Time: 40 Mins, Serves: 2, Skill: Easy*

**Ingredients**
- Onion (1/4 cup), chopped
- Sugar (1 tbsp)
- Oil (1 tbsp)
- Mozzarella cheese (6 oz.), shredded
- Green pepper (1/4 cup), chopped
- Water (1/2 cup)
- Ground beef (1/2 lb.), cooked, well-drained
- Dough
- Warm water (1 cup)
- Dry yeast (1 1/4 teaspoon), 1/2 package
- Sugar (1 tbsp)
- Oil (1 tbsp)
- Flour (2 cups)

**For Sauce**
- Oregano (1/2 tsp)
- Tomato paste (3 oz.), salt-free
- Garlic powder (1/4 tsp)

**Instructions**
- Put the yeast in a tub of warm water. Add 1 tablespoon of oil, 1 tablespoon of butter, sugar, and enough flour to make a smooth dough. Using 20 strokes to combine.
- Put it in a greased 17' x 14' tray, turn to moisten surfaces, cover, and set in a warm spot.
- In a saucepan, combine 1/2 cup water, tomato paste, oregano, garlic powder, 1 tablespoon of butter, and 1 tablespoon of oil. Combine and cook for 5 minutes.
- Evenly spread the sauce over the dough.
- Add green pepper, onion, beef, and cheese. Preheat oven to 400°F and bake for 20 to 30 minutes, or until the dough and cheese are golden brown.
- Using a sharp knife, cut into 12 pieces.

*Calories 201, Protein 11 g, Sodium 75 mg, Potassium 176 mg, Phosphorus 115 mg, Calcium 13 mg*

## Pork Pasties
*Time: 1 hour and 20 Mins, Serves: 4, Skill: Hard*

**Ingredients**
- Potato (1 medium/100g)
- White/ Black pepper
- Carrot (1 medium)

- Pork (200g), minced
- Dried herbs
- Short crust pastry (500g), one packet
- Onion (1 small)

**Instruction:**
- Preheat oven to 400 °F.
- Brown the pork in a saucepan (non-stick). Cook for 15 minutes, or until the meat is halfway cooked. Eliminate any residual liquid from the meat.
- Boil the potatoes, carrots, and onion for 10 minutes, then drain well and break into small bits. Toss the mince in a big mixing tub. As required, season the meat with pepper and herbs.
- On a saucer, roll out the pastry to produce 6 circles.
- Divide the meat among the pastry rings, dampen the pastry corners, fold in half, and press the pastry corners together to seal. Rub it with milk and place it on a baking tray.
- Bake for 25-30 minutes in the center of the oven.

*Calories 191, Protein 30.9 g, Sodium 159 mg, Potassium 81 mg, Phosphorus 92 mg, Calcium 10 mg*

## Barbecue Beef

*Time: 8 hours and 30 Mins, Serves: 4, Skill: Hard*

**Ingredients**
- Beef (2 lbs.), for roast
- Red chili (1)
- Chipotle chili (1/4)
- Barbeque sauce
- Black pepper (1 tsp)
- Onion (1), chopped into large slices
- Garlic clove (1)
- Bay leaf (1)

**Instructions**
- Cut the beef into strips.
- Thoroughly dry it.
- Place in a crockpot or microwave roasting bag.
- Combine the onion, pepper, bay leaf, barbeque sauce, garlic, and chilis in a blender. Combine all the products thoroughly.
- Place the beef strips in the slow cooker and stir to combine.
- Remove any excess air from the baking bag (if applicable) and seal it as tightly as possible.
- Cook for 1 hour on high, then reduce to low and cook for another 4 hours.

*Calories 343, Protein 40 g, Sodium 381 mg, Potassium 171 mg, Phosphorus 66 mg, Calcium 32 mg*

## Beef Casserole

*Time: 40 Mins, Serves: 2, Skill: Easy*

**Ingredients**
- Salt (1/4 tsp)
- Fresh parsley (1 tbsp), chopped
- Lean beef (500g)
- Water (350ml)
- Onion (1 medium), chopped
- Vegetable oil (1 tbsp)
- Carrots (2 medium), peeled and sliced
- White pepper (1/4 tsp)

**Instructions**
- Fry the onion in a limited volume of vegetable oil.
- Add the beef and cook until it is browned.
- Then add some water and cook until the beef is tender.
- Add the carrots and onions to the meat and proceed to cook until the vegetables and the meat are cooked through.
- Apply salt, pepper, and finely chopped parsley to taste.

*Calories 351, Protein 29 g, Sodium 124 mg, Potassium 381 mg, Phosphorus 216 mg, Calcium 77 mg*

## Spicy Beef Stir-Fry

*Time: 45 Mins, Serves: 4, Skill: Easy*

**Ingredients**
- Sugar (1/2 tsp)
- Sesame oil (1/4 tsp)
- Egg (1 large), beaten
- Water (2 tbsp), separated
- Beef round tip (12 oz.), sliced
- Canola oil (3 tbsp), separated
- Cornstarch (2 tbsp), separated
- Onions (1 cup), sliced
- Green bell pepper (1), sliced
- Sherry (1 tbsp)
- Red chili pepper (1/4 tsp), or to taste, ground
- Parsley, optional garnish
- Soy sauce (2 tsp), reduced-sodium

### Instructions
- Whisk together 1 large egg, 1 tablespoon of cornstarch, 1 tablespoon of water, 1 tablespoon of canola oil, and the beef in a large mixing bowl. Set it aside to marinate for 20-minute.
- In a different pan, combine the leftover water and cornstarch.
- In a skillet, add 2 tablespoons of oil and the marinated meat mixture. Cook the beef until it is golden brown.
- Add the green bell peppers, onion, and chili pepper. Drizzle the sherry over everything and cook for a minute. Then add the sesame oil, and soy sauce, cornstarch and water. Stir until it thickens before serving.

*Calories 270, Protein 29 g, Sodium 400 mg, Potassium 380 mg, Phosphorus 174 mg, Calcium 39 mg*

## Beef Curry
*Time: 3 hours, Serves: 4, Skill: Hard*

### Ingredients
- Vegetable oil (5 tbsp)
- Beef with bone (1-1/2 lb.), small
- Whole cumin seeds (3/4 tsp)
- Salt (3/4 tsp)
- Bay leaves (2)
- Whole peppercorns (1/4 tsp)
- Cayenne pepper (1-1/2 tsp)
- Cinnamon stick (1)
- Garam masala (1/2 tsp)
- Tomato (1 medium)
- Garlic cloves (2)
- Onions (2 medium)
- Ginger root (1" cube)

### Instructions
- Peel and chop the tomato. Mince the garlic, pepper, and ginger root.
- Heat the oil in a large, thick pot over medium-high heat. Add the cumin seeds, bay leaves, cinnamon sticks, and peppercorns, stirring occasionally.
- Add the garlic, ginger, and onion, and cook until brown specks appear on the onion.
- Add the beef, cabbage, cayenne pepper, flour, and a quarter cup of water to the pan and blend well. Bring to a low simmer, stirring regularly.
- Cover the pan, lower the heat to low, and simmer for 45 minutes, or until the beef is tender and juicy. Continue to stir during the cooking period.
- Remove the cover and maintain a low heat. To minimize the amount of oil used, season with garam masala and fry, stirring periodically, for around 5 minutes.

*Calories 337, Protein 29 g, Sodium 31 mg, Potassium 231 mg, Phosphorus 96 mg, Calcium 19 mg*

## Slow-Cooked Bavarian Pot Roast
*Time: 18 Hours, Serves: 2, Skill: Hard*

### Ingredients
- Apple juice (1/2 cup), or water
- Fresh apple slices, optional garnish
- Water (4 tbsp)
- Pepper (1/2 tsp)
- Beef chuck roast (3 lb.)
- Ginger (1/2 tsp), freshly ground
- Vegetable oil (1 tsp)
- Garlic cloves (3), whole
- Apples (2 cups), sliced
- Flour (4 tbsp)
- Onions (1/2 cup), sliced

### Instructions
- Trim the beef roast of any unnecessary fat. Using a napkin, wipe and dry the surface. Apply butter over the top of the roast, season with ginger and pepper, and wrap the roast in all the garlic cloves. Then sear all sides of the roast pot in a hot pan greased with oil.
- Add the onions and apple. Drizzle the apple juice over the roast in the pot.
- Cook for 10 to 12 hours on low heat, or 5 to 6 hours on high heat.
- Take the roast out of the slow cooker and set it aside. Put it away to keep it warm.
- Remove the pot roast juices and put them directly into the slow cooker. To suppress and thicken the liquid, increase the heat to a high setting.
- Create a smooth paste with the flour and water, then whisk it into the slow cooker.
- Cook until the mixture thickens, sealed. Pour the sauce over the roast just before serving.

*Calories 370, Protein 40 g, Sodium 521 mg, Potassium 525 mg, Phosphorus 287 mg, Calcium 47 mg*

# Roast Pork Loin with Sweet and Tart Apple Stuffing

*Time: 1 hour and 20 Mins, Serves: 6, Skill: Medium*

**Ingredients**

**Cherry Marmalade Glaze:**
- Orange marmalade (1/2 cup), sugar-free
- Nutmeg (1/8 tsp)
- Apple juice (1/4 cup)
- Dried cherries (1/4 cup)
- Cinnamon (1/8 tsp)

**Apple Stuffing:**
- Hawaiian rolls, or any white bread (2 cups), cubed
- Canola oil (2 tbsp)
- Butter (2 tbsp), unsalted
- Granny smith (1/2 cup), finely diced (honey crisp)
- Celery (2 tbsp), finely diced,
- Onions (2 tbsp), finely diced,
- Black pepper (1 tsp)
- Fresh thyme (1 tbsp), or dried thyme (1/2 tsp)
- Chicken stock (1/2 cup), low-sodium

**Roast Pork Loin:**
- Pork loin (1 lb.), boneless
- Butcher twine (2), 18-inch pieces

**Instructions**

**Cherry Marmalade Glaze:**
- Heat all the glaze components in a small saucepan over medium-high heat

before the marmalade liquifies and begins to bubble. Set the mixture aside.
- Preheat the oven to 400 °F.

**Apple Stuffing:**
- In a big sauté pan over medium-high heat, fry all ingredients in oil for 2-3 minutes, except the chicken stock.
- Gradually add the chicken stock until the mixture is sticky but not soggy. (Depending on how much juice is released from the apples during preparation, this might or may not be enough.)
- Switch off the heat and set aside, allowing the stuffing to cool down to room temperature.

**Loin de pork:**
- Cut five 1-inch apart slits down the length of the loin to shape pockets.
- Fill each pocket with around 2 tablespoons of stuffing (saving about half a cup).
- Secure the stuffing in place by looping the twine around the loin as desired.
- Spread the remaining stuffing on a baking dish, cover with the tied, stuffed pork, and bake for 45 minutes at 400 °F, or until an internal temperature of 160 °F is achieved.
- Glaze the loin, switch off the heat, and leave it in the oven with the dried cherry marmalade for 10-15 minutes. Take a pork loin and cut it into pieces. Warm it up and serve it.

*Calories 263, Protein 14 g, Sodium 137 mg, Potassium 275 mg, Phosphorus 154 mg, Calcium 68 mg*

# Pasta with Cheesy Meat Sauce

*Time: 40 Mins, Serves: 4, Skill: Easy*

**Ingredients**
- Pasta (1/2 box), large-shaped
- Black pepper (1/2 tsp), ground
- Worcestershire sauce (2 tbsp), reduced-sodium
- Onions (1/2 cup), diced
- Ground beef (1 lb.)
- Onion flakes (1 tbsp)
- Beef bouillon (1 tbsp), no salt added
- Beef stock (1 1/2 cups), reduced-sodium
- Pepper jack or Monterey cheese (3/4 cup), shredded
- Tomato sauce (1 tbsp), no salt added
- Italian seasoning (1/2 tsp)
- Cream cheese (8 oz.), softened

**Instructions**
- Prepare the pasta as directed on the box.
- Brown the ground beef in a frying pan. Fry the meat until it is tender and golden, adding onion and onion flakes if required.
- Remove the pasta and combine the browned beef, stock, bouillon, and tomato sauce in a pan.
- Cook, stirring constantly until the mixture boils. Turn off the heat and combine the cooked pasta, melted cream cheese, shredded cheese, and seasonings in a large mixing bowl (Italian seasoning, black pepper, and Worcestershire sauce).
- Combine the pasta and meat mixture in a mixing bowl until the cheese is fully melted.

*Calories 143, Protein 24 g, Sodium 81 mg, Potassium 31 mg, Phosphorus 96 mg, Calcium 13 mg*

## Hawaiian-Style Slow-Cooked Beef
*Time: 6 Hours, Serves: 4, Skill: Hard*

**Ingredients**
- Onion powder (1 tsp)
- Paprika (1/2 tsp)
- Liquid smoke (2 tbsp)
- Boneless Beef (4 lb.)
- Black pepper (1/2 tsp), freshly ground
- Pickled or radishes red onions (optional garnish)
- Garlic powder (1/2 tsp)

**Instructions**
- In a bag, add black pepper, paprika, garlic powder, and onion.
- Rub the beef with the flavoring paste all over. In a slow cooker or a cooker, position the beef. Sprinkle with liquid smoke.
- Pour sufficient water into the crock-pot or slow cooker to fill it to a depth of 14–12 inches. Cook for 4–5 hours on high pressure.
- Shred the beef with two forks after extracting it from the cooker.
- Serve it warm.

*Calories 370, Protein 40 g, Sodium 521 mg, Potassium 525 mg, Phosphorus 287 mg, Calcium 47 mg*

## Stuffing of Tacos with Beef
*Time: 40 Mins, Serves: 3, Skill: Easy*

**Ingredients**
- Lean ground beef (1 1/4 lb.)
- Red pepper (1/2 tsp), ground
- Black pepper (1/2 tsp)
- Italian seasoning (1 tsp)
- Garlic powder (1 tsp)
- Onion powder (1 tsp)
- Vegetable oil (2 tbsp)
- Tabasco sauce (1/2 tsp)
- Nutmeg (1/2 tsp)

**Will also need:**
- Taco shells (1 packet)
- Lettuce (1/2 head), shredded

**Instructions**
- Bring the oil to a simmer. Combine the ground beef and all other ingredients (except the lettuce) in a mixing bowl.
- In a skillet, cook until all the components, including the beef, are fully mixed and cooked through.
- Fill each taco shell with 4 tablespoons of meat and finish with chopped lettuce.

*Calories 191, Protein 20.9 g, Sodium 152.5 mg, Potassium 31 mg, Phosphorus 96 mg, Calcium 13 mg*

## Spicy Barbecue Sauce
*Time: 40 Mins, Serves: 2, Skill: Easy*

**Ingredients**
- Dark corn syrup (1/4 cup)
- All-purpose flour (1 tbsp)
- Mrs. Dash, of your choice (1 tsp)
- Red wine vinegar (1/4 cup)
- Onion (1/4 cup), chopped
- Water (1 cup)
- Dry mustard (2 tsp)
- Tomato paste (2 tbsp)
- Tabasco pepper sauce (1 tsp)
- Vegetable oil (2 tbsp)

**Instructions**
- Combine all the ingredients in a saucepan, except the flour and vegetable oil.
- Render a paste of flour and vegetable oil in a separate pan.
- Put it in the saucepan and simmer on low heat before it reaches the ideal thickness.
- Brush or smear on beef that has been cooked or grilled.

*Calories 43, Protein 4 g, Sodium 21 mg, Potassium 31 mg, Phosphorus 16 mg, Calcium 12 mg*

## Fiesta Lime Tacos
*Time: 14 Mins, Serves: 12, Skill: Easy*

**Ingredients**
- Water (3/4 cup)
- Lean ground beef or turkey (1 lb.)
- Mrs. Dash Fiesta Lime Seasoning Blend (4 tbsp)
- Taco shells (12), or 6-inch flour tortillas

**Instructions**
- Brown the ground beef in a large skillet over medium-high heat.
- Get rid of the excess fat.
- Add the water and Mrs. Dash Fiesta Lime Seasoning Mixture.

- Bring the water to a boil. Reduce the heat to low and simmer, stirring occasionally, for 5 minutes.
- Scoop the meat mixture into taco shells or tortillas that are already soft. If chosen, serve with additional toppings.

*Calories 213, Protein 20 g, Sodium 31 mg, Potassium 121 mg, Phosphorus 216 mg, Calcium 10 mg*

## Pork Steak
*Time: 7 Hours, Serves: 4, Skill: Hard*

### Ingredients
- Garlic cloves (2), minced
- Pepper (1/4 tsp)
- Chuck steak (1 1/2 lb.), pork
- Beer (12 oz.), 1 can
- Green onion (1/2 cup), sliced
- Green pepper (1/4 cup), chopped
- Vinegar (2 tbsp)
- Teriyaki sauce (1 tbsp)
- Sugar (2 tbsp)

### Instructions
- Put the steak in a serving bowl (shallow), pour the remaining ingredients over it and mix well.
- Marinate in the refrigerator for 6 to 8 hours, stirring once or twice to enable the essences to absorb.
- Drain and put aside the steak marinade.
- Broil the steak for 15 to 20 minutes over medium coals, coating it often with the reserved marinade.

*Calories 548, Protein 30 g, Sodium 144 mg, Potassium 261 mg, Phosphorus 126 mg, Calcium 45 mg*

## Spicy Lamb
*Time: 8 hours and 20 Mins, Serves: 4, Skill: Hard*

### Ingredients
- Leg of lamb (1), trimmed for roasting
- Garlic powder (1 1/2 tbsp)
- Vegetable oil (1/4 cup)
- Dry mustard (3 tbsp)

### Instructions
- In a mixing cup, combine the mustard, garlic powder, and oil.
- Marinate the lamb legs in the marinade for 6-8 hours. You could also leave it overnight.
- Roast the beef for 30 minutes a pound on the barbecue spit. When basting the meat with the marinade, use a beef thermostat to raise the temperature to 170 °F.

*Calories 417, Protein 48 g, Sodium 8 mg, Potassium 129 mg, Phosphorus 96 mg, Calcium 10 mg*

## Homemade Pan Sausage (Beef)
*Time: 40 Mins, Serves: 2, Skill: Easy*

### Ingredients
- Basil (1 tbsp), optional
- Fresh lean ground beef (1 lb.)
- Cooking spray
- Black pepper (1 tbsp), ground
- Sage (2 tbsp), ground
- Granulated sugar (2 tbsp)
- Red pepper (1/2 tbsp), ground

### Instructions
- Grind a loin of beef.
- Carefully mix all the ingredients to make sausages.
- Shape 2 teaspoons of the meat mixture into a patty.
- In a skillet or under the broiler, cook until thoroughly cooked.

*Calories 243, Protein 12 g, Sodium 88 mg, Potassium 212 mg, Phosphorus 106 mg, Calcium 10 mg*

## Seasoned Pork Chops
*Time: 1 hour and 10 Mins, Serves: 3, Skill: Hard*

### Ingredients
- Lean pork chops (4 x 4-ounce), fat removed
- Vegetable oil (2 tbsp)
- Thyme (1/2 tbsp)
- All-purpose flour (1/4 cup)
- Black pepper (1 tsp)
- Sage (1/2 tbsp)

### Instructions
- Preheat the oven to 350 °F.
- Spray the skillet with cooking spray.
- In a mixing dish, combine the flour, sage, black pepper, and thyme.
- Dredge the chops in the flour mix and drop them in the baking tray with the oil.
- Put it in the oven for about 40 minutes, or until it is juicy on all sides.

*Calories 191, Protein 30.9 g, Sodium 159 mg, Potassium 81 mg, Phosphorus 92 mg, Calcium 10 mg*

## Classic Beef Stroganoff with Egg Noodles

*Time: 1 hour 20 Mins, Serves: 4, Skill: Hard*

**Ingredients**
- Onions (1 cup), finely diced
- Egg (1), beaten
- Worcestershire sauce (2 tbsp), reduced-sodium
- Breadcrumbs (1/4 cup)
- Mayonnaise (1 tbsp)
- Tomato sauce (1 tbsp), no salt added
- Flour (2 tbsp)
- Black pepper (1 tsp), freshly ground
- Better than bouillon beef (4 tsp), reduced-sodium
- Sour cream (1/4 cup)
- Wide egg noodles (12oz. package), 1/2 package, cooked
- Chives (2 tbsp)
- Parsley (1/4 cup)
- Butter (2 tbsp), cold and cubed, unsalted
- Rosemary (1 tbsp), chopped
- Ground beef (1 lb.)
- Canola oil (3 tbsp)
- Water (3 cups)

**Instructions**
- Add the first 6 ingredients in a mixing cup with 1/2 teaspoon black pepper. Include the ground beef fully into the mixture. Make a total of 16 meatballs of the same size.
- In a frying pan over medium heat, brown the stroganoff meatballs. Move all the meatballs to one side of the plate and add the flour and oil. For 10 minutes, or until the sauce thickens, stir in the remaining water, black pepper, and bouillon.
- Remove the skillet from the heat and mix in the chives and sour cream before serving over egg noodles.

**Pasta**
- Combine the egg noodles and 2 tablespoons of water in a bowl
- Heat and combine the water until it is well moistened, then switch off the heat.
- Add the rosemary, sugar, and parsley in a large mixing cup.

*Calories 200, Protein 150 g, Sodium 81 mg, Potassium 50 mg, Phosphorus 116 mg, Calcium 23 mg*

## Taco Stuffing

*Time: 1 hour 25 Mins, Serves: 3, Skill: Medium*

**Ingredients**
- Lettuce (1/2 head), shredded
- Onion powder (1 tbsp)
- Vegetable oil (2 tbsp)
- Taco shells (1 medium)
- Lean ground beef or turkey (1 1/4 lb.)
- Nutmeg (1/2tbsp)
- Ground red pepper (1/2 tbsp)
- Black pepper (1/2 tbsp)
- Tabasco sauce (1/2 tbsp)
- Italian seasoning (1 tbsp)
- Garlic powder (1 tbsp)

**Instructions**
- Bring the oil to a simmer. Combine the ground beef and all other ingredients in a tub, reserving the lettuce and taco shells. Cook until the beef is finished and all the ingredients are thoroughly mixed.
- Serve the filled the beef taco shells with sliced lettuce.

*Calories 100, Protein 50 g, Sodium 181 mg, Potassium 250 mg, Phosphorus 180 mg, Calcium 43 mg*

## Open-Faced Steak & Onion Sandwich

*Time: 1 hour and 20 Mins, Serves: 2, Skill: Medium*

**Ingredients**
- Black pepper (1 tbsp)
- Hoagie rolls (4), sliced
- Steaks (4 x 4-oz. each), chopped
- Onion (1 medium), sliced into rings
- Lemon juice (1 tbsp)
- Vegetable oil (1 tbsp)
- Italian seasoning (1 tbsp)

**Instructions**
- Combine the steak, lemon juice, Italian seasoning, and black pepper in a mixing bowl.
- Heat the oil in a frying pan over low heat.
- Sear all sides of seasoned steaks before cooking to your preference. Remove the steak from the pan and pat dry with paper towels.
- Lower the heat to low and introduce the onion, cooking until it is soft.

- Serve with onion rings or on a sliced hoagie sandwich open-faced.

*Calories 313, Protein 31 g, Sodium 121 mg, Potassium 312 mg, Phosphorus 92 mg, Calcium 9 mg*

## Parsley Burger
*Time: 1 hour and 10 Mins, Serves: 1, Skill: Medium*

**Ingredients**
- Oregano (1/4 tbsp)
- Slender ground turkey or beef (1 lb.)
- Thyme (1/4 tbsp), ground
- Lemon juice (1 tbsp)
- Black pepper (1/4 tbsp)
- Parsley flakes (1 tbsp)

**Instructions**
- Gently blend all the ingredients in a large mixing cup.
- Shape into four small patties, each around 3/4 inches in diameter.
- Put in a skillet or broiler pan that has been finely greased.
- Broil for 10 to 15 minutes after turning, about 3" from the flame.

*Calories 443, Protein 49 g, Sodium 311 mg, Potassium 315 mg, Phosphorus 72 mg, Calcium 31 mg*

## Eggplant Casserole
*Time: 1 hour and 15 Mins, Serves: 2, Skill: Medium*

**Ingredients**
- Onion (1/2 cup), finely chopped
- Lean ground beef or turkey (1 lb.)
- Red pepper (1/2 tbsp), optional
- Eggplant (1 large)
- Egg (1 large), slightly beaten
- Vegetable oil (2 tbsp)
- Plain bread crumbs (2 cups)
- Green pepper (1/2 cup), chopped

**Instructions**
- Preheat the oven to 350 °F.
- Cook the eggplant until it is soft, then drain and mash it.
- Heat the oil in a big skillet and add the meat, onion, and green and red pepper. Before they turn golden brown, sauté them.
- In a big mixing cup, combine the eggplant, bread crumbs, and egg.
- Taste and season with red pepper flakes if required.
- In a casserole bowl combine all ingredients, bake for 30 to 45 minutes.

*Calories 331, Protein 25 g, Sodium 120 mg, Potassium 368 mg, Phosphorus 206 mg, Calcium 81 mg*

## Easy Beef Burgers
*Time: 1 hour 10 Mins, Serves: 2, Skill: Medium*

**Ingredients**
- Dried mixed herbs (a pinch)
- Onion (1), chopped
- Black pepper
- Beef or pork (500 g), low in fat, minced

**Instruction:**
- Ready the grill or barbecue by preheating it. Combine all the ingredients in a big mixing cup.
- Using clean, damp hands, split it into 8 small or 4 large patties. Cut the beef into flattish rounds of similar depth to ensure even and detailed cooking.
- Cook for 5 to 10 minutes on either side on the grill.
- Both the inside and outside of the burgers must be brown. Serve on pita bread or a sandwich bun with sliced lettuce and a spoonful of mayonnaise, tomato sauce, or vinegar.

*Calories 214, Protein 19 g, Sodium 211 mg, Potassium 215 mg, Phosphorus 122 mg, Calcium 21 mg*

## Pork Chops with Herb Crust
*Time: 45 Mins, Serves: 2, Skill: Medium*

**Ingredients**
- Garlic clove (1), chopped
- Oil (2 tbsp)
- Mixed dried herbs, or chopped parsley (1 pinch)
- Mustard (1 tbsp)
- Spring onions (2), or shallot (1), chopped
- Breadcrumbs (2 tbsp)
- Pork chops (2)

**Instruction:**
- Preheat the oven to 400°F.
- Place each pork chop in a roasting pan or baking dish with one side spread with mustard.
- In a mixing cup, combine the oil, garlic, onions, dried herbs, spring onion, and breadcrumbs to create the herb crust. Press the herb crust mixture

onto the surface of each pork chop and cover it with tin foil.
- Bake for 25 minutes, taking off the foil for the last 5 minutes. Serve with boiled potatoes, rice, or boiled vegetables.

*Calories 263, Protein 19 g, Sodium 237 mg, Potassium 175 mg, Phosphorus 141 mg, Calcium 18 mg*

## Pork Carne

*Time: 1 hour 20 Mins, Serves: 4, Skill: Hard*

### Ingredients
- Red kidney beans in water (200g/8oz), canned, rinsed, and drained
- Pork (500g/1lb), minced, low in fat
- Vegetable oil (1 tbsp)
- Paprika (1/2 tsp)
- Sugar (1/2 tbsp)
- Onion (1), chopped
- Vinegar (1/2 tbsp)
- Garlic clove (1), crushed
- Chili powder (1/2 tbsp)
- Tinned tomatoes (200g/8oz)

### Instruction
- In a small saucepan, heat the oil and cook the garlic and onion for 5 minutes over low heat.
- Add the minced pork and cook, stirring occasionally, until lightly browned.
- Add all the other ingredients, except the kidney beans. Cook on low heat for around 30 minutes, adding a little more water if necessary, to save it from sticking.
- Add the kidney beans and continue to cook for another 10 minutes or so.
- Using a slotted spoon, serve with rice or crusty bread.

*Calories 367, Protein 36 g, Sodium 232 mg, Potassium 321 mg, Phosphorus 96 mg, Calcium 13 mg*

## Jamaican Curried Goat

*Time: 2 Hours and 25 Mins, Serves: 6, Skill: Hard*

### Ingredients
- Vegetable oil (3 tbsp)
- Goat mutton/lamb boneless (600g/1lb)
- Ground black pepper
- Allspice (1 tbsp), Jamaican pimiento
- Thyme (1-2 sprigs)

**Marinade:**
- Scotch bonnet or chili pepper (1 small), seeds removed but left whole
- Ginger (1 finger piece), grated, or Ginger powder (1 tbsp)
- Spring onions (6), chopped
- Stock cube (1), reduced salt, crumbled
- Garlic cloves (2), chopped

### Instructions
- Cut the meat into 3 cm (1 inch) pieces after removing the fat. Toss the beef carefully with all the marinade components to coat it. To marinate, lock, and store overnight in the refrigerator.
- Heat the remaining oil in a big, heavy kettle and add the marinated beef. Cook, rolled, for 2 to 3 hours, until the meat is soft, including a little hot water if necessary, to prevent sticking. Reduce the temperature to low.
- Toss with a slotted spoon and serve with plain rice.

*Calories 329, Protein 43 g, Sodium 229 mg, Potassium 608 mg, Phosphorus 69 mg, Calcium 48 mg*

## Mince with Basil

*Time: 45 Mins, Serves: 2, Skill: Easy*

### Ingredients
- Garlic clove (1), crushed
- Fresh basil (1 handful/10g), chopped
- Vegetable oil (1 tbsp)
- Beef (500g), minced, low in fat if possible
- Soy sauce (1 tbsp), reduced-salt
- Chili (1), chopped
- Onion (1), chopped

### Instruction:
- In a small saucepan, heat the oil and add the garlic and chili.
- Add the minced beef and deep-fried under high pressure. Cook for 15 to 20 minutes, or until the mince is well browned. Combine the remaining ingredients and add them to the mix.
- Toss with a leafy green salad or a cooked vegetable of your choice, and serve with rice or pasta.

*Calories 243, Protein 24 g, Sodium 208 mg, Potassium 231 mg, Phosphorus 216 mg, Calcium 173 mg*

## Tortilla Beef Rollups

*Time: 25 Mins, Serves: 2, Skill: Easy*

### Ingredients
- Romaine lettuce leaves (2)

- Roast beef (5 oz.), cooked
- Red onion (1/4 cup), chopped
- Cucumber (8 slices)
- Flour tortilla (2), 6" size
- Red/Green or Yellow bell pepper (1/4), cut in strips
- Cream cheese (2 tbsp), whipped
- Herb seasoning blend (1 tbsp)

**Instructions**
- Place the tortillas on a plate and spread cream cheese on top.
- Split the products in half to produce two tortillas. On each tortilla, layer the roast beef, pepper strips, red onion, cucumbers, & lettuce.
- Season with a pinch of salt and pepper.
- Fold tortillas.
- Serve each tortilla whole or cut into 4 parts.

*Calories 209, Protein 21 g, Sodium 281 mg, Potassium 131 mg, Phosphorus 126 mg, Calcium 13 mg*

## Meat Pasties
*Time: 1 hour and 20 Mins, Serves: 2, Skill: Easy*

**Ingredients**
- Potato (1 medium/100g)
- White/ Black pepper
- Carrot (1 medium)
- Beef (200gm), minced
- Dried herbs
- Short crust pastry (500g), one packet
- Onion (1 small)

**Instruction:**
- Preheat oven to 400 °F.
- Brown the beef in a saucepan (non-stick). Cook for 15 minutes, or until the meat is halfway cooked. Rinse the beef to eliminate any residual liquid.
- Boil the potatoes, carrots, and onion for 10 minutes, then drain well and break into small bits. Toss the mince and vegetables in a big mixing tub. As required, season the meat with pepper and herbs.
- On a saucer, roll out the pastry to produce 6 circles.
- Divide the meat among the pastry rings, dampen the pastry corners, fold in half, and press the pastry corners together to seal. Rub it with milk and place it on a baking tray.

- Bake for 25-30 minutes in the center of the oven.

*Calories 191, Protein 30.9 g, Sodium 159 mg, Potassium 81 mg, Phosphorus 92 mg, Calcium 10 mg*

## Brewery Burger
*Time: 40 Mins, Serves: 1, Skill: Easy*

**Ingredients**
- Herb Seasoning Blend (1 tsp), salt-Free
- Rice milk (3 tbsp)
- Egg (1)
- Soda crackers (5), salt-free
- Beef (1 lb.), 85% lean

**Instructions**
- Break the soda crackers in a cup and combine with the milk. Allow the crackers to puff up for a few minutes.
- Beat and stir the egg into the cracker mixture. Add the herb mixture to the crackers and stir well, breaking them up as required. Add the ground beef and blend it in thoroughly.
- Shape the ground beef mixture into 4 patties of approximately similar thickness.
- Cook until the internal temperature exceeds at least 160 °F over medium heat.
- Serve on a bun or a potato and starch patty of your choice with desired toppings.

*Calories 315, Protein 29 g, Sodium 211 mg, Potassium 215 mg, Phosphorus 172 mg, Calcium 32 mg*

## Jamaican Beef Patties
*Time: 1 hour and 20 Mins, Serves: 2, Skill: Medium*

**Ingredients**
- Garlic clove (1), chopped
- Fresh chili (1), minced
- Chili powder (1 tbsp.)
- Thyme (1/2 tbsp), dried
- Short crust pastry (500g or 1 lb.), one packet
- Beef (200g or 8oz.), minced
- Breadcrumbs (4 tbsp), 2 slices of bread
- Onion (1 small), chopped
- Curry powder (1 tbsp)

**Instruction:**
- Preheat the oven to 400°F.
- Cook the chopped garlic and onion with the minced beef in a nonstick frying pan until the meat is nearly brown. Cook for 15 minutes with the breadcrumbs and seasoning, covered, over a low

flame. Using a colander or sieve, drain and remove any remaining liquid.
- On a saucer, roll out the pastry to make 6 circles.
- Divide the beef evenly among the pastry rings. To close the pastry, dampen the sides, cut it in half, and press the corners together. Rub it with milk and place it on a baking tray.
- Bake for 25-30 minutes, or until golden brown, in the center of the oven.

*Calories 170, Protein 30 g, Sodium 59 mg, Potassium 213 mg, Phosphorus 102 mg, Calcium 18 mg*

## Chili Rice with Beef
*Time: 50 Mins, Serves: 1, Skill: Easy*

### Ingredients
- Rice (2 cups), cooked
- Onion (1 cup), chopped
- Black pepper (1/8 tsp)
- Chili con carne seasoning powder (1 1/2 tsp)
- Sage (1/2 tsp)
- Ground beef (1 lb.), lean
- Vegetable oil (2 tbsp)

### Instructions
- In a skillet, heat the oil and add the beef and onion. Fry until golden brown, stirring constantly.
- Apply fried rice and spices to the combination. S
- Remove the combination from the flames. Cover with a lid and set aside for 10-14 minutes.

*Calories 143, Protein 24 g, Sodium 81 mg, Potassium 31 mg, Phosphorus 96 mg, Calcium 13 mg*

## Cajun Pork Chops
*Time: 1 hour and 40 Mins, Serves: 4, Skill: Hard*

### Ingredients
- Parsley flakes (1 tsp)
- Hot pepper sauce (2 to 3 drops)
- Garlic powder (1/8 tsp)
- Cumin (1/4 tsp), ground
- Garlic powder (1/4 tsp)
- Thyme (1/4 tsp)
- Dry mustard (1/4 tsp)
- Paprika (1/4 tsp)
- Sage (1/4 tsp), ground
- Pepper (1/8 tsp)
- Margarine (1 tbsp)
- Pork chops (4 x 4 oz. each), cut 1/2-inch thick
- Onion (1), sliced

### Instructions
- On waxed paper, mix together the paprika, 1/4 teaspoon of garlic powder, sage, thyme, mustard, cumin, and pepper. This sauce can be added on all sides of the pork chops.
- Arrange chops on a square 8" microwave-safe dish in a single sheet. Garnish each chop with onion slices.
- Cover the board with waxed sheets. Microwave for 5 minutes on high. Microwave on low for 25 to 30 minutes (30 percent) or until the vegetables are soft, turning the dish often during this period.
- Take your time while preparing the sauce and let it cook. Combine parsley, Margarine, 1/8 teaspoon of pepper sauce, and garlic powder in a glass bowl.
- Microwave for 30 to 40 seconds on heavy, or until melted. Drizzle the sauce over the chops before ready to serve.

*Calories 291, Protein 29 g, Sodium 159 mg, Potassium 135 mg, Phosphorus 221 mg, Calcium 10 mg*

## Homemade Pan Sausage (Pork)
*Time: 50 Mins, Serves: 4, Skill: Easy*

### Ingredients
- Cooking spray
- Sage (2 tsp), ground
- Fresh lean ground pork (1 lb.)
- Granulated sugar (2 tsp)
- Black pepper (1 tsp), ground
- Red pepper (1/2 tsp), ground
- Basil (1 tsp), optional

### Instructions
- Preferably purchase pork that has already been grinded, if not this is your first step.
- In a large mixing bowl, combine all the ingredients to form a sausage.
- Take accurate measurements using 2 teaspoons of the meat mixture to produce a patty.
- Cook until it is cooked through.

*Calories 130, Protein 20 g, Sodium 118 mg, Potassium 391 mg, Phosphorus 165 mg, Calcium 23 mg*

## Egg Fried Rice
*Time: 1 hour and 40 Mins, Serves: 4, Skill: Hard*

### Ingredients
- Green peas (1/2 cup), frozen
- Dry mustard (1/4 tsp)

- Green onion (1/4 cup), chopped
- Pork (1/2 cup), cooked, chopped
- Garlic cloves (2), minced
- Rice (4 cups), cooked
- Oil (3 tbsp)
- Soy sauce (1 tsp), low sodium
- Eggs (6), scrambled and chopped

**Instructions**
- Heat the oil in a pan over low heat. Add the garlic and proceed to cook until the vegetables are tender. After adding the onion, cook for 2 minutes.
- In a mixing cup, combine the pork, soy sauce, and rice. Simmer for 3 minutes, stirring sometimes.
- Add the remaining ingredients and cook until all is finished.

*Calories 231, Protein 19 g, Sodium 297 mg, Potassium 310 mg, Phosphorus 123 mg, Calcium 16 mg*

## Lamb Chops and Mustard Sauce
*Time: 45 Mins, Serves: 2, Skill: Medium*

**Ingredients**
- Garlic clove (1), minced
- Orange (1 tsp), grated and peeled
- Dry rosemary (1 tsp)
- Water (1 tbsp)
- Lamb chops (2/12 oz.)
- Seasoning of Mrs. Dash herb (1/2 tsp)
- Brown mustard (1 tsp), spicy
- Orange marmalade (2 tbsp), reduced-sugar

**Instructions**
- In a mixing cup, finely chop the garlic and combine it with seasoning of Mrs. Dash and rosemary.
- Scatter on the top of the lamb chops.
- Broil for 5 minutes on either side, 6 inches apart.
- In a shallow dish combine the mustard, orange peel, water, and marmalade.
- Combine all ingredients in a microwave-safe bowl and heat for 1 minute.
- Brush the sauce over the broiled chops and broil for 1 minute.

*Calories 449, Protein 43 g, Sodium 484 mg, Potassium 633 mg, Phosphorus 79 mg, Calcium 53 mg*

## Spicy Pork Tenderloin
*Time: 2 Hours and 30 Mins, Serves: 8, Skill: Hard*

**Ingredients**
- Pork loin roast (2 lbs.), boneless
- Vegetable oil (2 tsp)
- Garlic cloves (3-4), minced
- Black pepper (1/2 tsp), grounded
- Allspice (2 tsp)
- Cumin (1/2 tsp)
- Onion powder (2 tsp)

**Instructions**
- In a cup, combine the minced garlic, allspice, black pepper, cumin, and onion powder, and use the combination to marinate the tenderloin.
- Combine all ingredients in a bowl and set aside for 2 hours.
- Preheat the oven to 347 °F.
- Pour the oil from the marinade into the roasting pan.
- Place the tenderloin on top, shaking off any remaining ingredients.
- Roast it for 45 minutes to an hour, uncovered.

*Calories 135, Protein 23 g, Sodium 350 mg, Potassium 89 mg, Phosphorus 59 mg, Calcium 13 mg*

## Hawaiian-Style Slow-Cooked Pulled Pork
*Time: 6 Hours, Serves: 4, Skill: Hard*

**Ingredients**
- Garlic powder (1/2 tsp)
- Liquid smoke (2 tbsp)
- Onion powder (1 tsp)
- Pork roast (4 lbs.)
- Paprika (1/2 tsp)
- Black pepper (1/2 tsp), freshly ground
- Pickled radishes or red onions (optional garnish)

**Instructions**
- In a bag, add black pepper, paprika, garlic powder, and onion.
- Rub the pork with the flavoring paste. In a slow cooker or a cooker, position the pork. Add 2 tablespoons of liquid smoke.
- Pour sufficient water into the crock-pot or slow cooker to fill it to a depth of 14–12 inches. Cook for 4–5 hours on high pressure.

- Shred the pork with two forks after extracting it from the cooker.

*Calories 350, Protein 44 g, Sodium 511 mg, Potassium 515 mg, Phosphorus 227 mg, Calcium 40 mg*

## Runzaa Tasty Meat and Bread Pocket

*Time: 2 Hours and 40 Mins, Serves: 12, Skill: Hard*

**Ingredients**
- Onion (1/4 cup)
- Lamb (1 lb.), grounded
- Cabbage (4 cups), shredded
- Black pepper (1/8 tsp)
- Pinch of salt
- Loaf of bread dough (1), frozen

**Instructions**
- Preheat the bread dough from frozen.
- Preheat oven to 350 °F.
- Cook the cabbage until it is soft in mildly salted water.
- Cook the onion, pepper, and ground lamb, until the meat turns brown.
- Add the cabbage to the burger mixture and blend properly.
- Using your fingertips, form the bread dough into a rectangular shape.
- Put the burger mixture on top of the bread dough, flip it over, and pinch the corners together.
- Bake for 20 to 25 minutes, or until the surface is golden brown.

*Calories 246, Protein 11 g, Sodium 254 mg, Potassium 71 mg, Phosphorus 82 mg, Calcium 5 mg*

## Sweet and Spicy Meatballs

*Time: 1 hour and 25 Mins, Serves: 4, Skill: Medium*

**Ingredients**
- Liquid creamer (1/4 cup), non-dairy
- Grape jelly (1/2 cup)
- Lemon juice (1 tsp)
- Onion (1/4 cup), chopped
- Lean ground chuck (1 lb.)
- Fine dry bread crumbs (1/3 cup)
- Vegetable cooking spray
- Fresh parsley (1/4 cup), chopped
- Nutmeg (1/8 tsp)
- Egg white (1), beaten
- Cranberries (1/2 cup), finely chopped
- Dry mustard (2 tsp)
- Cayenne pepper (1/8 tsp)

**Instructions**
- Spray a medium-sized saucepan with cooking spray and place it on the stovetop. Add the onion to the pot and cook until it is soft.
- In a mixing cup, combine the lean ground chuck, onions, bread crumbs, egg white, pepper, parsley and mustard. Make 36 meatballs from the mixture, each about 1 inch in diameter.
- Put them on a baking sheet that has been gently treated with nonstick cooking spray. Preheat the oven to 375 °F and bake for 18 minutes.
- In a saucepan, combine the cranberries with the remaining ingredients to make the sauce. Cook over medium heat, stirring sometimes until the time is thoroughly heated.
- Arrange the meatballs in a serving dish and top with the sauce. Toothpicks are used to serve.

*Calories 209, Protein 21 g, Sodium 281 mg, Potassium 131 mg, Phosphorus 126 mg, Calcium 13 mg*

## Slow Cook Chuck Roast

*Time: 8 hours and 30 Mins, Serves: 8, Skill: Hard*

**Ingredients**
- Canola oil (2 tbsp)
- Onion (1 large)
- Chuck roast (2-3 lbs.)
- Cayenne pepper, to taste
- Dried basil (1 tsp)
- Garlic powder (1 tsp)
- Desired spice

**Instructions**
- Place the canola oil in the slow cooker.
- Chop the onion finely and add it to the crockpot.
- Apply garlic powder, dried basil, and cayenne pepper to the onion.
- Lower the heat.
- Cover and cook the beef for 20 minutes on top of the onion.
- Remove the cover and turn the meat; cover and cook for another 10 or 15 minutes, or until the meat is fully cooked.
- Remove from the slow cooker and switch to a serving platter.
- Place the onions over the roast.

*Calories 542, Protein 47 g, Sodium 1039 mg,
Potassium 1435 mg, Phosphorus 49 mg, Calcium 99 mg*

## Basic Meat Loaf

*Time: 1 hour and 35 Mins, Serves: 2, Skill: Medium*

**Ingredients**
- Water (1/4 cup)
- Italian seasoning (1/2 tbsp)
- Black pepper (1/4 tbsp)
- Lean ground turkey (1 lbs.)
- Egg white (1)
- Green bell pepper (1/2 cup), diced
- Lemon juice (1 tbsp)
- Plain bread crumbs (1/2 cup)
- Onions (1/2 cup), chopped
- Onion powder (1/2 tbsp)

**Instructions**
- Preheat the oven to 400 °F.
- Combine the beef and lemon juice in a mixing cup.
- In a mixing bowl, combine all the ingredients.
- Add the beef and thoroughly combine.
- Bake the loaf in a skillet for 45 minutes.

*Calories 372, Protein 18.2 g, Sodium 334.6 mg,
Potassium 120 mg, Phosphorus 68 mg, Calcium 25 mg*

## Smothered Pork Chop

*Time: 1 hour and 35 Mins, Serves: 6, Skill: Hard*

**Ingredients**
- Black pepper (1 tbsp)
- Pork loin chops (6), center-cut, natural, bone-in
- Fresh onions (1 1/2 cups), sliced
- Onion powder (2 tsp), granulated
- Paprika (2 tsp)
- Flour (1 cup and 2 tbsp)
- Garlic powder (2 tsp), granulated
- Beef stock (2 cups), low-sodium
- Canola oil (1/2 cup)
- Scallions (1/2 cup) fresh, sliced on the bias

**Sautéed Greens:**
- Olive oil (2 tbsp)
- Collard greens (8 cups) fresh, chopped and blanched
- Onions (1/4 cup), finely diced
- Butter (1 tbsp), unsalted
- Red pepper flakes (1 tsp), crushed
- Fresh garlic (1 tbsp), chopped
- Vinegar (1 tsp), optional
- Black pepper (1 tsp)

**Instructions**
- Preheat the oven to 350 °F.

**Pork chops (chops de pork):**
- In a big mixing cup, combine the paprika, black pepper, garlic powder, and onion powder. Marinate the pork chops on both sides with half of the paste, while the other half is mixed with 1 cup of rice.
- Set aside 2 tablespoons of the flour mixture for later use.
- Coat the pork chops with a thin layer of flour.
- Heat the oil in a big Dutch oven or an oven-ready sauté pan on medium-high (with no rubber handles).
- Fry the pork chops on both sides for 2-4 minutes, or until optimal crispness is achieved.
- Remove it from the pan and drain all the fat save 2 teaspoons.
- Cook the onions until they are translucent, around 4-6 minutes. Add 2 tablespoons of reserved flour, along with the onions, and thoroughly blended for 1 minute.
- Slowly drizzle in the beef stock, stirring constantly until it thickens.
- Return the pork chops to the skillet with the sauce and baste them. In a 350° F oven, cook for at least 30-45 minutes, wrapped or coated in foil.
- Take the dish out of the oven and put it aside for at least 5-10 minutes before serving.

**Sautéed greens:**
- Blanch the greens by submerging them for at least 30 seconds in boiling water.
- Strain the boiling water and place them into a tub of ice and water as soon as possible.
- Keep the greens aside until they've cooled, strained, and dried.
- Melt the butter and oil together in a large sauté pan over medium-high heat. Cook until the garlic and onions are finely browned, around 4-6 minutes.
- With the collard greens and red and black pepper, roast for 5-8 minutes on high heat, stirring continuously.
- Remove the pan from the heat and, if desired, stir in the vinegar.

*Calories 191, Protein 30.9 g, Sodium 159 mg, Potassium 81 mg, Phosphorus 92 mg, Calcium 10 mg*

## Black Bean Burger and Cilantro Slaw

*Time: 2 Hours, Serves: 6, Skill: Hard*

**Ingredients**

- Bulgur wheat (1/2 cup), to prepare mix 1/2 cup bulgur wheat with 1/2 cup hot water and set aside for at least 30 minutes
- Black beans (1/2 cup), low sodium, drained, rinsed, mashed, and dried
- Granulated garlic (1 tsp)
- Lime juice (1/4 cup)
- Hamburger rolls (6)
- Mayonnaise (1/4 cup)
- Black pepper (1 tsp), ground
- French's Worcestershire sauce (1 tbsp), reduced sodium
- Smoked paprika (1/2 tsp)
- Better Than Bouillon beef (1 tbsp), reduced-sodium
- Onion flakes (1 tsp)
- Scallions (1/4 cup)
- Onions (1/2 cup), sautéed until translucent
- Slaw mix (3 cups), 10-oz. bag
- Flour (2 tbsp)
- Cilantro (2 tbsp)
- Balsamic vinegar (1/4 cup)
- Canola oil (2 tbsp), for searing
- Sesame oil (2 tbsp)
- Lime zest (1)

**Instructions**

- Preheat the oven to 400 °F.
- Mix bulgur wheat, black beans, ground black pepper, smoked paprika, granulated garlic, onion flakes, Worcestershire sauce, beef bouillon, half-cup scallions, and onions in a medium-sized mixing bowl.
- Make burgers out of around half a cup of the mixture and freeze or refrigerate until firm (not frozen).
- Mix together sesame seed, 1 tablespoon of cilantro, lime juice, and vinegar to produce a vinaigrette. Combine all but 2 teaspoons of vinaigrette in a small tub and put aside in the fridge.
- Mix the mayonnaise and the remaining 2 teaspoons vinaigrette in a separate shallow dish and set aside.
- Gently coat the black bean burgers with flour, brushing off any residue. Spray the burger tops as well as the tray that has already been sprayed. Preheat the oven to 350 °F and bake the burgers for at least 14 minutes, flipping halfway through.
- Toast the rolls and sprinkle mayonnaise on top in an equal quantity. Cover the black bean burger with a quarter cup of slaw (or as much as you like).

If you're in a rush, lightly grill the black bean burger on both sides on medium-high for 3-4 minutes with the canola oil.

*Calories 315, Protein 29 g, Sodium 211 mg, Potassium 215 mg, Phosphorus 172 mg, Calcium 32 mg*

## Cranberry Pork Roast

*Time: 12 Hours and 45 Mins, Serves: 4, Skill: Hard*

**Ingredients**

- Salt (1/2 tsp)
- Pork roast (4 lb.), center-cut
- Orange peel (1 tsp), zest, grated
- Cranberries (1 cup), chopped
- Nutmeg (1/8 tsp)
- Black pepper (1 tsp)
- Honey (1/4 cup)
- Brown sugar (1 tbsp)
- Garlic cloves (1/8 tsp), ground

**Instructions**

- Sprinkle the pork roast with pepper and salt. Put it in a crock-pot or slow cooker.
- Add the rest of the ingredients and pour over roast.
- Cover and simmer for 8-10 hours on low.
- From the crock-pot or slow cooker, cut the roast and slice it into 24 pieces. Cover it with a spoonful of drippings.

*Calories 370, Protein 40 g, Sodium 521 mg, Potassium 525 mg, Phosphorus 287 mg, Calcium 47 mg*

## Beef Ribs

*Time: 1 hour and 50 Mins, Serves: 8, Skill: Medium*

**Ingredients**

- Pineapple juice (1/4 cup)
- Mustard powder (1/4 tsp)

- Beef ribs (4 lb.), large
- Red pepper (1/8 tsp)
- Chili powder (2 tsp)
- Paprika (1 tbsp)
- Garlic powder (1/2 tsp)

**Instructions**
- Place the ribs in two small roasting pans in a single layer, meat side down on the racks. Preheat the oven to 450 °F and roast the vegetables for 30 minutes. Drain all the water.
- Pour pineapple juice all over the ribs.
- In a large mixing cup, combine the remaining ingredients. Distribute the seasonings uniformly across the ribs.
- Preheat the oven to 350 °F. Roast the ribs for another 45 to 60 minutes with the meaty side up.

*Calories 191, Protein 20.9 g, Sodium 152.5 mg, Potassium 31 mg, Phosphorus 96 mg, Calcium 13 mg*

## Sukiyaki and Rice
*Time: 2 Hours, Serves: 10, Skill: Hard*

**Ingredients**
- Vegetable oil (1 tbsp)
- Lean beef chuck (2 1/2 lb.), slice into thin paper pieces
- Celery (1/2 cup), diced into 1/2-inch slices
- Soy sauce (2 tbsp), low sodium
- White rice (5 cups), cooked
- Water (1 tbsp)
- White turnip (1 cup), diced into 1/8-inch pieces
- Scallions (3 medium), sliced thin
- Green pepper (1 medium), diced in rings
- Onion (1 medium), dice into 1/8-inch pieces
- Cabbage (1 cup), shredded
- Mushrooms (3/4 cup), sliced
- Tomato (1 medium), sliced
- Broccoli (1/2 cup), chopped and frozen
- Sugar (1 tbsp)

**Instructions**
- In a big heavy skillet (mostly electric), heat the oil and brown the meat on both sides gently.
- Lower the heat to low and add the vegetables to the skillet (in layers).
- In a big mixing cup, combine the sugar, water, and soy sauce; spill over the vegetables.
- Steam for 10-15 minutes, sealed, over a low flame.
- Serve with rice that has been simmering for a few minutes (half cup of rice per serving).

*Calories 143, Protein 24 g, Sodium 81 mg, Potassium 31 mg, Phosphorus 96 mg, Calcium 13 mg*

## Spicy Pork Chops with Apples
*Time: 2 Hours and 10 Mins, Serves: 6, Skill: Hard*

**Ingredients**
- Salt (3/4 tsp)
- Garlic cloves (2), minced, pared
- Red onion (1 large), sliced into 3/4-inch slices, and pared
- Sugar (1/2 tsp)
- Ginger (1/2 tsp), ground
- Cumin (1/4 tsp), ground
- pepper (1/4 tsp)
- Rome Beauty apples (2 medium), unpaired, cored, diced into 1-inch slices
- Pork chops, (6 large)

**Instructions**
- In a mixing dish, combine the garlic cloves, sugar, ground ginger, salt, pepper, and ground cumin.
- Season each pork chop on both sides with the seasoning mixture.
- Put it in a big glass baking dish.
- Sandwich the chops between strips of onion and fruit.
- Crumple the aluminum foil and position it at the pan's opposite ends to press the ingredients together.
- Cover with foil and cook for 20 minutes at 400°F.
- Reduce heat to 325°F and cook for 30-35 minutes.
- Bake for 15 minutes, or until light brown, after removing the crumpled foil from the chops.
- Mix all ingredients in a bowl and toss with rice.

*Calories 291, Protein 29 g, Sodium 59 mg, Potassium 335 mg, Phosphorus 221 mg, Calcium 17 mg*

## Beef Enchiladas
*Time: 1 hour and 50 Mins, Serves: 6, Skill: Hard*

**Ingredients**
- Corn tortillas (12)
- Garlic clove (1), chopped
- Onion (1/2 cup), chopped
- Enchilada sauce (1 can)
- Lean ground beef (1 lb.)
- Black pepper (1/2 tsp)

- Cumin (1 tsp)

**Instructions**
- Preheat the oven to 375 °F.
- Brown the beef in a saucepan.
- In a mixing cup, combine the garlic, onion, pepper, and cumin. Cooking can be continued. Stir constantly until the onions are soft.
- Cook the tortillas in a small volume of oil in a different pan.
- Sprinkle enchilada salsa on each tortilla.
- Stuff the beef mixture into the rolls and fold them up.
- In a shallow container, place the enchilada and cover with cheese and salsa, if desired.
- Bake the enchiladas until the cheese has melted and the enchiladas have become golden brown.
- Serve with sliced olives, whipped cream, or other desired toppings.

*Calories 253, Protein 21 g, Sodium 151 mg, Potassium 321 mg, Phosphorus 519 mg, Calcium 63 mg*

## Chili Verde, Crock Pot
*Time: 8 hours and 15 Mins, Serves: 6, Skill: Hard*

**Ingredients**
- Garlic powder (3/4 tsp)
- Beef broth (1/2 cup), low-sodium
- Green bell pepper (1), sliced into 1-inch squares
- Red chili flakes (1/2-3/4 tsp.)
- Onions (2 large), sliced into wedges
- Pork loin chops or pork (2-2 1/2 lbs.), trim fat
- Red bell pepper (1), sliced into 1-inch squares
- Corn starch (1 1/2 tbsp)
- Tomatillos, (2 cups or 1 jar/16 oz.), fresh
- Green Tomatillo Salsa and 1/2 cup vinegar

**Instructions**
- In a slow cooker with a 3 1/2 to 4-quart capacity. Layer the pork chops, tomatillos or green tomatillo sauce, and onions.
- Combine the cornstarch and water in a crockpot, then add the vinegar, red chili flakes, and garlic powder (only if using new tomatillos).
- Cover and cook on low heat for 6 1/2-7 hours, or until tender.
- Increase the temperature to the maximum setting.
- Add the green and red bell peppers to the mix.
- Cook for 15 to 30 minutes on high with the cover on. Serve with rice or toss the corn chips with a pinch of seasoning.

*Calories 350, Protein 44 g, Sodium 511 mg, Potassium 515 mg, Phosphorus 227 mg, Calcium 40 mg*

## Hungarian Goulash
*Time: 2 Hours and 30 Mins, Serves: 6, Skill: Hard*

**Ingredients**
- Sweet paprika (2 tsp)
- Wine vinegar or red wine (1 tbsp)
- Beef round steak (2 lbs.)
- Flour (1/4 cup)
- Oil or butter (1/4 cup)
- Onions (1 1/2 cups), chopped
- Beef stock (1 cup), low sodium

**Instructions**
- Flour the meat and cut it into 1-inch cubes.
- In a thick pot, brown the meat on all sides with oil or butter.
- Simmer for a few minutes after introducing the onion.
- Pour the contents the beef stock into the pot. Add more if required. It should be dense and stew-like inconsistency, but easily stirrable.
- Cover the pot.
- Cook the beef for 1 1/2 hours at a low temperature.
- Take the meat out of the pot and set it aside to keep it soft.
- Season the stock with paprika and thicken with corn starch or flour.
- Vinegar or wine should be applied to the mix. Layer lettuce and pasta or spaetzle on top of the goulash.

*Calories 427, Protein 25 g, Sodium 662 mg, Potassium 1188 mg, Phosphorus 106 mg, Calcium 92 mg*

## Italian Meatballs
*Time: 2 Hours, Serves: 12, Skill: Medium*

**Ingredients**
- Onion (1/2 cup), chopped
- Oregano (1 tsp), dried
- Eggs (2 large), beaten
- Ground beef (1 1/2 lbs.)
- Black pepper (1/2 tsp)
- Parmesan cheese (3 tbsp)

- Oatmeal flakes (1/2 cup), dry
- Garlic powder (1/2 tbsp)
- Olive oil (1/2 tbsp)

**Instructions**
- Preheat the oven to 375 °F.
- In a large mixing bowl, combine all the ingredients.
- Roll them into 1" balls and place them on a baking sheet
- Bake the meatballs for 10 to 15 minutes, or until cooked through.
- Serve with a side of your choice.

*Calories 143, Protein 24 g, Sodium 81 mg, Potassium 31 mg, Phosphorus 96 mg, Calcium 13 mg*

## Beef Chops
*Time: 1 hour and 50 Mins, Serves: 4, Skill: Hard*

**Ingredients**
- Parsley flakes (1 tsp)
- Hot pepper sauce (2 to 3 drops)
- Garlic powder (1/8 tsp)
- Cumin (1/4 tsp), ground
- Garlic powder (1/4 tsp)
- Thyme (1/4 tsp)
- Dry mustard (1/4 tsp)
- Paprika (1/4 tsp)
- Sage (1/4 tsp), ground
- Pepper (1/8 tsp)
- Margarine (1 tbsp)
- Beef chops (4 x 4 oz. each), cut 1/2-inch thick
- Onion (1), sliced

**Instructions**
- On waxed paper, mix together the paprika, 1/4 teaspoon of garlic powder, sage, thyme, mustard, cumin, and pepper. This sauce can be added on all sides of the beef chops.
- Arrange chops on a square 8" microwave-safe dish in a single sheet. Garnish each chop with onion slices.
- Cover the board with waxed sheets. Microwave for 5 minutes on high. Microwave on low for 25 to 30 minutes (30 percent) or until the vegetables are soft, turning the dish often during this period.
- Take your time while preparing the sauce and let it cook. Combine parsley, margarine, 1/8 teaspoon of pepper sauce, and garlic powder in a glass bowl.
- Microwave for 30 to 40 seconds on heavy, or until melted. Drizzle the sauce over the chops before ready to serve.

*Calories 419, Protein 33 g, Sodium 484 mg, Potassium 613 mg, Phosphorus 179 mg, Calcium 43 mg*

## Herb Crusted Roast Leg of Lamb
*Time: 3 hours and 15 Mins, Serves: 12, Skill: Hard*

**Ingredients**
- Lemon juice (3 tbsp)
- Ground black pepper (1/2 tsp)
- Leg of lamb (1 4-lb.)
- Garlic cloves (2), minced
- Vermouth (1/2 cup), dry
- Curry powder (1 tbsp)
- Onions (1 cup), sliced

**Instructions**
- Preheat the oven to 400 °F.
- In the roasting pan, position the leg of the lamb. Add 1 teaspoon of lemon juice.
- Mix 2 teaspoons of lemon juice with the remaining seasoning to make the paste. Rub the paste all over the lamb.
- Roast the lamb for 30 minutes.
- Strip the fat from the pan and include the onions and vermouth in its absence.
- Reduce the heat to 325°F and simmer for a further 1-2 hours. Enable bastings on the lamb's neck on a regular basis. Remove from the oven when the internal temperature reaches 145°F and set aside for at least 3 minutes before serving.

*Calories 143, Protein 24 g, Sodium 81 mg, Potassium 31 mg, Phosphorus 96 mg, Calcium 13 mg*

## Herb-Crusted Pork Loin
*Time: 1 hour and 30 Mins, Serves: 4, Skill: Medium*

**Ingredients**
- Dill seed (2 tbsp)
- Caraway seed (2 tbsp)
- Soy sauce (2 tbsp), low sodium
- Pork loin roast (1 x 3½ pounds), boneless
- Fennel seed (2 tbsp)
- Anise seed (2 tbsp)

**Instructions**
- Drizzle soy sauce over the roast until it's fully coated. Combine the fennel, anise seed, dill seed, and caraway in a 13' x 10' x 1' baking sheet. To

cover the pork roast, roll it in seeds. Refrigerate the pork for 2 hours or overnight after covering it in plastic.
- Preheat the oven to 325°F. In a shallow open roasting pan, put the meat fat side up on the rack. Place the tip of the meat thermometer in the center of the thickest section of the meat.
- Roast the pork loin for 35-40 minutes per pound. When the roast cooked, the meat thermometer will read 145 °F. Enable 3 minutes resting time. Serve by cutting into slices.

*Calories 350, Protein 44 g, Sodium 511 mg, Potassium 515 mg, Phosphorus 227 mg, Calcium 40 mg*

# Soup & Stew Recipes

## Baked Potato Soup
*Time: 45 Mins, Serves: 6, Skill: Medium*

**Ingredients**
- Skim milk (4 cups)
- Pepper (1/2 tsp)
- Monterey jack cheese (4 oz.), reduced fat, shredded
- Sour cream (1/2 cup), fat-free
- Potatoes (2 large)
- Flour (1/3 cup)

**Instructions**
- Preheat the oven to 400°F and roast the potatoes until they are fork-tender.
- Allow time for them to cool.
- Scoop out the pulp and slice lengthwise.
- Add the flour to a big saucepan. Drizzle in the milk gently, stirring vigorously until it is fully mixed.
- Add the potato pulp and season with salt and pepper.
- Cook, stirring continuously, until thick and bubbly over medium heat.
- Whisk in the cheese until it melts.
- Take the pan from the heat and add the sour cream, whisking constantly.

*Calories 307, Protein 04 g, Sodium 412 mg, Potassium 712 mg, Phosphorus 100 mg, Calcium 20 mg*

## Beef Barley Soup
*Time: 2 Hours, Serves: 10, Skill: Hard*

**Ingredients**
- Beef stew meat (2 lbs.), diced, 1-"cubes
- Vegetable oil (1/4 cup), divided
- Onion (1 cup), chopped
- Mushrooms (1/2 cup), sliced
- Carrots (2), diced
- Garlic (1/2 tsp), minced
- Black pepper (1/2 tsp)
- Chicken broth (14.5 oz.), 1 can, low sodium
- Water (3 cups)
- Vegetables (16 oz.), 1 frozen package
- Potatoes (2), soaked and diced
- Barley (1/2 cup)
- Thyme (1/4 tsp), dried

**Instructions**
- Season the beef with pepper.
- Cook for about 5 minutes with 2 tablespoons of oil in the stew pot.
- Add the onions, 2 carrots, oil, and mushrooms.
- Cook, stirring constantly, for 5 minutes.
- Add the thyme and garlic, cook for 3 minutes.
- Cover the pot halfway with water and chicken broth.
- Add the mixed vegetables, barley, and potatoes.
- Bring the mixture to a low boil, then reduce to low heat.
- After covering with a lid, you may reduce the heat.
- Cook on low heat for 1 to 1 1/2 hours.

*Calories 146, Protein 24 g, Sodium 350 mg, Potassium 366 mg, Phosphorus 12 mg, Calcium 2 mg*

## Turkey Broth
*Time: 2 Hours and 30 Mins, Serves: 8, Skill: Hard*

**Ingredients**
- Water (16 cups)
- Celery (2 stalks)
- Carrots (2)
- Onion (2), quartered
- Bay leaves (2)
- Ground black pepper (1/2 tsp)
- Dried (1/2 tsp) or fresh thyme (4 stems)
- Turkey/turkey breast carcass (1 small)

**Instructions**
- In a large pot, combine all the ingredients.
- Bring to a simmer, then reduce to low heat and continue to simmer for 2 hours, stirring occasionally.
- Remove the foam from the stock.
- Remove the carrots, skin, and bones from the broth with a strainer.

*Calories 15, Protein 100 g, Sodium 924 mg, Potassium 45 mg, Phosphorus 40 mg, Calcium 0 mg*

## Thai Chicken Soup
*Time: 50 Mins, Serves: 4, Skill: Easy*

**Ingredients**
- Sugar (1 tbsp), brown/white

- Chili sauce/chili flakes (1 tsp)
- Lemongrass stalk (1), chopped
- Ginger (1"), sliced
- Lite coconut milk (1 can)
- White button mushrooms (10), quartered
- Red bell pepper (1), sliced
- Yellow onion (1/2), sliced
- Lime juice (2 tbsp)
- Chicken breast (1 lb.), or shrimp
- Simple Chicken Broth (4 cups), other low sodium broth
- Fish sauce (1/2 tbsp)

**Instructions**

- In a large pot coated with nonstick cooking oil, brown the shrimp or chicken until evenly browned.
- Add the broth, fish sauce, chili sauce, ginger, and lemongrass.
- Reduce the heat to medium-low and cook for 10 to 15 minutes, stirring periodically.
- Add the coconut milk, bell pepper, mushrooms, and onions. Simmer for 5 minutes.
- Lime juice can be added just before serving.

*Calories 185, Protein 24 g, Sodium 816 mg, Potassium 311 mg, Phosphorus 30 mg, Calcium 5 mg*

# Renal-friendly cream of mushroom soup

*Time: 50 Mins, Serves: 2, Skill: Easy*

**Ingredients**

- Onion/shallot (1/4 cup), finely minced
- Mushrooms (1/4 cup), finely minced
- All-purpose flour (2 1/2 tbsp)
- Chicken broth (1/2 cup), reduced or low sodium
- Almond milk (1/2 cup), unsweetened
- Sea salt
- Pepper
- Butter (3 tbsp), unsalted

**Instructions**

- In a 10-inch skillet, melt the butter over medium heat.
- Fry the onion until it is clear.
- Cook for 5 to 6 minutes after adding the mushrooms and blending it together. After sprinkling flour over the vegetables, simmer for 2 minutes.
- Blend in the milk and broth until fully smooth. Carry to a simmer, then reduce to low heat and steam for 5 minutes, or until the sauce has thickened

*Calories 333, Protein 4.9 g, Sodium 35 mg, Potassium 260 mg, Phosphorus 15 mg, Calcium 6 mg*

# Yogurt-Cucumber Soup

*Time: 50 Mins, Serves: 4, Skill: Easy*

**Ingredients**

- Garlic (2 cloves), coarsely chopped
- Cucumbers (2 medium/402g), peeled and cubed, 1/4 inch wide
- Water (1 cup/235 ml), divided
- Whole milk yogurt/low-fat yogurt (2 cups/475 ml)
- Black/white pepper (1/4 tsp), freshly ground
- Sea salt (1/2 tsp), optional
- Flower petals edible (pansy, nasturtium, borage, geranium) for garnishing, optional
- Red onion (1/4 medium/27g), coarsely chopped
- Green bell pepper (1/2 small/59g), coarsely chopped
- Assorted herbs (1 handful), dill, mint, parsley, basil, fresh

**Instructions**

- Combine the onion, garlic, and bell pepper in a blender. Remove the herb leaves from the stems and place them in a separate container.
- Combine half of the cubed cucumbers and the remaining herbs in a blender (leave some for garnish).
- Before thoroughly mixing, add 12 cups of water.
- Blend in the yogurt until it reaches a smooth consistency.
- If required, season with salt and pepper. Half-fill a mixing dish with the soup.
- Toss in the remainder of the cucumber slices into the sauce.
- If you are not serving immediately, freeze some of the blended mix in ice cube trays.
- Serve in pots, garnished with edible flowers and fresh herbs.

*Calories 88.4, Protein 8.1 g, Sodium 87.9 mg, Potassium 388.4 mg, Phosphorus 10 mg, Calcium 14.1 mg*

# Wild Rice Soup

*Time: 1 hour and 5 Mins, Serves: 4, Skill: Medium*

**Ingredients**
- Red onion (1 cup), diced small
- Garlic powder (1 1/2 tsp)
- Dried thyme (1/2 tsp)
- Pepper (1/4 tsp)
- Salt (1/2 tsp)
- Wild rice (1/2 cup), dry
- Water (6 cups)
- Olive oil (1 tbsp)
- Celery (1/2 cup), sliced
- Kale (2 cups), stemmed & leaves chopped
- Parsley (1/4 cup), chopped
- Lemon juice (1 tbsp)

**Instructions**
- In a wide pot, heat the oil, then add the onions and celery and cook, stirring occasionally, for 3 to 4 minutes, or until slightly brown.
- Add the seasonings, garlic powder, salt, dried thyme, and pepper. Cook for about 30 seconds, or until fragrant, stirring constantly.
- Toast the wild rice for at least 2 minutes after mixing it in.
- In the water, mix it together. Bring to a simmer, sealed, over high flame.
- Reduce heat to low and simmer for around 50 minutes, stirring regularly, until it starts to boil.
- Cook for another 5 minutes after adding the kale.
- Add the parsley and lemon juice. Pots may be used to prepare the soup.

*Calories 291.8, Protein 5 g, Sodium 660 mg, Potassium 561 mg, Phosphorus 30 mg, Calcium 99.9 mg*

# Mushroom Stew with Creamy Polenta

*Time: 1 hour and 10 Mins, Serves: 6, Skill: Medium*

**Ingredients**

**Polenta:**
- Water (2 cups)
- Sea salt (1/2 tsp)
- Garlic (1 clove)
- Polenta (3/4 cup)
- Rice milk (2 cups), unsweetened

**Stew:**
- Olive oil (3 tbsp)
- Garlic (2 cloves), minced
- Tomato paste (3 tbsp)
- Water (1 1/2 cup)
- Sherry vinegar (1 tsp)
- Butter (2 tbsp)
- Parsley (2 tbsp), chopped
- Sea salt (2 tsp), optional
- Onion (1 medium), sliced thinly
- Rosemary (2 tsp), chopped
- Freshly grounded black pepper
- Portobello mushrooms (1/2 lb.), sliced
- White champignon mushrooms (1 lb.), sliced

**Instructions**
- Combine water, rice milk, and salt in a medium-high-heat saucepan.
- Add the garlic.
- Add the polenta as soon as the rice milk mixture begins to boil.
- Whisk the ingredients together quickly with a wire mixer, making sure there are no lumps. Stir constantly until the sauce thickens.
- Cook the onion slices in 1 tablespoon of olive oil over low heat until soft, around 10 minutes.
- Apply the rosemary and pepper to the fried onions (as well as salt, if desired). Move the mixture to a small bowl and put it aside after a minute.
- Toss both of the mushrooms in the pan with the remaining olive oil. Cook for 5 minutes, or until golden brown on both sides.
- Return the onions to the skillet with the remaining ingredients and mix to blend (except parsley and butter). Cook on low pressure for 10 minutes.
- Add the butter. Serve with polenta.
- Cover each serving with a sprig of parsley.

*Calories 179.2, Protein 7.3 g, Sodium 482 mg, Potassium 419.2 mg, Phosphorus 15.2 mg, Calcium 2.2 mg*

# Mushroom and Barley Soup

*Time: 1 hour and 5 Mins, Serves: 4, Skill: Easy*

**Ingredients**
- Celery ribs (2), sliced
- Water (3 cups)
- Barley (1 cup)
- Porcini/other mushrooms (2 tbsp)
- Olive oil (2 tbsp)
- Onion (1 large), diced

- Carrot (1), sliced
- Garlic cloves (3), minced
- Fresh cremini mushrooms (1 lb.), sliced
- Flour (1 tbsp)
- Beef broth/water (8 cups)
- Italian parsley (1/4 cup), minced
- Tomato Paste (1 tbsp), optional
- Salt (2 tsp), optional

**Instructions**
- In warm water, soak dried mushrooms for 15 minutes.
- Drain and save the liquid from the mushrooms.
- Heat the olive oil in a large pot, then add the onion, carrot, celery, fresh mushrooms, and garlic. Cook for 5 minutes, or until the vegetables are soft.
- Add the flour to the vegetables and whisk constantly over low heat until the mixture thickens.
- Slice the mushrooms that have been soaking.
- Add the mushroom liquid, beef broth, onions, tomato paste (if using), and barley. Cook, stirring occasionally, for around 8 minutes, or until the broth has thickened.
- Serve with sliced parsley as a garnish.

*Calories 186, Protein 6.1 g, Sodium 3195 mg,*
*Potassium 525 mg, Phosphorus 14.3 mg, Calcium 3.3 mg*

## Minestrone Soup
*Time: 1 hour and 20 Mins, Serves: 4, Skill: Medium*

**Ingredients**
- Onion (1/2 large), diced
- Garlic cloves (4), minced
- Italian seasoning (1 tsp)
- Black pepper (1/2 tsp)
- Vegetable stock (4 cups), no-salt-added
- Tomatoes (14.5 oz.), diced, no-salt-added, 1 can
- Mixed vegetables (10 oz.), frozen
- Olive oil (2 tbsp)
- Short, dried pasta, like ditalini (3 oz.)

**Instructions**
- Heat the liquid in a broad pot over medium-low heat. Cook the garlic, onion, pepper, and Italian seasoning, stirring occasionally. About 8 minutes.
- Allow the onions, mixed vegetables, and tomatoes to boil in the cooker. Cook until the dry pasta is just under al dente.
- Serve immediately.

*Calories 103.6, Protein 3.6 g, Sodium 125 mg,*
*Potassium 345.5 mg, Phosphorus 4.8 mg, Calcium 6.3 mg*

## Carrot Ginger Soup
*Time: 40 Mins, Serves: 4, Skill: Easy*

**Ingredients**
- Carrots (1 lb.), chopped
- Onion (1 cup), chopped
- Black pepper (1/4 tsp)
- Ginger (1 tbsp), minced
- Garlic cloves (2), minced
- Canola oil (2 tbsp)
- Vegetable stock (4 cups), no salt added

**Instructions**
- Add the onion, carrots, and pepper to the hot oil and roast, stirring often, for around 15 minutes, or until the vegetables begin to brown. Add the garlic and ginger, cook for a few minutes longer.
- Cover and bring to a low boil with the vegetable stock. Cook until the carrots are soft, about 10 to 15 minutes, then set aside to cool.
- Blend the mixture until it is smooth. Serve.

*Calories 130, Protein 1 g, Sodium 70 mg, Potassium 31 mg,*
*Phosphorus 5.3 mg, Calcium 0 mg*

## Butternut Squash and Cider Soup
*Time: 55 Mins, Serves: 8, Skill: Easy*

**Ingredients**
- Zucchini (1 med), peeled & diced
- Olive oil (3 tbsp)
- Onion (1 medium), chopped
- Butternut squash (1 1/2 lb.) small peeled, seeded & diced
- Water (1 1/2 cups)
- Apple cider (1 1/2 cups)
- Butter (1 tbsp)

**Garnish:**
- Feta cheese (1/4 cup)
- Dill sprigs (4)

**Instructions**
- Cook for 10 minutes, or until the onions are transparent, in hot olive oil.

- Bring the water, squash, and cider to a boil at the same time.
- Reduce the fire to the lowest setting and simmer for 10 minutes. Cook for another 5 minutes, or until the squash is really soft, after adding the zucchini.
- In a mixer, blend the Purée mixture in batches.
- Thin the purée with more water or cider until it achieves the desired consistency, depending on how sweet you like it.
- Heat the mixture in a saucepan until it starts to boil.
- Add the butter and stir until it is melted.
- Serve in individual containers. Sprinkle feta cheese and dill sprigs on top, if desired.

*Calories 187.7, Protein 1 g, Sodium 640.6 mg, Potassium 455.1 mg, Phosphorus 4.5 mg, Calcium 6.3 mg*

## Chestnut Celery Root Soup
*Time: 1 hour and 20 Mins, Serves: 12, Skill: Medium*

### Ingredients
- Water (3 1/2 cups)
- Olive oil (3 tbsp)
- Fresh chestnuts (2 cups), precooked & peeled
- Celery root (3 2/3 cups), diced
- Celery (1/4 cup), chopped
- Onion (1/4 cup), chopped
- Sea salt (1/4 tsp)
- Freshly grounded black pepper
- Rice milk or whole milk (1 cup), unsweetened
- Chopped chives, for garnish

### Instructions
- In a pot, combine the celery root, fried chestnuts, onion, and celery. Season with salt and pepper if necessary.
- Until the vegetables soften, cook for around 10 minutes on medium heat.
- Cook, stirring regularly, for 20-30 minutes after including the water, or until the vegetables are thoroughly cooked. Get the milk to a rolling boil.
- In a mixer, puree the products.
- To remove any unblended pieces, strain via a fine mesh strainer before ready to serve.
- Serve with a sprinkling of sliced chives on top.

*Calories 119, Protein 2 g, Sodium 105 mg, Potassium 297 mg, Phosphorus 92 mg, Calcium 52 mg*

## Yellow Lentil Stew
*Time: 1 hour, Serves: 6, Skill: Easy*

### Ingredients
- Water (4 cups)
- Coconut oil (3 tbsp)
- Onion (1), diced
- Jalapeño pepper (1), diced
- Cumin seeds (1/2 tsp), ground
- Turmeric (1/2 tsp), grounded
- Coriander seeds (1/2 tsp), freshly crushed
- Ginger (1 tbsp), grated
- Yellow lentils (1 cup)
- Russet potato (1), peeled & diced
- Fresh cabbage leaves (2 cups)
- Fresh cilantro leaves (1/4 cup)
- Lemon juice (1/2 tsp)
- White rice (4 cups), cooked
- Sea salt (optional)

### Instructions
- Cook the onion, spices, and jalapeno in a pot with coconut oil on low heat for 5 to 10 minutes, or until the vegetables are soft and tender.
- Before including the lentils and water, cook the ginger. Bring the water to a simmer, and include the potatoes.
- Cook for 20 minutes, sealed, or until the vegetables and lentils are tender.
- Add the cilantro and cabbage. Before the cabbage wilts, combine the ingredients. To taste, season with salt and lemon juice.
- Serve with a side of fried rice.

*Calories 259, Protein 14 g, Sodium 16 mg, Potassium 440 mg, Phosphorus 54 mg, Calcium 16 mg*

## Shiitake, Soba Noodles, and Miso Bowl
*Time: 40 Mins, Serves: 2, Skill: Easy*

### Ingredients
- Shiitake mushrooms (1/2 cup), dried
- Soba noodles (4 oz.)
- White miso (1 tbsp)
- Water (3 cups)

### Instructions
- Bring the water to a boil, then add the mushrooms and cook until they're soft around 15 minutes.

- Boil the noodles until they are al dente (firm to the bite).
- Pour roughly 1/4 cups of noodle oil into a measuring cup.
- Using a whisk or fork, gently mix the miso in the cup.
- Load the miso mixture back into the saucepan.

*Calories 156, Protein 8 g, Sodium 390 mg, Potassium 196 mg, Phosphorus 68 mg, Calcium 10 mg*

## Chicken and Corn Chowder

*Time: 40 Mins, Serves: 12, Skill: Easy*

**Ingredients**
- Chicken breasts (8), boneless, diced
- Fresh thyme (6 tbsp), chopped
- Bacon (12 slices), low sodium
- Onions (2), chopped
- Chicken broth (7 cups), low sodium
- Potatoes (4), diced & soaked
- Corn (8 cups)
- Mocha Mix (4 cups)
- Black pepper (1/2 tsp)
- Green onions (8), chopped

**Instructions**
- Fry the bacon. Remove the bacon from the pan and place it on a plate to cool.
- Fry the onions in the bacon fat.
- After including the potatoes and broth, cover and simmer for 10 minutes.
- Add the chicken, corn, and thyme to the pot and cook until the chicken is thoroughly baked, (15 mins).
- Add the Mocha Mix to the broth, cook for 2 minutes.
- Toss in the bacon, green onions, and season to taste with salt and pepper.

*Calories 349.2, Protein 26.6 g, Sodium 658.4 mg, Potassium 787.7 mg, Phosphorus 40.8 mg, Calcium 17.3 mg*

## Chicken and Dumplings

*Time: 8 hours and 10 Mins, Serves: 2, Skill: Hard*

**Ingredients**
- Mace/nutmeg (1/2 tsp)
- Chicken (1 whole), or chopped chicken (3 lbs.)
- Water or low sodium chicken broth (2 cups)
- Celery with leaves (1 stalk), cut fine
- Carrots (2-3), sliced
- Black pepper (1/2 tsp)
- Flour (1/4 cup)
- Eggs (2)
- Milk (2/3 cup)
- Baking powder (3 tsp)
- Flour (2 cups)
- Butter/margarine (2 tbsp), unsalted

**Instructions**
- Combine the carrots, chicken, spices, and broth or water in a slow cooker.
- One inch of water should be enough to cover the chicken.
- Set the timer low for 6-8 hours.
- In a baking dish that can be used in the oven, position the chicken. Bones should be cast out.
- Increase the slow cooker's temperature to high. To avoid lumps, use 1/4 cup flour to whisk quickly.
- Split the butter into the two cups of flour in a food processor.
- Combine the wet ingredients and drop spoonful of dough into the boiling broth to create a solid dough.
- To avoid overheating, reduce the heat to low and cover it. Without removing the lid, cook for 15 minutes.
- In a large serving dish, serve with dumplings and a thickened sauce over the chicken.

*Calories 350, Protein 28 g, Sodium 300 mg, Potassium 363 mg, Phosphorus 36 mg, Calcium 6 mg*

## Chicken Seafood Gumbo

*Time: 1 hour and 20 Mins, Serves: 12, Skill: Medium*

**Ingredients**
- Flour (1/2 cup)
- Chicken broth (2 quarts), low sodium
- Shrimp (1/2 lb.), cooked
- Canola oil (1 tbsp)
- Celery stalks (3), chopped
- Yellow onion (1), chopped
- Red bell pepper (1), chopped
- Chicken breasts (2), skinless, chopped
- Lean smoked turkey sausage (8 oz.), sliced
- Canola oil (1/2 cup)
- Cajun seasoning (1 tbsp), salt-free
- Canned crab (6 oz.), drained
- Frozen okra (3 cups), chopped

## Instructions

- One tablespoon of oil, heated in a larger pot over medium heat (4.5 quarts).
- After including the onion, celery, bell pepper, turkey sausage, and chicken, cook for at least 10 minutes.
- Combine the ingredients.
- Lower the heat to a medium environment.
- To create a roux, add 1/2 cup of oil and the flour.
- After adding the Cajun spice, cook for another minute or two. Add more if you like your gumbo to be darker.
- Slowly pour in the chicken broth, mixing constantly to prevent lumps.
- Over medium-high heat, get the mixture to a simmer. Continue to cook for another 10 minutes, or before it thickens somewhat.
- Turn the heat down to low and stir in the crab, shrimp, and okra.
- Cook for 10 minutes, or until well cooked.

*Calories 267, Protein 41.3 g, Sodium 2007.7 mg, Potassium 761.1 mg, Phosphorus 36.3 mg, Calcium 16.7 mg*

## Mediterranean Roasted Red Pepper Soup

*Time: 1 hour and 5 Mins, Serves: 6, Skill: Medium*

### Ingredients

- Fresh red peppers (3), roasted
- Olive oil (2 tbsp)
- Onions (2 large), diced
- Garlic cloves (6), minced
- Paprika (1 tsp)
- Lentils (1/2 cup), rinsed & sorted
- Chicken broth or water (2 cups), low sodium
- Dry milk (2/3 cup), nonfat
- Red wine vinegar (1 tbsp)
- Cashews/almonds (1/4 cup), toasted

### Instructions

- Softly caramelize the onions in a shallow saucepan with olive oil. After adding the garlic and paprika, cook for another 2 minutes.
- Add lentils, garlic, peppers, and 1 cup of broth.
- Bring to a boil, then reduce to low heat, cover, and cook until the lentils are tender, around 20 minutes.
- In a mixer, puree the soup in batches until it is nearly smooth.
- Add vinegar and dried milk to the last batch.
- Combine all.
- Add more vinegar if desired and, if it's too thick, a little broth.
- If desired, garnish with a sliver of cashews or almonds and a drizzle of oil.

*Calories 110, Protein 2 g, Sodium 10 mg, Potassium 31 mg, Phosphorus 24 mg, Calcium 80 mg*

## Quick Mushroom Broth

*Time: 40 Mins, Serves: 2, Skill: Easy*

### Ingredients

- Dried mushrooms (5-8)
- Water (2-4 cups)
- Onions (1/2 cup), chopped
- Carrots & celery (1/2 cup), chopped

### Instructions

- In a saucepan, bring all ingredients to a boil, then reduce heat to low and enable to simmer for 10 minutes.

*Calories 24, Protein 1 g, Sodium 20 mg, Potassium 62 mg, Phosphorus 8 mg, Calcium 4 mg*

## Simple Chicken Broth

*Time: 3 hours 45 Mins, Serves: 10, Skill: Hard*

### Ingredients

- Chicken wings or whole chicken (3 lbs.)
- Thyme (2 tsp), dried
- Onions (2), halved
- Celery rib (1), halved
- Carrots (2), halved
- Peppercorns (8), whole
- Bay leaves (2)

### Instructions

- Combine all the ingredients in a large container of around 18 cups of cold water.
- Bring to a simmer, then turn down to low.
- Continue skimming the froth that has formed at the top.
- Simmer for almost 3 hours.
- Strain the broth into a sieve, reserving the chicken meat thus discarding the remaining solids.
- In a pan, combine the chicken, onions, and grains.
- Cook on low heat for 30 minutes.

- It may be preserved in portions for up to 3 months.

*Calories 12, Protein 1 g, Sodium 860 mg, Potassium 0 mg, Phosphorus 12 mg, Calcium 0 mg*

## Simple Soup Base
*Time: 1 hour, Serves: 4, Skill: Easy*

### Ingredients
- Paprika (1/4 tsp)
- Flour (2 tbsp)
- Margarine or butter (2 tbsp)
- Milk (2 cups)
- Dry mustard (1/4 tsp)
- Parsley, basil or any other herbs (1/2 tsp)

### Instructions
- Mix margarine and flour in a microwave-safe dish.
- Microwave for 30 seconds on high, stir, then microwave for another 30 seconds on high.
- Add the spices and milk, and cook for another minute in the microwave.
- To thicken, microwave for another minute. Microwave for a further minute if the sauce isn't thick enough.
- It may be used in lieu of cream soups.

*Calories 15, Protein 1 g, Sodium 1670 mg, Potassium 31 mg, Phosphorus 20 mg, Calcium 0 mg*

## Slow Cooker Gumbo
*Time: 8 hours and 45 Mins, Serves: 8, Skill: Hard*

### Ingredients
- Cajun Seasoning (1 tbsp)
- Celery (3 stalks), chopped
- Onion (1), chopped
- Chicken breasts (3), Skinless, boneless, chopped
- Chicken broth (2 cups), low sodium
- Lean smoked turkey sausage (4-8 oz.), sliced
- Canola oil (1/2 cup)
- Flour (1/2 cup)
- Red bell pepper (1), chopped
- Shrimp (1/4 lb.), cooked, optional
- Okra (3 cups) frozen, chopped, optional

### Instructions
- Combine the onion, celery, sausage, and chicken in a slow cooker.
- Add a low-sodium chicken broth to the pot.
- Add more water to cover the chicken if possible.
- Simmer for 6–8 hours.
- In a wash, mix 1/2 cup of canola oil and 1/2 cup of flour to create a roux.
- Add the Cajun seasoning and proceed to cook for another minute or so. Stir in a limited volume of the slow cooker broth at a time to avoid lumps.
- Add the cut-up shrimp, red pepper, and okra to the slow cooker with the thin paste (if desired).
- Cook for 10 minutes, or until the chicken is completely cooked, before serving with rice.

*Calories 189.6, Protein 14.5 g, Sodium 757.9 mg, Potassium 391.8 mg, Phosphorus 21.5 mg, Calcium 8.4 mg*

## Texas-Style Chili
*Time: 1 hour and 25 Mins, Serves: 6, Skill: Hard*

### Ingredients
- Onion (1 large)
- Tomato sauce (8 oz.), 1 can, unsalted if possible
- Water (2 cups)
- Green chili pepper (4 oz.), 1 can
- Red bell pepper (1), chopped
- Chili powder (2 tbsp)
- Lean ground beef (1 lb.)
- Garlic powder (1 tbsp)
- Cumin (1/4 tsp), ground
- Dried oregano (1/2 tsp)
- Dried thyme (1/2 tsp)
- Dried basil (1 tsp)
- Cajun seasoning (1/4 tsp)

### Instructions
- In a big pot over medium heat, brown the beef.
- Add the onion and cook until it is soft, around 5 minutes.
- In a big mixing bowl, add 2 cups water, tomato sauce, bell pepper, green chilies, and spices.
- Bring to a simmer, then reduce to low heat and proceed to cook for around 1 hour.

*Calories 267, Protein 21.2 g, Sodium 453.9 mg, Potassium 459.1 mg, Phosphorus 16.9 mg, Calcium 12.8 mg*

## Chilled Pea and mint soup
*Time: 40 Mins, Serves: 4, Skill: Easy*

### Ingredients
- Butter (2 tbsp)
- Vegetable broth (2 cups)
- Lime juice (1 tsp)
- Water (2 cups)

- Green peas (2 lb.)
- Parsley (1/4 cup)
- Cayenne (1/2 tsp)
- Onion (1), diced
- Mint leaves (1/4 cup)
- Mint leaves for garnish, as required

**Instructions**
- In melted butter, fry the onion for 7 minutes.
- In a saucepan, mix the water and broth and bring to a boil.
- Transfer half the stock mixture to the skillet with the roasted onions.
- Carry to a simmer over high heat before adding the peas.
- After 1 minute of boiling, extract the pan from the heat.
- Add the parsley, mint, cayenne, and the remaining stock mixture.
- Combine all the ingredients in a blender and blend until smooth.
- Refrigerate the mixture after the lime juice has been added.
- Garnish with a mint sprig and serve.

*Calories 220, Protein 7 g, Sodium 830 mg, Potassium 600 mg, Phosphorus 14 mg, Calcium 15 mg*

## Vibrant carrot soup
*Time: 1 hour, Serves: 4, Skill: Easy*

**Ingredients**
- Olive oil (1 tbsp)
- Ginger (2 tsp), grated
- Sweet onion (1/2), chopped
- Garlic (1 tsp), minced
- Carrots (3), chopped
- Water (4 cups)
- Coconut milk (1/2 cup)
- Turmeric (1 tsp), ground
- Cilantro (1 tbsp), chopped

**Instructions**
- Sauté the garlic, onion, and ginger in a saucepan of hot olive oil for 3 minutes over a high flame.
- Bring the turmeric, water, and carrots to a boil in a saucepan.
- Reduce the heat to low and proceed to cook for another 20 minutes.
- Put the soup mixture and vegetables into a blender and add the coconut milk to produce a smooth broth.
- Return the smooth soup mixture to the pan and heat until it has thickened to the consistency of a deep soup.
- Garnish with chopped cilantro.

*Calories 113, Protein 2 g, Sodium 34 mg, Potassium 242 mg, Phosphorus 58 mg, Calcium 31 mg*

## Creamy broccoli soup
*Time: 40 Mins, Serves: 4, Skill: Easy*

**Ingredients**
- Onion (1/2), chopped
- Extra virgin olive oil (1 tsp)
- Broccoli (2 cups), chopped
- Black pepper, to taste
- Vegetable broth (4 cups)
- Rice milk (1 cup)
- Parmesan cheese (1/4 cup), grated

**Instructions**
- Heat olive oil in a pan and fry the onions for 5 minutes.
- After 5 minutes, add the broth, pepper, and broccoli.
- Bring the broth to a low boil. Reduce the heat to low and continue to cook for another 10 minutes.
- Put the soup mixture in a food processor, then add the rice milk and process until smooth.
- Move the mixture to a pan, apply the cheese, and cook for 5 minutes before eating.

*Calories 151.5, Protein 9.5 g, Sodium 720.6 mg, Potassium 836.3 mg, Phosphorus 18.2 mg, Calcium 11 mg*

## Green Breakfast Soup
*Time: 40 Mins, Serves: 2, Skill: Easy*

**Ingredients**
- Vegetable broth (2 cups)
- Coriander (1 tsp), ground
- Turmeric (1 tsp), Ground
- Cumin (1 tsp), ground
- Lettuce (1 cup)
- Black pepper, to taste

**Instructions**
- Mix the lettuce, coriander, turmeric, broth, and cumin in a food processor.

- Transfer the mixture to a skillet and cook over medium heat for 3 minutes.
- Season to taste with pepper and serve.

*Calories 227, Protein 4.3 g, Sodium 192 mg, Potassium 572 mg, Phosphorus 73 mg, Calcium 63 mg*

## Vegetable Stew
*Time: 50 Mins, Serves: 8, Skill: Easy*

**Ingredients**
- Cayenne pepper (1 pinch)
- Garlic (1 tsp), chopped
- Red bell pepper (1), diced
- Tomatoes (2), chopped
- Coriander (1 tsp)
- Carrots (2), chopped
- Cumin (1/2 tsp)
- Zucchini (2), chopped
- Broccoli florets (2 cups)
- Onion (1), chopped
- Black pepper, to taste
- Olive oil (1 tsp)
- Cilantro (2 tbsp), chopped
- Vegetable stock (2 cups)

**Instructions**
- Heat the olive oil in a medium saucepan and sauté the garlic and onion.
- After adding the bell pepper, zucchini, and carrots, cook for another 5 minutes.
- Add the tomatoes, cumin, broccoli, cayenne pepper, and coriander.
- Reduce it to a low heat.
- Proceed to cook the vegetables for another 5 minutes.
- Garnish with cilantro and black pepper before serving.

*Calories 159, Protein 5.8 g, Sodium 1219 mg, Potassium 381 mg, Phosphorus 57 mg, Calcium 3.3 mg*

## Cream of Corn Soup
*Time: 50 Mins, Serves: 2, Skill: Easy*

**Ingredients**
- Flour (2 tbsp)
- Water (1 cup)
- Cream-style corn baby food (2 jars /128 g each), strained
- Liquid non-dairy creamer (1 cup)
- Pepper (1/8 tsp)
- Margarine (2 tbsp)

**Instructions**
- In a saucepan over low pressure, melt the margarine. Combine the flour and spices in a mixing dish. Stir until the mixture is almost smooth.
- Slowly add in the non-dairy creamer and water. Cook, stirring continuously until the mixture starts to bubble.
- Blend in the corn until it is fully smooth.

*Calories 294.6, Protein 12.9 g, Sodium 541.9 mg, Potassium 1074.5 mg, Phosphorus 27.5 mg, Calcium 5.6 mg*

## Chicken Tortilla Soup
*Time: 1 hour, Serves: 4, Skill: Medium*

**Ingredients**
- Hominy (1 cup)
- Green chili peppers (1 x 4 oz. can), chopped
- Cilantro (1/4 cup), chopped
- Chicken breasts (3), cooked & chopped
- Lemon juice, to taste
- Cumin, to taste
- Green onion (1), chopped for garnishing
- Onion (1 medium), chopped
- Garlic cloves (3), minced
- Olive oil (1 tbsp)
- Chili powder (2 tsp)
- Italian seasoning or oregano (1 tsp)
- Chicken broth (1x 10 oz. can), low sodium
- Water (1x 10 oz. can)
- Corn (1 cup)

**Instructions**
- Sauté the garlic and onion in a limited amount of oil.
- Simmer for 30 minutes on medium-high heat with chili powder, chicken breasts, chicken broth, onions, oregano, water, hominy, corn, cilantro, and chili peppers.
- If required, cumin and lemon juice may be added.

*Calories 188.9, Protein 24.3 g, Sodium 1721.3 mg, Potassium 795.1 mg, Phosphorus 31.8 mg, Calcium 6.3 mg*

## Lower Potassium Potato Soup
*Time: 1 hour, Serves: 4, Skill: Easy*

**Ingredients**
- Nondairy creamer (2 tbsps.)

- Garlic cloves (2 small), minced
- Potatoes (3 medium)
- Chicken broth (2 1/4 cups), low sodium
- Onion (1/4 cups), chopped
- Celery (1/2 cups), chopped
- Parsley (1/2 tbsps.), dried
- Butter, (1 1/4 tbsps.), unsalted
- Green onion (1/2 cups), chopped

**Instructions**
- In a pan, heat the butter and add the garlic, onion, and celery. Cook until the vegetables are tender, about 15 minutes.
- In a saucepan, combine the latter with the broth, nondairy creamer, potatoes, and parsley.
- Cook on low heat for another 20 to 30 minutes.
- Continue to cook when breaking up the potatoes until it has simmered. Half-fill a soup bowl with the soup and garnish with green onions.

*Calories 140, Protein 4 g, Sodium 52 mg, Potassium 224 mg, Phosphorus 79 mg, Calcium 41 mg*

## Rotisserie Chicken Noodle Soup
*Time: 45 Mins, Serves: 4, Skill: Easy*

**Ingredients**
- Carrots (1 cup)
- Wide noodles (6 oz.), uncooked
- Onion (1/2 cup)
- Rotisserie chicken (1), prepared
- Chicken broth (8 cups), low-sodium
- Celery (1 cup)
- Fresh parsley (3 tbsps.)

**Instructions**
- After deboning the chicken, cut it into bite-sized pieces. Prepare 4 cups of broth for the soup.
- Fill a stockpot halfway with chicken broth and bring to a boil.
- Cut the celery and carrots into thin slices and dice the onion.
- Add the chicken, vegetables, and noodles.
- Bring to a boil, then reduce to low heat and cook for around 15 minutes, or until the noodles are finished.
- Serve with sliced parsley as a garnish.

*Calories 271.7, Protein 16 g, Sodium 390.6 mg, Potassium 186 mg, Phosphorus 9.2 mg, Calcium 2.7 mg*

## Hearty Vegetable Soup
*Time: 53 Mins, Serves: 2, Skill: Easy*

**Ingredients**
- White rice (1 cup), can be replaced with 2 cup noodles
- Green beans (2 cups), frozen
- Onion (1), diced
- Chicken broth (2 x 16 oz. cans), sodium-free
- Celery stalks (3), diced
- Carrots (2), sliced

**Instructions**
- Prepare the celery, onion, and carrots by slicing them into small pieces.
- In a 2-quart saucepan, add 2 cans of salt-free chicken broth and frozen green beans.
- Fill the pan with rice. On a low fire, cook the carrots until they are tender.
- To include in noodle dishes, add the noodles after the carrots have been broiled and cook on low heat until they are tender.

*Calories 56, Protein 4 g, Sodium 502.2 mg, Potassium 444.8 mg, Phosphorus 7.4 mg, Calcium 4.7 mg*

## Kidney-Friendly Cream of Mushroom Soup
*Time: 1 hour and 15 Mins, Serves: 4, Skill: Medium*

**Ingredients**
- Butter (3 tbsp), unsalted
- Almond milk (1/2 cup), unsweetened
- Sea salt, to taste
- Chicken broth (1/2 cup), low sodium,
- Onion (1/4 cup), finely minced
- Pepper, to taste
- Mushrooms (1/4 cup), finely minced
- All-purpose flour (2 1/2 tbsp)

**Instructions**
- In a 10-inch pan, melt the butter over medium heat. Add the onions and cook until they are smooth and transparent.
- Cook, stirring regularly, for 5 minutes after adding the mushrooms. After sprinkling flour on the vegetables, simmer for another minute or two.
- In a separate cup, whisk together the milk and broth until creamy. Cook on low heat for 5 minutes, or until the sauce has thickened.

*Calories 127, Protein 3 g, Sodium 109 mg, Potassium 299 mg, Phosphorus 71 mg, Calcium 56 mg*

## Spring Vegetable Soup
*Time: 1 hour and 10 Mins, Serves: 2, Skill: Medium*

**Ingredients**
- Carrots (1/2 cup)
- Olive oil (2 tbsp)
- Mushrooms (1/2 cup)
- Vegetable broth (4 cups), low-sodium
- Oregano leaves (1 tsp), dried
- Green beans (1 cup), fresh
- Frozen corn (1/2 cup)
- Celery (3/4 cup)
- Onion (1/2 cup)
- Roma tomato (1 medium)
- Garlic powder (1 tsp)
- Salt (1/4 tsp)

**Instructions**
- After separating the strings and tips, cut the green beans into 2-inch fragments. Slice tomatoes, onions, carrots, celery, and mushrooms.
- Heat the olive oil in a medium-sized kettle and gently cook the celery and onion until tender.
- Add and bring the rest of the ingredients to a boil with the rest of the ingredients. Reduce the heat to a mild simmer and continue to cook for another 45 to 60 minutes.

*Calories 279.3, Protein 3 g, Sodium 931 mg, Potassium 450 mg, Phosphorus 12 mg, Calcium 39.2 mg*

## Easy Low Sodium Pumpkin Soup
*Time: 40 Mins, Serves: 4, Skill: Easy*

**Ingredients**
- Cinnamon (1/2 tbsp), ground
- Pepper (1/4 tbsp), ground
- Nutmeg (1/4 tbsp), ground
- Pumpkin puree (1 can/15oz)
- Water (3/4 cup), divided
- Onion (1 small), chopped
- Skim milk (1 cup)
- Vegetable broth (2 cups), unsalted

**Instructions**
- Bring 1/4 cup water to a boil in a large saucepan over medium heat. Then add the onion and simmer for another 3 minutes.
- Add the remaining water, pumpkin puree, vegetable broth, cinnamon, nutmeg, and pepper. Give it a good stir before it gets to a boil. Reduce the heat to low and continue to cook for another 5 minutes. After adding the milk, boil for 10 minutes.

*Calories 34, Protein 1.3 g, Sodium 13.4 mg, Potassium 130.1 mg, Phosphorus 30.7 mg, Calcium 13.5 mg*

## Mediterranean Soup Jar
*Time: 40 Mins, Serves: 2, Skill: Easy*

**Ingredients**
- Bell pepper and onion strips (1/2 cup), fresh or frozen
- Black olives (3 large), reduced sodium
- Ricotta cheese (1 tbsp), whole milk
- Canned chickpeas (1/3 cup), no salt added
- Garlic and herb seasoning blend (1/2 tbsp)
- Black pepper (1/2 tsp)
- Red pepper flakes (1/8 tbsp)
- Extra-virgin olive oil (1 tbsp)
- Coleslaw mix (1/2 cup)

**Instructions**
- Rinse the chickpeas and cut the black olives in half.
- In a 16-ounce glass jar, layer all the ingredients in the order mentioned above.
- Refrigerate it before you're able to cook and serve it.
- Remove the container from the refrigerator 15 minutes before serving.
- Fill the container halfway with boiling water, shut the lid, and shake to mix. Allow 2 minutes for the ingredients to settle in the jar.
- Fill a large bowl halfway with the contents and serve.

*Calories 140, Protein 5.4 g, Sodium 70 mg, Potassium 15 mg, Phosphorus 11 mg, Calcium 5 mg*

## Friendly Noodle Soup with Chicken
*Time: 55 Mins, Serves: 6, Skill: Easy*

**Ingredients**
- Black Pepper (1/4 tbsp)
- Carrots (1 cup), sliced
- Dry egg noodles (2 cups)
- Butter (1 tbsp), unsalted
- Oregano (1/2 tbsp), ground

- Onion (1 cup), minced
- Celery (1/2 cup), chopped
- Basil (1/2 tsp), ground
- Chicken stock (5 cups)
- Fried Chicken Breast (8 oz.)

**Instructions**
- Cook the chicken and shred it into small bits. Clean and cut all your vegetables after that.
- In a low-heat oven, melt the butter (5 quarts Dutch). Cook the onion and celery in the butter until tender, about 5 minutes. The chicken stock is added with the chicken, carrots, basil, noodles, and oregano. Get the water to a rolling boil. Reduce to low heat and cook for about 20 minutes.
- It serves 6 people (approximately 2 cups per serving).

*Calories 330, Protein 20 g, Sodium 2000 mg, Potassium 430 mg, Phosphorus 15 mg, Calcium 0 mg*

## Kidney-Friendly Navy Bean Stew
*Time: 8 hours and 20 Mins, Serves: 6, Skill: Hard*

**Ingredients**
- Pepper, (2 ¼ oz.), seasoned
- Taste of Louisiana (1/2 tbsp)
- Navy Beans (1 lb.), raw, mature seeds, rinsed thoroughly
- Onion (1 medium), chopped
- Garlic cloves (3)
- Carrots (1 cup), raw, grated
- Chicken Bouillon (2 cups), sodium Free

**Instructions**
- As guided, soak 1 lb. navy beans overnight.
- Fill a slow cooker halfway with the saturated water.
- Add the garlic, beans, sliced carrots, onions, black pepper, taste of Louisiana Rub, and chicken broth.
- Mix well and cook for 6-8 hours on low heat.
- Serve immediately.
- The stew can be refrigerated for up to 3 days if there are any leftovers.

*Calories 264.2, Protein 16.8 g, Sodium 23.44 mg, Potassium 16 mg, Phosphorus 18 mg, Calcium 13 mg*

## Chicken Pot Pie Stew
*Time: 1 hour 10 Mins, Serves: 6, Skill: Medium*

**Ingredients**
- Canola oil (1/4 cup)
- Chicken breast (1 1/2 lb.), boneless, skinless
- Heavy cream (1/2 cup)
- Sweet peas (1/2 cup), frozen, thawed
- Piecrust (1), frozen, cooked, and broken into bite-size pieces
- Chicken stock (2 cups), low-sodium
- Fresh onions (1/2 cup), diced
- Flour (1/2 cup)
- Fresh carrots (1/2 cup), diced
- Black pepper (1/2 tsp)
- Chicken bouillon (2 tsp), low sodium
- Cheddar cheese (1 cup), low-fat
- Fresh celery (1/4 cup), diced
- Italian seasoning (1 tbsp), sodium-free

**Instructions**
- Pound the chicken and cut it into tiny cubes to tenderize it.
- Cook for half an hour over medium-high heat with the chicken and stock in a large stockpot. In the meantime, blitz the flour and oil together in a blender until smooth.
- Slowly stir in the flour and pour it into the chicken broth mixture until it slightly thickens. For 15 minutes, reduce the heat to medium-low or low.
- Add the bouillon, onions, celery, carrots, Italian seasoning, and black pepper. Cook for 15 minutes more.
- Take the pan from the heat and whisk in the milk and peas. Mix until it's absolutely smooth. Serve in mugs filled with equal parts cheese and piecrust.

*Calories 240, Protein 11 g, Sodium 850 mg, Potassium 0 mg, Phosphorus 12 mg, Calcium 0 mg*

## Beef and Cabbage Vegetable Soup
*Time: 1 hour and 30 Mins, Serves: 4, Skill: Hard*

**Ingredients**
- Garlic clove (1), chopped
- Beef chuck (1 1/2 lb.), chopped
- Water (10 cups)
- Potato (1), cut into small pieces
- Fresh cilantro (1/2 cup), chopped
- Cabbage (1/2 lb.), cut into small pieces
- Tomato sauce (1/2 cup), low-salt
- Onion (1/2 cup), chopped
- Celery stalks (3), cut into small pieces
- Carrots (2), cut into small pieces

**Instructions**
- In a pot boil the garlic, beef, and water for an hour.
- Add the remaining ingredients.
- Cook on low heat until the vegetables are soft.

*Calories 85.8, Protein 4.7 g, Sodium 133.8 mg, Potassium 619.8 mg, Phosphorus 6.8 mg, Calcium 7.1 mg*

## Chicken and White Bean Chili Stew
*Time: 8 hours and 25 Mins, Serves: 5, Skill: Hard*

**Ingredients**
- White beans (1 cup), canned
- Onions (6 whole), white pearl
- Garlic powder (2 tsp)
- Chili powder (2 tsp)
- Oregano (1 tsp)
- Cayenne pepper (1/4 tsp)
- Chicken breasts (1 lb.), boneless, skinless
- Carrot (3/4 cup)
- Garlic cloves (4)
- Black pepper (1 tsp)
- Celery (3/4 cup)
- Onion (3/4 cup)
- Chicken broth (4 cups), low-sodium
- Green chilies (4 1/2 oz.), canned, diced
- Golden hominy (15 1/2 oz.), 1 can
- Cumin (2 tsp), ground

**Instructions**
- Using a sharp knife, cut the chicken into tiny cubes. Place in crock-pot and season with black pepper.
- The carrot, celery, and onion can all be cut into small pieces. Garlic can be sliced finely. To extract salt, rinse and wash the beans and hominy.
- Toss the diced carrots, onion, garlic, hominy, pearl onions, celery, beans, chicken broth, and green chilies in the crock-pot.
- Season with cayenne pepper, garlic powder, cumin, curry powder, and oregano.
- Cook on low for 8 hours in the crock-pot with the lid closed.

*Calories 212, Protein 19 g, Sodium 241 mg, Potassium 512 mg, Phosphorus 237 mg, Calcium 41 mg*

## Chicken and Groundnut Stew
*Time: 1 hour and 45 Mins, Serves: 6, Skill: Medium*

**Ingredients**
- Eggplant (1), peeled and cubed
- Vegetable oil (1 tbsp)
- Onion (1), chopped
- Fresh okra (2 cups), sliced
- Hot chilies (2), chopped or cayenne pepper (1) tsp
- Whole chicken (1), skinned, cut in pieces
- Peanut butter (2 tbsp)
- Ginger (1), peeled
- Tomatoes (2), chopped
- Onion (1/2)

**Instructions**
- Soak the okra & eggplant for 1 to 2 hours in a bowl of water. Please drain.
- Boil the pieces of chicken with the ginger and half of the onion in two cups of water.
- Heat the oil in a separate kettle over low heat and fry the remaining chopped onion until tender. Add the tomatoes to the mixture.
- Return the partially cooked chicken parts to the pot, along with about half the broth.
- Salt, peanut butter, cayenne pepper, and chili peppers can be added now. Then add the drained okra and eggplant after 5 minutes of simmering.
- Cook the chicken and vegetables until they are tender.
- If required, add more broth to save the stew from being too thin.
- Serve with rice bread, wheat dumplings, or corn flour to fill out the dinner.

*Calories 438, Protein 38.1 g, Sodium 534.1 mg, Potassium 268.4 mg, Phosphorus 5.7 mg, Calcium 5.6 mg*

## Potato Soup, Irish Baked
*Time: 40 Mins, Serves: 6, Skill: Easy*

**Ingredients**
- Potatoes (2 large)
- Cheese (4 oz.), cubed
- Sour cream (1/2 cup), fat-free
- Flour (1/3 cup)
- Skim milk (4 cups)
- Pepper (1/2 tsp)

**Instructions**
- Roast the potatoes in the oven or bake them at 400°F until tender.
- Let them cool before slicing them lengthwise and scooping out the pulp.

- Cook the flour over medium heat until it turns a light brown color, then slowly pour in the milk, stirring constantly until thoroughly combined.
- Add the pepper and potato pulp and mix well.
- Boil, stirring constantly, over medium heat until it is bubbly and thick.
- Mix in the cheese until it is fully melted.
- Remove the skillet from the heat and add the sour cream to it.

*Calories 229, Protein 8.6 g, Sodium 183.3 mg,*
*Potassium 755.7 mg, Phosphorus 19.1 mg, Calcium 15 mg*

## Ground Beef Soup

*Time: 1 hour 20 Mins, Serves: 4, Skill: Medium*

**Ingredients**
- Ground beef (1/2 lb.)
- Beef broth (14 oz.), 1 can, low salt
- Flour, all-purpose (1/2 cup)
- Pepper, to taste
- Mixed vegetables (3 cup), frozen
- Water (2 cup)
- Tomatoes (14 oz.), stewed, 1 can
- Onion (1 cup), chopped
- Celery (1 cup), sliced
- Bouillon (1 cube), low salt

**Instructions**
- In a big saucepan, brown the beef for 6 to 8 minutes over medium heat, stirring to break up the meat, then rinse.
- In a saucepan, combine the beef, mixed vegetables, onion, celery, stewed tomatoes, garlic, and bouillon cube.
- Whisk the broth and flour together in a small cup until smooth, then pour into the mixture while continuously stirring.
- Bring the water to a boil. Reduce the heat to low and simmer for 15 to 25 minutes, covered. Stir every now and then.

*Calories 165, Protein 13.15 g, Sodium 1410 mg,*
*Potassium 385 mg, Phosphorus 9.7 mg, Calcium 7.5 mg*

## Beef & Vegetable Soup

*Time: 1 hour and 20 Mins, Serves: 6, Skill: Medium*

**Ingredients**
- Beef stew (1 lb.)
- Green peas (1/2 cup), frozen
- Frozen okra (1/2 cup)
- Frozen corn (1/2 cup)
- Basil (1/2 tsp)
- Onions (1 cup), raw, sliced
- Water (3 1/2 cups)
- Black pepper (1 tsp)
- Carrots (1/2 cup), frozen, diced
- Thyme (1/2 tsp)

**Instructions**
- Mix the black pepper, beef stew, thyme, basil, and water in a pot. On a medium flame, cook for 45 minutes.
- Cook on low heat until the meat is moist, then add the frozen vegetables. Before eating, reheat the soup.

*Calories 488, Protein 32 g, Sodium 181 mg,*
*Potassium 1341 mg, Phosphorus 32 mg, Calcium 8 mg*

## Beef Barley Stew

*Time: 4 hours and 25 Mins, Serves: 4, Skill: Hard*

**Ingredients**
- Pearl barley (1 cup), uncooked
- White flour (2 tbsps.), all-purpose
- Onion herb seasoning (1 tsp)
- Canola oil (2 tbsp)
- Salt (1/2 tsp)
- Onion (1/2 cup)
- Carrots (2 medium)
- Celery stalk (1 large)
- Garlic clove (1)
- Bay leaves (2)
- Beef stew meat, 1 (lb.), lean
- Black pepper (1/4 tsp)

**Instructions**
- Soak the barley for 1 hour in 2 cups of water.
- Cut the celery and onion into small bits. Carrots can be sliced into 1/4-inch-thick rounds. Garlic cloves should be ground before being used. Cube the beef into 1-1/2" pieces.
- Mix the flour, stew beef, and black pepper in a plastic bag. Shake the beef vigorously before coating it with starch.
- In a 4-quart jar, heat the oil and brown the beef. Place the beef on a plate after removing it from the pot.
- 2 minutes of stirring and sautéing garlic, onion, and celery in the beef drippings. Bring to a boil by

adding 2 quarts of water. Put the meat back in the pan. Reduce the heat to low and begin to cook the bay leaves and salt.
- Before applying the barley to the pot, drain and rinse it. With the lid on, cook for an hour. Give it a nice stir every 15 minutes.
- Add the sliced carrots and season with herb seasoning after an hour. Enable for an extra hour of simmering time. Additional water can be added to discourage sticking.

*Calories 110, Protein 6 g, Sodium 680 mg, Potassium 657 mg, Phosphorus 28.9 mg, Calcium 2 mg*

## Simple Beef Stew

*Time: 1 hour and 15 Mins, Serves: 6, Skill: Hard*

**Ingredients**
- Carrots (1 x 10-oz bag), frozen
- Okra (1x 10-oz bag), frozen, Sliced
- Dried basil (1/4 tsp)
- Onions (1 cup), sliced
- Beef (2 lb.), boneless, cut into bite-size pieces
- Vegetable oil (3 tbsp)
- Garlic cloves (2), minced
- All-purpose flour (2 tbsp)
- Green peppers (3/4 cup)
- Black pepper (1/4 tsp)
- Beef broth (2 x 10 1/2oz. cans), low-sodium

**Instructions**
- In the pan, heat 2 tablespoons oil; add boneless beef and fry on medium-high heat.
- Remove the meat from the pan and place it on a plate to cool. Add 1 tablespoon of oil to the pan.
- Add the garlic, onion, and pepper in a pan and cook together.
- Add the flour and simmer for 2 to 3 minutes, stirring regularly.
- Add the beef and broth and continue to cook until it boils.
- Cook for about 10 minutes, wrapped, with the black pepper, carrots, and basil. When the gravy cooks, it will thicken.
- After adding the okra, cook for another 5-10 minutes.
- Arrange on a bed of hot white rice.

*Calories 356, Protein 25 g, Sodium 511 mg, Potassium 31 mg, Phosphorus 0 mg, Calcium 0 mg*

## Beef Tortilla Soup

*Time: 1 hour and 10Mins, Serves: 4, Skill: Medium*

**Ingredients**
- Hominy (1 cup)
- Green chili peppers (4 oz. can), chopped
- Cilantro (1/4 cup), chopped
- Beef (1/2 kg), boneless, cooked & chopped
- Lemon juice
- Cumin
- Green onions, chopped for garnishing
- Onion (1 medium), chopped
- Garlic cloves (3), minced
- Olive oil (1 tsp)
- Chili powder (2 tsp)
- Italian seasoning or oregano (1 tsp)
- Tomatoes (2), chopped, fresh
- Chicken broth (10 oz. can), low sodium
- Water (10 oz. can)
- Corn (1 cup)

**Instructions**
- Sauté the garlic and onion in a limited amount of oil.
- Simmer for 45 minutes on medium-high heat with chili powder, beef, chicken broth, onions, oregano, water, hominy, corn, coriander, and chili peppers.
- If required, cumin and lemon juice may be added.

*Calories 203, Protein 11.3 g, Sodium 1399.7 mg, Potassium 232.2 mg, Phosphorus 8.5 mg, Calcium 3.1 mg*

## Cream of Crab Soup

*Time: 1 hour, Serves: 4, Skill: Medium*

**Ingredients**
- Cornstarch (2 tbsp)
- Chicken broth (1-quart), low-sodium
- Onion (1/2 medium), chopped
- Imitation crab meat (1/2 lb.), shredded
- Margarine (1 tbsp), unsalted
- Non-dairy coffee creamer (1 cup)
- Dillweed (1/8 tsp)

**Instructions**
- Melt the margarine in a frying pan over low heat. Cook, stirring continually until the onion is smooth and translucent. Place the crab meat in the pan and cook for 3 minutes, stirring continuously.

- Bring the mixture to a boil with the chicken broth. Reduce the intensity of the heat to a minimum.
- In a mixing cup, combine cornstarch and non-dairy creamer. Stir until the mixture is almost smooth.
- Stir in the cornstarch and simmer, stirring constantly, until the mixture thickens and boils. Add the dillweed.

*Calories 340, Protein 9 g, Sodium 530 mg, Potassium 0 mg, Phosphorus 9.1 mg, Calcium 15 mg*

## Côte d'Ivoire Fish

*Time: 1 hour and 5 Mins, Serves: 6, Skill: Medium*

### Ingredients
- Tomato puree (1 tbsp)
- Stock cube (1), reduced salt
- Aborigines (2), diced
- Garlic cloves (5), crushed
- White fish fillets 02 medium
- Hot chili pepper (1)
- Onion (1), chopped

### Instructions
- Submerge the aborigine in a huge pan of ice water.
- Combine all the ingredients, except the stock cube, in a large pot.
- After filling with water, bring to a boil for 45 minutes. Place the stock cube in the pot and cook, uncovered, until the soup has thickened and reduced.
- Serve with a spoon and simple boiled rice.

*Calories 280, Protein 39.2 g, Sodium 86 mg, Potassium 36 mg, Phosphorus 6.5 mg, Calcium 40 mg*

## Winter minestrone

*Time: 55 Mins, Serves: 4, Skill: Easy*

### Instructions
- Small macaroni (5 oz.)
- Cauliflower florets (1 cup)
- Celery (1/2 cup), diced
- Butternut squash (1 cup)
- Carrot (1/2 cup), diced
- Water (8 cups)
- Cabbage (2 cups), chopped
- Onion (1/2 cup), diced
- Parmesan cheese (1/4 cup), grated
- Black beans (1/2 cup)
- Olive oil (1/4 cup)

### Instructions
- In a Dutch pan, mix all the vegetables and cook for 2 minutes.
- Half-fill the pan with water, cover, and keep warm.
- Add the grated cheese, flour, olive oil, and macaroni.
- Bring to a boil.
- Reduce the heat to low and simmer for another 60 minutes.
- Season to taste with black pepper and salt. Pour the soup into a serving bowl and top with cheese.

*Calories 157.7, Protein 4.3 g, Sodium 162.2 mg, Potassium 544.2 mg, Phosphorus 6.6 mg, Calcium 5.6 mg*

## Turkey Paprikash

*Time: 1 hour and 5 Mins, Serves: 5, Skill: Easy*

### Ingredients
- Paprika (2 tsp)
- Turkey (1 cup)
- Egg yolks (2)
- Sour cream (1 cup)
- Turkey (2 cups), cooked
- Noodles (1/2 cup), cooked
- Butter (2 tbsp)
- Poppy seeds (1 tsp)
- Onion (1), sliced
- Mushrooms (1/2 cup)
- Butter (3 tbsp)
- Flour (2 tbsp)

### Instructions
- Sauté the mushrooms and onion in butter in a saucepan until tender.
- Add the flour, paprika, and salt; add in the broth (try the homemade chicken broth and turkey broth).
- Cook, stirring continuously, for around 1 minute, or until the mixture thickens and bursts.
- Whisk the egg yolks with a small amount of the hot mixture in a small bowl; apply to the hot mixture.
- Continue to cook on low heat for another minute.
- Add in the sour cream when thoroughly blended.
- Heat it slowly until the desired temperature is achieved.

*Calories 635.2, Protein 40.6 g, Sodium 407.7 mg, Potassium 512 mg, Phosphorus 35.3 mg, Calcium 12.3 mg*

## Baked Cauliflower Soup
*Time: 45 Mins, Serves: 6, Skill: Medium*

**Ingredients**
- Skim milk (4 cups)
- Pepper (1/2 tsp)
- Shredded Monterey jack cheese (4 oz.), reduce fat
- Sour cream (1/2 cup), fat-free
- Cauliflower (2 large)
- Flour (1/3 cup)

**Instructions**
- Preheat the oven to 400°F and roast the cauliflower until they are fork-tender.
- Allow time for them to cool.
- Scoop out with a lengthwise slicing.
- Add the flour to a big saucepan. Drizzle in the milk gently, stirring vigorously until it is fully mixed.
- Season with salt and pepper.
- Cook, stirring continuously, until thick and bubbly over medium heat.
- Whisk in the cheese until it melts.
- Take the pan from the heat and add the sour cream, whisking constantly.

*Calories 352.7, Protein 13.9 g, Sodium 1036.7 mg, Potassium 1011.6 mg, Phosphorus 27.4 mg, Calcium 15.3 mg*

## Simple Pork Stew
*Time: 1 hour and 25 Mins, Serves: 6, Skill: Hard*

**Ingredients**
- Carrots (10-oz bag), frozen
- Okra (10-oz bag), frozen, Sliced
- Basil (1/4 tsp), dried
- Onions (1 cup), sliced,
- Pork (2 lb.), boneless, cut into bite-size pieces
- Vegetable oil (3 tbsp)
- Garlic cloves (2), minced
- All-purpose flour (2 tbsp)
- Green peppers (3/4 cup)
- Black pepper (1/4 tsp)
- Beef broth (2 x 10 1/2-oz. cans), low-sodium,

**Instructions**
- In the oven, heat 2 tablespoons of oil; add boneless pork and fry on medium-high heat.
- Remove the meat from the pan and place it on a plate to cool. Add 1 tablespoon of oil to the pan.
- Add the garlic, onion, and pepper and cook together.
- Add the flour and simmer for 2 to 3 minutes, stirring regularly.
- Add the pork and broth and continue to cook until it boils.
- Cook for about 10 minutes, wrapped, with the black pepper, carrots, and basil. When the gravy cooks, it will thicken.
- After adding the okra, cook for another 5-10 minutes.
- Arrange on a bed of hot white rice.

*Calories 247.2, Protein 7.5 g, Sodium 85.4 mg, Potassium 1076.2 mg, Phosphorus 16.4 mg, Calcium 6.2 mg*

## Cream of Prawn Soup
*Time: 1 hour, Serves: 4, Skill: Medium*

**Ingredients**
- Cornstarch (2 tbsp)
- Chicken broth (1-quart), low-sodium
- Onion (1/2 medium), chopped
- Prawns' meat (1/2 lb.), shredded
- Margarine (1 tbsp), unsalted
- Non-dairy coffee creamer (1 cup)
- Dillweed (1/8 tsp)

**Instructions**
- Melt the margarine in a frying pan over low heat. Cook, stirring continually until the onion is smooth and translucent. Place the prawn's meat in the pan and cook for 3 minutes, stirring continuously.
- Bring the mixture to a boil with the chicken broth. Reduce the heat to low.
- In a mixing cup, combine cornstarch and non-dairy creamer. Stir until the mixture is almost smooth.
- Stir in the cornstarch and simmer, stirring constantly, until the mixture thickens and boils. Add the dillweed.

*Calories 219.6, Protein 6.8 g, Sodium 2089.3 mg, Potassium 143.4 mg, Phosphorus 79.3 mg, Calcium 42.7 mg*

## Turkey Tortilla Soup
*Time: 40 Mins, Serves: 4, Skill: Easy*

**Ingredients**
- Hominy (1 cup)
- Green chili peppers (1 x 4 oz. can), chopped

- Cilantro (1/4 cup), chopped
- Turkey breasts (3), cooked, chopped
- Lemon juice
- Cumin
- Green onions, chopped for garnishing
- Onion (1 medium), chopped
- Garlic cloves (3), minced
- Olive oil (1 tbsp)
- Chili powder (2 tsp)
- Italian seasoning or oregano (1 tsp)
- Tomatoes (2), chopped, fresh
- Chicken broth (10 oz. can), low sodium
- Water (10 oz. can)
- Corn (1 cup)

**Instructions**
- Sauté the garlic and onion in a limited amount of oil.
- Simmer for 30 minutes on medium-high heat with chili powder, turkey breast, tomatoes, seasoning, chicken broth, onions, oregano, water, hominy, corn, cilantro, and chili peppers.
- If required, cumin and lemon juice may be added.

*Calories 130.7, Protein 10.4 g, Sodium 560.8 mg, Potassium 364 mg, Phosphorus 14.3 mg, Calcium 2 mg*

## Vibrant Potato soup
*Time: 1 hour, Serves: 4, Skill: Easy*

**Ingredients**
- Olive oil (1 tbsp)
- Ginger (2 tsp), grated
- Sweet onion (1/2), chopped
- Garlic (1 tsp), minced
- Potatoes (3), diced
- Water (4 cups)
- Coconut milk (1/2 cup)
- Turmeric (1 tsp), ground
- Cilantro (1 tbsp), chopped

**Instructions**
- Sauté the garlic, onion, and ginger in a saucepan of hot olive oil for 3 minutes over a high flame.
- Bring the turmeric, water, and potatoes to a boil in the saucepan.
- Reduce the heat to low and proceed to cook for another 20 minutes.
- Put the soup mixture into a blender and add the coconut milk to produce a smooth broth.
- Return the smooth soup mixture to the pan and heat until it has thickened to the consistency of a deep soup.
- Garnish with chopped cilantro.

*Calories 110, Protein 1 g, Sodium 81 mg, Potassium 620 mg, Phosphorus 4 mg, Calcium 8 mg*

## Simple Beef Broth
*Time: 4 hours and 50 Mins, Serves: 2, Skill: Hard*

**Ingredients**
- Beef (3 lbs.), with bone
- Thyme (2 tsp), dried
- Onions (2), halved
- Celery rib (1), halved
- Carrots (2), halved
- Peppercorns (8), whole
- Bay leaves (2)

**Instructions**
- Combine all the ingredients in a large pot of around 18 cups of cold water.
- Bring to a simmer, then turn down to low.
- Continue skimming the froth that has formed at the top.
- Simmer for almost 3 hours.
- Strain the broth into a sieve, reserving the beef meat thus discarding the remaining solids.
- In a big mixing bowl, combine the beef, onions, and grains.
- Cook on low heat for 30 minutes.
- It may be preserved in portions for up to 3 months.

*Calories 141.3, Protein 6 g, Sodium 633.2 mg, Potassium 832.2 mg, Phosphorus 12.6 mg, Calcium 12.8 mg*

# Drink and Beverage Recipes

## Apple Cup Cider
*Time: 25 Mins, Serves: 4, Skill: Easy*

**Ingredients**
- Cinnamon sticks (2)
- Whole cloves (1/2 tsp)
- Nutmeg (1 pinch)
- Allspice (1 tsp)
- Apple juice (2 quarts 100%)

**Instructions**
- In a large saucepan, heat the apple juice over medium-high heat.
- Add the remaining ingredients.
- Reduce to low heat after bringing to a low boil. Allow for a 10-minute "steeping" period.
- Pour the cider into a mug or thermos using the fine metal sieve.

*Calories 120, Protein 0.3 g, Sodium 60 mg, Potassium 140 mg, Phosphorus 4.6 mg, Calcium 2 mg*

## Fresh Fruit Lassi
*Time: 15 Mins, Serves: 2, Skill: Easy*

**Ingredients**
- Rosewater (1/2 tsp)
- Lime juice (1/4 cup)
- Plain yogurt (1 cup)
- Milk (1/2 cup)
- Mango juice (1/2 cup), or apricot, nectar, or peach
- Sugar (1-3 tbsp)
- Cardamom (1/4 tsp)

**Instructions**
- Combine all the ingredients in a blender until creamy.

*Calories 137.8, Protein 3.8 g, Sodium 46.5 mg, Potassium 310 mg, Phosphorus 10 mg, Calcium 12.4 mg*

## Katie Shake
*Time: 15 Mins, Serves: 1, Skill: Easy*

**Ingredients**
- Vanilla ice cream (1/4 cup)
- Prepared Jell-O (1/4 cup)
- Plain yogurt (1/4 cup), or cottage cheese

**Instructions**
- Combine all the ingredients in a blender until creamy.

*Calories 144, Protein 5 g, Sodium 97 mg, Potassium 209 mg, Phosphorus 137 mg, Calcium 4 mg*

## Chocolate Smoothie
*Time: 10 Mins, Serves: 2, Skill: Easy*

**Ingredients**
- Ice (2 cups)
- Southern comfort liqueur (2 tbsp)
- Evaporated milk (1/2 cup)
- Condensed milk (1/4 cup)
- Ground cinnamon (1/4 tsp)
- Nutmeg (1 pinch)
- Whey protein chocolate-flavored (2 scoops)

**Instructions**
- Combine all the ingredients in a blender until creamy.

*Calories 386.1, Protein 15.5 g, Sodium 287.9 mg, Potassium 987.6 mg, Phosphorus 7.5 mg, Calcium 32 mg*

## Apple Smoothie
*Time: 12 Mins, Serves: 1, Skill: Easy*

**Ingredients**
- Plain yogurt (1/2 cup)
- Applesauce (1/2 cup), unsweetened
- Skim milk (1/4 cup)
- Honey (1 tbsp)
- Oat bran (2 tbsp)
- Apple (1/2), peeled and in chunks

**Instructions**
- Combine all the ingredients in a blender until creamy.

*Calories 431.6, Protein 38.4 g, Sodium 248.4 mg, Potassium 587.1 mg, Phosphorus 27.2 mg, Calcium 38.6 mg*

## Watermelon Bliss
*Time: 14 Mins, Serves: 1, Skill: Easy*

**Ingredients**
- Mint sprigs (2), leaves only
- Celery stalk (1)
- Ice
- Squeeze of lime
- Watermelon (2 cups)
- Cucumber (1 medium), peeled and sliced

**Instructions**

- Combine all the ingredients in a blender until creamy.

*Calories 1530, Protein 12 g, Sodium 1030 mg, Potassium 0 mg, Phosphorus 4 mg, Calcium 12 mg*

## Bahama Breeze
*Time: 13 Mins, Serves: 2, Skill: Easy*

**Ingredients**
- Pineapple (1/2 cup)
- Ice cubes
- Strawberries (1/2 cup)
- Orange (1 small), peeled
- Rice milk (1/2 cup)
- Handful of spinach (optional)

**Instructions**
- Combine all the ingredients in a blender until creamy.

*Calories 130, Protein 1 g, Sodium 30 mg, Potassium 14 mg, Phosphorus 6 mg, Calcium 12 mg*

## Very Berry Goodness
*Time: 13 Mins, Serves: 3, Skill: Easy*

**Ingredients**
- Blueberries (1/2 cup), fresh
- Strawberries (1/2 cup), fresh or frozen
- Rice milk (1/2 cup), unsweetened
- Stevia (optional)
- Cucumber (1 medium), peeled and sliced

**Instructions**
- Combine all the ingredients in a blender until creamy.

*Calories 152, Protein 6 g, Sodium 5 mg, Potassium 186 mg, Phosphorus 25 mg, Calcium 7 mg*

## Cran-tastic
*Time: 12 Mins, Serves: 1, Skill: Easy*

**Ingredients**
- Parsley (a handful)
- Cranberries (1 cup), frozen
- Cucumber (1 medium), peeled and sliced
- Celery (1 stalk)
- Squeeze of lime

**Instructions**
- Combine all the ingredients in a blender until creamy.

*Calories 240, Protein 7 g, Sodium 4 mg, Potassium 5 mg, Phosphorus 25 mg, Calcium 40 mg*

## What a Peach
*Time: 10 Mins, Serves: 1, Skill: Easy*

**Ingredients**
- Almond milk (1 cup), vanilla flavored, unsweetened
- Raspberries (1 cup), frozen
- Peach (1 medium), pit removed, or, sliced/frozen peaches (1/2 cup)
- Silken tofu (1/2 cup)
- Honey (1 tbsp)

**Instructions**
- Combine all the ingredients in a blender until creamy.

*Calories 50, Protein 1 g, Sodium 15 mg, Potassium 20 mg, Phosphorus 7.6 mg, Calcium 2 mg*

## Easy Pineapple Protein Smoothie
*Time: 15 Mins, Serves: 1, Skill: Easy*

**Ingredients**
- Ice cubes (2), optional
- Pineapple sherbet (3/4 cup), or sorbet
- Whey protein powder, vanilla flavor (1 scoop)
- Water (1/2 cup)

**Instructions**
- Combine all the ingredients in a blender until creamy.

*Calories 369.1, Protein 29.1 g, Sodium 50.2 mg, Potassium 1099 mg, Phosphorus 13.9 mg, Calcium 17.4 mg*

## Mixed Berry Protein Smoothie
*Time: 12 Mins, Serves: 2, Skill: Easy*

**Ingredients**
- Cream topping (1/2 cup), whipped
- Whey protein powder (2 scoops)
- Coldwater (4 oz.)
- Mixed berries (1 cup), fresh/frozen
- Ice cubes (2)
- Crystal Light (1 tsp), flavor enhancer drops (liquid, any berry flavor)

**Instructions**
- Combine all the ingredients in a blender until creamy.
- Load the protein powder into a broad mixing cup.
- Stir in the cream topping thoroughly.

*Calories 288.3, Protein 21.6 g, Sodium 58.3 mg, Potassium 545.5 mg, Phosphorus 6.2 mg, Calcium 15 mg*

## Kidney Nourishing Smoothie
*Time: 15 Mins, Serves: 2, Skill: Easy*

**Ingredients**
- Ice (1 cup)
- Stevia, to taste
- Cucumber (1/2 large), peeled and sliced
- Blueberries (1 cup), fresh/frozen
- Coconut water (1 cup), or any nut milk or plain filtered water
- Chia seeds or ground flax (1-2 tbsp)
- Cinnamon (pinch)
- Fresh lime juice

**Instructions**
- Combine all the ingredients in a blender until creamy.

*Calories 188, Protein 8 g, Sodium 6 mg, Potassium 163 mg, Phosphorus 30 mg, Calcium 8 mg*

## Blueberry Blast Smoothie
*Time: 15 Mins, Serves: 4, Skill: Easy*

**Ingredients**
- Apple juice (14 oz.), no added sugar
- Blueberries (1 cup), frozen
- Splenda (8 packets)
- Protein powder (6 tbsp)
- Ice cubes (8)

**Instructions**
- Combine all the ingredients in a blender until creamy.

*Calories 479, Protein 14 g, Sodium 160 mg, Potassium 80 mg, Phosphorus 24 mg, Calcium 250 mg*

## Four Ingredient Simple Blueberry Smoothie
*Time: 12 Mins, Serves: 1, Skill: Easy*

**Ingredients**
- Ice cubes (for obtaining desired thickness)
- Blueberries (1/4 cup), frozen
- Rice milk (1 cup)
- Honey (1 tsp), or stevia
- Mint (1 sprig), fresh

**Instructions**
- Combine all the ingredients in a blender until creamy.

*Calories 416, Protein 10 g, Sodium 330 mg, Potassium 756 mg, Phosphorus 174 mg, Calcium 426 mg*

## Watermelon Summer Cooler
*Time: 15 Mins, Serves: 1, Skill: Easy*

**Ingredients**
- Watermelon wedges (2 small), for garnish
- Ice (1 cup), crushed
- Watermelon (1 cup), seedless, cubes
- Lime juice (2 tsp)
- Sugar (1 tbsp)

**Instructions**
- Combine all the ingredients in a blender until creamy.

*Calories 52, Protein 2 g, Sodium 1 mg, Potassium 96 mg, Phosphorus 9 mg, Calcium 6 mg*

## Lemonade
*Time: 10 Mins, Serves: 2, Skill: Easy*

**Ingredients**
- Ice cubes
- Water (2-1/2 cups)
- Sugar (1-1/4 cups)
- Lemon (1/2 tsp), finely shredded
- Fresh lemon or lime juice (1-1/4 cups)

**Instructions**
- Heat the water and sugar in a medium saucepan until the sugar has dissolved. Remove the pan from the heat and put it aside to cool for 20 minutes.
- In a large mixing cup, combine the lemon peel and juice. Allow to cool in a covered pitcher or pot. This can be held for up to three days.
- In a glass packed with ice, combine 3 oz. of base and 3 oz. of water to make a lemonade cocktail. Shake it up a little and serve.

*Calories 70, Protein 1.1 g, Sodium 20 mg, Potassium 0 mg, Phosphorus 6 mg, Calcium 3 mg*

## Strawberry-Apple Smoothie
*Time: 10 Mins, Serves: 2, Skill: Easy*

**Ingredients**
- Oat/wheat bran (2 tbsp)
- Strawberries (1/2 cup)
- Plain yogurt (1/2 cup)
- Applesauce (1/2 cup), unsweetened
- Almond/rice milk (1/4 cup)
- Honey (1 tbsp)

**Instructions**

- Combine all the ingredients in a blender until creamy.

*Calories 106.8, Protein 1.9 g, Sodium 26 mg, Potassium 347.6 mg, Phosphorus 6 mg, Calcium 7.7 mg*

## Easy No Milk Shake
*Time: 8 Mins, Serves: 1, Skill: Easy*

### Ingredients
- Berries, banana or apple (1/2 cup), or peanut butter (2 tbsp)
- Pasteurized Liquid Egg Product (1/2 cup)
- Non-Dairy Whipped Topping Frozen (1/2 cup)
- The flavor of choice – vanilla extract, lemon juice, almond extract

### Instructions
- Combine all the ingredients in a blender until creamy.

*Calories 120.8, Protein 8.4 g, Sodium 437.4 mg, Potassium 406.7 mg, Phosphorus 24.7 mg, Calcium 30.1 mg*

## Berry Smoothie
*Time: 10 Mins, Serves: 1, Skill: Easy*

### Ingredients
- Vanilla extract (1 tsp)
- Cranberry juice cocktail (1/4 cup)
- Silken tofu (2/3 cup), firm
- Raspberries (1/2 cup), frozen, unsweetened
- Blueberries (1/2 cup), frozen, unsweetened

### Instructions
- Combine all the ingredients in a blender until creamy.

*Calories 94.8, Protein 6 g, Sodium 80.5 mg, Potassium 360.6 mg, Phosphorus 16.9 mg, Calcium 20.9 mg*

## Lemon-Strawberry Punch
*Time: 10 Mins, Serves: 1, Skill: Easy*

### Ingredients
- Ginger ale (1 l. bottle)
- Lemonade concentrate (3cans), frozen, thawed
- Frozen strawberries (1 box 10 oz), in a light syrup, undrained and thawed

### Instructions
- Whisk together the lemonade concentrate and 9 cans of water in a four-quart tub until well mixed.
- Fill a punch bowl halfway of lemonade. Strawberries may be combined in a number of ways.
- Apply the ice and ginger ale and whisk softly.

*Calories 160, Protein 0 g, Sodium 120 mg, Potassium 60 mg, Phosphorus 3.9 mg, Calcium 0 mg*

## Pineapple Lime Punch
*Time: 25 Mins, Serves: 16, Skill: Easy*

### Ingredients
- Ginger ale (1 L/4 1/4 cups), chilled
- Sugar (2 cups)
- Coldwater (2 quarts)
- Lime-flavored soft drink mix (2 packages 0.13 oz. each), unsweetened
- Pineapple juice (1 cup/46 oz), chilled

### Instructions
- Combine the water and sugar in a punch bowl or large pitcher and stir until the sugar is fully dissolved.
- Combine the remaining components in a small dish.
- Serve.

*Calories 139.2, Protein 0.7 g, Sodium 19.6 mg, Potassium 49.3 mg, Phosphorus 0.3 mg, Calcium 3.3 mg*

## Berry yogurt smoothie
*Time: 10 Mins, Serves: 1, Skill: Easy*

### Ingredients
- Non-dairy milk (1/4 cups), water to thin
- Plant-based yogurt (3/4 cup), unsweetened
- Mixed berries (1 ½ cups), frozen
- Maple syrup (1 tsp)

### Instructions
- Combine all the ingredients in a blender until creamy.

*Calories 186.8, Protein 16.2 g, Sodium 50.8 mg, Potassium 691.5 mg, Phosphorus 22.1 mg, Calcium 15.6 mg*

## Kidney friendly masala chai tea
*Time: 25 Mins, Serves: 8, Skill: Easy*

### Ingredients
- Star anise (2–3)
- Whole nutmeg (2–3)
- Water (6 cups)
- Heavy whipping cream (1 1/2 cups)
- Rice milk (2 1/2 cups)
- Black tea leaves (2 tbsp), broad leaf-like Ceylon
- Cinnamon sticks (2)
- Black peppercorns (2)

- Whole cloves (10)
- Cardamom pods (6)
- Brown sugar (1/2 c)

**Instructions**

- Combine the spices and one cup of water in a 2-quart saucepan, bring to a boil, then remove from the heat and rest for 5 to 20 minutes, depending on how hot you want it.
- In a mixing bowl, combine the cream, rice milk, spices, and water. Bring the cream and spice mixture to a boil, and switch off the fire.
- In a cup, mix the tea and milk and set aside for 5 to 10 minutes to taste (reheat to a boil and remove from the heat at this stage.) At this point, you may either add sugar or serve without it, enabling people to add as much as they choose.
- Strain into a pot and serve with sugar to taste.

*Calories 145, Protein 1 g, Sodium 28.2 mg, Potassium 85.1 mg, Phosphorus 24.5 mg, Calcium 13 mg*

## Italian lemonade (distinctive kidney-friendly liquid refreshment)

*Time: 15 Mins, Serves: 6, Skill: Easy*

**Ingredients**

- Lemon juice (2 cups), about 12-15 lemons
- Cold/sparkling water (2 cups)
- Fresh basil (1 bunch), washed & stemmed
- Sugar (2 cups)
- Water (1 cup)

**Instructions**

- Basil syrup: In a saucepan, add the basil, sugar (2 cups), and water (1 cup) and simmer for 5 minutes, or until the sugar is dissolved. Allow to cool before using.
- In a pitcher, add the basil syrup, lemon juice, and 2 cups cold/sparkling water. Refrigerate until ready to serve.

*Calories 107.7, Protein 24 g, Sodium 25 mg, Potassium 32 mg, Phosphorus 8.1 mg, Calcium 0 mg*

## Pineapple coconut turmeric smoothie

*Time: 10 Mins, Serves: 1, Skill: Easy*

**Ingredients**

- Turmeric powder (1 tsp)
- Almond milk (1 cup) Unsweetened
- Canned coconut milk (1 cup)
- Pineapple (2 cups), diced in chunks
- Ginger (1 tbsp), peeled, grated

**Instructions**

- Combine all the ingredients in a blender until creamy.

*Calories 221, Protein 3 g, Sodium 102.8 mg, Potassium 435.6 mg, Phosphorus 86 mg, Calcium 6 mg*

## Homemade kidney-friendly apple cider

*Time: 3 hour and 30 Mins, Serves: 8, Skill: Hard*

**Ingredients**

- Ground allspice (1 tbsp)
- Apples (10), quartered
- White sugar (1/2 cup)
- Cinnamon (1 tbsp), ground

**Instructions**

- Put the apples in a big stockpot and cover with 2 cups of water "At the very least, there should be ample water to cover it." Add the sugar, cinnamon, and allspice. Carry to a low boil, uncovered, for around 1 hour. Cover the pot, decrease the heat to a minimum, and simmer for 2 hours.
- Strain the apple liquid through a finer mesh sieve, discarding the solids. Drain the cider through a cheesecloth-lined sieve and chill until fully frozen.

*Calories 114, Protein 0.2 g, Sodium 9.9 mg, Potassium 250.5 mg, Phosphorus 17.4 mg, Calcium 2 mg*

## Vegan Hot Chocolate

*Time: 15 Mins, Serves: 1, Skill: Easy*

**Ingredients**

- Vanilla extract (1/2 tsp)
- Oat milk (1 cup)
- Cocoa powder (1 tbsp)
- Honey (2 tsp)

**Instructions**

- Heat the milk in a small saucepan over medium-high heat.
- Combine the cocoa powder, vanilla extract, and honey in a mixing cup.
- To mix, carefully whisk all the products together.
- Carry to a simmer before scalding (when bubbles emerge along the edges of the liquid in the pot).
- Extract it from the pan, put it into a mug, and serve.

*Calories 120, Protein 1 g, Sodium 45 mg, Potassium 94 mg, Phosphorus 19.2 mg, Calcium 20 mg*

## Strawberry Cheesecake Smoothie
*Time: 12 Mins, Serves: 2, Skill: Easy*

**Ingredients**
- Vanilla extract (1 tsp)
- Ice cubes (3-5)
- Rice milk (1 cup), unsweetened
- Strawberries (1 cup), hulled
- Cream cheese (2 tbsp), at room temperature
- Honey (1/2 tsp)

**Instructions**
- Combine all the ingredients in a blender and process until smooth.

*Calories 155, Protein 18 g, Sodium 490 mg, Potassium 285 mg, Phosphorus 0 mg, Calcium 0 mg*

## Aromatic Tea
*Time: 40 Mins, Serves: 5, Skill: Easy*

**Ingredients**
- Black peppercorns (5)
- Water (5 cups)
- Cinnamon sticks (2)
- Ginger (1 piece), 2-", peeled & sliced
- Turmeric (1 piece), 2-", peeled & sliced

**Instructions**
- In a medium saucepan, heat the water over medium heat.
- Mix all the ingredients in the saucepan and carry to a medium simmer.
- Cook on low pressure for 30 minutes.
- Serve at room temperature or cold.

*Calories 114, Protein 0.2 g, Sodium 9.9 mg, Potassium 250.5 mg, Phosphorus 17.4 mg, Calcium 2 mg*

## Watermelon Cooler
*Time: 16 Mins, Serves: 3, Skill: Easy*

**Ingredients**
- Sea salt (pinch)
- Grapefruit (1 small)
- Watermelon (2 cups), cubed
- Ice cubes (8)
- Water (1 1/2 cups)
- Honey (1 tsp)

**Instructions**
- Remove the white membrane on the grapefruit and cut it into pieces.
- In a mixer, combine all ingredients (except the honey) and process until smooth.
- Process for another 15 seconds after adding the honey, then serve immediately.

*Calories 69, Protein 1.3 g, Sodium 31.7 mg, Potassium 180.5 mg, Phosphorus 44.3 mg, Calcium 4 mg*

## Watermelon Lime Refresher
*Time: 25 Mins, Serves: 6, Skill: Easy*

**Ingredients**
- Basil leaves (6 large)
- Watermelon (4 cups), cubed
- Strawberries (2 cups)
- Limes (2)
- Ice (2 cups)

**Instructions**
- Combine all the ingredients in a blender and process until smooth.

*Calories 56, Protein 1 g, Sodium 2 mg, Potassium 226 mg, Phosphorus 29 mg, Calcium 24 mg*

## Coco Coffee Frappe
*Time: 15 Mins, Serves: 2, Skill: Easy*

**Ingredients**
- Cinnamon (1/4 tsp)
- Coffee (3/4 cup), brewed strong, room temperature
- Ice (1/4 cup)
- Coconut milk (1/2 cup)
- Maple syrup (2 tsp)

**Instructions**
- Add all the ingredients in a blender and mix until smooth.

*Calories 37, Protein 1 g, Sodium 14 mg, Potassium 134 mg, Phosphorus 10 mg, Calcium 37 mg*

## Rose Hibiscus Limeade
*Time: 25 Mins, Serves: 6, Skill: Easy*

**Ingredients**
- Hibiscus flowers (1/3 cup), dried
- Water (8 cups)
- Maple syrup (1/4 cup)
- Ginger (2 inches), freshly grated
- Rose petals (1/2 cup), dried
- Limes (2), juiced

### Instructions
- Bring the water to a boil in a stockpot over medium-high heat.
- Add the maple syrup and ginger to the boiling pot.
- Cook on low pressure for 15 minutes.
- Cook for an additional 5 minutes after adding the dried hibiscus flowers and rose petals to the ginger-infused broth (dried).
- Strain the water from the grated ginger and dried flowers into a separate pitcher.
- Apply the lime juice and serve at room temperature or cool.

*Calories 56, Protein 1 g, Sodium 2 mg, Potassium 226 mg, Phosphorus 29 mg, Calcium 24 mg*

## Mexican Coconut Drink
*Time: 25 Mins, Serves: 6, Skill: Easy*

### Ingredients
- Lime (4 slices)
- Water (2 cups)
- White rice (2 cups)
- Coconut water (2 cups), unsweetened
- Coconut milk (1 can), unsweetened
- Sugar (1/3 cup)

### Instructions
- Fill a saucepan halfway with water (2 cups), bring to a boil, and remove from heat as soon as possible.
- In a medium mixing bowl, combine the coconut water and rice; cover and set aside at room temperature for the night.
- Blend the rice and coconut water mixture until smooth the next day.
- Wrap a medium-sized dish in cheesecloth and secure it with a rubber band or twine.
- Using cheesecloth, strain the liquid from the rice puree.
- Pour the rice water into a strainer and discard the rice sediment.
- In a small saucepan, heat the coconut milk and sugar over low heat for 4 minutes, or until the sugar is fully dissolved.
- Pour the sweetened coconut mixture over the rice and chill before ready to serve.
- Serve with ice and lime juice, garnished with lime slices.

*Calories 161.2, Protein 2.6 g, Sodium 65.9 mg, Potassium 46.8 mg, Phosphorus 1.5 mg, Calcium 7.2 mg*

## Iced Tea with Mint
*Time: 3 hours and 30 Mins, Serves: 8, Skill: Hard*

### Ingredients
- Sprigs fresh mint leaves (2 large), washed
- Boiling water (1/2 gallon)
- Black tea bags (4)

### Instructions
- In a mixing cup, combine the tea bags and boiling water; allow 3 to 5 minutes for the tea to brew to the desired strength.
- Set aside for 2-3 hours in the refrigerator.
- Combine with mint in a large mixing bowl, then chill for a few hours or overnight.

*Calories 25, Protein 0 g, Sodium 4 mg, Potassium 96 mg, Phosphorus 15 mg, Calcium 10 mg*

## Papaya Smoothie
*Time: 10 Mins, Serves: 1, Skill: Easy*

### Ingredients
- Papaya (3 oz.), in small pieces
- Ice cubes (2)
- Almond milk/oat milk (1/2 cup), unsweetened
- Honey (1 tsp)
- Ginger (1/2 tsp), fresh, grated
- Lime juice (2 tbsp)

### Instructions
- Add all the ingredients in a blender and mix until smooth.

*Calories 224.6, Protein 6.9 g, Sodium 119.2 mg, Potassium 659.8 mg, Phosphorus 0.7 mg, Calcium 33.4 mg*

## Strawberry Sesame Milkshake
*Time: 16 Mins, Serves: 3, Skill: Easy*

### Ingredients
- Ice cubes (1 cup)
- Sesame seeds (1/2 tbsp), toasted
- Strawberries (1 lb.), halved
- Balsamic glaze (2 tbsp)
- Banana (1/2 small/50 grams), frozen, optional
- Coconut milk (1/2 cup)
- Tahini (2 tbsp)

### Instructions
- Preheat the oven to 400 °F.

- In a mixing bowl, toss the strawberries with the balsamic glaze.
- Spread it out on a baking dish lined with parchment paper and set aside for 5 minutes.
- Cook for 10 minutes, then remove from the oven and flip the strawberries over to roast for another 10 minutes, or until softened.
- In a blender, combine the strawberries, coconut milk, tahini, pineapple, and ice and blend until smooth.
- Pour the smoothies into three glasses and top with toasted sesame seeds and a dry strawberry.

*Calories 143, Protein 3 g, Sodium 16 mg, Potassium 358 mg, Phosphorus 121 mg, Calcium 87 mg*

## Cherry Citrus Mocktail
*Time: 12 Mins, Serves: 2, Skill: Easy*

### Ingredients
- Lime or Orange (2 rings), for garnish
- Tart cherry juice (1/4 cup), unsweetened
- Orange juice (1/2 cup), freshly squeezed
- Lime juice (1/4 cup), freshly squeezed
- Club soda (8 oz. can)

### Instructions
- In a big glass container, combine the juices.
- Cover with a lid and store in the refrigerator.
- To serve, take it out of the freezer and uncover it.
- Fill the cocktail bottles halfway with the mixture and top with a splash of club soda.
- Attach a lime or orange ring to the bottle.

*Calories 93, Protein 1.02 g, Sodium 2 mg, Potassium 296 mg, Phosphorus 108 mg, Calcium 14 mg*

## Pretty Pink Smoothie
*Time: 10 Mins, Serves: 1, Skill: Easy*

### Ingredients
- Flaxseed (2 tsp)
- Fresh ginger (1 tsp), peeled, grated
- Cooked beet (1/2 small), peeled, chopped
- Pear (1), cored, chopped
- Orange (1/2), peeled, chopped
- Homemade rice milk (1 cup)
- Ice cubes (3)

### Instructions
- Add all the ingredients in a blender and mix until smooth.

*Calories 277.4, Protein 27 g, Sodium 444.4 mg, Potassium 447.1 mg, Phosphorus 37.9 mg, Calcium 73.5 mg*

## Green Kiwi Smoothie
*Time: 10 Mins, Serves: 1, Skill: Easy*

### Ingredients
- Water (1 cup)
- Honey (1 tsp), optional
- Kiwi (1), peeled, chopped
- Kale (1/2 cup), fresh or frozen, stemmed & chopped
- Almonds (2 tbsp)
- Ice cubes (2)

### Instructions
- Add all the ingredients in a blender and mix until smooth.

*Calories 369.5, Protein 9.3 g, Sodium 87 mg, Potassium 2350 mg, Phosphorus 57 mg, Calcium 238.7 mg*

## Fruity Baked Tea
*Time: 45 Mins, Serves: 1, Skill: Medium*

### Ingredients
- Apricots (1/2 cup), dried, diced
- Cloves (25 pieces)
- Star anise (4 pieces)
- Apple (1), diced
- Pear (1), diced
- Orange (1), diced
- Lemon (1), diced
- Peaches (1 cup), diced
- Berries (2 cups), blackberries, raspberries, blueberries, cherries, diced
- Powdered cinnamon (2 tsp)
- Brown sugar (2 tbsp)

### Instructions
- Arrange all of the fruits in a baking bowl. Stir in all of the sugar and spices.
- Cover the bowl in aluminum foil to keep it dry. Bake for 40 minutes, stirring after 10 to 15 minutes.
- Remove the foil and bake for another 20 minutes to evaporate any juices and concentrate the taste.
- Extract the dish from the oven and automatically put the contents into four 8-ounce jars, or sixteen 2-ounce jars.
- Firmly seal the jars and encourage them to cool by standing on their lids with their bottoms up.

- Fill a medium saucepan halfway with water and bring to a boil. Boil for 15 minutes after inserting the bottoms of the jars.
- Remove the jars from the oven and put them aside to cool before placing them in the refrigerator.
- To serve, place 1 tablespoon of the mixture in a cup. Combine 8 oz. of boiling water in a glass and drink.

*Calories 62, Protein 1.2 g, Sodium 0 mg, Potassium 237 mg, Phosphorus 105 mg, Calcium 52.4 mg*

## Homemade Rice Milk
*Time: 25 Mins, Serves: 2, Skill: Easy*

**Ingredients**
- White rice (1 cup), cooked
- Filtered water (4 cups)

**Instructions**
- Combine the water and rice in a blender or food processor and blend for about 4 minutes, or until fluffy and smooth.
- Squeeze the remaining rice meal onto the fabric to collect the moisture, then pour the rice milk into a container using a double cheesecloth sheet or a strong sieve.
- Discard the rice meal and refrigerate the rice milk for up to one week in a lined glass jar.

*Calories 84, Protein 1 g, Sodium 1 mg, Potassium 25 mg, Phosphorus 26 mg, Calcium 6 mg*

## Fruit Julius
*Time: 10 Mins, Serves: 1, Skill: Easy*

**Ingredients**
- Egg substitute (1/2 cup)
- Juice (1/2 cup), orange, grape, cranberry, or other
- Ice cubes (3), crushed
- Tang powder (2 tsp)

**Instructions**
- In a blender, mix all the ingredients and mix until smooth.

*Calories 250, Protein 4 g, Sodium 85 mg, Potassium 46 mg, Phosphorus 20 mg, Calcium 14 mg*

## Rhubarb Lemonade Punch
*Time: 40 Mins, Serves: 5, Skill: Easy*

**Ingredients**
- Lemon-lime carbonated beverage (14 oz.), chilled
- Water (3 cups)
- Rhubarb (2 x 12 oz. packages), frozen
- Frozen lemonade concentrates (6 oz. can)
- Sugar (1/4 cup)

**Instructions**
- In a saucepan, combine the water, frozen condensed lemonade, frozen rhubarb, and sugar.
- Cover and simmer for 20 minutes, or until the rhubarb is tender.
- Drain the pulp with a strainer and cool the juice.
- Before serving, pour the rhubarb mixture over the ice.

*Calories 80.68, Protein 0.48 g, Sodium 6.49 mg, Potassium 163.52 mg, Phosphorus 15 mg, Calcium 62.6 mg*

## Blueberry Punch
*Time: 14 Mins, Serves: 2, Skill: Easy*

**Ingredients**
- Lemonade (1-quart), undiluted, frozen
- Ginger ale (3 x 28oz. bottles)
- Pineapple juice (3 quarts)
- Water (1quart)
- Blueberry juice (3 quarts)

**Instructions**
- Combine all of the ingredients in a big mixing bowl.

*Calories 367, Protein 0 g, Sodium 95 mg, Potassium 4.1 mg, Phosphorus 42 mg, Calcium 6 mg*

## Rhubarb Tea
*Time: 1 hour and 20 Mins, Serves: 8, Skill: Hard*

**Ingredients**
- Mint, to garnish
- Rhubarb stalks (8)
- Water (8 cups)
- Sugar (1/3 cup)

**Instructions**
- Cut 8 rhubarb stalks into 3" sections, put in a pot of 8 cups water, bring to a boil, then reduce to low heat, and simmer for 1 hour.
- Strain the drink, then apply about a third of a cup (or to taste) of sugar and put aside to cool.

*Calories 13, Protein 1 g, Sodium 4 mg, Potassium 288 mg, Phosphorus 14 mg, Calcium 86 mg*

## Every Berry Goodness
*Time: 12 Mins, Serves: 2, Skill: Easy*

**Ingredients**
- Strawberries (1/2 cup), fresh or frozen

- Blueberries (1/2 cup), fresh
- Stevia, to taste (optional)
- Rice milk (1/2 cup), unsweetened
- Cucumber (1 medium), peeled and sliced

**Instructions**
- In a blender, combine all ingredients and mix until smooth.

*Calories 43, Protein 1 g, Sodium 1 mg, Potassium 25 mg, Phosphorus 26 mg, Calcium 6 mg*

## Cranberry Blast Smoothie
*Time: 12 Mins, Serves: 2, Skill: Easy*

**Ingredients**
- Blueberries (1 cup), frozen
- Ice cubes (8)
- Protein powder (6 tbsp)
- Splenda (8 packets)
- Apple juice (14 oz.), no added sugar

**Instructions**
- In a blender, mix all the ingredients and blend until smooth.

*Calories 140.2, Protein 4.4 g, Sodium 76.7 mg, Potassium 227.7 mg, Phosphorus 11.4 mg, Calcium 15.9 mg*

## Blueberry Protein Smoothie
*Time: 10 Mins, Serves: 1, Skill: Easy*

**Ingredients**
- Ice cubes (2), optional
- Whey protein powder (1 scoop), vanilla flavor
- Blueberry sherbet (1 cup), frozen
- Water (1/2 cup)

**Instructions**
- Add whey protein powder, frozen blueberry, and water in a blender (with ice cubes if desired).
- Mix for 30 to 45 seconds before serving.

*Calories 162.9, Protein 8.3 g, Sodium 123.4 mg, Potassium 223.4 mg, Phosphorus 10.9 mg, Calcium 29 mg*

## Strawberry Blast Smoothie
*Time: 12 Mins, Serves: 2, Skill: Easy*

**Ingredients**
- Strawberries (1 cup), frozen
- Ice cubes (8)
- Protein powder (6 tbsp)
- Splenda (8 packets)
- Apple juice (14 oz.), no added sugar

**Instructions**
- In a blender, combine all the ingredients and process until smooth.

*Calories 65, Protein 2.2 g, Sodium 33 mg, Potassium 125 mg, Phosphorus 75 mg, Calcium 163 mg*

## Red Wine Vinaigrette
*Time: 10 Mins, Serves: 1, Skill: Easy*

**Ingredients**
- Extra virgin olive oil (1/2 cup)
- Lemon juice (1/2 tsp)
- Red wine vinegar (3 tbsp)
- Garlic powder (1/2 tsp)
- Oregano (1/2 tsp), dried

**Instructions**
- Mix together the red wine vinegar, oil, oregano, lemon juice, and garlic powder to produce the dressing.

*Calories 239.9, Protein 2.7 g, Sodium 201 mg, Potassium 50 mg, Phosphorus 3.2 mg, Calcium 1.7 mg*

## Scarlet Frozen Fantasy
*Time: 15 Mins, Serves: 2, Skill: Easy*

**Ingredients**
- Cranberry (1 cup), juice cocktail
- Strawberries (1 cup), fresh, whole, washed and hulled
- Strawberries, for garnish
- Sugar (1/4 cup)
- Lime juice (2 tbsp), fresh
- Ice cubes (8-9)

**Instructions**
- In a mixer, combine the strawberries, cranberry juice, sugar, and lime juice. All can be carefully combined.
- Add ice cubes into the mix. Blend until fully smooth.
- Pour the mixture into chilled cups. Serve with a garnish of strawberries.

*Calories 640, Protein 9 g, Sodium 330 mg, Potassium 110 mg, Phosphorus 6.5 mg, Calcium 7 mg*

## Pineapple Bliss
*Time: 15 Mins, Serves: 2, Skill: Easy*

**Ingredients**
- Mint (2 sprigs), leaves only
- Cucumber (1 medium), peeled and sliced
- Squeeze of lime

- Celery stalk (1)
- Pineapple (2 cups), drained
- Ice cubes

**Instructions**
- Mix all ingredients in a blender and process until smooth.
- Fill a glass with the mixture and serve.

*Calories 1854, Protein 38.2 g, Sodium 2268.1 mg, Potassium 96.4 mg, Phosphorus 1.9 mg, Calcium 76.1 mg*

## Peach Cobbler
*Time: 15 Mins, Serves: 2, Skill: Easy*

**Ingredients**
- Peaches (2 cups), sliced
- Plain flour (1/2 cup)
- Sugar (1/2 cup)
- Baking powder (1 tsp)
- Milk (1/2 cup), for lower phosphorus use coffee creamer

**Instructions**
- In a mixing bowl, combine the sugar, baking powder, and plain flour.
- Pour in the milk and give it a good mix.
- Add the peaches and the juice. Make a rigorous mix.
- Place in a baking dish.
- Bake until golden brown and thick, around 347 °F.

*Calories 432, Protein 4 g, Sodium 258 mg, Potassium 266 mg, Phosphorus 45 mg, Calcium 8 mg*

## Coffee Creamer
*Time: 15 Mins, Serves: 4, Skill: Easy*

**Ingredients**
- Milk (2 cups)
- Condensed milk (1 can x 14 oz.), sweetened

**Added options**
- Almond extract (1 tsp)
- Cocoa powder (2 tsp)
- Vanilla extract (2 tsp)
- Ice cream topping (2 tbsp), caramel
- Raspberry syrup (2 tbsp)

**Instructions**
- Combine the milk and condensed sweetened milk in a 32-ounce mixing cup.
- Apply the flavoring and whisk thoroughly.

*Calories 50.2, Protein 1.6 g, Sodium 20.3 mg, Potassium 0 mg, Phosphorus 0 mg, Calcium 2.2 mg*

## Party Punch
*Time: 25 Mins, Serves: 4, Skill: Easy*

**Ingredients**
- Liquid pineapple (1/2 cup)
- Lime-flavored sherbet (1 pint)
- Diet ginger ale (1 litre)

**Instructions**
- Add ginger ale and water in a big mixing cup.
- Stir in the condensed pineapple until it is well mixed.
- Apply the sherbet scoop to the blend.
- Serve the sherbet as soon as it has melted.

*Calories 107, Protein 0 g, Sodium 19 mg, Potassium 0 mg, Phosphorus 23 mg, Calcium 0 mg*

## Zippy Dip
*Time: 15 Mins, Serves: 2, Skill: Easy*

**Ingredients**
- Green onion (3 tbsp), chopped
- Cayenne pepper (dash)
- Cream cheese (1 package 8 oz.), softened
- Margarine (1/2 cup), softened
- Mayonnaise (2 tbsp)
- Lemon juice (1 1/2 tsp)
- Hot dry mustard (1 1/2 tsp)
- Vinegar (1 tbsp)
- Horseradish (1 tsp)
- Paprika (1 tsp)
- Tarragon (1/2 tsp)
- Garlic powder (1/2 tsp)

**Instructions**
- In a blender, combine all ingredients and mix until smooth.
- Serve with new veggies or unsalted crackers.

*Calories 64.52, Protein 2.12 g, Sodium 52.89 mg, Potassium 96.75 mg, Phosphorus 1.5 mg, Calcium 67.1 mg*

## Lemon Apple Honey Smoothie
*Time: 15 Mins, Serves: 4, Skill: Easy*

**Ingredients**
- Apple juice (1/2 cup)
- Apple (1), peeled & cored
- Banana (1/2), optional
- Honey (2-3 tsp)
- Vanilla yogurt (1 cup), frozen
- Lemon juice (1/4 cup)

**Instructions**
- Combine all the ingredients in a blender and mix until creamy.

*Calories 232.4, Protein 2.3 g, Sodium 4.5 mg, Potassium 661.8 mg, Phosphorus 4.2 mg, Calcium 3.8 mg*

# Berrylicious Smoothie
*Time: 15 Mins, Serves: 4, Skill: Easy*

**Ingredients**
- Silken tofu (2/3 cup), firm
- Raspberries (1/2 cup), unsweetened, frozen
- Blueberries (1/2 cup), unsweetened, frozen
- Vanilla extract (1 tsp)
- Powdered lemonade (1/2 tsp)
- Cranberry juice cocktail (1/4 cup)

**Instructions**
- Combine all the ingredients in a blender and mix until creamy.

*Calories 414, Protein 3 g, Sodium 65 mg, Potassium 0 mg, Phosphorus 14 mg, Calcium 13 mg*

# Snacks & Side Recipes

## BBQ Asparagus
*Time: 1 hour 10 Mins, Serves: 6, Skill: Easy*

**Ingredients**
- Pepper (1-1 1/2 tsp)
- Lemon juice (2-3 tbsp)
- Asparagus (1-1 1/2 lb.), fresh, 12 to 15 large spears
- Extra-virgin olive oil (2-3 tbsp)

**Instructions**
- In a shallow dish large enough to roll the asparagus in, combine the oil, pepper, and lemon juice and cover entirely with the mixture.
- Clean and trim the woody ends of the asparagus spears.
- Set aside in the tub after rolling the asparagus in the oil mixture. Place the tray on a platter in the refrigerator to marinate until the grill is primed.
- Prepare the barbecue or gas grill by lighting it and positioning it over a medium-high flame.
- To prevent the spears from sticking to the plate, gently spray the vegetable grilling tray or a grill basket into a shallow dish with olive oil spray.
- Arrange the asparagus spears on a vegetable grilling plate and drizzle the leftover oil from the dish over the other.
- Grill the asparagus in a skillet, or on tin foil until soft and starting to brown, around 5 minutes. At room temperature or a higher temperature, serve.

*Calories 45.9, Protein 2.6 g, Sodium 147.6 mg, Potassium 309.9 mg, Phosphorus 6.4 mg, Calcium 2.4 mg*

## BBQ Corn on the Cob
*Time: 45 Mins, Serves: 8, Skill: Easy*

**Ingredients**
- Thyme (1 tsp), dried
- Parsley (1 tsp)
- Black pepper (1/2 tsp)
- Corn on the cob (4)
- Olive oil (3 tbsp)
- Parmesan cheese, grated

**Instructions**
- In a big enough dish to roll the corn into and completely coat it with the mixture, combine the oil, cheese, parsley, thyme, and black pepper.
- Roll the corn cob in the mixture to fully coat it.
- All of the mix should be put in the middle of a heavy-duty aluminum foil sheet.
- Fold the foil sheet's sides together to create a pan, ensuring that no oil spills onto the grill.
- Place the foil tray on the grill over medium heat for 15-20 minutes, rotating halfway through to ensure even browning on both sides.

*Calories 102.4, Protein 2.9 g, Sodium 61 mg, Potassium 243 mg, Phosphorus 8 mg, Calcium 0.2 mg*

## Low Salt Macaroni and Cheese
*Time: 35 Mins, Serves: 4, Skill: Easy*

**Ingredients**
- Boiling water (2 to 3 cups)
- Cheddar cheese (1/2 cup), grated
- Margarine or salt-free butter (1 tsp)
- Noodles (2 cups)
- Dried mustard (1/4 tsp)

**Instructions**
- Bring the boiling water to a simmer, then add the noodles and simmer for 5-7 minutes, or until they are soft.
- Sprinkle in the cheese and whisk in the butter and mustard when it's still soft.

*Calories 314, Protein 19 g, Sodium 583 mg, Potassium 212 mg, Phosphorus 36 mg, Calcium 6 mg*

## Cauliflower in Mustard Sauce
*Time: 50 Mins, Serves: 4, Skill: Easy*

**Ingredients**
- White-wine vinegar (3 tbsp)
- Olive oil (1 tbsp)
- Black pepper (a dash)
- Cauliflower (2 cups)
- Dijon mustard (2 tsp)
- Honey (1 tsp)

**Instructions**
- In a mixing cup, add the mustard, honey, vinegar, and olive oil.
- Apply a tablespoon of black pepper to taste.
- Cook the cauliflower until it is soft in hot water.
- Drain all the water.
- Toss the grilled cauliflower with the dressing after it has been soaked.
- Allow to cool for 30-45 minutes before serving.

*Calories 188.3, Protein 2.9 g, Sodium 429.8 mg, Potassium 500.6 mg, Phosphorus 7.3 mg, Calcium 5.4 mg*

## 60-Second Salsa
*Time: 35 Mins, Serves: 8, Skill: Easy*

### Ingredients
- Plum tomatoes (4)
- Cilantro (1/2 bunch), fresh, chopped
- Cumin (1/2 tsp)
- Oregano (1/4 cup), fresh, chopped
- Green Onions (2), chopped
- Garlic cloves (3), minced
- Green bell pepper (1/2-1), chopped
- Jalapeño (1/2 – 1), fresh, chopped

### Instructions
- In a food processor or blender, combine all ingredients.
- Refrigerate for a couple of hours before serving.
- Serve cold with tortilla chips.

*Calories 11, Protein 0.4 g, Sodium 179 mg, Potassium 0 mg, Phosphorus 7 mg, Calcium 2 mg*

## Acorn Squash Baked with Pineapple
*Time: 1 hour 20 Mins, Serves: 2, Skill: Medium*

### Ingredients
- Butter (3 tbsp), unsalted
- Brown sugar (2 tsp)
- Pineapple (3 tbsp), crushed
- Acorn squash (1), cut in half and seeded
- Nutmeg (1/4 tbsp)

### Instructions
- Preheat the oven to 400 °F.
- In a greased baking tray, position the squash cut side up.
- Add one teaspoon of butter and one teaspoon of brown sugar to each half of an acorn.
- Cover the squash with aluminum foil and bake for 30 minutes, or until tender.
- Cook the squash and remove it from the shells, leaving 1/4 inch of the shell intact.
- In a wide mixing cup, add 1 tablespoon of butter, pineapple, and nutmeg. Blend until the mixture is fully smooth.
- Cover the shells halfway with the mixture and bake for 15 minutes at 425 °F.

*Calories 17.76, Protein 0.04 g, Sodium 0.29 mg, Potassium 1.97 mg, Phosphorus 0.6 mg, Calcium 3.8 mg*

## Alfredo Sauce
*Time: 1 hour and 20 Mins, Serves: 8, Skill: Medium*

### Ingredients
- Olive oil (1/4 cup)
- Lemon juice (1 tbsp)
- Cream cheese (4 oz.)
- Parmesan cheese (1/3 cup), shredded
- Nutmeg (1/4 tbsp), ground
- All-purpose flour (3 tbsp)
- Garlic clove (1), minced
- Rice milk (2 cups)

### Instructions
- Heat the olive oil in a broad skillet over medium heat. Combine flour and ground garlic to produce a paste.
- Drizzle in the rice milk slowly, whisking constantly to avoid lumps. When the mixture is simmering, cause it to thicken.
- Add the cream cheese and stir it in thoroughly. Set it aside.
- In a mixing dish, add 1/3 cup of Parmesan cheese, lemon juice, and nutmeg. To create a full mix, add all the ingredients to a blender.

*Calories 319, Protein 8 g, Sodium 1640 mg, Potassium 211 mg, Phosphorus 226 mg, Calcium 160 mg*

## Anytime Energy Bars
*Time: 1 hour and 15 Mins, Serves: 8, Skill: Hard*

### Ingredients
- Rolled oats (1 cup)
- Eggs (3 large)
- Applesauce (1/3 cup)
- Honey (3 tbsp)
- Cinnamon (1/2 tsp), ground
- Peanuts (3 tbsp), unsalted, chopped
- Semi-sweet small chocolate chips (1/4 cup)
- Coconut (1/3 cup), shredded

### Instructions
- Preheat the oven to 325 °F and spray a 9x9-inch baking pan with cooking oil.
- Combine the oats, cinnamon, peanuts, chocolate chips, and coconut in a large mixing cup.
- In a small mixing cup, whisk the eggs. Add the honey and applesauce.
- In a large mixing cup, completely blend the egg and oat mixture.

- Place the mixture evenly onto the rim of the greased pan.
- Cooking time is 40 minutes. Allow it to cool completely before cutting it into bars.

*Calories 250, Protein 15 g, Sodium 310 mg, Potassium 115 mg, Phosphorus 40 mg, Calcium 40 mg*

## Apple & Cherry Chutney
*Time: 50 Mins, Serves: 10, Skill: Easy*

### Ingredients
- Sugar (1 1/2 cups)
- Tart apple (1 medium)
- Tart cherries (1 cup), dried
- Red onion (1 small), thinly chopped
- Apple cider vinegar (1 cup)

### Instructions
- Leave the skin on the apple and take the core off before peeling and chopping it into thin strips.
- Combine the apples, cherries, onions, vinegar, and sugar in a wide saucepan. Cook, vigorously, whisking until the sugar has melted and the mixture has started to simmer.
- Cook, covered, over low heat for 8-10 minutes, or until the onions are soft and the dry cherries are plump.
- Remove the cap and lift the heat to maximum, then proceed to cook for another 5 minutes, or until the syrup has reduced to a glossy glaze around the berries. Chutney may be consumed right away, or stored in a sealed container in the refrigerator.

*Calories 55, Protein 1 g, Sodium 2 mg, Potassium 12 mg, Phosphorus 1 mg, Calcium 32 mg*

## BBQ Winter Squash
*Time: 55 Mins, Serves: 8, Skill: Easy*

### Ingredients
- Brown sugar (1-2 tbsp)
- Butter (1-2 tbsp)
- Butternut squash or acorn (1-2)
- Olive oil (1-2 tbsp)

### Instructions
- Preheat the grill to medium-high (around 400°F).
- Apply a thin layer of olive oil to the squash and place it on the grill for around 5 minutes before turning.
- Brush it with melted butter and brown sugar until its tender.
- On the barbecue, cook for 1 minute, then serve.

*Calories 115, Protein 2 g, Sodium 81 mg, Potassium 26 mg, Phosphorus 25 mg, Calcium 6 mg*

## Beef Jerky
*Time: 12 to 20 hours, Serves: 30, Skill: Hard*

### Ingredients
- Dark brown sugar (1/4 cup)
- Liquid smoke (2 tbsp)
- Worcestershire sauce (1 1/2 tsp)
- Tabasco sauce (2-3 drops)
- Garlic powder (1 tsp)
- Liquid pepper sauce (1 tsp)
- Flank steak (3 lb.)
- Soy sauce (3/4 cup), reduced sodium
- Red wine (1/2 cup)

### Instructions
- Trim fat and other lean beef from a 3-lb. flank steak.
- Slice it lengthwise into 30 strips.
- In a glass dish, arrange the strips.
- Combine all the ingredients in a mixing bowl and spill over the beef.
- Chill for at least 5 hours or overnight, sealed.
- Remove the beef from the marinade.
- Preheat the dehydrator to 144°F and dehydrate the meat for 4 to 20 hours (if you have one).
- Preheat the oven to 175 °F if you're using one.
- Arrange the strips so that they do not cross on wire racks on top of baking sheets.
- Roast the beef jerky for about 10 to 12 hrs. until it is crisp and brittle.

*Calories 369, Protein 30 g, Sodium 40 mg, Potassium 7 mg, Phosphorus 9 mg, Calcium 3 mg*

## Brown Bag Popcorn
*Time: 25 Mins, Serves: 1, Skill: Easy*

### Ingredients
- Canola oil (1 tsp)
- Lunch bag (1 brown paper)
- Popcorn kernels (1/4 cup)

### Instructions
- Combine the popcorn and oil in a mixing cup.
- Fill a brown bag halfway with popcorn, fold it in two, and staple the end twice.
- Microwave for 3 minutes on heavy, or until pops are 5 seconds apart.

*Calories 284.3, Protein 7.7 g, Sodium 2328 mg, Potassium 193.1 mg, Phosphorus 19.2 mg, Calcium 0.8 mg*

## Dry-Rubbed Barbecue Turkey Wings

*Time: 1 hour and 10 Mins, Serves: 7, Skill: Medium*

**Ingredients**
- Turkey wings (7), whole
- Smoked paprika (1 tsp)
- Granulated garlic (2 tsp)
- Dehydrated onion flakes (2 tsp)
- Dark chili powder (2 tsp)
- Packed brown sugar (1 cup)
- Black pepper (1 tsp)
- Red pepper flakes (1 tsp)

**Instructions**
- Preheat the oven to 375 °F.
- Clean the wings and pierce both ends with a fork.
- Mix together all seasonings.
- One tablespoon of the seasoning rub can be set aside for later usage while seasoning the wings.
- Wrapped in foil, roast the wings in a baking dish for 30 minutes. Cook for another 30 minutes after taking the wings from the oven and discarding the foil. Season the rest of the wings with salt and pepper before flipping them.
- Remove the wings from the oven and set aside for 15 minutes before serving with a low-sodium barbecue sauce.

*Calories 272, Protein 19 g, Sodium 371 mg, Potassium 321 mg, Phosphorus 155 mg, Calcium 54 mg*

## Not Very Spicy Chipotle Wings

*Time: 1 hour, Serves: 4, Skill: Easy*

**Ingredients**
- Butter (1/4 cup), unsalted, slightly melted
- Black pepper (1 tsp)
- Chives (1 tbsp), chopped
- Jumbo chicken wings (1 lb.), fresh
- Chipotle peppers (1 1/2 tbsp), diced, in adobo sauce*
- Honey (1/4 cup)

**Instructions**
- Preheat the oven to 400 °F.
- Arrange the precut wings on a baking tray lined with greased baking sheets.
- Bake for 20 minutes, or until crisp on the outside and an internal temperature of 165 °F, using an instant-read thermometer halfway through.
- In a mixing cup, combine the remaining ingredients and whisk briefly with a rubber spatula before mixing.
- Take the wings out of the oven and toss them in the sauce to cover them equally. Serve immediately on a big platter.

*Calories 384, Protein 20 g, Sodium 99 mg, Potassium 266 mg, Phosphorus 146 mg, Calcium 21 mg*

## Cinnamon Biscotti

*Time: 1 hour and 20 Mins, Serves: 18, Skill: Medium*

**Ingredients**
- Eggs (2 large)
- Vanilla extract (1 tsp)
- Peel of oranges (a pinch)
- All-purpose flour (2 cups)
- Cream of tartar (1 tsp)
- Baking soda (1/2 tsp)
- Sugar (1 cup)
- Butter (1/2 cup), unsalted
- Salt (1/4 tsp)
- Cinnamon (1 tsp), ground

**Instructions**
- Preheat the oven to 325 °F.
- Brush nonstick cooking oil onto two baking sheets.
- Combine the sugar and unsalted butter in a big mixing bowl.
- One at a time, whisk in the eggs, whisking well after each inclusion.
- In a mixing cup, combine the orange peel and vanilla extract.
- In a medium mixing dish, combine the flour, tartar cream, cinnamon, baking soda, and salt.
- Whisk the dry ingredients into the butter mixture until thoroughly combined.
- Dividing the dough in half. Place each half on a sheet that has already been prepared. Form each half into a 3 inch wide by three-quarters of an inch tall log using lightly floured palms. Bake the dough logs for 35 minutes, or until solid.
- Remove the dough logs from the oven and put them aside for 10 minutes to cool.

- Cut diagonally into 12-inch-thick slices using serrated blades. Put on baking sheets, cut side up.
- Bake for 12 minutes, or until golden brown on the bottoms.
- Turn and bake for a further 12 minutes, just until the bottoms are crispy.
- Cool on a wire rack before serving.

*Calories 104.6, Protein 2.4 g, Sodium 50.3 mg, Potassium 22.1 mg, Phosphorus 3.1 mg, Calcium 3.0 mg*

## Crispy Cauliflower Phyllo Cups
*Time: 1 hour and 20 Mins, Serves: 10, Skill: Medium*

**Ingredients**
- Onions (1/4 cup), finely diced
- Jalapeños (2 tbsp), diced
- Red pepper flakes (1/2 tsp)
- Parsley (1 tbsp)
- Black pepper (1/2 tsp), ground
- Phyllo dough (3 sheets)
- Eggs (3), beaten and lightly scrambled
- Swiss cheese (1/2 cup), shredded, reduced-sodium
- Cheddar cheese (1/2 cup), shredded
- Butter (2 tbsp)
- Bacon (4 slices), natural and uncured
- Cauliflower (1 1/2 cups), diced, cooked and drained well

**Instructions**
- Preheat the oven to 375 °F.
- Lightly scramble the eggs in a large sauté pan, then extract them from the pan and put them aside.
- Melt the butter in the same pan. Sauté the bacon before frying it. Once the onions turn translucent, add the jalapenos, cauliflower, and red pepper flakes. Add parsley and black pepper to taste.
- Take the skillet from the heat and add the scrambled eggs and two kinds of cheese.
- The third sheet should be put on top of the previous one.
- Split the sheets into 24 squares and position them in a mini muffin tin tray that has been lightly sprayed.
- Fill each muffin cup halfway with the mixture and bake on the back shelf of the oven for 12-15 minutes, or until the edges are slightly crisp. Switch off the oven and leave it to cool for 2 to 3 minutes.

*Calories 68, Protein 3 g, Sodium 107 mg, Potassium 42 mg, Phosphorus 49 mg, Calcium 45 mg*

## Sweet & Nutty Protein Bars
*Time: 45 Mins, Serves: 12, Skill: Easy*

**Ingredients**
- Flaxseeds (1/2 cup)
- Peanut butter (1/2 cup)
- Cherries, blueberries, or raisins (1 cup), dried
- Honey (1/2 cup)
- Rolled oats (2 ½ cups), toasted
- Almonds (1/2 cup)

**Instructions**
- Place the rolled oats on a baking sheet and toast for 10 minutes, or until golden brown.
- In a mixing cup, combine all the ingredients and whisk until well combined.
- In a tightly greased 9" x 9" plate, place the protein mixture flat. Refrigerate for at least 1 hour or overnight, sealed.
- Serve the protein bars sliced into desired squares.

*Calories 283, Protein 7 g, Sodium 49 mg, Potassium 258 mg, Phosphorus 177 mg, Calcium 51 mg*

## Homemade Herbed Biscuits
*Time: 1 hour and 10 Mins, Serves: 10, Skill: Medium*

**Ingredients**
- Baking soda (1/2 tsp)
- Mayonnaise (1/4 cup)
- Skim milk (2/3 cup)
- Chives or any other herb (3 tbsp), fresh or dry, to taste
- Cooking spray
- All-purpose flour (1 3/4 cups)
- Cream of tartar (1 tsp)

**Instructions**
- Preheat the oven to 400 °F. The baking sheet can then be coated with nonstick cooking oil.
- Combine the flour, tartar, and baking soda in a mixing cup. Then, using a fork, whisk in the mayonnaise until the paste resembles coarse cornmeal.
- Combine the milk and herbs in a shallow cup and stir them into the flour mixture. Stir before it is well combined.
- Scoop a tablespoon of the mixture into the baking bowl. Cook for 10 minutes in the oven.

- Keep refrigerated until ready to serve.

*Calories 128.6, Protein 2.7 g, Sodium 655.2 mg, Potassium 58.1 mg, Phosphorus 2.3 mg, Calcium 3.6 mg*

## Oregano Salsa (canned)
*Time: 2 Hours and 25 Mins, Serves: 15, Skill: Hard*

**Ingredients**
- Garlic cloves (2), crushed
- Onions (5 cups), chopped
- Sugar (1 tbsp)
- Oregano leaves (2 tbsp)
- Cilantro leaves (1 cup)
- Cumin (1 tsp), ground
- Jalapeno peppers (4), seeded and chopped
- Green chilies (4 long), seeded, and chopped
- Vinegar or lemon juice (2 1/2 cups)
- Pepper (1 tbsp)

**Instructions**
- Mix all the ingredients in a saucepan.
- Carry to a simmer, then reduce to low heat and proceed to cook for 20 minutes.
- Proceed to mix for about an hour, or until the sauce thickens.
- Pour the spicy salsa halfway into pint jars, leaving 1/2 inch of headspace.
- Cover it with canning lids.
- Using a jar lifter, place the jars in a pot of boiling water for around 20 minutes.
- Bring a pot of water to a boil.
- Remove them from the boiling pot.

*Calories 90.5, Protein 5.1 g, Sodium 92.5 mg, Potassium 697.9 mg, Phosphorus 7.7 mg, Calcium 4.6 mg*

## Tomatillo, Corn and Black Bean Chutney
*Time: 45 Mins, Serves: 20, Skill: Easy*

**Ingredients**
- Tomatillos (1 lb.), chopped,
- Whole kernel corn (1/4 cup)
- Black beans (1/4 cup), cooked
- Black olives (1/4 cup), sliced
- Red wine vinegar (2/3 cup)
- Brown sugar (1/4 cup)
- Fresh cilantro (1 tbsp), chopped
- Red bell pepper (1 cup), chopped,
- Green bell pepper (1 cup), chopped
- Jalapeños (4), seeded and minced
- Onions (1 cup), chopped
- Cayenne pepper (1/4 tsp)
- Cumin (1/4 tsp), ground

**Instructions**
- Bring all the ingredients to a boil in a large saucepan, stirring continuously.
- Decrease the heat to low and proceed to cook, stirring regularly.
- It may be preserved for up to a year or held in the refrigerator for 4-6 weeks.

*Calories 20, Protein 0 g, Sodium 25 mg, Potassium 75 mg, Phosphorus 11 mg, Calcium 0 mg*

## Teriyaki Flavor Sauce
*Time: 25 Mins, Serves: 1, Skill: Easy*

**Ingredients**
- Garlic cloves (3), crushes
- Ginger (1/4 tsp), ground
- Soy sauce (1 cup), low sodium
- Sesame oil (2 tbsp)
- Sake or mirin (2 tbsp)
- Granulated sugar (1/2 cup)

**Instructions**
- For this, use a light soy sauce.
- In a saucepan, combine all the ingredients and simmer until the sugar has dissolved.
- Keep it refrigerated.

*Calories 42.5, Protein 0.2 g, Sodium 191.8 mg, Potassium 26.2 mg, Phosphorus 0.5 mg, Calcium 0.5 mg*

## Taco Seasoning
*Time: 35 Mins, Serves: 5, Skill: Easy*

**Ingredients**
- Onion powder (1 tbsp)
- Oregano (1 tsp), dried
- Garlic powder (1 tsp)
- Red pepper (1 tsp), crushed
- Cinnamon (1/2 tsp)
- Chili powder (1/4 cup)
- Cumin (1 tbsp), ground

**Instructions**
- In an airtight jar, combine all the ingredients and store until usage.

*Calories 15, Protein 0 g, Sodium 300 mg, Potassium 55 mg, Phosphorus 115 mg, Calcium 4 mg*

# Thai Lettuce Wraps

*Time: 55 Mins, Serves: 6, Skill: Medium*

**Ingredients**
- Shrimp paste (1/2 tsp)
- Granulated sugar (2 tsp)
- Fresh cilantro (4 tbsp), finely sliced
- Fresh basil (4 tbsp), finely sliced
- Vegetable oil (1 tbsp)
- Onions or shallots (3 green)
- Thai chili (1), diced
- Garlic cloves (3), minced
- Ground pork (1 1/2 lb.)
- Soy sauce (1 tbsp), low sodium
- Iceberg or butter lettuce (8 leaves)

**Instructions**
- Heat the oil in a large skillet or wok over medium heat.
- Add the green onions, ginger, and Thai chili.
- Cook for 2 minutes.
- Roast the ground pork in the skillet for 15 minutes, or before it is thoroughly cooked.
- Add a portion of the basil and cilantro, as well as the low-sodium soy sauce, butter, and shrimp paste.
- Cook for 5 minutes.
- Garnish with the rest of the cilantro and basil.
- Spread around 2 oz. of the pork mixture over the lettuce leaves.

*Calories 284.1, Protein 4.8 g, Sodium 1816.5 mg, Potassium 400.6 mg, Phosphorus 7.9 mg, Calcium 5.6 mg*

# Slovakian Sauerkraut and Egg Noodles

*Time: 55 Mins, Serves: 5, Skill: Easy*

**Ingredients**
- Egg noodles (6 oz.)
- Sauerkraut (4 oz.), drained
- Black pepper (1/2 tsp), ground
- Butter (2 tbsp), unsalted
- Onion (1/2 small/35g), diced
- Dill (1 tbsp), fresh, chopped

**Instructions**
- Melt one tablespoon of butter over medium heat in a large skillet
- Add the onions. Cook, stirring regularly, until the onions are smooth and transparent, around 5 minutes.
- Put a broad pot halfway full of water to a boil.
- Add the egg noodles to the boiling broth and cook as directed on the box.
- Add the sauerkraut and 1/2 tablespoon more butter to the fried onions. Since thoroughly blending, boil for 3 minutes.
- Combine the noodles, sauerkraut, and the remaining 1/2 tablespoon of butter in the same pan. Blend well after seasoning with black pepper.
- Garnish with dill on top. You should serve it with a side salad.

*Calories 298, Protein 9 g, Sodium 262 mg, Potassium 225 mg, Phosphorus 150 mg, Calcium 38 mg*

# Cucumber Dill Cream Cheese Bites

*Time: 45 Mins, Serves: 4, Skill: Easy*

**Ingredients**
- Cucumbers (2 medium)
- Whole milk Greek yogurt (4 oz.)
- Dill (2 tbsp)
- Cream cheese (8 oz.), softened

**Instructions**
- Thinly slice the cucumber strips into 2 and a 1/2-inch slices.
- Add the cream cheese and Greek yogurt with a large spoon or a hand blender. Mix in the dill thoroughly.
- Split one tablespoon of cream cheese equally among the 4 cucumber slices.

*Calories 86, Protein 1 g, Sodium 35 mg, Potassium 141 mg, Phosphorus 55 mg, Calcium 26 mg*

# Cinnamon Sugar Popcorn

*Time: 25 Mins, Serves: 4, Skill: Easy*

**Ingredients**
- Butter (2 tbsp), unsalted, melted
- Popcorn kernels (1/4 cup)
- Granulated sugar (3 tbsp)
- Cinnamon (1 1/2 tsp), ground

**Instructions**
- Preheat a 4-quart nonstick pot over medium heat with a tight-fitting lid. Add the popcorn kernels when the pot is warm.

- Cover and shake the pot for a few seconds with the lid. In 1-2 minutes, the kernels should start bursting. Continue to softly shake the pot every 2 seconds until the interval between kernel pops is at least 3 seconds.
- Stay out of the heat as far as possible. Allow the popcorn to cool completely in a large mixing bowl.
- Mix the sugar and cinnamon in a shallow dish.
- Drizzle the butter over the popcorn and turn it to evenly cover it.
- Drizzle the cinnamon-sugar mixture over the kernels and cover evenly.

*Calories 60.6, Protein 1.6 g, Sodium 148.4 mg, Potassium 17 mg, Phosphorus 0.2 mg, Calcium 4.2 mg*

# Sriracha Popcorn
*Time: 40 Mins, Serves: 8, Skill: Easy*

## Ingredients
- Butter (2 tbsp), unsalted, melted
- Sriracha sauce (4 tsp)
- Popcorn kernels (1/4 cup)

## Instructions
- Over medium heat, warm a 4-quart nonstick container with a tight-fitting lid. Add the popcorn kernels until the pot is warmed.
- Cover and shake the pot for a few seconds with the lid. In 1-2 minutes, the kernels should start bursting. Continue to softly shake the pot every 2 seconds until the interval between kernel pops is at least 3 seconds.
- Place the popcorn in a mixing bowl and put it aside to cool.
- Combine the butter and Sriracha in a tiny bowl.
- Toss the popcorn with Sriracha butter to cover it.

*Calories 190, Protein 4 g, Sodium 420 mg, Potassium 39 mg, Phosphorus 37 mg, Calcium 40 mg*

# Cream Cheese and Tomatillo Spread
*Time: 2 Hours, Serves: 6, Skill: Hard*

## Ingredients
- Olive oil (1 tbsp)
- Packed cilantro (1/2 cup)
- Fresh lime juice (2 tbsp)
- Sugar 1 tbsp
- Cream cheese (8 oz. package), low-fat
- Tomatillos (1 lb.)
- Anaheim chili pepper
- Pepper (1), jalapeño
- Onions (1 cup), cut in chunks
- Garlic clove (1), peeled

## Instructions
- To make the salsa, coat the tomatillos in warm water in a medium bowl. Allow 20 minutes for preparation. This isn't necessary, but it makes husking the husks easier.
- Preheat the oven to 400 °F.
- Remove the tomatillos' husks and wash out the oily resin from the skins. Arrange the husks on the baking dish.
- Toss the tomatillos, Anaheim peppers, jalapeno, onion, and garlic with olive oil. This mixture can be spread out on a rimmed baking sheet lined with foil or parchment paper.
- Roast in the oven for 18-20 minutes, turning halfway through, until soft and slightly crispy.
- Remove it from the oven and set it aside for a few minutes to cool. Remove the peppers' stem, seeds, and outer skin.
- Place the herbs in a food processor along with their juices. In a bowl, add cilantro, sugar, and lime juice. Pulse until the mixture is almost smooth and there are no large bits of tomatillos left, scraping down the sides of the bowl when required. The salsa can be a little thin at first, but if it remains in the refrigerator for a few hours, it will thicken.
- Place the cream cheese on a plate to create a spread. Enable 30 minutes for it to soften at room temperature.
- Place 1 cup of tomatillo salsa on top of the cream cheese. Refrigerate the leftover salsa in an airtight bag for up to a week.

*Calories 170, Protein 4 g, Sodium 128 mg, Potassium 315 mg, Phosphorus 73 mg, Calcium 53 mg*

# American Favorite Blend
*Time: 20 Mins, Serves: 30, Skill: Medium*

## Ingredients
- Garlic powder (1 tbsp)
- White pepper (1/2 tsp)
- Paprika (1 tbsp)
- Celery seeds (1/2 tsp)
- Dry mustard (1 tbsp)
- Onion powder (5 tsp)
- Salt (1/2 tsp)

- Thyme (1 tsp)

**Instructions**
- Combine all ingredients in a sealable container and shake vigorously.

*Calories 330, Protein 3 g, Sodium 650 mg, Potassium 70 mg, Phosphorus 23 mg, Calcium 7.7 mg*

## Low Sodium Deviled Eggs
*Time: 45 Mins, Serves: 8, Skill: Easy*

**Ingredients**
- Cider vinegar (1 tsp)
- White sugar (1 tsp)
- Yellow mustard (1 tsp)
- Onion powder (1/2 tsp)
- Eggs (6), hard-boiled
- Mayonnaise (2 tbsp)

**Instructions**
- Halve the eggs and set aside the whites and yolks separately.
- In a shallow bowl, mash the yolks with a fork. Add the mayonnaise, vinegar, onion powder, and mustard. Blend until fully smooth.
- Place the mixture in a piping bag and pipe it into the egg white halves.
- If necessary, garnish with paprika. Refrigerate before serving.

*Calories 197.3, Protein 9.6 g, Sodium 201.1 mg, Potassium 101.6 mg, Phosphorus 13.2 mg, Calcium 4.1 mg*

## Strawberry Shortcake Chia Seed Pudding
*Time: 35 Mins, Serves: 4, Skill: Easy*

**Ingredients**
- Maple syrup (2 tbsp)
- Vanilla extract (1 tsp)
- Strawberries (1 cup)
- Cookies (4), crumbled, shortbread
- Almond milk (2 cups), unsweetened
- Chia seeds (1/2 cup)

**Instructions**
- In a mixing cup, add the almond milk, maple syrup, chia seeds, and vanilla. Whisk the ingredients together to combine them.
- Refrigerate overnight, sealed (or at least 4 hours). Since chia seeds maintain moisture, the chia pudding is supposed to be moist when eaten. If necessary, add more of the chia seeds, mix it, and chill again.
- Add crumbled shortbread cookies and sliced strawberries on top.

*Calories 228, Protein 11.9 g, Sodium 34.8 mg, Potassium 501.3 mg, Phosphorus 17.6 mg, Calcium 6.7 mg*

## Sweet Spice Cottage Cheese
*Time: 25 Mins, Serves: 4, Skill: Easy*

**Ingredients**
- Cottage cheese (4 oz.), no-salt-added, 1%
- Cinnamon (1/2 tsp)
- Honey (2 tsp)
- Apple (1/2 small), chopped

**Instructions**
- Add the cottage cheese, apple, and cinnamon to a mixing dish. To create a full mix, add all the ingredients to a blender.
- Serve with honey drizzled on top.

*Calories 163, Protein 28 g, Sodium 30 mg, Potassium 37 mg, Phosphorus 24 mg, Calcium 11 mg*

## Fruit Salsa
*Time: 35 Mins, Serves: 4, Skill: Easy*

**Ingredients**
- Red onion (1/4 cup), diced
- Jalapeño (1), finely diced
- Mint leaves (2 tbsp), chopped
- Orange juice (2 tbsp)
- Lime juice (1 tbsp)
- Pineapple (3/4 cup), diced
- Mango (3/4 cup), diced
- Strawberries (1/2 cup), diced

**Instructions**
- Add all the ingredients to a medium ceramic or glass dish and stir to combine.
- Cover the Salsa in plastic wrap and put it aside to marinate for 20-30 minutes before serving.

*Calories 39.3, Protein 0 g, Sodium 0 mg, Potassium 2.7 mg, Phosphorus 0 mg, Calcium 1 mg*

## Energy Bites
*Time: 45 Mins, Serves: 10, Skill: Easy*

**Ingredients**
- Peanut butter (1/2 cup), creamy
- Honey (1/2 cup)
- Oats (1 1/2 cups), regular or quick

- Peanuts (1/2 cup), crushed, unsalted
- Flax seeds (3/8 cup), ground
- Mini chocolate chips (3/8 cup)
- Vanilla extract (1 1/2 tsp)

**Instructions**
- Add all the ingredients to a large mixing bowl and fold them together until well mixed.
- Cover a 9x13 board of parchment paper, make sure it stretches up and down the sides for quick removal.
- Rub your hand with coconut oil and press the paste into the pan. Until cooling and cutting, roll the bars in nuts and seeds.
- Allow 1 hour in the refrigerator before serving. Remove the parchment from the pot and cut it into squares.
- Keep refrigerated to maintain shape. It will keep for about 5-7 days.

*Calories 109.6, Protein 2.5 g, Sodium 45.5 mg, Potassium 64.2 mg, Phosphorus 5.4 mg, Calcium 1.1 mg*

## Swiss Chard Crostini
*Time: 35 Mins, Serves: 10, Skill: Easy*

**Ingredients**
- Olive oil (2 tbsp)
- Garlic cloves (3)
- Water (3 tbsp)
- Baguette (1/2), sliced into 10, ½-inch slices
- Swiss chard (1/2 bunch/6 oz.)
- Ricotta cheese (1/2 cup)

**Instructions**
- Toast the baguette slices until finely browned in a toaster oven or a standard oven at 300°F.
- Extract the Swiss chard's roots. To build a leaf mound, arrange the leaves in four layers. Roll horizontally and slice into the rolls to create leaf ribbons.
- Continue until all the leaves are trimmed.
- Melt the olive oil in a large skillet over medium heat. For 2 minutes, stirring halfway through, roast the Swiss chard and garlic. Reduce to a low heat and place in boiling water. Cook until the chard is soft but still has a light green color.
- Position the toasted baguette slices on a serving tray to assemble. Spread a thin layer of ricotta on each piece. Place the cooked chard on top of the ricotta toast with tongs. Serve as a snack or an appetizer.

*Calories 14, Protein 0.6 g, Sodium 76.7 mg, Potassium 136 mg, Phosphorus 3.9 mg, Calcium 18.4 mg*

## Cinnamon Scented Applesauce
*Time: 35 Mins, Serves: 10, Skill: Easy*

**Ingredients**
- Lemon juice (2 tbsp)
- Sugar (1/4 cup)
- Granny Smith apples (1 lb.)
- Fuji apples (1 lb.)
- Nutmeg (1/4 tsp)
- Water (3/4 cup)
- Cinnamon (1/2 tsp)

**Instructions**
- Peel, core, and dice the apples.
- In a big pot, mix all the ingredients and bring to a boil over high heat.
- Lower the heat to medium-high and cook for 20-30 minutes, or until the water has evaporated and the apples have begun to stick to the plate's rim.
- Remove the pan from the heat and gently ground the apples with a fork, potato masher, or food processor to the perfect consistency.
- Set it aside to cool before serving it.

*Calories 129, Protein 1 g, Sodium 1 mg, Potassium 175 mg, Phosphorus 21 mg, Calcium 13 mg*

## Muhammara Dip
*Time: 35 Mins, Serves: 2, Skill: Easy*

**Ingredients**
- Breadcrumbs (1/2 cup), finely ground
- Lemon juice (1 tbsp), freshly squeezed
- Walnuts (1/3 cup), chopped,
- Garlic cloves (2 to 4), minced
- Jar roasted red peppers (7 oz.), drained
- Hot red pepper flakes (1/2 tsp), dried
- Olive oil (3 oz.)
- Pita bread (7)
- Sea salt (1/4 tbsp), optional
- Pomegranate molasses (2 tbsp)
- Cumin (1 tbsp), ground

**Instructions**
- In a small dry skillet over medium heat, toast the walnuts until finely colored. Stir them continually to save them from burning.

- Mince the garlic and mash it into a paste with 1/4 teaspoon of salt if required.
- In a food processor or mixer, combine the remaining ingredients and additional salt to taste. The mixture should be silky smooth.
- Slowly pour in the oil. Making sure you use enough to create a sloppy dip (depending on the amount of liquid in your roasted peppers, you can need oil).
- Serve.

*Calories 110, Protein 2 g, Sodium 130 mg, Potassium 0 mg, Phosphorus 6 mg, Calcium 2 mg*

## Cinnamon Spiced Cornbread
*Time: 45 Mins, Serves: 10, Skill: Easy*

**Ingredients**
- Ginger (1 tbsp), finely grated
- Cinnamon (1 tsp), grounded
- Sugar (3 tbsp)
- Eggs (5)
- Pumpkin puree (2 cans/15 oz.)
- Yogurt (15 oz.)
- Butter (3 tbsp), melted
- Anise (1/2 tsp), grounded
- Allspice (1/2 tsp), grounded
- Cornmeal (2 cups), coarsely grounded
- Baking soda (1 tsp)

**Instructions**
- Preheat the oven to 425 °F.
- Using olive or coconut oil to coat a 13-inch oven-safe cast-iron skillet.
- In a cup, combine the ginger and all the dry ingredients.
- In a mixing cup, whisk together the eggs, pumpkin, milk, and melted butter. To create a full mix, add all the ingredients to a blender. Season with salt if necessary.
- Bake for 35 minutes, or until set.
- Serve slightly wet, split into 10 equal wedges.

*Calories 208.5, Protein 38 g, Sodium 3052 mg, Potassium 1575 mg, Phosphorus 826.2 mg, Calcium 564 mg*

## Tangy Coleslaw
*Time: 40 Mins, Serves: 8, Skill: Easy*

**Ingredients**
**Slaw:**
- Fennel bulb (1 small/234g), shredded
- Red cabbage (1/4 small head/142g), thinly sliced
- Red pepper (1 small/74g), thinly sliced
- Parsley (1 cup), chopped
- Dill (1 cup), chopped
- Pecans (3/4 cup), chopped and toasted
- Carrot, julienned (1 medium/61g each)

**Dressing:**
- Lemon juice (1/3 cup)
- Buttermilk (1/3 cup)
- Dijon mustard (1 tbsp)
- Apple cider vinegar (1 tsp)
- Jalapeño (14g), diced and seeded
- Sugar (2 tsp)

**Instructions**
- Preheat the oven to 350 °F and cover a shallow baking tray with parchment paper.
- Place the pecans on a baking sheet and roast for 15 minutes, rotating halfway through.
- Place the pecans in a small bowl and set them aside until ready to use. In a wide serving dish, mix the carrots, red cabbage, fennel, and red pepper.
- Mix in the sliced herbs thoroughly.
- In a shallow mixing cup, whisk together all the ingredients except the sugar to make the dressing.
- Apply the sugar with a fork and mix well.
- Drizzle on the slaw dressing. Serve each piece in a separate bowl of toasted pecans on top.

*Calories 115.9, Protein 1.8 g, Sodium 461.3 mg, Potassium 310.7 mg, Phosphorus 3.8 mg, Calcium 5.4 mg*

## Spiced Pepitas
*Time: 40 Mins, Serves: 8, Skill: Easy*

**Ingredients**
- Brown sugar (1 tbsp)
- Cumin seed (1 tsp), grounded
- Butter (1 1/2 tbsp), unsalted
- Pepitas (1 1/2 cups)

**Instructions**
- In a skillet over low heat, melt the butter, then stir in the sugar and cumin until well combined.
- To fairly spread the pepitas, apply them and combine for 1 to 2 minutes.
- Remove the pan from the heat and set it aside to cool.
- Any serving may be enjoyed alone, or with a slice of fruit or cheese as a snack.

*Calories 126, Protein 5.3 g, Sodium 5 mg, Potassium 31 mg, Phosphorus 0 mg, Calcium 0 mg*

## Watermelon Ice Cream
*Time: 3 hours and 30 Mins, Serves: 4, Skill: Hard*

**Ingredients**
- Vanilla extract (1/4 tsp)
- Sea salt (a pinch)
- Honey (1 tbsp)
- Watermelon (3 cups), cubed
- Coconut milk (2/3 cup)

**Instructions**
- In a mixer, combine all ingredients and transfer to a shallow baking dish.
- Thaw the watermelon for 3 hours.
- Once the watermelon has thawed, put it in the blender with the rest of the ingredients.
- Combine all until it's sleek and creamy.
- Move the mixture to a jar and freeze for around 25 minutes, or until it achieves the perfect consistency.
- Function as ice cream with the toppings if necessary.

*Calories 90, Protein 2 g, Sodium 25 mg, Potassium 80 mg, Phosphorus 6 mg, Calcium 8 mg*

## Date Indulgence
*Time: 45 Mins, Serves: 2, Skill: Easy*

**Ingredients**
- Medjool dates (2 large/48g each)
- Dark chocolate (1/2 oz.), divided
- Sunflower seed butter (1 tbsp/16g)

**Instructions**
- Remove the pits from the dates and halve.
- On each date, sprinkle 1/2 tbsp sunflower seed butter.
- Cut a 1/4-inch-thick dark chocolate slice and place it on top of the butter in the center of the date.
- Arrange the stuffed dates on a tray to serve.
- Half-submerge the remaining chocolate in a bigger saucepan of hot water.
- Remove the chocolate from the saucepan once it has fully melted.
- Pour molten chocolate over each date as well as the tray.
- Serve immediately.

*Calories 118, Protein 1.03 g, Sodium 1 mg, Potassium 276 mg, Phosphorus 31 mg, Calcium 6 mg*

## Easy Blueberry – Lemon Parfait
*Time: 25 Mins, Serves: 8, Skill: Easy*

**Ingredients**
- Blueberries (2 cups), fresh
- Lemon yogurt (2 x 8 oz. Cartons)
- Gingersnaps (10), crumbled

**Instructions**
- Dive the gingersnaps, blueberries and lemon yogurt into four cups.
- Repeat step 1 in the same tub to create two layers of each product.

*Calories 319, Protein 7 g, Sodium 221 mg, Potassium 437 mg, Phosphorus 167 mg, Calcium 227 mg*

## Gingerbread Christmas log
*Time: 50 Mins, Serves: 12, Skill: Easy*

**Ingredients**
**Christmas log**
- Balls stem ginger (2)
- Golden syrup (50g)
- Butter (50g), unsalted
- Eggs (4 large)
- Treacle (50g)
- Muscovado dark sugar (100g)
- Baking powder (1/2 tsp)
- Stem ginger syrup (2 tbsp)
- Ginger (2 tsp), ground
- Additional butter for greasing
- Plain flour (100g)

**Icing**
- Butter (200g), unsalted and softened
- Icing sugar (250g)
- Vanilla extract (2 tsp)
- Stem ginger syrup (3 tbsp)

**Instructions**
- Preheat the oven to 375 °F. Using the baking paper, spray and cover a 20x30cm Swiss roll plate. The parchment could then be lightly oiled. In a cup, heat the vanilla extract, sugar, butter, and grated stem ginger until melted, then whisk to blend. Enable to cool before serving.
- Whisk the eggs and sugar in a mixing cup for 10 minutes, or until moist, doubled in size, and mousse-like. The mixture is prepared if the ribbon

trace from the beaters is held for 3 seconds. Rain the molten butter mixture across the bowl's sides, causing it to run through the whisked eggs. Sift the flour, seasoning, and baking powder into a mixing cup.

- Fold all together with caution. Put the mixture into a Swiss roll tin and smooth out the corners until it's blended. Bake for 12 minutes, or until just finished. Prepare a baking parchment lay sheet that is big enough to complement the cake on the work surface and is finely dusted with sugar when the sponge is frying.
- Take the cake out of the oven and put it on parchment paper right away. With a serrated knife, score a line around 2 cm from one shorter end. From here, roll up the parchment layers. Allow it to cool for a few minutes on the wire rack to help it keep its shape.
- To produce the icing, whisk together the first two ingredients in a mixing bowl until smooth. Using a piping bag fitted with a large circular nozzle, unroll the sponge and drizzle the surface with ginger syrup (2 tbsp). Apply the ginger buttercream coating to the inside of the roll, then tightly re-roll it to the roulade with paper underneath. Both ends are cut off for a tidy finish.
- Place the log on a plate or shelf to serve. Pipe a thick layer on top of the sponge with the remaining icing, zigzagging back and forth to create a pattern.

*Calories 52, Protein 1.4 g, Sodium 38.5 mg, Potassium 13 mg, Phosphorus 3.2 mg, Calcium 0.6 mg*

## Traditional mince pies

*Time: 1 hour and 20 Mins, Serves: 12, Skill: Medium*

### Ingredients
**Mincemeat**
- Mixed spice (1 tsp)
- Mixed fruit peel (100g)
- Brandy/rum (1 tbsp)
- Bramley apple (1 large)
- Margarine (25g), low fat
- Glace cherries (50g)
- Dark brown sugar soft (50g)

**Pastry**
- Plain flour (225g)
- Butter (150g)
- Caster sugar (2 tbsp)
- Egg (1)
- Cold water (3 tbsp)

### Instructions
- Sift the flour into a mixing bowl and use your fingers to roll in the butter so the mixture resembles coarse breadcrumbs. Add the sugar. The egg yolk is mixed with water and then added to the dry ingredients to create a smooth dough.
- Refrigerate the dough for 30 minutes after wrapping it in cling film. Meanwhile, finely slice the cherries and grind the apple. In a mixing cup, combine all of the mincemeat goods. It must be thoroughly mixed.
- Half of the puff pastry can be rolled out on the table (3mm thick). With a fluted knife, cut out 12 7.5 to 9cm circles of pastry, and gently press into an oiled patty tin. The remaining pastry is then used to remove 12 smaller circles using the 6cm cutter.
- Place a teaspoon of mincemeat in each round, brush the sides with water, and place the lids on top, gently pressing together to seal.
- Clean the tops with the egg white and make a little hole in the roof to let the air out.
- Finally, bake it at 374 °F for around 20 minutes. Before switching to the wire rack, allow 5 minutes in the tin.

*Calories 188, Protein 1.2 g, Sodium 0 mg, Potassium 16 mg, Phosphorus 0.6 mg, Calcium 0 mg*

## Easy baked pears

*Time: 45 Mins, Serves: 4, Skill: Easy*

### Ingredients
- Cinnamon (1/2 tsp), ground
- Clear honey (4 tbsp)
- Ginger biscuits (8)
- Ripe pears (4)
- Crème Fraiche (4 level tbsp), reduced-fat

### Instructions
- To start, preheat the oven to 374 °F.
- Split each pear in 1/2. Using a teaspoon, scrape out the cores. In the center of each make a dip. Place them, sliced side up, on the baking sheet.
- Drizzle honey over the top and season with cinnamon.
- Roast the pears for 10 to 15 mins, or until tender. Crush some biscuits of ginger and sprinkle them

on top, and serve along with a cream fraiche (spoonful).
*Calories 114.9, Protein 0.7 g, Sodium 21.7 mg, Potassium 216 mg, Phosphorus 1.9 mg, Calcium 3.9 mg*

## Eton mess
*Time: 40 Mins, Serves: 6, Skill: Easy*

**Ingredients**
- Vanilla extract (1 tsp)
- Raspberries (150g), fresh
- Blueberries (150g), fresh
- Meringue nests (4 individual)
- Double cream (400ml)

**Raspberry coulis**
- Raspberries (200g), frozen
- Caster sugar (30g)
- Lemon juice (1 tbsp)

**Instructions**
- In a saucepan, combine all the ingredients and cook for 5-7 minutes to make the coulis. In a food processor, puree until creamy, then press through a sieve to remove the pips. Set it aside before you're ready to serve.
- Remove the meringues from the oven and set them aside in tiny sections. Lightly whip the cream before soft peaks emerge. Gently fold in the blueberries, raspberries, and meringue pieces.
- Add the vanilla extract and, if using, the ginger cordial. Then whisk in some of the raspberry coulis. You should see a ripple effect of raspberry running through it.
- Drizzle the raspberry coulis on top. For a final flourish, crumble the ginger biscuits on top.

*Calories 165, Protein 7 g, Sodium 0 mg, Potassium 0 mg, Phosphorus 0.6 mg, Calcium 0 mg*

## Crème brûlée
*Time: 3 hours, Serves: 6, Skill: Hard*

**Ingredients**
- Egg yolks (5)
- Double cream (500ml)
- Vanilla pods (2)
- Milk (100ml), full-fat
- Caster sugar (75g)

**Instructions**
- Preheat the oven to 140 °F. Scrape the seeds out of the vanilla pod by splitting them in two. Bring the milk, cream, vanilla pods, and seeds to a boil in a saucepan.
- The egg yolks and 75g of sugar can now be whisked in until the mixture is dense and pale in color. Pour the hot cream into the mixture slowly.
- Stir well, then reduce to low heat for a few minutes. Before pouring the mixture into six ramekins, strain it to remove the vanilla pods.
- Fill the ramekins with hot water until the water hits 2/3 of the way up the sides of the ramekins in a roasting pan.
- Bake for 30 to 40 minutes, or until solid and wobble-free. Allow to cool completely before storing in the refrigerator for 2 hours, or overnight.
- Remove it from the fridge and spread the remaining 50g of caster sugar over the top in a small, even sheet. To caramelize the end, position it under a really hot grill or use a blow torch. You should have a golden crackling topping. Place it in the refrigerator for 3-4 minutes before serving.

*Calories 274, Protein 7 g, Sodium 15.2 mg, Potassium 72 mg, Phosphorus 4 mg, Calcium 183.8 mg*

## Lemonade scones
*Time: 55 Mins, Serves: 12, Skill: Medium*

**Ingredients**

**For the Scones**
- Flour self-raising (450g)
- Double cream (250ml)
- Lemonade (250ml)

**Instructions**
- To start, preheat the oven to 400 °F. In a mixing bowl, combine all the ingredients to make the dough.
- Before switching to the floured surface, knead for a few seconds. Using your fingers, press the dough down to a depth of 3cm. Cut 12 scones with a standard circular cutter and place on a lined baking or greased tray.
- Bake for 10-12 minutes, or until golden brown and risen.
- To eat, spread 1 tablespoon of jam (your choice) and 2 tablespoons of clotted cream on each scone.

*Calories 109.8, Protein 2.8 g, Sodium 6.3 mg, Potassium 45.1 mg, Phosphorus 3.8 mg, Calcium 1.8 mg*

## Chicken and Lime Salad Sandwich
*Time: 45 Mins, Serves: 6, Skill: Easy*

**Ingredients**
- Green pepper (1/2 cup), chopped
- Celery (1/2 cup), diced
- Onion (1/4 cup), sliced
- Mayonnaise (1/3 cup)
- Chicken (1 cup), chopped, cooked
- Mandarin lime (1 cup)

**Instructions**
- Combine the chicken, onion, and green pepper in a mixing bowl.
- Toss the mandarin into the chicken mixture, then add the mayonnaise and mix it together carefully.
- Serve the chicken mixture on top of fried bread.

*Calories 279, Protein 20.3 g, Sodium 75.6 mg, Potassium 1198 mg, Phosphorus 24.8 mg, Calcium 3.6 mg*

## Sunshine Carrots
*Time: 20 Mins, Serves: 4, Skill: Easy*

**Ingredients**
- Carrots (3 cups), sliced
- Parsley (1 tsp), chopped, fresh, for garnish
- Sugar (1 tbsp)
- Lemon juice (1 tbsp)
- Lemon peel (1/4 tsp), grated
- Margarine (2 tbsp)

**Instructions**
- Cook the carrots until soft in boiling water; rinse well.
- In a mixing cup, combine the butter, sugar, lemon juice, margarine, and lemon peel.

*Calories 70, Protein 1 g, Sodium 329.8 mg, Potassium 26 mg, Phosphorus 67 mg, Calcium 20.4 mg*

## Overnight oats
*Time: 40 Mins, Serves: 2, Skill: Easy*

**Ingredients**
- Rolled Oats (5 cups)
- Almond Milk (1 1/2 cups)
- Cinnamon (1/2 tsp)
- Coconut milk (1 cup)
- Chia Seeds (2 tbsp)

**Instructions**
- Combine all the ingredients in a skillet and mix well.
- To improve the flavor, keep the jar refrigerated overnight.
- Serve by pouring the mixture into serving dishes and filling it with preferred toppings.

*Calories 188.1, Protein 10.4 g, Sodium 87.4 mg, Potassium 416.4 mg, Phosphorus 38.1 mg, Calcium 27.1 mg*

## Roasted grape crostini with ricotta and balsamic reduction
*Time: 45 Mins, Serves: 4, Skill: Easy*

**Ingredients**
- Bread (12 slices)
- Balsamic vinegar (1/3 cups)
- Brown sugar (1 tsp)
- Seedless grapes (1/2 lb.)
- Olive oil (3 tbsp)
- Thyme (1 tsp)
- Mascarpone cheese (96 oz.)
- Black pepper (1/2 tsp)

**Instructions**
- In a mixing cup, combine the thyme, grapes, 2 tablespoons of olive oil, and black pepper.
- In a preheated oven, roast the grape mixture for 15 minutes at 400 °F with occasional stirring.
- Toast the bread for 8 minutes after spraying it with olive oil.
- In a shallow saucepan, heat balsamic vinegar over medium heat until it thickens.
- Combine black pepper and sugar in a vinegar solution.
- On toasted bread, spread half a tablespoon of ricotta cheese, then finish with grapes and a balsamic layer.
- Serve with a rosemary garnish.

*Calories 96, Protein 6 g, Sodium 144 mg, Potassium 31 mg, Phosphorus 13 mg, Calcium 2 mg*

## Sour candy grapes
*Time: 3 hours and 25 Mins, Serves: 3, Skill: Easy*

**Ingredients**
- Green grapes (4 cups)
- Sweetener (3/4 cup)
- Lime juice (3 tbsp)

**Instructions**
- Combine the grapes and lime juice in a mixing cup. Allow 10 minutes for it to rest.

- Combine sweetener and grapes in a mixing bowl; fold each grape in the sweetener to coat fully, then put on foil paper.
- Freeze the foil paper with the grapes for 3 hours.

*Calories 110, Protein 1 g, Sodium 9 mg, Potassium 0 mg, Phosphorus 16 mg, Calcium 0 mg*

## Raspberry pear sorbet
*Time: 4 hours and 15 Mins, Serves: 6, Skill: Hard*

### Ingredients
- Pear sliced (2)
- Lime juice (1/3 cup)
- Pear liqueur (1 tbsp)
- Raspberries (1 pint), fresh
- Sugar (1/2 cup)
- Raspberries (1 pint)

### Instructions
- Make the syrup by bringing water and sugar to a boil in a saucepan.
- Bring the sugary solution to a boil before the sugar has dissolved in the broth.
- Put in the refrigerator to cool.
- In a food processor, combine the raspberries, liqueur, lime juice, and pear.
- Apply the sugar to the raspberries and mix for a couple of seconds more.
- Put the mixture in a freezer-safe jar and freeze for 4 hours.
- Split up the solid mixture and combine it in a food processor after 4 hours.
- Freeze the smooth mixed mixture for another 8 hours before serving.

*Calories 181.35, Protein 5.5 g, Sodium 4.31 mg, Potassium 251.97 mg, Phosphorus 9.6 mg, Calcium 21.1 mg*

## Cherry brown butter bars
*Time: 1 hour 15 Mins, Serves: 16, Skill: Hard*

### Ingredients
Crust
- Butter (3/4 cup)
- Sugar (2/3 cup)
- Salt (1/8 tsp)
- Sugar (2/3 cup)
- Vanilla extract (1/2 tsp)
- Flour (2 cups + 2 tbsp)
- Salt (1/8 tsp)
- Creamy Top and Cherry Filling
- Butter (1 cup)
- Eggs (3)
- Flour (1/2 cup)
- Vanilla extract (1 tsp)
- Almond extract (1 tsp)
- Flour tossed cherries (4 cups)

### Instructions
- In a mixing dish, blend the sugar, butter, and vanilla extract, then include the salt and flour.
- Put the dough in a baking tray lined with parchment paper and push it down.
- Melt butter in a skillet over medium heat for 6 minutes, or before it becomes orange. Remove from the heat.
- Combine the flour, sugar, eggs, salt, and vanilla extract in a mixing cup.
- After the flour mixture has been blended into a thick batter, apply the butter gently and thoroughly.
- Arrange a layer of cherries on top of the dough, then a layer of filling.
- Bake for 30 minutes at 375 °F in a preheated oven.
- Leave it to cool then break into pieces and store in the refrigerator.

*Calories 190, Protein 1 g, Sodium 20 mg, Potassium 75 mg, Phosphorus 11 mg, Calcium 2 mg*

## Grilled blackened tilapia
*Time: 40 Mins, Serves: 4, Skill: Easy*

### Ingredients
- Oregano (1 tsp), dried
- Olive oil (2 tbsp)
- Garlic powder (1 tsp)
- Cumin (3/4 tsp)
- Tilapia filets (4)
- Smoked paprika (2 tsp)
- Cayenne pepper (1/2 tsp)

### Instructions
- In a mixing dish, combine the seasonings and coat the tilapia.
- Cook the fish for 3 minutes on either side on a preheated grill.
- Garnish with cilantro and serve.

*Calories 159.8, Protein 20.6 g, Sodium 631.3 mg, Potassium 28.1 mg, Phosphorus 0.8 mg, Calcium 1.5 mg*

## Honey garlic kebab marinade
*Time: 1 hour and 20 Mins, Serves: 16, Skill: Easy*

**Ingredients**
- Black pepper (1/4 tsp)
- Honey (1/3 cup)
- Bragg's Liquid Aminos (1/4 cup)
- Garlic cloves (3), chopped
- Olive oil (1/4 cup)

**Instructions**
- Combine all the ingredients in a plastic bag and blend well.
- Marinate kebabs of your choice overnight in the marinade.
- Serve kebabs fried in olive oil over medium heat.

*Calories 281.3, Protein 34.9 g, Sodium 635.6 mg, Potassium 157 mg, Phosphorus 3.5 mg, Calcium 1.6 mg*

## Southern-fried okra
*Time: 45 Mins, Serves: 6, Skill: Easy*

**Ingredients**
- Salt (1/8 tsp)
- Sunflower oil (1/3 cup)
- Yellow cornmeal (1/2 cup)
- Cayenne pepper (1/4 tbsp)
- Black pepper (1/4 tbsp)
- Milk (2 tbsp)
- Egg (1)
- Flour (1/2 cup)
- Okra (3 cups), sliced

**Instructions**
- Combine the black pepper, flour, salt, cayenne pepper, and cornmeal in a mixing dish.
- In a separate dish, mix the milk and egg.
- Drop the okra parts into the egg mixture, then roll them in the flour mixture before putting them aside.
- In a pan, heat sunflower oil and fry coated okra bits for 2 minutes.
- Or, bake the fried bits for 3 minutes at 300°F in a preheated oven.

*Calories 98.5, Protein 5.3 g, Sodium 150.3 mg, Potassium 29 mg, Phosphorus 0.6 mg, Calcium 6.2 mg*

## Champ – Side Dish Irish Potato
*Time: 35 Mins, Serves: 2, Skill: Easy*

**Ingredients**
- Potatoes (600 g)
- Black pepper, ground
- Onions (2), chopped
- Milk (1-2 tbsp)

**Instructions**
- In a big saucepan of water, boil the potatoes until soft.
- Mash the potatoes once you have added the black pepper, milk, and spring onions.

*Calories 318.52, Protein 6.55 g, Sodium 443.15 mg, Potassium 868.76 mg, Phosphorus 7.1 mg, Calcium 148.2 mg*

# DESSERT RECIPES

## Strawberry Sorbet
*Time: 5 Mins, Serves: 2, Skill: Easy*

**Ingredients**
- Water (1/4 cup)
- Ice (1 1/4 tbsp), crushed/cubed
- Sugar (1/4 cup)
- Lemon juice (1 tbsp)
- Strawberries (1 cup), frozen or fresh

**Instructions**
- Fill a blender halfway with ice.
- Raise the pace of the blender to smash and liquefy the remaining ingredients.

*Calories 67, Protein 0 g, Sodium 01 mg, Potassium 79 mg, Phosphorus 12 mg, Calcium 09 mg*

## Triple Berry Protein Parfait
*Time: 15 Mins, Serves: 4, Skill: Easy*

**Ingredients**
- Honey (1 tsp)
- Whipped topping (1-1/2 cups)
- Whey protein powder (2 tbsp)
- Blueberries (1/2 cup)
- Strawberries (1/2 cup)
- Blackberries (1/4 cup)

**Instructions**
- Using a sharp knife, quarter the strawberries. Blend the berries together and, to taste, drizzle with a sweetener of your choice, such as honey.
- Set aside for 10 minutes.
- In a mixing bowl, combine whipped topping and protein powder gently.
- Layer the berries and whipped topping in a bowl or parfait glass in contrasting layers.

*Calories 188, Protein 6 g, Sodium 42 mg, Potassium 194 mg, Phosphorus 68 mg, Calcium 29 mg*

## Sweet Cherry Cobbler
*Time: 1 hour 10 Mins, Serves: 12, Skill: Easy*

**Ingredients**

**Cherry Filling**
- Cornstarch (2 tbsp)
- Salt (1/4 tsp)
- Lemon juice (2 tbsp)
- Sweet Red Cherries (5 cups) about 1.7 pounds, pitted and halved
- Granulated sugar (2/3 cup)
- Almond extract (1/4 tsp)
- Vanilla extract (1 tsp)

**Cobbler Topping**
- Sugar (1/2 cup)
- Baking powder (1 tsp)
- Salt (1/4 tsp)
- Cinnamon (1/4 tsp), ground
- All-purpose flour (1 cup)
- Butter (2 tbsp), unsalted, cold and cubed
- Milk (1/2 cup), non-fat, cold

**Instructions**
- Preheat the oven to 450 °F.

**Compote de Cherries**
- Prepare the cherries. To create a void in the cherries, break them in half and extract the pits, or use a hard straw. Push the straw up from the tip of the cherry from the root. The pit is on the verge of bursting open. Then, in the middle, cut the cherries in half. This technique is a bit messy, but it saves time by chopping the cherries in half.
- Toss the cherries with the sugar, salt, and cornstarch in a saucepan, and include the lemon juice, almond extract, and vanilla extract.
- Cook, stirring occasionally, for 5 to 7 minutes, or until the cherries are soft and the liquids have thickened, then bring to a boil over medium-high heat.
- Pour the cherry filling into an 8-inch baking pan that hasn't been greased.

**Cobblers as a garnish**
- In a medium cup, combine the flour, salt, baking powder, sugar, and cinnamon.
- Cut through the batter with a fork or a pastry cutter until the mixture resembles coarse crumbs.
- Drizzle a tiny volume of milk over the dough to lubricate it.
- Lower the tablespoon of dough on top of the filling using a soup spoon. Allow some breathing space between the dough scoops for the stuffing to rise to the surface.

- Bake for 10–15 minutes, or until well browned on top. Also, scan for crispness using a toothpick.
- Allow it to come to room temperature for 30 minutes before heating it for 10 to 15 minutes at 350°F. Refrigerate for up to a week.

*Calories 143, Protein 4 g, Sodium 81 mg, Potassium 31 mg, Phosphorus 16 mg, Calcium 13 mg*

## Sugarless Pecan and Raisin Cookies
*Time: 55 Mins, Serves: 8, Skill: Medium*

### Ingredients
- Salt (1/2 tsp)
- Oil (1/4 cup)
- Egg (1)
- Pecans (1/2 cup)
- Raisins (1/2 cup)
- Flour (3/4 cup)
- Baking powder (2 tsp)
- Cinnamon (1/2 tsp)
- Canned orange juice (3/4 cup), unsweetened
- Orange rind (1/2 tsp)

### Instructions
- In a big mixing bowl, combine the flour, baking powder, salt, and cinnamon.
- Add and combine the remaining ingredients.
- Drop by the teaspoonful onto a baking sheet that hasn't been greased.
- Preheat oven to 375°F and bake for 15 to 20 minutes.

*Calories 144, Protein 19 g, Sodium 21 mg, Potassium 36 mg, Phosphorus 63 mg, Calcium 15 mg*

## Spicy Raisin Cookies
*Time: 1 hour 20 Mins, Serves: 4, Skill: Medium*

### Ingredients
- Egg (1 large), beaten
- Vanilla extract (1/2 tsp)
- Almond extract (1/4 tsp)
- Cinnamon (1/2 tsp), ground
- Nutmeg (1/2 tsp), ground
- Ginger (1/4 tsp), ground
- Cloves (1/8 tsp), ground
- Salt (1/8 tsp)
- Fruit cocktail (1 cup), in syrup
- All-purpose flour (1-1/2 cups)
- Baking soda (1/2 tsp)
- Margarine or butter (1/2 cup), unsalted
- White sugar (1/2 cup)
- Light brown sugar (1/2 cup)
- Raisins (1/2 cup)

### Instructions
- Preheat the oven to 375 °F. Lightly oil and line the mats with flour.
- In a big mixing dish, combine the margarine and white sugar. The paste is thickened with brown sugar. Add and whisk together the egg, vanilla, and almond extracts until smooth.
- Combine the dry ingredients and distribute them evenly into the smooth mixture. Add the raisins and fruit cocktail.
- Place tablespoons of dough on baking trays in a stack. Bake for 11-12 minutes, or until golden brown. Place them on wire racks to cool for 2-3 minutes.
- Store it in a tightly sealed container.

*Calories 144, Protein 1.9 g, Sodium 92.1 mg, Potassium 73.6 mg, Phosphorus 26 mg, Calcium 14.5 mg*

## Crispy Butterscotch Cookies
*Time: 40 Mins, Serves: 10, Skill: Easy*

### Ingredients
- Sugar (1/2 cup)
- Egg alternative (3 tbsp)
- Milk (1 tbsp)
- Vanilla extract (1 tsp)
- Margarine (1/2 cup)
- Packed brown sugar (1/2 cup)
- Cream of Wheat (1 cup)
- Butterscotch chips (1 cup)
- All-purpose flour (1 cup + 3 tbsp)
- Baking powder (1 tsp)
- Cinnamon (1/2 tsp), ground

### Instructions
- Preheat the oven to 350 °F.
- In a mixing tub, cream together the sugar and butter.
- Add and whisk together the egg, chocolate, and milk. Using a blender, soften the mixture.
- In a mixing cup, combine the flour, cinnamon, and baking powder.
- Pour into the butter mixture and whisk well.

- Add in the butterscotch chips and cereal thoroughly.
- Drop teaspoons one at a time onto the prepared baking dish.
- Bake for 9–12 minutes, or until golden brown.
- Allow to cool on the baking sheet for 1 minute before switching to cooling racks.

*Calories 223, Protein 01 g, Sodium 275 mg, Potassium 21 mg, Phosphorus 96 mg, Calcium 8 mg*

## Gooey, Carmel-Filled Butterscotch Cookies

*Time: 35 Mins, Serves: 4, Skill: Easy*

**Ingredients**
- Egg alternative (3 tbsp)
- Vanilla extract (2 tsp)
- All-purpose flour (1-3/4 cups)
- Margarine (1/2 cup/1 stick), unsalted
- Light brown sugar (1 cup)
- Baking powder (1/2 tsp)
- Granulated sugar (3 tbsp)
- Butterscotch morsels (1-1/2 cups)
- Caramel cubes (1/2 bag)
- Baking soda (1/2 tsp)

**Instructions**
- Preheat the oven to 350 °F.
- Using a hand blender, mix the melted butter and sugar until smooth.
- After including the egg and vanilla extract, beat for another 30 seconds.
- Sift the dry ingredients into a mixing cup and beat in the butter mixture on low speed for around 15 seconds.
- Add the butterscotch chips and mix well.
- Lower the cookie dough, approximately 3 inches apart, onto an oiled sheet pan or a baking sheet creased with the paper of parchment using a 1 teaspoon ice cream scoop.
- In the middle, place one caramel square and cover it with another tablespoon of dough.
- Roll it around in your palm until a smooth disc emerges.
- Bake for 12-20 minutes, or until well browned on the outside.
- Unlike most types of cookies, the cookies will be dense and not spaced apart.

*Calories 243, Protein 02 g, Sodium 275 mg, Potassium 29 mg, Phosphorus 68 mg, Calcium 09 mg*

## Dutch Apple Pancake

*Time: 45 Mins, Serves: 4, Skill: Easy*

**Ingredients**
- Eggs (3)
- All-purpose flour (1/2 cup)
- Milk (1/2 cup)
- Sour cream (1 tbsp)
- Salt (1/4 tsp)
- Butter (2 tbsp), unsalted
- Granny Smith apples (3 large)
- Granulated sugar (6 tbsp)
- Cinnamon (1 tsp), ground
- Lemon zest (1 tsp), grated

**Instructions**
- Melt the butter in an oven-safe tub over medium-high heat.
- Add the apples, sugar, and cinnamon and simmer, stirring regularly, for 3-5 minutes.
- Whisk the eggs in a cup until foamy. In a mixing dish, combine the flour, cinnamon, sour cream, zest, and juice.
- Combine all the ingredients in a mixing bowl so they form a batter-like consistency.
- Pour over apples and bake at 400°F for 25 minutes, or until mildly puffed and orange.
- Slice into wedges and serve straight away.

*Calories 445.9, Protein 10.3 g, Sodium 182.2 mg, Potassium 243.2 mg, Phosphorus 72 mg, Calcium 138.1 mg*

## Butterscotch Apple Crisp

*Time: 1 hour and 20 Mins, Serves: 9, Skill: Medium*

**Ingredients**
- Lemon juice (1 tsp)
- Water (1 tsp)
- Cinnamon (2 tsp), ground
- Light brown sugar (1/4 cup)
- All-purpose flour (1/2 cup)
- Cooking apples (6 cups), peeled, sliced
- Rolled oats (1/2 cup)
- Package butterscotch pudding and pie filling mix (3-1/4 oz.)
- Margarine or butter (1/2 cup), unsalted

**Instructions**
- Preheat the oven to 375 °F. Arrange the apples in a circular 8 or 9-inch tray. Add 1 teaspoon of sugar, 1 teaspoon of lemon juice, and 1 teaspoon of cinnamon.
- In a small container, combine the brown sugar, remaining cinnamon, flour, and the mixture.
- In a saucepan, melt the butter or margarine.
- Blend the pudding mixture until it is crumbly. They can be sprinkled on top of the apples.
- Bake the apples for 40-45 minutes, or until soft.
- Serve at room temperature or chilled. Serve with dairy-free creamer or dairy-free desserts if needed.

*Calories 233, Protein 01 g, Sodium 251 mg, Potassium 29 mg, Phosphorus 58 mg, Calcium 8 mg*

## Low Sodium Pound Cake
*Time: 55 Mins, Serves: 4, Skill: Easy*

**Ingredients**
- Sugar (3/4 cup)
- Eggs (2 large)
- Bread flour (1 1/4 cup)
- Milk (3 oz.)
- Butter (1/4 lb.), unsalted

**Instructions**
- Cream together the butter and sugar until smooth.
- Add and whisk together the eggs, milk, and flour.
- Stir it thoroughly.
- Line a saucepan with pan paper to make it 18×13.
- Preheat oven to 375°F and bake for 30 minutes.

*Calories 2043, Protein 124 g, Sodium 21.2 mg, Potassium 39 mg, Phosphorus 51.6 mg, Calcium 13 mg*

## Harvest Apple Cake with Cinnamon Yogurt Sauce
*Time: 1 hour and 20 Mins, Serves: 12, Skill: Medium*

**Ingredients**
- Cinnamon (1 tsp)
- Salt (1/2 tsp)
- Ginger (1/4 tsp)
- Cloves (1/4 tsp), ground
- Eggs (2)
- Vanilla extract (1 tsp)
- Vegetable oil (1/4 cup)
- Flour (3/4 cup)
- Whole wheat flour (3/4 cup)
- Baking soda (1 tsp)

**Instructions**
- Whisk together 2 large eggs, 1/4 cup of vegetable oil, and 1 teaspoon vanilla extract in a large mixing bowl
- Add the flour and apples.
- Pour into a well-oiled baking pan and bake at 350°F for 40 to 45 minutes.
- Allow to cool on a baking sheet for 10 minutes.
- Sugar is sprinkled on the cake.
- Mix 1 1/2 teaspoon cinnamon into 1 cup low-fat natural yogurt.
- Combine the cake and yogurt in a serving bowl.

*Calories 214.3, Protein 04 g, Sodium 116 mg, Potassium 91 mg, Phosphorus 29 mg, Calcium 3 mg*

## Easy Spicy Angel Cake
*Time: 40 Mins, Serves: 18, Skill: Easy*

**Ingredients**
- Nutmeg (1/2 tsp), ground
- Ginger (1/4 tsp), ground
- Cloves (1/4 tsp), ground
- Angel food cake mix (1 pkg)
- Cinnamon (1 tsp), ground

**Instructions**
- In a bowl, combine all the ingredients.
- Begin cooking and baking as directed on the box.
- Set aside to cool.
- Cut each segment into one-inch pieces.
- Include a whipped topping and strawberry or pineapple to finish.

*Calories 214, Protein 12 g, Sodium 125 mg, Potassium 119 mg, Phosphorus 12 mg, Calcium 31 mg*

## Easy Fruit Dip
*Time: 10 Mins, Serves: 8, Skill: Easy*

**Ingredients**
- Cream cheese (1 package/8 oz.)
- Marshmallow cream (1 jar/7 oz.)
- Dried orange peel (1 tbsp)

**Instructions**
- In a blender, combine all ingredients and mix until smooth.
- Add fresh and healthy fruits like strawberries and grapes to the mix.

*Calories 67, Protein 02 g, Sodium 01 mg, Potassium 69 mg, Phosphorus 20 mg, Calcium 09 mg*

## Chocolate Covered Strawberries
*Time: 25 Mins, Serves: 2, Skill: Easy*

**Ingredients**
- Corn syrup (1 tbsp)
- Margarine (5 tbsp)
- Strawberries (1 qtr.)
- Chocolate chips (1/2 cup), semi-sweet

**Instructions**
- Over a low flame, melt the first three ingredients.
- Blend until fully smooth.
- Switch off the heat and cover the pan with water.
- Put strawberries on waxed paper after dipping them in chocolate.
- Place the food in the fridge to cool before serving.

*Calories 431, Protein 14 g, Sodium 37 mg, Potassium 135 mg, Phosphorus 216 mg, Calcium 11 mg*

## Strawberry Pie
*Time: 35 Mins, Serves: 8, Skill: Easy*

**Ingredients**
- Sugar (1 cup)
- Cornstarch (3 tbsp)
- Lemon juice (2 tbsp)
- Unbaked pie shell (1 single-crust 9-inch)
- Strawberries (4 cups)

**Instructions**
- Preheat the oven to 350°F and bake the pie shell until it is both hot and brown.
- In a mixing dish, combine 2 cups of strawberries, sugar, lemon juice, and cornstarch. In a frying pan, fire the mixture over low heat. Stir the mixture until it becomes thick and transparent.
- Cut the remaining strawberries into small pieces and add them to the cooled mixture. Fill the pie shell halfway with the mixture.
- Cover with plastic wrap and refrigerate until fully chilled. If required, top with whipped cream.

*Calories 265, Protein 1.5 g, Sodium 109.3 mg, Potassium 146.7 mg, Phosphorus 98.1 mg, Calcium 26.2 mg*

## Almond Pecan Caramel Corn
*Time: 1 hour and 25 Mins, Serves: 8, Skill: Hard*

**Ingredients**
- Corn syrup (1/2 cup)
- Cream of tartar (pinch)
- Baking soda (1 tsp)
- Popped popcorn (20 cups)
- Almonds (2 cups), unblanched
- Granulated sugar (1 cup)
- Pecan halves (1 cup)
- Butter (1 cup), unsalted

**Instructions**
- Popcorn is finely sliced and baked in a large roasting pan with almonds and pecans.
- Mix the sugar, corn syrup, butter, and tartar cream in a big, heavy-bottomed frying pan.
- Bring to a low boil, stirring continuously, over medium-high heat. Allow for a five-minute boil without stirring.
- Turn off the heat and stir in the baking soda.
- Pour the caramel over the popcorn and mix it so it is uniformly colored.
- Bake for 1 hour at 200°F, mixing after 10 minutes.
- Cool for up to one week in an airtight tin, shaking occasionally.

*Calories 144, Protein 19 g, Sodium 21 mg, Potassium 36 mg, Phosphorus 63 mg, Calcium 15 mg*

## Apple Filled Crepes
*Time: 30 Mins, Serves: 6, Skill: Easy*

**Ingredients**
- Eggs (2)
- Sugar (1/2 cup)
- Flour (1 cup)
- Oil (1/4 cup)
- Milk (2 cups)
- Egg yolks (4)
- Apples (4 pieces)
- Brown sugar (1/2 cup)
- Cinnamon (1/2 tsp)
- Nutmeg (1/2 tsp)
- Butter (1 stick or 1/2 cup), unsalted

**Instructions**
- Whisk together the egg yolks, entire whites, sugar, flour, butter, and milk in a big mixing bowl until smooth.
- In a tiny nonstick pan, melt the oil over medium heat.
- Coat the bowl with nonstick cooking spray.
- Spoon 1 scoop of batter into the tub with a 2-ounce ladle or 1/4 cup, and roll the pan to evenly scatter the crepe batter on the bottom.

- Cook for 20 seconds, on one side, then flip and cook for another 10 seconds on the other. While we prepare the filling, set the crepes aside.
- Peel and core the apples, and cut them into 12 slices each.
- Steam the apples in a medium sauté pan.
- Eventually, apply the brown sugar to the melting butter.
- In a mixing dish, combine the cinnamon, apples, and nutmeg.
- Cook until the apples are tender but not soggy. Remove from the heat and set aside to cool.
- Fill each crepe's center with approximately two tablespoons of apple filling.

*Calories 445, Protein 13 g, Sodium 122 mg, Potassium 224.3 mg, Phosphorus 112 mg, Calcium 38.1 mg*

## Asian Pear Crisp
*Time: 60 Mins, Serves: 8, Skill: Hard*

**Ingredients**
- Nuts (3/4 cup), chopped
- Butter (5 tsp), unsalted
- Cornstarch (1 tbsp)
- Lemon (1)
- Asian pears (3 lb.), peeled & cored
- Unbleached all-purpose flour (1/2 cup)
- Light brown sugar (1/4 cup)
- Granulated sugar (4 tbsp), divided
- Cinnamon (1/4 tsp), ground
- Nutmeg (1/8 tsp), ground

**Instructions**
- Preheat the oven to 375 °F.
- In a food processor, combine the cornstarch, nuts, brown sugar, two teaspoons of granulated sugar, nutmeg, and cinnamon.
- Pour the melted butter mixture on top and stir until it resembles moist sand.
- In a big mixing bowl, combine the remaining two teaspoons of granulated sugar, lemon juice, and cornstarch.
- Pears should be peeled, halved, and centered. Cut through half-moons and wedges.
- Move the pears to an 8-inch square baking dish and toss with the sugar mixture.
- Place the pears on top of the toppings.
- Bake for 45 minutes, or until the fruit has burst at the sides and the top has turned a rich golden color.
- Allow for a 15-minute cooling time for the wire stand. Place the food on the table.

*Calories 354, Protein 12 g, Sodium 81 mg, Potassium 31 mg, Phosphorus 96 mg, Calcium 13 mg*

## Asian Pear Torte
*Time: 1 hour and 20 Mins, Serves: 10, Skill: Medium*

**Ingredients**
- Sugar (2/3 cup)
- Lemon zest (1 tbsp)
- Cinnamon (1 tsp)
- Almond extract (1 tsp)
- Flour (1 1/2 cups)
- Almonds (1 1/2 cups) plus for garnish (1/4 cup)
- Butter (1 cup), cold, unsalted, cut into cubes
- Egg yolks (2)
- Apple, currant jelly, or lemon marmalade (1/2 cup)
- Asian pears (2-3 pieces)
- Maraschino cherry and powdered sugar, for garnish

**Instructions**
- Preheat the oven to 350 °F.
- Pulse 1 1/2 cups of nuts, lemon, sugar, flour, & cinnamon in a food processor until the nuts are thinly sliced.
- Add the butter, almond extract, and egg yolks.
- Pulse to combine.
- Grease the 9 "springform bowl's bottom layer and cover with dough, pulling up to the sides. Set aside 1/4-1/2 cups of batter.
- Slice any 1/4 "big Asian Pears."
- Layer slices in the sequential ring out from the center, beginning in the middle of the batter. Make two complete rings across the top of the torte.
- To create a crust of sorts, distribute the reserved batter over the pie's side over the pears' end.
- Melt the jelly in the microwave for 1 min and brush it over the Asian pear slices.
- Sprinkle with the leftover sliced almonds on the edges and middle.
- Bake for 30-35 minutes.
- Before removing the torte from the pan, let it cool.

- Sprinkle with powdered sugar & marinade with a maraschino cherry in the middle.

*Calories 341, Protein 10 g, Sodium 111 mg, Potassium 61 mg, Phosphorus 119 mg, Calcium 10 mg*

## Apple Oat Shake
*Time: 30 Mins, Serves: 4, Skill: Easy*

**Ingredients**
- Wheat germ (1 tbsp)
- Vanilla extract (1 1/2 tsp)
- Frozen apple (1/2 pieces), cut into chunks
- Oatmeal (1/2 cup), cooked, chilled
- Skim milk (2/3 cup)
- Brown sugar (2 tbsp)

**Instructions**
- Blend the oatmeal for a couple minutes in a blender.
- In a large mixing cup, whisk together the milk, vanilla, brown sugar, wheat germ, and half of the apple mixture.
- Blend until the mixture has reached a creamy, dense consistency.

*Calories 67, Protein 0 g, Sodium 01 mg, Potassium 79 mg, Phosphorus 12 mg, Calcium 09 mg*

## Blueberry Squares
*Time: 1 hour and 25 Mins, Serves: 16, Skill: Medium*

**Ingredients**
- Oats (1 cup)
- Cinnamon (1 tsp)
- Sugar (1 cup)
- Butter (3/4 cup or 1 1/2 sticks), melted
- Blueberries (3 cups)
- Zest of a lemon (1)
- Sugar (3/4 cup)
- Water (1 cup)
- Flour (1 1/2 cups)
- Cornstarch (3 tbsp)

**Instructions**
- Preheat oven to 350ºF.
- Combine the flour, sugar, cinnamon, oats, and butter in a medium mixing bowl and whisk until the mixture is crisp and crunchy.
- Half of the flour and oat mixture should be pressed into a 9-inch square baking dish.
- To coat the tray's base, swirl blueberries, and lemon zest together.
- In a microwave-safe tub, whisk together cornstarch and sugar, then steadily whisk in water until it boils.
- Pour a water, sugar, and cornstarch combination over the blueberries.
- Over the end, sprinkle the remaining flour/oat mixture.
- The cooking time varies between 45 and 1 hour.

*Calories 114.3, Protein 12.4 g, Sodium 68.1 mg, Potassium 39.1 mg, Phosphorus 119.6 mg, Calcium 13.2 mg*

## Blueberry Whipped Pie
*Time: 1 hour and 30 Mins, Serves: 9, Skill: Medium*

**Ingredients**
- Graham cracker crumbs (2 cups)
- Cinnamon (1 tsp)
- Granulated sugar (1/4 cup)
- Lemon juice (2 tsp)
- Vanilla extract (1 tsp)
- Whipped cream (8 oz. tub), non-dairy
- Blueberries (3 cups)
- Butter (1/2 cup), melted, unsalted
- Cream cheese (8 oz.), softened

**Instructions**
- Preheat oven to 375ºF.
- Put the cinnamon sticks, graham cracker crumbs, and melted butter in a medium mixing cup.
- To make a crust, thinly scatter the mixture in the bottom of a 9-inch circular or square baking dish.
- After baking, allow for 7 minutes of cooking time.
- In a big mixing tub, using a hand processor, smooth out the melted cream cheese.
- In a mixing cup, combine the vanilla and lemon juice.
- Before applying the blueberries, fold in the whipped topping softly.
- Cover the whole surface with the paste.
- After covering, place in the refrigerator for at least 1 hour.

*Calories 265, Protein 1.5 g, Sodium 109.3 mg, Potassium 146.7 mg, Phosphorus 98.1 mg, Calcium 26.2 mg*

## Molten Mint Chocolate Brownies
*Time: 40 Mins, Serves: 8, Skill: Easy*

**Ingredients**
- Andes mint chocolates (12 pieces)

- Optional garnish: cocoa powder, powdered sugar, fresh mint springs,
- Betty Crocker brownie mix (1 box)

**Instructions**
- Preheat the oven to 350°F and follow the product instructions for cooking the brownie mix.
- In a 12-cup muffin pan that has been lined or lightly oiled, flour the bottom sheet. Bake for 25 minutes after putting the brownie mix in the pans.
- After placing one slice of mint candy in the middle, bake for an additional 5 minutes. Remove the brownies from the oven and place them on a cooling rack to cool. Allow for 5–10 minutes of cooling before serving.

*Calories 307, Protein 3 g, Sodium 147 mg, Potassium 120 mg, Phosphorus 61 mg, Calcium 23 mg*

## Dried Cranberry Fruit Bars
*Time: 1 hour and 25 Mins, Serves: 24, Skill: Hard*

**Ingredients**
**Crust**:
- All-purpose flour (1 1/2 cups)
- Sugar (3/4 cup)
- Eggs (4 large)
- Vanilla extract (1 tsp)
- Powdered sugar for dusting (optional)
- Sugar (1 1/3 cups)
- Butter (3/4 cup), unsalted

**Topping**:
- All-purpose flour (1/2 cup)
- Baking powder (1 tsp)
- Dried cranberries (1 cup)

**Instructions**
- Preheat oven to 350°F.
- Combine all the sugar and flour in a medium-sized mixing cup; cut in unsalted butter so the mixture comes together. In a 9" x 13" baking sheet, pat onto an ungreased surface. 10 minutes in the oven, or until finely browned.
- To produce the topping, sift the flour and baking powder together in a wide dish. Add the cranberries from a can.
- Combine sugar, vanilla, and eggs in a medium-sized mixing cup. Use the flour mixture to coat the surface. Place the fried crust on top of that. Preheat the oven to 200 °F and bake for 20 to 25 minutes.
- While the bars are still hot, cut them into 24 pieces and dust them with powdered sugar.

*Calories 139.2, Protein 04 g, Sodium 21 mg, Potassium 48 mg, Phosphorus 16 mg, Calcium 3.8 mg*

## Sunburst Lemon Bars
*Time: 1 hour and 20 Mins, Serves: 24, Skill: Medium*

**Ingredients**
**Crust**:
- All-purpose flour (2 cups)
- Powdered sugar (1/2 cup)
- Butter (1 cup)

**Glaze**:
- Powdered sugar (1 cup)
- Lemon juice (2 tbsp)

**Filling**:
- Eggs (4 pieces)
- Sugar (1 1/2 cups)
- All-purpose flour (1/4 cup)
- Cream of tartar (1/2 tsp)
- Baking soda (1/4 tsp)
- Lemon juice (1/4 cup)

**Instructions**
**Crust**
- Preheat oven to 350°F.
- In a big mixing dish, combine the flour with the melted butter and powdered sugar. To make the mixture crumbly, add all the ingredients together in a big mixing bowl. Fill a 9" x 13" baking pan halfway with the paste and smooth it out.
- Preheat oven to 350°F and bake for 15–20 minutes, or until golden brown.

**Arrangement**
- In a medium mixing cup, lightly whisk the eggs.
- Mix the flour, baking soda, sugar, and tartar cream together in a separate dish. Add together the eggs and dry ingredients. Add and beat the lemon juice as it reaches a small peak.
- On the warm soil, bake for an additional 20 minutes, or until the filling has hardened.
- Remove the pan from the heat and place it on a cooling rack.

**Glaze**
- In a small cup, sift the powdered sugar and gently whisk in the lemon juice before it's ready to use. Use as much or as little lemon juice as you choose.

- Glaze the cooling filling with the glaze. Break the cake into 24 bars after adding the glaze. Refrigerate some leftover lemon strips.

*Calories 114, Protein 2.4 g, Sodium 86.1 mg, Potassium 93 mg, Phosphorus 109.6 mg, Calcium 1.3 mg*

## Filled Phyllo Pastries with Rustic Apple Cinnamon

*Time: 45 Mins, Serves: 6, Skill: Easy*

**Ingredients**

**Apple mixture:**
- Butter (1/4 cup)
- Cinnamon (1 tsp)
- Nutmeg (1/4 tsp)
- Vanilla extract (2 tbsp)
- Cornstarch (1/4 tsp)
- Phyllo dough (1 package/6 sheets)
- Powdered sugar (3 tbsp)
- Cinnamon (2 tbsp)
- Apples (3 1/2 cups), diced and peeled
- Brown sugar light (1/4 cup)
- Butter (2 tbsp)
- Optional garnish: fresh mint sprigs, powdered sugar, & whipped cream

**Instructions**

**Apples in a mixture**
- Preheat the oven to 350°F.
- Cook the apples in the butter for 6 to 8 mins in a big saucepan over medium-high heat.
- In a large mixing cup, whisk together the nutmeg, cinnamon, and brown sugar. 3–4 minutes more cooking time
- Before dissolving the cornstarch, whisk together the vanilla extract in a tiny cup. Cook for 2 minutes more over medium-high heat, stirring in the apple mixture.
- Remove the mixture from the heat & set it aside.

**Pastries made from phyllo dough:**
- Oil on the rim a large tin pan (6-muffin).
- Dust the first layer of phyllo pastry with molten butter, then sprinkle with powdered sugar & cinnamon mixture. Stack one layer on top of the other before all six layers of sugar and cinnamon mixture have been buttered and dusted.
- Cut 6 even squares out of the pile. Each muffin cup can be lined on the sides and bottom with one pile of squares, with several squares hanging around the edges.
- Fill every phyllo-lined cup of muffin halfway to 3/4 complete with apple mixture, making sure that the volume of apple mixture in every phyllo-lined cup of muffin is consistent.
- In each muffin cup, fold the extra phyllo dough on to the apples.
- Preheat oven to 350 °F and bake for 8 to 10 mins.

*Calories 280, Protein 02 g, Sodium 97 mg, Potassium 177 mg, Phosphorus 33 mg, Calcium 44 mg*

## Yellow Cake

*Time: 1 hour and 25 Mins, Serves: 8, Skill: Medium*

**Ingredients**
- Sugar (2/3 cup)
- Water (1/2 cup)
- Egg (1)
- Vanilla (1/2 tsp)
- Master Mix (1 1/2 cups)

**Instructions**
- Preheat the oven to 375 °F.
- For Master Mix, follow the steps outlined.
- Add some sugar to the mixture.
- In a separate dish, whisk together the egg, water, and vanilla extract.
- Beat for 2 minutes after adding half of the solvent to the mixture.
- Pour in the remaining liquid and continue to beat for 2 minutes.
- Bake for 25 minutes in a tray lined with wax paper.
- One 8-inch layer is made for this recipe.

*Calories 143, Protein 04 g, Sodium 91.2 mg, Potassium 31 mg, Phosphorus 61 mg, Calcium 13.1 mg*

## Tropical Fruit Salad with Basil Lime Syrup

*Time: 1 hour and 10 Mins, Serves: 10, Skill: Medium*

**Ingredients**
- Strawberries (1 1/2 cup), sliced
- Mango (1 cup), cubed
- Pineapple (2 cups), cubed
- Water (1/4 cup)
- Sugar (1/4 cup)
- Lime zest (1 1/2 tsp)
- Packed basil leaves (1/4 cup)

**Instructions**

- Bring water to a boil in a small frying pan and stir in sugar.
- Boil and cook until the sugar melts.
- Take the pan off the heat and stir in the lime zest and basil.
- In a large mixing cup, combine the fruits while the syrup cools.
- Soak the cheesecloth or strainer in the syrup to remove the solids.
- Serve as a side dish of fruits or as a snack.

*Calories 67, Protein 02 g, Sodium 01 mg, Potassium 69 mg, Phosphorus 20 mg, Calcium 09 mg*

## Pineapple Pudding
*Time: 1 hour and Mins, Serves: 12, Skill: Medium*

**Ingredients**

- Sugar (1/2 cup)
- Egg (1 large)
- Eggs (3), divided
- Milk 2% (1 cup)
- Water (1 cup)
- Vanilla extract (1 tsp)
- Pineapple chunks (2 cups)
- Sugar (1/4 cup)
- Vanilla wafers (25-30 pieces)
- All-purpose flour (3 tbsp)

**Instructions**

- Pre-heat the oven to 425 °F.
- In a double boiler, combine 3 egg yolks, flour, 1 whole egg, and sugar.
- Add the milk and water. Cook, stirring continuously, until it hardens, untreated, over hot water.
- Whisk in the vanilla extract after removing the pan from the oven.
- Distribute a tiny quantity of custard in a 1 1/2-quart casserole dish, and finish with 12 vanilla wafers and 12 pineapple slices.
- Continue layering the custard wafers, custard, and pineapple pieces in that order.
- Beat the remaining egg whites with a hand blender or an egg beater after applying the starch, until you get those hard peaks.
- Pour the hard egg whites over the layered pudding. Preheat the oven to 350°F and bake for 5 minutes, or until golden brown.

*Calories 214, Protein 12 g, Sodium 125 mg, Potassium 119 mg, Phosphorus 12 mg, Calcium 31 mg*

## Old Fashioned Pound Cake
*Time: 15 hours and 25 Mins, Serves: 24, Skill: Hard*

**Ingredients**

- All-purpose flour (3 1/2 cups)
- Lemon rind (2 tbsp), grated
- Lemon extract (1 tsp)
- Eggs (6)
- Butter (2 cups)
- Powdered sugar (4 cups)

**Instructions**

- Preheat the oven to 350 °F.
- Using a hand blender, blend the butter for 3 minutes on low pressure, until smooth and light.
- Gradually drizzle in the sugar, followed by the lemon rinds, and beat well.
- Include the lemon and egg extracts one at a time, combining thoroughly with each addition.
- Stir in the flour slowly and thoroughly.
- Put the batter into a 10-Bundt pan halfway filled with oil and flour.
- Bake for 1 hour and 20 minutes, or until a toothpick inserted in the center of the cake comes out clean.
- Remove the baking sheet from the oven and put it aside to cool.

*Calories 204.3, Protein 12.4 g, Sodium 112 mg, Potassium 39 mg, Phosphorus 56 mg, Calcium 39 mg*

## Vanilla Strudel
*Time: 1 hour and 40 Mins, Serves: 12, Skill: Hard*

**Ingredients**

- Vanilla extract (1 tsp)
- Sugar (4 tbsp)
- Cinnamon (1/2 tsp), ground
- Butter (4 tbsp), unsalted
- Phyllo dough (12 sheets)
- Pumpkin (1 1/2 cups), unsweetened
- Nutmeg (1/2 tsp), grated

**Instructions**

- Preheat the oven to 380 °F. Place an oven shelf in the oven's middle.
- Whisk together the pumpkin, nutmeg, vanilla extract, 12 tablespoons of cinnamon, and 2

teaspoons of sugar in a medium mixing cup until well mixed.

- Butter a medium non-stick baking tray with a pastry knife. On a smooth work surface, spread a sheet of basic phyllo dough and cover with butter. Then, one by one, stack the buttered phyllo tubes, coating each one with melted butter. Before using the leftover phyllo sheets, cover them in foil wrap.
- After completed all 12 sheets, scatter the mixture uniformly on one of the stack's longer sides. Begin rolling from the filling edge to a blank end, seam-side down.
- Place the roll, seam-side down, on the oiled sheet plate, and dust with the remaining butter.
- In a small cup, combine the remaining cinnamon and sugar. Distribute it evenly over the top and sides of the strudel.
- Bake for 12 to 15 minutes on the center rack of the oven, until well browned.
- Remove the baked strudel from the oven and put it aside for 5 to 10 minutes.
- Enable the center to cool before cutting and serving with a sharp knife.

*Calories 351, Protein 14 g, Sodium 181 mg, Potassium 93.1 mg, Phosphorus 86 mg, Calcium 19 mg*

## Apple Muffins
*Time: 1 hour and 35 Mins, Serves: 12, Skill: Hard*

**Ingredients**
- Raw apple (1 1/2 cup)
- Eggs (2)
- Sugar (1 cup)
- Muffin papers (12 pieces)
- Canola oil (1/2 cup)
- All-purpose white flour (1 1/2 cup)
- Baking soda (1 tsp)
- Cinnamon (1 1/2 tsp)
- Water (1/2 cup)
- Vanilla (1 tbsp)

**Instructions**
- Preheat the oven to 400°F and cover a muffin tin with muffin foil. Peel and slice the apple into small pieces.
- In a big mixing cup, whisk together the eggs. In a blender, combine the sugar, water, and oil and blend until smooth. In a small bowl, combine the vanilla extract and the water.
- Combine the flour, 1 teaspoon of cinnamon, and baking soda in a separate cup.
- Blend the flour and salt into the egg mixture. The batter is lumpy in form. Fold the apple in half and cut it into pieces.
- Fill muffin tins 3/4 full. In a shallow mixing cup, combine the remaining half teaspoon of cinnamon and 1 teaspoon of sugar. Sprinkle on top of the muffins.

*Calories 162, Protein 3 g, Sodium 117 mg, Potassium 46 mg, Phosphorus 34 mg, Calcium 10 mg*

## Cornbread Muffins
*Time: 1 hour, Serves: 12, Skill: Easy*

**Ingredients**
- Sugar (1/4 cup)
- Baking powder (2 tsp)
- Liquid egg substitute (1/2 cup)
- Rice milk (1 cup), unenriched
- Butter (2 tbsp), unsalted
- All-purpose white flour (1 cup)
- Plain cornmeal (1 cup)

**Instructions**
- Preheat the oven to 400 °F.
- Combine the flour, sugar, cornmeal, and baking powder in a mixing dish.
- Whisk together the egg substitute, melted butter, and rice milk in a separate container.
- Combine the dry and wet products just after they've been moistened.
- Fill muffin cups halfway. In oiled or paper-lined muffin tins, pour 2/3 of the batter.
- Bake for 15–20 minutes, or when a toothpick inserted in the center comes out clean.
- Serve immediately.

*Calories 160, Protein 3 g, Sodium 115 mg, Potassium 49 mg, Phosphorus 30 mg, Calcium 12 mg*

## Dessert Cups with Fresh Fruit
*Time: 1 hour and 10 Mins, Serves: 8, Skill: Medium*

**Ingredients**
- Blueberries (1 cup), fresh
- Blackberries (1 cup), fresh
- Raspberries (1 cup), fresh
- Strawberries (1 cup), fresh
- Cool whip (3 cups)
- Phyllo pastry dough (4 sheets)

- Nonstick cooking spray

**Instructions**
- Preheat the oven to 400 °F.
- Spray a 12-cup muffin tray with cooking spray containing butter.
- Arrange four phyllo dough sheets on a baking sheet and lightly brush each layer with cooking spray. To make the cake cups, cut the phyllo dough into 3-1/2" squares and place them in a muffin tray.
- Bake for 10-12 minutes, or until the phyllo cups are well browned in the muffin tin. Allow to cool to room temperature before serving.
- Fill each of the phyllo dessert containers with 1/3 cup fresh berries after they have finished baking. Cover with 1/4 cup Cool Whip cake coating.

*Calories 67, Protein 02 g, Sodium 01 mg, Potassium 69 mg, Phosphorus 20 mg, Calcium 09 mg*

## Honey-Maple Trail Mix
*Time: 1 hour 5 Mins, Serves: 32, Skill: Easy*

**Ingredients**
- Cinnamon Teddy Grahams snack cookies (10 ounces)
- Pretzel Crisps (6 oz.)
- Butter (1/2 cup), unsalted
- Dark brown sugar (1/3 cup)
- Honey (1/4 cup)
- Maple syrup (1/4 cup)
- Sweetened cranberries (5 oz.), dried
- Crispy Apple Chips of Granny Smith (3 oz.)
- Golden Grahams cereal (3 cups)
- Rice Chex cereal (5 cups)

**Instructions**
- In a big mixing cup, combine the Golden Grahams, Teddy Grahams, Rice Chex, and pretzels.
- In a shallow saucepan, melt the butter and add brown sugar, maple syrup, and honey. Cook until the sugar has melted over low pressure.
- Pour over the cereal mixture and toss well to cover all the pieces.
- Preheat the oven to 325 °F.
- Preheat oven to 350°F. Line three jelly roll pans with aluminum foil and brush with cooking spray. (You should do this in three different batches.) Distribute the cereal mixture evenly in the containers using a spatula. Bake for 20 minutes, stirring halfway through.
- In a mixing cup, combine the cranberries and apple chips; split and stir equally between the two serving dishes.
- Bake for 5 more minutes, then cool completely before placing in an airtight container.

*Calories 262, Protein 3 g, Sodium 178 mg, Potassium 84 mg, Phosphorus 66 mg, Calcium 63 mg*

## Berry Oatmeal Muffins
*Time: 1 hour and 20 Mins, Serves: 12, Skill: Medium*

**Ingredients**
- Eggs (2)
- Apple sauce (1/2 cup)
- Canola oil (1/4 cup)
- Orange (1), the grated zest only
- Lemon (1), the grated zest
- Lemon juice (1 tbsp)
- Raspberries (3/4 cup), fresh or frozen
- Unbleached all-purpose flour (1 cup)
- Quick-cooking oatmeal (1/2 cup)
- Lightly packed brown sugar (2/3 cup)
- Baking soda (1/2 tsp)
- Blueberries (3/4 cup), fresh or frozen

**Instructions**
- Preheat the oven to 400 °F and place the rack in the middle. In a muffin tray, position 12 paper or silicone muffin cups.
- Combine the flour, brown sugar, oatmeal, and baking soda in a mixing dish.
- Whisk together the eggs, oil, apple sauce, lemon juice, and citrus zest in a large mixing cup. Stir in the dried goods with a wooden spoon. Add the berries and blend them in thoroughly.
- Scoop the muffin mixture into the muffin cups. Cook for 20–22 minutes, or until a toothpick inserted in the center comes out clean. Allow to cool before serving.

*Calories 162, Protein 3 g, Sodium 117 mg, Potassium 46 mg, Phosphorus 34 mg, Calcium 10 mg*

## Festive Raspberry Meringue Trifle
*Time: 2 Hour and 30 Mins, Serves: 6, Skill: Hard*

**Ingredients**
**Meringues**
- Egg whites (2)

- Granulated sugar (1/2 cup)
- Vanilla extract (1/4 tsp)
- Candy canes (1/4 cup), crushed

**Raspberry Mousse**
- Raspberries (1 cup), frozen
- Water (1/4 cup)
- Raspberry Jell-O powder (2 tsp), no sugar added
- Cool whip (1 1/2 cup)
- Raspberries (1 package), fresh

**Instructions**
- Preheat the oven to 350 °F and line a baking tray with parchment paper to create the meringues.
- Whip the egg whites in a stick blender or a mixing cup until frothy. Drizzle in the sugar gradually when beating the egg whites until they are light and strong. Cover with crushed candy canes and vanilla extract.
- Bake on a baking sheet lined with meringue in a hot oven. Enable the meringue to cool for 2-3 hours after turning off the oven. Crumble the meringue into bite-sized bits until it has dried.
- In a small frying pan, mix the frozen raspberries and water to produce the mousse. Steam the raspberries until they thaw or soften. Fill a mixing cup halfway with the raspberry mixture. Stir in the diluted jello until it is well combined. Fold in the Cold Whip after the raspberry mixture has cooled fully.
- In a larger trifle cup, layer the raspberry mousse, fresh berries, and crumbled meringue to compose the seasonal trifles. Repeat the layers. Chill for several hours before serving.

*Calories 114.3, Protein 12.4 g, Sodium 68.1 mg, Potassium 39.1 mg, Phosphorus 119.6 mg, Calcium 13.2 mg*

## Saskatoon Berry Pudding
*Time: 1 hour and 15 Mins, Serves: 6, Skill: Hard*

**Ingredients**
- White sugar (1/3 cup)
- Water (2 cups)
- Flour (1/2 cup)
- Saskatoon berries (2 cups)

**Instructions**
- In a medium-sized pot, add the berries, 1 1/2 cups water, and the sugar.
- Bring it to a simmer over high flame.
- Reduce to low heat and allow to boil for 30 minutes.
- Pour flour into a small dish. Add 1/2 cup of water.
- Apply the flour mixture to the berries and cook for 10 minutes to thicken the paste.

*Calories 766.8, Protein 9.4 g, Sodium 856.6 mg, Potassium 31 mg, Phosphorus 64 mg, Calcium 43 mg*

## Cherry filo pastry tarts
*Time: 55 Mins, Serves: 6, Skill: Easy*

**Ingredients**
- Pitted cherries (250g), frozen
- Water (1 tbsp)
- Filo pastry (250g approx.), 1 box ready to use
- Oil (1 tbsp)
- Butter (60g)
- Icing sugar (1 tbsp)
- Granulated sugar (75g)
- Vanilla essence (1 tsp)
- Arrowroot powder (1 tbsp)

**Instructions**
- Combine the frozen cherries, sugar, and vanilla essence in a saucepan. Cook, stirring constantly, for 5 minutes over medium heat. Gently remove the cherries with a spatula. Add arrowroot powder and water to make a paste.
- As you pour in the mixture, blend it in with the dried cherries. Bring the water to a boil, then remove it from the heat. Allow for cooling time. Preheat the oven to 374 °F and gently grease a muffin tray.
- Cut three puff pastry sheets into halves to make four triangles. Brush all sides of the puff pastry with molten butter, then fill each space with two squares. One tablespoon of cherry filling can be used for each. Fold the filo pastry edges over the top of the cherry filling to partially cover.
- Spread the remaining butter on top of each tart. Bake for 10 to 15 minutes, or until golden brown on top. Place it on a cooling rack after removing it from the heat. Sprinkle with powdered sugar after it has cooled. It's best served at room temperature or warm.

*Calories 445.9, Protein 10.3 g, Sodium 182.2 mg, Potassium 243.2 mg, Phosphorus 72 mg, Calcium 138.1 mg*

## Reduced Sugar Carrot Cupcakes
*Time: 1 hour and 35 Mins, Serves: 16, Skill: Hard*

**Ingredients**
- Mixed spice (2 tsp)
- Orange (1)
- Eggs (2)
- Sunflower oil (150ml)
- Carrots (200g)
- Light muscovado sugar (125g)
- Whole meal flour (100g)
- White flour (50g)
- Bicarbonate of soda (1 tsp)

**Icing**
- Butter (70g), softened
- Soft cheese (200g), low fat
- Vanilla extract (1/2 tsp)
- Icing sugar (50g), sifted

**Instructions**
- Preheat the oven to 350 °F and line 12 muffin tins with paper liners.
- In a mixing cup, combine the flour, mixed seasoning, bicarbonate of soda, and orange zest.
- In a separate cup, whisk together the eggs, oil, and sugar, then stir them into the dry ingredients. Grated and peeled carrots should be added to the mixture and thoroughly blended in.
- Put the mixture into the muffin tins and bake for 20-22 minutes, or until a skewer inserted in the middle comes out clean. After that, set it aside to cool on a wire rack.
- Melt the butter, and add the soft cheese, sifted icing sugar, and vanilla extract to produce the icing. Using a palette/cutlery knife, swirl icing on top of cakes.

*Calories 243, Protein 02 g, Sodium 101 mg, Potassium 91 mg, Phosphorus 119.6 mg, Calcium 41.8 mg*

## Christmas Turkey Crown with All the Trimmings
*Time: 1 hour and 45 Mins, Serves: 8, Skill: Hard*

**Ingredients**
**Carrots with tarragon & fennel seeds**
- Carrots (340g)
- Butter (25g)
- Fennel seeds (1 tsp)
- Tarragon (2 tbsp), chopped
- Brussel sprouts (300g), pan-fried & with nutmeg
- Olive oil (2 tbsp)
- Butter (25g)
- Red onion (1)
- Parsley (1 tbsp)
- Nutmeg seed (1)

**Roast turkey with gravy**
- Butter (75g)
- Garlic clove (1)
- Flat-leaf parsley (1 tbsp), fresh
- Orange zest
- Thyme (1 tsp), fresh
- Sunflower oil (50ml)
- Plain flour (1 tbsp)
- Chicken stock (300ml), low salt
- Sage & onion stuffing
- Butter (75g)
- Turkey crown (1.5kg)
- Turkey, bones & giblets
- Onion (1 small)
- Sage (1 tsp), fresh
- White breadcrumbs (175g), fresh

**Potato (crispy) with rosemary & red onion**
- Rosemary (1 tsp), fresh
- Olive oil (50ml)
- Red onion (1)
- Potatoes (800g)
- Plain flour (75g)

**Instructions**
- For the filling, peel, and dice the onion. Combine the onion, flour, and chopped sage in a frying pan. When the onion is soft, apply the breadcrumbs and whisk to blend. Pour into a buttered tin foil, firmly coil, and refrigerate until ready to use.
- Preheat oven to 375°F. Flavored butter is made by combining the orange zest, crushed garlic, and sliced herbs. Using your hands, scatter the butter under the turkey's crown skin. In the roasting pan, drizzle oil over the turkey and giblets. Cover with foil & cook for the amount of time defined by the weight. The cooking time for one & a half kg turkey crown is 1 hour and 40 minutes.
- For the last 30 minutes of preparation, remove the foil and baste often. Remove the dish from the oven and cover it with foil before it is finished.

- When you cook the potatoes, stuffing, and onions, let the meat sit for at least 30 minutes.
- Turn the oven to 200°F. Carrots should be peeled and diced into balls, while potatoes should be peeled and diced. Cook the veggies discretely in water (boiling) for 5 to 10 mins, or until tender. The potatoes should be drained and dried. Sprinkle them with rosemary & toss in flour before adding it to a roasting tin with some oil.
- Roast potatoes & stuffing for 30 minutes. Slice red onion & sprinkle over potatoes in the last 10 minutes of cooking. Add the blanched sprouts, spices, butter, and sliced onions, as well as the nutmeg, in a pan. Combine the blanched carrots, fennel seeds and butter in a skillet. Cook each side for 5 to 10 mins. Sprinkle tarragon on to the carrots just before eating.
- Remove the giblets & cooking juices from the roasting pan and position it over medium heat to create a gravy. After adding the flour, whisk in the chicken stock for 5 minutes before straining.

*Calories 495, Protein 103 g, Sodium 3 mg, Potassium 183 mg, Phosphorus 206 mg, Calcium 40 mg*

## Jam sponge cake
*Time: 1 hour, Serves: 8, Skill: Medium*

**Ingredients**
- Baking powder (1 tsp)
- Eggs (4)
- Caster sugar (150g)
- Corn flour (30g)
- Plain flour (50g)
- Oil and greaseproof paper, to line and grease cake tins.
- Jam (3 tbsp)

**Instructions**
- Grease and line two 1/8 cm sandwich tins with parchment paper. Preheat the oven to 350 °F.
- In a mixing cup, sift together the flour and baking powder.
- Whisk the egg whites until stiff, then add the sugar and whisk for a few seconds more. Beat the egg yolks in a separate bowl and then add to the egg whites.
- Fold the flour mixture into the egg mixture with a large metal spoon, then distribute between the two muffin tins.
- Bake for 18-20 minutes, or until the sponges are golden and raised. Allow to cool in the tins for 10 minutes before turning out into a cooling shelf.
- Once the cake has cooled, spread jelly on half of it and add the other half on top. Sift a tiny amount of icing sugar over the top before eating.

*Calories 204.3, Protein 12.4 g, Sodium 112 mg, Potassium 39 mg, Phosphorus 56 mg, Calcium 39 mg*

## Cornflake and ginger cookies
*Time: 45 Mins, Serves: 5, Skill: Easy*

**Ingredients**
- Egg (1)
- Golden caster sugar (75g)
- Cornflakes (40g)
- Butter (100g), unsalted
- Stem ginger (60g)
- Flour (130g)

**Instructions**
- Preheat the oven to 200°F. Two baking sheets can be lined with greaseproof paper.
- Cream together the butter and sugar until light and fluffy. After that, whisk in the egg until it's completely smooth. In a mixing bowl, combine flour, cornflakes, and chopped stem ginger. Then, to make a smooth dough, combine all the ingredients.
- Shape into 12 walnut-sized balls, place on a baking sheet, and gently press down with fingertips, create plenty of space between cookies.
- Bake for 15 minutes, or until golden brown, before transferring to a wire rack to cool.

*Calories 223, Protein 01 g, Sodium 275 mg, Potassium 21 mg, Phosphorus 96 mg, Calcium 8 mg*

## Chocolate profiteroles with Chantilly cream
*Time: 1 hour, Serves: 8, Skill: Easy*

**Ingredients**
**Profiteroles**
- Eggs (2 medium)
- Plain flour (75g)
- Coldwater (150ml)
- Butter (50g), unsalted

**Chantilly cream**
- Vanilla extract (1 tsp)
- Double cream (300ml)

- Caster sugar (1 tbsp)

**Chocolate sauce**

- Dark chocolate (100g)

**Instructions**

- Preheat the oven to 338 °F, and lightly grease a baking sheet (non-stick). Sift the flour into a mixing cup. Bring water and diced butter to a boil in a large saucepan.
- Slowly drizzle in the flour until the paste clings to the whisk. Replace the whisk with a wooden spoon and stir for 2-3 minutes, or before it comes away from the pan's sides and falls off a spoon.
- Take it off the burner. Beat in the eggs one at a time. Combine the ingredients with a wooden spoon or an electric whisk. The finished product should be smooth and polished.
- Using a dessert spoon/ piping bag with a 1 cm nozzle, pipe 18 equal-sized balls of pastry onto a baking tray. Preheat oven to 180°F and bake for 18-20 minutes, or until golden and puffy. Remove it from the oven and set it aside to cool until its done cooking.
- To make Chantilly cream, add cream, sugar, and vanilla extract in a mixing cup. Combine them with an electric whisk or a hand whisk to form soft peaks. Cut a slit in each profiterole with a nozzle, then pipe cream filling into each one.
- To melt the chocolate, break it up and drop it in a heatproof bowl set over a pan of simmering water (do not let the bowl touch the water). Serve molten chocolate profiteroles with a drizzle of melted chocolate on top.

*Calories 136, Protein 18 g, Sodium 108.1 mg, Potassium 31 mg, Phosphorus 316 mg, Calcium 28 mg*

## Meringue with mango & lime cream

*Time: 1 hour 40 Mins, Serves: 9, Skill: Hard*

**Ingredients**

- Eggs (5 large)
- Caster sugar (300g)
- Corn flour (2 tsp)
- Icing sugar (1 tsp)
- Mango & lime cream
- Fresh cream (600ml)
- Mango (150g)
- Lime (1)
- Meringues

**Instructions**

- For the meringues, draw eight 6cm circles on parchment paper, leaving spaces between each circle. Preheat oven to 350°F. Line a baking tray with parchment paper.
- Separate the eggs until the yolks are removed. Place the egg whites in a dry, clean pan. The egg whites should be hard enough to form stiff peaks when whisked. Combine the caster sugar and corn flour in a separate bowl. Whisk in 1 tablespoon of sugar at a time until it is fully dissolved.
- Spread a 2cm thick layer of meringue thinly over the parchment paper rings. Apply the mixture along the circular sides of the meringue nests with a piping or bag spoon for the raised edge. Bake for 1 hour and 30 minutes, or until the meringue is crisp and well-colored.
- Whip the cream and apply the icing sugar to make the lime ice and raspberry. It's time to apply the lime juice and zest (12). Finish with the sliced, minced, and de-stoned mango and lime cream in the meringue nests. On top, sift the icing sugar.

*Calories 143, Protein 24 g, Sodium 81 mg, Potassium 31 mg, Phosphorus 96 mg, Calcium 13 mg*

## Chicken, leek & tarragon pie

*Time: 1 hour and 10 Mins, Serves: 4, Skill: Medium*

**Ingredients**

- Chicken stock cube (1), low salt
- Boiling water (150ml)
- Double cream (142ml)
- White wine (150ml), optional
- Fresh tarragon (1 tbsp)
- Puff pastry (375g pack), ready-rolled
- Vegetable oil (2 tbsp)
- Onion (1)
- Leeks (2 medium), 300g approx.
- Chicken breasts (4), 600g approx., skinless
- Garlic clove (1)
- Savoy cabbage (1/2 small), 320g approx.
- Egg (1 medium)

**Instructions**

- Preheat the oven to 430 °F. Heat the oil in a frying pan over low heat.
- The onion can be finely diced and sliced. Leeks should be cleaned, cut, and thinly sliced before

frying. Cook until the leeks and onion are softened, about 4 to 5 minutes.
- Cut the chicken into bite-size bits and simmer for another 4 to 5 minutes with the leeks and onions. Crush the garlic and whisk it in, then add the wine and reduce it to two-thirds of its original volume. Prepare the chicken stock, then put it into the pan and cook it down to half its original volume. Bring the cream and finely sliced tarragon to a boil, then reduce to low heat for 5 to 6 minutes, or until the sauce thickens. Place in a pie dish and place in the refrigerator to cool.
- The edge of the pie dish can be rubbed with water. Unroll the puff pastry and cut a slice to cover the dish. By pushing the edges down, cut off the excess with a knife. To let the steam out, cut a tiny hole in the middle of the pastry. After setting it on the baking tray, refrigerate for 15 minutes.
- Beat an egg in a separate bowl and brush it over the puff pastry. Bake for 40-45 minutes, or until the pastry is crisp. Shred the cabbage leaves and put them in a saucepan with enough water to cover them halfway. Bring to a boil, then reduce to low heat and cook for 5 minutes, or until the vegetables are tender. The water has been drained and disposed of.

*Calories 214, Protein 12 g, Sodium 125 mg, Potassium 119 mg, Phosphorus 12 mg, Calcium 31 mg*

## Christmas Cake

*Time: 240 Mins, Serves: 24, Skill: Hard*

### Ingredients
- Honey (2 tbsp)
- Almond essence (1 tsp)
- Eggs (4), beaten
- Brandy (2 tsp)
- Plain flour (250g)
- Soft brown sugar (250g)
- Butter (250g), unsalted
- Nutmeg (1 tsp)
- Glacé cherries (250g), halved
- Mixed peel (250g)
- Prunes (200g tinned), drained and chopped
- Mixed spice (1 tsp)
- Water (25ml)
- Caramel coloring (A few drops)

### Instructions
- To start, beat together the butter and sugar until light and fluffy. Add the spices and flour.
- Combine the flour and eggs to the creamed mixture in batches. Mix in the cherries, mixed peel, and prunes until all is uniformly spread.
- Add brandy, honey, and water. Before it approaches a dropping consistency, it should be thoroughly blended.
- In a well-greased, greaseproof-paper-lined baking pan, bake it for 3 - 4 hours at 302 °F.

*Calories 264.3, Protein 04 g, Sodium 91.2 mg, Potassium 31 mg, Phosphorus 61 mg, Calcium 13.1 mg*

## Easter Cake

*Time: 5 hours, Serves: 16, Skill: Hard*

### Ingredients
- Nutmeg (1 tsp)
- Almond essence (1 tsp)
- Mixed spice (1 tsp)
- Eggs (4)
- Water (25ml)
- Glacé cherries (250g), halved
- Plain flour (250g)
- Mixed peel (250g)
- Soft brown sugar (250g)
- Tinned prunes (200g)
- Butter (250g), unsalted
- Honey (2 tbsp)

### Instructions
- To start, cream together the butter and sugar until light and fluffy. Add the spices and flour. After halving the cherries, and chopping the prunes, set aside.
- The eggs are pounded and applied in batches to the flour and creamed mixture. Apply the peel, cherries, and prunes after it has been properly mixed.
- Remember to add the honey and water. Before it meets the dropping consistency, it has to be thoroughly combined.
- Bake for 3 to 4 hours at 300 °F in an 18cm well-greased and greaseproof baking tray (paper-lined).

*Calories 431, Protein 10.4 g, Sodium 110.2 mg, Potassium 93.1 mg, Phosphorus 61 mg, Calcium 11 mg*

# Raspberry and passion fruit mousse
*Time: 8 hours, Serves: 4, Skill: Medium*

**Ingredients**
- Egg yolks (3)
- Egg whites (3)
- Caster sugar (100g)
- Double cream (300ml), fresh and softly whipped
- Water (2 tbsp)
- Passion fruits (4), 150g approx., pulp
- Raspberries (300g), fresh or frozen
- Gelatin (2 leaves), vegetarian alternatives are possible

**Instructions**
- Add the pulp in a saucepan with the raspberries, gently heat until the raspberries are soft.
- Put aside to cool slightly after draining the seeds with a sieve. Soak the gelatin in water for about 5 minutes. After that, squeeze them dry entirely before adding them to the raspberry/passion fruit puree and whisking until the gelatin is completely dissolved. Set them aside.
- Whisk the sugar and egg yolks together over a simmering broth until the mixture is pale and thick. Add the raspberry/passion fruit puree and gently mix in the freshly whipped cream.
- In addition, whisk the egg whites until they develop rigid peaks. Gently fold the mixture in.
- Fill 6 glasses halfway with the mixture and chill for 2-3 hours, covered in cling film.

*Calories 136, Protein 18 g, Sodium 108.1 mg, Potassium 31 mg, Phosphorus 316 mg, Calcium 28 mg*

# Pineapple upside-down cake
*Time: 1 hour and 20 Mins, Serves: 4, Skill: Medium*

**Ingredients**
**Topping**
- Butter (50g), unsalted
- Light soft brown sugar (50g)
- Pineapple (9 x rings), in fruit juice
- Glace cherries (9-10)

**Cake**
- Flour self-raising (150g)
- Baking powder (1 1/2 tsp)
- Eggs (3)
- Butter (150g), soft & unsalted
- Golden caster sugar (150g)

**Instructions**
- Preheat the oven to 350 °F.
- To make the filling, mix the butter and soft brown sugar together until creamy, then sprinkle it over the bottom and sides of the brownie pan or a well-greased dish.
- Fill in the holes with glace cherries after dropping 8-9 pineapple rings on the bottom of the pan. Any remaining juice should be set aside for later use.
- Mix the remaining ingredients in a blender with 3 teaspoons of pineapple juice until a soft consistency is obtained.
- Spread the mixture over the pineapple rings and smooth it out until it is completely flat.
- Remove it from the oven after 35 minutes and set it aside to cool for 5 minutes. Turn out and serve.

*Calories 214, Protein 12 g, Sodium 125 mg, Potassium 119 mg, Phosphorus 12 mg, Calcium 31 mg*

# Pear crumble
*Time: 1 hour and 10 Mins, Serves: 6, Skill: Medium*

**Ingredients**
**Crumble filling**
- Pears (5 large)
- Butter (25g), unsalted
- Caster sugar (50g)

**Crumble topping**
- Plain flour (160g)
- Soft dark brown sugar (40g)
- Sugar (40g)
- Ginger (pinch), ground
- Butter (75g), unsalted
- Almonds (40g), ground
- Porridge oats (40g)

**Instructions**
- Preheat the oven to 320 °F and center, peel, and finely chop both of the pears.
- Melt 25g butter in a skillet and add the pears. Cook, stirring occasionally, until the liquid has nearly evaporated. Stir in the sugar until it has fully dissolved. Remove from the heat and set aside.
- Combine the crumble topping ingredients in a food processor, mixer, or in a cup, and rub together with your fingertips until the mixture resembles breadcrumbs. In the finished dish, leave a few lumpy bits because they add texture.

- Cover the fruit mixture halfway in an oven-safe serving bowl, then spoon the crumble topping on top.
- Cook for 20 minutes, or until golden brown and bubbling on top.

*Calories 367, Protein 5 g, Sodium 59 mg, Potassium 31 mg, Phosphorus 96 mg, Calcium 42 mg*

# Shepherd's pie with swede & carrot mash

*Time: 1 hour, Serves: 10, Skill: Easy*

### Ingredients
- Onion (1 large)
- Garlic cloves (2)
- Bay leaf (1)
- Thyme (2 tsp), fresh
- Celery (2 sticks)
- Lean lamb mince (500g)
- Passata (300g)
- Beef stock cube, low salt
- Boiling water (150ml)
- Vegetable oil (1 tbsp)
- Swede (1 small), 450g approx.
- Carrots (375g)
- Peas (150g), frozen
- Wholegrain mustard (2 tsp)
- Worcestershire sauce (1 tbsp)

### Instructions
- Preheat the oven to 375 °F. In a large nonstick pan that has been prepared over medium heat, pour in the oil. The onion and celery can now be sliced and diced. Cook, stirring regularly, for 6–8 minutes, or until the onion, bay leaf, celery, crushed garlic, and chopped thyme are tender.
- Add the mince. Cook for about 5 minutes, or until the mince is browned, breaking it up with a wooden spoon. Stock is made with boiling water. In a mixing dish, combine the passata, stock, mustard, and Worcestershire sauce. Bring to a boil, then reduce to low heat and continue to simmer for an additional 25 minutes.
- In the meantime, peel and dice the swede, then slice the carrots and put them in a large saucepan with enough water to cover them, then bring to a boil. Reduce the heat to low and simmer for 20 minutes, or until the vegetables are tender.
- Drain it, then return it to the pan and remove it from the heat. Season with black pepper and set aside.
- Spoon the mixture into the baking dish after pouring the peas into the filling. Arrange the swede and carrot topping on top in a uniform pattern, then grate the parmesan on top.
- Bake for 20 minutes, or until the surface is golden brown. Take it out of the oven and let it cool for 5 minutes.

*Calories 214, Protein 12 g, Sodium 125 mg, Potassium 119 mg, Phosphorus 12 mg, Calcium 31 mg*

# Jamaican Cornmeal Pie

*Time: 2 Hours and 10 Mins, Serves: 8, Skill: Hard*

### Ingredients
- Egg (1 medium)
- Spring onions (2)
- Cheddar cheese (250g), grated
- Onion (1/2)
- Semi-skimmed milk (500ml)
- Celery (1 stalk)
- Sweetcorn (325g tin), drained
- Garlic cloves (2)
- Fine cornmeal (600g)
- Red pepper (1/2)
- Plain flour (1 tbsp)
- Vegetable oil (2 tbsp)
- Green pepper (1/2)

### Instructions
- Break the egg in a large mixing cup, then add the flour, milk, half of the sweetcorn, and half of the grated cheese. Blend it for a few minutes with a hand blender to give it a gritty texture. Preheat the oven to 375 °F.
- Now finely chop the spring onions, cabbage, celery, red, and green peppers. Garlic cloves should be peeled and ground before being used. Heat the oil in a big skillet, add the garlic and the vegetables, and cook for about 5 minutes.
- Add the remaining sweetcorn to the pot. Slowly whisk in the cornmeal, then stir for another 5 minutes or until the texture is firm.
- Fill a greased baking pan or proof dish to the required size with the mixture. Sprinkle the remaining grated cheese on top. After putting it in the oven, cook for 35 minutes.

*Calories 469, Protein 6 g, Sodium 308 mg, Potassium 311 mg, Phosphorus 26 mg, Calcium 26 mg*

## Blackberry crumble
*Time: 45 Mins, Serves: 6, Skill: Easy*

**Ingredients**
### Crumble filling
- Butter (25g), unsalted
- Blackberries (100g), fresh/frozen
- Caster sugar (50g)

### Crumble topping
- Butter (75g), unsalted
- Porridge oats (40g)
- Plain flour (160g)
- Soft dark brown sugar (40g)
- Sugar (40g)
- Ginger (pinch), ground
- Almonds (40g), ground

**Instructions**
- Preheat the oven to 320ºF.
- Melt 25g butter in a skillet. Cook, stirring occasionally, until the liquid has nearly evaporated. Stir in the sugar and blackberries until the sugar has fully dissolved. Switch off the heat.
- Combine the crumble topping ingredients in a food processor or mixer, or in a cup, and rub together with your fingertips until the mixture resembles breadcrumbs. In the finished dish, leave a few lumpy bits because they add texture.
- Place the fruit mixture halfway in an oven-safe serving bowl, then spoon the crumble topping on top.
- Cook for 20 minutes, or until golden brown and bubbling on top.

*Calories 367.3, Protein 4 g, Sodium 59.8 mg, Potassium 43.1 mg, Phosphorus 101.6 mg, Calcium 24.2 mg*

## Chewy Lemon-Ginger-Coconut Cookies
*Time: 1 hour and 20 Mins, Serves: 12, Skill: Medium*

**Ingredients**
- Sugar (1/2 cup)
- Egg (1)
- Baking soda (1/2 tsp)
- Lemon juice (2 tbsp)
- Lemon zest (1 tbsp)
- Ginger (1 tbsp), fresh
- Flour (1 1/4 cups)
- Butter (1/2 cup), unsalted
- Coconut (1 cup), toasted

**Instructions**
- Preheat the oven to 350 ºF.
- Put the coconut on a baking sheet pan and bake for 5-10 minutes, or until the sides are light brown.
- Place it in a serving bowl after removing it from the oven.
- Using a hand mixer, cream together the sugar and butter until light and fluffy. Combine the egg, lemon zest, lemon juice, and chopped ginger in a large mixing bowl.
- Combine the flour and baking soda. Toss the flour mixture into the butter mixture until well combined.
- Allow for at least 30 minutes of resting time after covering.
- Scoop tablespoon-sized dough balls and roll them in the toasted coconut. Place the balls on a lightly oiled baking sheet tray at least 2 inches apart.
- Bake for 10-12 minutes, or until the edges are lightly browned.

*Calories 223, Protein 01 g, Sodium 275 mg, Potassium 21 mg, Phosphorus 96 mg, Calcium 8 mg*

## Mini Pineapple Upside down Cakes
*Time: 1 hour and 25 Mins, Serves: 12, Skill: Hard*

**Ingredients**
- Sugar (2/3 cup)
- Milk (2/3 cup), fat-free
- Canola oil (3 tbsp)
- Egg (1)
- Vanilla extract (1/2 tsp)
- Cake flour (1-1/3 cups)
- Baking powder (1-1/4 tsp)
- Salt (1/4 tsp)
- Lemon juice (1 tsp)
- Butter (3 tbsp), unsalted
- Packed brown sugar (1/3 cup)
- Pineapple slices (12 canned), unsweetened
- Fresh cherries (6 pieces), cut into halves and pitted

**Instructions**
- Apply butter on the muffin tray for 12 servings.
- Each section should be lightly dusted with brown sugar.

- Press one pineapple slice into each section to form a cup shape. Set one-half of the cherry aside and one in the center of each pineapple slice.
- Whisk the sugar, oil, milk, lemon juice, vanilla extract and egg together. In a large mixing bowl, combine the flour, salt, and baking powder; add to the sugar mixture, beat until smooth. Half-fill a muffin tin with the batter you've made.
- Preheat oven to 350°F and bake for 35-40 minutes, or until a toothpick inserted in the center comes out clean. Place the baked cakes on a serving tray after reversing the muffin tin. If required, carefully pry the edges away from the plate with a butter knife or a tiny spatula.

*Calories 204.3, Protein 12.4 g, Sodium 112 mg, Potassium 39 mg, Phosphorus 56 mg, Calcium 39 mg*

## Independence Day Jell-O Flag Layer Cup

*Time: 5 hours and 20 Mins, Serves: 16, Skill: Hard*

**Ingredients**
- Boiling water (7 1/2 cups)
- Blueberries (1 small package)
- Whipped topping (1 16 oz. tub), non-dairy
- Pineapple juice (3 3/4 cups)
- Red Jell-O (2 x 6 oz. packages)
- Blue Jell-O (2 x 6oz. packages)
- Lemon Jell-O (1 oz. package)

**Instructions**
- Fill a 13-inch-by-9-inch spray pan with nonstick cooking oil. A flag mold, if you have one, may be used to create a more flag-like result.
- Increase the color of the jelly by adding a few drops of food coloring, 3 cups boiling water & 3 cups red gelatin. It will take approximately 2 minutes to complete.
- Mix in 1 1/2 cups of pineapple juice. Pour into the mold of a 13-inch x 9-inch pan.
- Refrigerate the mixture for 1 hour in a pan.
- To produce the next gelatin sample, either clean the big bowl or begin with a fresh one. To produce a lemon Jell-O, add 1/2 cup of hot water and the lemon Jell-O, stirring until it has dissolved.
- Stir in 3/4 cups of chilled pineapple juice until it is fully diluted. In a tub, cool for 30 minutes. The Jell-O should thicken, but not completely set. It should have the consistency of egg whites.
- In the tub, blend 8 ounces of cool whip with the moistened lemon Jell-O. This will aid in the preparation of the Jell-O turning white and enhance its flavor and texture. Pour the mixture on top of the Jell-O red set.
- Enable another 30 minutes in the refrigerator.
- Make the blue Jell-O with 3 cups of boiling water until it has dissolved.
- Add 1/2 cup of pineapple juice.
- Pour over the hardened Jell-O.
- Refrigerate for a further 3 hours, or overnight
- Slide a butter knife down the sides of the Jell-O bowl to remove it. Place the gelatin on a serving platter and softly shift it around.
- Shave the Jell-O edges with a large, sharp knife to offer it a more defined, flag-like look.
- Fill a rectangle of blueberries and decorate the top left corner. The white lines would can be drawn. Tube flag-like lines around the Jell-O with a pipe bag halfway full of non-dairy whipped cream.

*Calories 230, Protein 4 g, Sodium 128 mg, Potassium 92 mg, Phosphorus 78 mg, Calcium 23 mg*

## Pineapple Cream Cake

*Time: 1 hour and 20 Mins, Serves: 18, Skill: Hard*

**Ingredients**
- Sugar (1/4 cup)
- Eggs (5)
- Crushed pineapple (8-oz can)
- Yellow cake mix (1 box)
- Vegetable oil (1/3 cup)
- Water (1 cup)
- Vanilla flavoring (1 tsp)
- Cream cheese (8-oz package), softened

**Instructions**
- Preheat the oven according to the instructions on the cake mix package.
- Mix the cream cheese, 2 eggs, and sugar together in a cup. Drain and put aside the pineapple.
- Combine the yellow cake mix, water, oil, vanilla extract, and the other 3 eggs in a big mixing cup. Blend on high for 2 minutes with a hand blender.
- Before putting the flour in a Bundt pan or a 9 x 3.5-inch tube dish, coat it with cooking spray.
- Apply the cheese mixture to the cake batter and blend well. After that, add the batter into the greased and floured pan.

- Bake for 55 to 65 minutes, or until the center is set.
- Set aside to cool for 10 minutes before serving.

*Calories 431, Protein 10.4 g, Sodium 110.2 mg, Potassium 93.1 mg, Phosphorus 61 mg, Calcium 11 mg*

## Festive Cream Cheese Sugar Cookies

*Time: 2 Hours and 40 Mins, Serves: 48, Skill: Hard*

**Ingredients**
- Egg (1 large), separated
- Salt (1/2 tsp)
- Almond extract (1/4 tsp)
- Vanilla extract (1/2 tsp)
- Sugar (1 cup)
- All-purpose flour (2 1/4 cups)
- Optional garnish: colored sugar
- Butter (1 cup), unsalted, softened
- Cream cheese (3 oz.), softened

**Instructions**
- Sugar, flour, cream cheese, egg yolk, almond extract, vanilla extract, and butter can all be mixed in a big mixing cup. All should be thoroughly combined.
- Allow 2 hours to chill the cookie dough.
- Preheat oven to 350ºF.
- On a finely floured board, roll out a third of the dough at a time to a thickness of 14 inches. Perfectly cut out forms of finely floured cookie cutters.
- On ungreased baking sheets, space them 1 inch apart. Dust them with a gently beaten egg white and, if needed, colored sugar.
- Bake for 7–9 minutes, or until lightly browned on top. Set aside to cool before serving.

*Calories 79, Protein 1 g, Sodium 33 mg, Potassium 11 mg, Phosphorus 16 mg, Calcium 4 mg*

## Hot Fruit Compote

*Time: 1 hour and 15 Mins, Serves: 10, Skill: Medium*

**Ingredients**
- Slices of pear, juice packed
- Chunks of pineapple, juice packed
- Slices of peach, juice packed
- Cherry pie filling
- Margarine (1/4 cup), melted
- Corn flakes (2 cups), crushed

**Instructions**
- Drain the fruit first. Before applying the pie filling, grease a 9" x 13" plate and powder the fruit.
- In a dish, combine the corn flakes and margarine and drizzle over the fruit.
- Preheat the oven to 350 ºF and bake for 30 minutes.

*Calories 67, Protein 02 g, Sodium 01 mg, Potassium 69 mg, Phosphorus 20 mg, Calcium 09 mg*

# 4-WEEKS MEAL PLAN

Following a diet without a plan is not an easy task to follow.
In this 4-week renal diet plan, we show you what a healthy low-potassium, low-sodium diet for kidney disease looks like.

## Week 1

**Day 1** — Friday
Breakfast: Mexican Egg & Tortilla Skillet  25
Lunch: Beef Casserole  119
Dinner: Italian Eggplant Salad  42
Snacks: Southern-Fried Okra  184
**Day 2**
Breakfast: Fresh Fruit Compote
Lunch: Grilled Chicken Sesame
Dinner: Brewery Burger
Snacks: Overnight Oats
**Day 3**
Breakfast: Burritos with Eggs and Mexican Sausage
Lunch: Easy low sodium salmon with lime and herbs
Dinner: Oven-Fried Chicken
Snacks: BBQ Corn on the Cob
**Day 4**
Breakfast: Fig and Goat Cheese Quesadilla
Lunch: Curry Chicken
Dinner: Meat Loaf
Snacks: Low Salt Macaroni and Cheese
**Day 5**
Breakfast: Puffy Chili Rellenos Casserole
Lunch: Shrimp Salad with Cucumber Mint
Dinner: Baked Tuna
Snacks: Tropical Fruit Salad with Basil Lime Syrup
**Day 6**
Breakfast: Sudden Quiche
Lunch: Cool Coconut Marshmallow Salad
Dinner: Simple Beef Broth
Dessert: Spicy Raisin Cookies
Snacks: Fried Onion Rings
**Day 7**
Breakfast: Oriental Egg Rolls
Lunch: Cucumber Cups Stuffed with Buffalo Chicken Salad
Dinner: Salt-Free Pizza
Snacks: 60-Second Salsa

## Week 2

**Day 1**
Breakfast: Mexican Brunch Eggs
Lunch: Creamy Tuna Twist
Dinner: Hawaiian-Style Slow-Cooked Beef
Snacks: Brown Bag Popcorn
**Day 2**
Breakfast: Buckwheat Pancakes
Lunch: Chicken Tikka
Dinner: Spicy Beef Stir-Fry
Snacks: Dry-Rubbed Barbecue Turkey Wings
**Day 3**
Breakfast: 40-Second Omelet
Lunch: Yogurt-Cucumber Soup
Dinner: Sukiyaki and Rice
Snacks: Crispy Cauliflower Phyllo Cups
**Day 4**
Breakfast: Apple Bran Muffins
Lunch: Spanish Paella
Dinner: Pasta with Cheesy Meat Sauce
Snacks: Sweet & Nutty Protein Bars
**Day 5**
Breakfast: Biscuits with Master Mix
Lunch: Salmon Veggie Salad
Dinner: Lemon Chicken
Snacks: Sriracha Popcorn
**Day 6**
Breakfast: Bran Breakfast Bars
Lunch: Thai Chicken Soup
Dinner: Beef Curry
Dessert: Low Sodium Pound Cake
Snacks: Homemade Herbed Biscuits
**Day 7**
Breakfast: Burritos Rapido's
Lunch: Pork Carne
Dinner: Cream of Prawn Soup
Snacks: Energy Bites

# Week 3

**Day 1**
Breakfast: Spicy Tofu Scrambler
Lunch: Adobo Marinated Tilapia Tapas
Dinner: Parsley Burger
Snacks: BBQ Asparagus
**Day 2**
Breakfast: Homemade Muesli
Lunch: Pork Chops with Herb Crust
Dinner: Herb-Crusted Pork Loin
Snacks: Low Sodium Deviled Eggs
**Day 3**
Breakfast: Southwest Baked Egg Breakfast Cups
Lunch: Fish Sticks
Dinner: Jamaican Curried Goat
Snacks: Fresh Fruit Lassi
**Day 4**
Breakfast: Curried Egg Pita Pockets
Lunch: Baked Potato Soup
Dinner: Pork Steak
Snacks: Seafood Croquettes
**Day 5**
Breakfast: Huevos Rancheros
Lunch: Tuna-Noodle Skillet
Dinner: Easy Beef Burger
Snacks: Fruity Chicken salad
**Day 6**
Breakfast: Toad in a Hole
Lunch: Honey Glazed Salmon
Dinner: Chicken Cabbage Stir Fry
Dessert: Butterscotch Apple Crisp
Snacks: Cinnamon Biscotti
**Day 7**
Breakfast: Summer harvest egg muffin cups
Lunch: Turkey Paprikash
Dinner: Nathan Outlaw's baked sea bass
Snacks: Cinnamon Sugar Popcorn

# Week 4

**Day 1**
Breakfast: Asparagus and Swiss Cheese Frittata
Lunch: Baked Salmon
Dinner: Chicken'N Rice
Snacks: Sour Candy Grapes
**Day 2**
Breakfast: Quinoa Porridge
Lunch: Chicken Stir-Fry
Dinner: Shrimp Fried Rice
Snacks: Grilled Blackened Tilapia
**Day 3**
Breakfast: Fruit and Oat Pancakes
Lunch: Special Pizza
Dinner: Super Tuesday Shrimp
Snacks: Cherry Brown Butter Bars
**Day 4**
Breakfast: German Pancake
Lunch: Herb-Roasted Chicken Breasts
Dinner: Salisbury steak
Snacks: Crème brûlée
**Day 5**
Breakfast: Savory Egg Muffins
Lunch: Herb Rice Casserole
Dinner: Minestrone Soup
Snacks: Watermelon Ice cream
**Day 6**
Breakfast: Veggie Mug Omelet
Lunch: Creamy Broccoli Soup
Dinner: Chicken Curry
Dessert: Gooey, Carmel-Filled Butterscotch Cookies
Snacks: Pineapple Coleslaw
**Day 7**
Breakfast: Egg Sandwich
Lunch: Eggplant Casserole
Dinner: Easy Chicken and Pasta Dinner
Snacks: Veggie Strata

# CONCLUSION

Chronic Kidney Disease (CKD) means the kidneys are at risk and blood filtration may be compromised. The condition is referred as "chronic" because the injury continues to progress over time. This harm could lead to a buildup of waste in your body. Kidney failure can also be caused by a variety of health issues. One of the challenges that most kidney patients face is finding simple, tasty CKD recipes that help them regulate the amount of chemicals and fluid in their blood.

This book aims to strike a balance between savoring your food's taste and making the required dietary changes. It is specially written for people who choose to follow a normal renal diet, but it is useful regardless of the therapy degree. The dishes in this cookbook include low sodium, potassium, phosphate and a moderate number of nutritious proteins. There are also low-carb meals available for weight-loss participants.

This diet's aim is to keep your body's electrolyte, nutrient, and fluid levels stable while you're on dialysis for CKD. Dialysis patients must follow this diet in order to minimize the concentration of waste materials in their bodies.

Too much salt can be harmful for patients with renal disease because their kidneys are unable to adequately filter excess fluid and sodium from the body. Edema, heart disease, elevated blood pressure, and other conditions may result from the accumulation of fluid and sodium in the bloodstream and tissues. People with kidney disease must eat a kidney-friendly diet in order to live a healthier life.

---

*Thanks for reading this book.*

*I would be extremely grateful if you would take 1 minute of your time to leave a review on Amazon about my work.*

*April Ellis*

## SCAN THE QR CODE WITH YOUR MOBILE

**Customer reviews**

★★★★★ 4.9 out of 5

44 global ratings

| | | |
|---|---|---|
| 5 star | | 90% |
| 4 star | | 10% |
| 3 star | | 0% |
| 2 star | | 0% |
| 1 star | | 0% |

˅ How are ratings calculated?

Printed in Great Britain
by Amazon